Judicial Activism in Comparative Perspective

Global Perspectives on Judicial Politics

Richard Pacelle, Raul Sanchez Urribarri, and Lori Hausegger

Series Editors

Vol. 1

Judicial Activism in Comparative Perspective

Edited by Lori Hausegger and
Raul Sanchez Urribarri

PETER LANG
New York - Berlin - Bruxelles - Chennai - Lausanne - Oxford

Library of Congress Cataloging-in-Publication Control Number: 2023015386

Bibliographic information published by the Deutsche Nationalbibliothek.
The German National Library lists this publication in the German
National Bibliography; detailed bibliographic data is available
on the Internet at http://dnb.d-nb.de.

Cover design by Peter Lang Group AG

ISSN 2993-3897 (print)
ISBN 9781433198120 (hardback)
ISBN 9781433198137 (ebook)
ISBN 9781433198144 (epub)
DOI 10.3726/ b19826

Published by Peter Lang Publishing Inc., New York, USA
info@peterlang.com - www.peterlang.com

This publication has been peer reviewed.

CONTENTS

LIST OF ILLUSTRATIONS AND TABLES

ACKNOWLEDGMENTS

First, we would like to thank all our contributors who, despite the difficulties of the last few years, believed in the project and participated in its different iterations, all the way to completion. Special thanks to Richard Pacelle, who pioneered both this project and the new Book Series where it belongs, and who supported this project throughout all its phases.

This project started in 2020, with a collaborative 'conference within a conference' at the Southern Political Science Association Annual Meeting in San Juan, Puerto Rico, followed by an online workshop hosted at the 2021 Annual Meeting a year later. We would like to thank the Association for the opportunity, and acknowledge the input of all our participants in the conference. We also thank our respective home institutions - Boise State University and La Trobe University- for the financial and logistic support to complete this project.

In these challenging pandemic times, we would also like to acknowledge our family, friends, and esteemed colleagues, who have been an invaluable source of support to complete a long-term project of this nature. Our heartfelt gratitude to all of you.

Finally, thanks to Peter Lang International Publishers, and especially to Anthony Mason and everyone involved in the production of this book, for both their confidence in this project, and their patience to see it to completion.

· 1 ·

STUDYING JUDICIAL ACTIVISM IN COMPARATIVE PERSPECTIVE

Lori Hausegger and Raul Sanchez Urribarri

This book focuses on judicial activism in comparative perspective. Judicial activism is a contested concept frequently used by scholars, journalists, lawyers, and even politicians, to broadly describe the courts' deliberate action that transcends the judiciary's role as a neutral conflict-adjudicator. A quick glance at any news source regarding the use of 'judicial activism', shows how the term is used to describe a wide variety of examples in which courts or judges behave in a way that is perceived to overstep or violate "their cultural standards of judicial role" (Green, 2009, p. 1199). This occurs, across different socio-political contexts, legal systems, types of proceedings and other circumstances. Whilst the term is common in U.S. parlance about the courts' intervention in politics and policy-making—often with a negative or pejorative connotation—it comes up in Australia, Brazil, Colombia, Great Britain, Israel, Turkey, and a wide variety of other nations, through different types of actors with various political proclivities.

When described in a negative way, an 'activist judiciary' is understood to be an abusive, politicized, overzealous or unprofessional institution that disregards its true mission in a democratic context, and its role as a guarantor of the rule of law. As Kermit Roosevelt points out, claiming that a court or decision is 'activist' has become "a rhetorically charged way of saying that you disagree with a decision or think a decision is wrong" (Rodia, citing Roosevelt, 2022). But there also seems to be 'good activism', described as virtuous from the eye of the beholder, with courts then being described as rising to the occasion and going beyond legal, institutional, or political constraints to do 'what is right' in a case. Some proponents of this perspective see judicial activism as a corrector to the excesses of democracy. For instance, Sherry argues, "too little activism produces worse consequences than does too much. If we cannot assure that the judges tread the perfect middle ground (and we cannot), it is better to have an overly aggressive judiciary than an overly restrained one" (2013, 1).

Yet, despite the common use of the term in popular discourse and research on law, courts, and judicial decision-making, works about judicial activism seldom engage in analyses that have in mind more than one court, judge, or decision. Often, commentary on judicial activism fails to link discussions about the phenomena to rigorous conceptual frameworks. Scholarly debates centered on the experiences of specific judicial systems seldom address the transferability of their definitions or refer to an overarching comparative theoretical reference. Without such, it is hard to study judicial activism in ways that assist comparative inquiry. Moreover, since the term has been frequently used in the U.S. context, some debates that take place in other jurisdictions are, consciously or not, informed by an institutional reality and socio-political circumstances that might differ significantly from the one under study. As a result, we are left with debates that fail to communicate with one another effectively.

To bridge this gap, this volume seeks to articulate a comparative perspective on judicial activism, bringing together a series of theoretical and empirical studies across different socio-political and institutional contexts. We hope that this exercise not only demonstrates the complexity of the concept, but also helps us make sense of the different meanings of judicial activism, while achieving a more nuanced picture about the conditions under which it tends to emerge, in what ways, and to what effect. We ground the discussion on a selection of countries across different types of political regimes and legal systems, developed by scholars specialized in these jurisdictions. Each contributes to the common goal of going beyond isolated case study analyses to explore judicial activism in ways that will contribute to a genuine comparative debate. In particular, the present volume focuses on three examples from Western democracies that have varying experiences with the more U.S.-Centric form of judicial activism: the U.S., Canada, and the U.K. After grounding the discussion in the more often studied common law experience, the volume then turns to six Latin American countries with very different experiences with judicial activism, democracy and liberal constitutionalism: Brazil, Colombia, Costa Rica, Mexico, Paraguay, and Venezuela. This focus on a wide variety of Latin American countries, allows for a more complete consideration of the complexity of judicial activism, using a part of the world where debates on the concept have been widespread in popular discourse and academia in recent years. These case studies are analyzed with reference to a common conceptual core, assisted by a beginning theoretical essay and two concluding cross-national studies highlighting different theoretical and methodological approaches.

Based on those premises, the present volume has sought to develop a conversation focused on the following key questions: What is understood by judicial activism in different jurisdictions? Beyond a superficial agreement, are we talking about the same phenomenon across countries and systems (or over time in a specific jurisdiction), and to what extent? How do we measure judicial activism? Do these measurements, and the assumptions upon which they rest, travel well in different contexts and times? How, and to what degree, can different actors expect that courts will go beyond their expected roles to engage in rights protection? Given rising trends of growing authoritarian and political polarization world-wide—and the political manipulation of courts in the U.S. and over the world—to what degree are these efforts affecting the propensity of courts to engage in judicial activism? How is judicial activism related to processes of democratization or, conversely, democratic backsliding? This book brings together original works by scholars with expertise in different thematic areas, methodological approaches, and regional expertise to address these questions. We have strived to bring together scholars specialized in comparative judicial politics and comparative constitutionalism –two fields that have grown increasingly intertwined, and which require increasing collaboration and cross-fertilization to study law and politics cross-nationally. We have developed this book based on a vibrant exchange among peers, by gathering the contributors to this book on two different occasions, allowing us to exchange views on the project's mission, goals, and key debates. We hope the result is a book that is sensitive to the wide variety of experiences with judicial activism across the jurisdictions studied and beyond.

Approaching Judicial Activism in Comparative Perspective

There are many conceptual studies on judicial activism that have been developed over the years, since Schlesinger Jr. first coined the term (1947, see also

Kmiec, 2004 and works discussed in Roux, 2021). Whilst there are works that, from the get-go, warn us about the lack of rigor with which the concept tends to be employed, and even discourage its use (e.g., Roosevelt, 2008), there is abundant scholarly literature that defines, critiques, and deliberately uses the term. These works have made a substantial effort to define judicial activism and, usually, make sense of the terms of the debate, particularly in the U.S. context. These studies not only include scholarly debates, but also uses of the term in popular culture or by legal actors themselves (Kmiec, 2004; Josev, 2017), covering one or more 'dimensions' of the different phenomena that 'judicial activism' encompasses, addressing the concept's multiple meanings (Canon, 1982). A good example of this line of scholarship is Cohn and Kremnitzer (2005), who build on Canon to develop a multidimensional analysis of judicial activism that encompasses different instances of the phenomenon, at different stages of the judicial process and in relation with multiple players with which the judiciary interacts.

Waller and Sterling (2020) analyze judicial activism from a political theory perspective, focusing on 'activist decisions' as rulings based on personal or political convictions over legal considerations. This speaks directly to the issue of what is the acceptable range of judicial discretion, while leaving a pending task of assessing where (and how) to draw the line in terms of what decisions would be considered activist. On the other hand, Lindquist and Cross (2009) focus on vital methodological issues of relevance for empirical legal studies researchers of judicial activism/restraint, but yet again mainly deal with debates anchored in the U.S. context. In both cases, there is substantial room for enhancing the discussion by expanding it to different institutional and socio-political realities.

What about works that specifically grapple with the concept with a comparative lens? A notable example of judicial activism scholarship specifically seeking to develop a comparative approach is Holland's 1991 edited collection. This book was an important innovation that not only advanced conceptual discussions on the topic, but also included chapters on a variety of jurisdictions across the world, with an emphasis on industrial democracies with different institutional configurations and trajectories. An important exception to this focus was the chapter on the Soviet Union, which was included back then as a country in the process of liberalization and political reform. This is important since, as we will see in some of the cases under analysis in this book, the extent to which courts are willing to sideline previous interpretations of the law in democratizing contexts, embracing a role that protects rights against political abuse, is an important part of the story of the global rise of judicial power. Of course, Holland's edited volume is now over three decades old—a time where much has happened in terms of variations of political regime and the courts' role across the world. The book also does not include major reflections on jurisdictions in democratizing societies in the Global South, countries that provide valuable insight into activism as a concept. Perhaps relatedly, the book focused on limited understandings of aspects of judicial activism, i.e., courts 'adventuring' to make social policies (Holland, 1991, p. 1) or engaging in lawmaking. Our project has sought to address this by not starting the project with a narrow understanding of judicial activism, but rather to let the project's contributors bring to the analysis their own approaches, as long as they critically engaged with the term.

Other classic books from the nascent field of comparative judicial politics in the 1990s—such as Charles Epp's classic *The Rights Revolution* (1998) and Tate and Vallinder's collection *The Global Expansion of Judicial Power* (1995)—documented and analyzed a variety of cases of increasing judicial power across the world, yet for the most part did not address judicial activism and restraint trends or examples. Both books, though, had important lessons to offer to students of judicial activism comparatively. Tate and Vallinder's volume highlighted the need to pay closer attention to judicial institutions as venues and deciders of major political debates, at a time when there was still wide resistance to accept the role of courts as political actors in many jurisdictions across the world. It also encouraged scholars to consider the wide variety of experiences globally against a surging narrative of rights protection in a growingly liberal context. Epp's excellent book (1998) also pushed forward this view, while paying closer attention to the broader legal support network responsible for instances of judicialization of politics and policymaking. More importantly, both books engaged conceptually and methodologically with the different ways in which judges exercised their powers against a variety of institutional frameworks and socio-political conditions, whether as a selection of case studies (Tate and Vallinder) or in a small-n research design (Epp). Thus, while neither book sought to tackle conceptual and measurement questions pertaining to judicial activism, scholars can take important lessons from them.

More recently, there has been a surge of interest in studying judicial activism across different jurisdictions, reflecting an increasing awareness about the expansion of judicial authority and ensuing debates, especially at a time when courts are often put in the position of having to decide major cases of political import (i.e., mega-political cases, Hirschl, 2008). For instance, Dickson's edited volume (2007) examines judicial activism across nine different common law jurisdictions (including the three included in this book), through the lens of their high court's role in the protection of fundamental rights. Coutinho, La Torre and Smith's (2015), edited collection focuses on the American and European experiences and takes an interdisciplinary look at judicial activism. The volume reunites perspectives from different fields, including legal, philosophical, and political science, taking a genuine comparative interest from both theoretical and empirical standpoints.

Beyond some similarities in terms of interest in judicial activism and the comparative scope of both projects, there are substantial differences between the contributions of both volumes and our own. For example, Dickson's collection only includes common law countries and is more narrowly focused on activism in terms of the protection of rights. We argue by bringing in a wide variety of Latin American civil law jurisdictions we are able to provide a more complex and comprehensive picture of the contested concept of activism. Coutinho et al.'s approach is more theoretical and normative based and is focused on the American and European experience, while ours seeks to engage with questions of conceptualization and measurement and explore how judicial activism operates in different realities and contexts.

Other recent works are expanding the confines of global debates on judicial activism to include the experiences of judges in conditions of political instability, crisis, regime change or other socio-political circumstances in which the role of judges could shift as a result. For example, Belov's edited collection (2021) brings together examples centered on judicial activism understood as the judicialization of politics, with a particular focus on constitutional courts (see Zamboni's chapter in the book, 2021). The book covers a variety of contexts, including select cases in Western Europe, international courts, judicial activism in illiberal polities (Poland, Romania, Morocco, and Jordan) and the role of courts in situations of emergency in Bulgaria and Croatia. Although these two projects are similar in some ways—and seem to respond to common concerns regarding the need for additional conceptual and empirical clarity on activism, broadly defined—there are differences in terms of theory, methods, and cases of interest.

Beyond these comparative projects, there is a variety of small-n books or case study works that explore judicial activism in a small selection of countries or focused on a specific jurisdiction. For instance, Petersen (2017) studies judicial activism taking into account whether courts go beyond the roles assigned to them in their jurisdictions to correct 'market failures' in the democratic

process. His work focuses on Canada, Germany, and South Africa, looking at the exercise of judicial review in different jurisdictions and going beyond the usual single-case approach to studying activism. Additionally, there are works that have surveyed judicial activism at the level of transnational courts. For example, Dawson, De Witte, and Muir's compilation (2013) looks at judicial activism in the European Court of Justice, assessing and questioning the role of the Court for Europe's governance. All of these are valuable, but more limited than what we hope to accomplish with a large variety of countries and experiences.

Some of these other smaller works have been written and published in languages other than English, showing the need for greater engagement with experts based in each country to study judicial activism comparatively. For example, in Chile, García García and Verdugo Ramírez analyze whether new modalities of judicial intervention in environmental policy, health policy, education and other areas can be considered excessive, engaging with the debate of the proper role of judges in a troubled democratic context (García García and Verdugo Ramírez, 2013). One danger when approaching comparative research is missing important domestic contributions for a country. Edited volumes like those described above and our own, can help mediate that danger through the inclusion of scholars who work extensively within these jurisdictions and who are familiar with the work of local scholars.

This succinct overview of relevant literature does not intend to offer a thorough scholarly background to the question of judicial activism. Instead, it seeks to introduce the debate and show the need for additional comparative work on the topic. We argue the quick survey demonstrates that this book is timely and fills an existing gap in the literature on judicial activism, through its collection of countries with dramatically different democratic and judicial experiences, and through each scholar's careful conceptual approach allowing for a more complex picture of this contested concept.

Our Contributions to Analyzing Judicial Activism

We set out to develop a book that helped illustrate specific instances of judicial activism in different social, political, and legal contexts, grounded on clear conceptual understandings and a variety of methodologies. At the beginning, we wished to cover as many jurisdictions as possible, based on the assumption that a greater number of cases would allow us to have a more detailed account of the global reach of the concept of judicial activism. However, as we developed the project, we found the scattershot approach less useful than focusing on more coherent regions that allowed us to explore the themes that emerged from discussions. Our focus on the common law legal jurisdictions allows us to illustrate the importance of different governmental and institutional arrangements as we explore the different judicial activism experiences of countries as similar as the U.K., Canada and the U.S., all countries with strong, independent courts. The Latin American legal jurisdictions under study then allow us to explore the differences between countries with more or less assertive and independent courts, and the role they play vis a vis their governmental systems. The variety of experiences included here provide a clearer picture of the many faces of activism beyond U.S.-centric definitions, helping to challenge assumptions about what judicial activism is (or is not) that are based on that country's experience and institutional framework. This provides a stronger starting point to engage in debates about the concept's systematic analysis in comparative perspective.

Judicial Activism as a Contested Concept

After this brief introduction, we begin with a theoretical chapter setting the stage for all the analysis that follows. Jeff Staton's thorough introduction to the concept of Judicial Activism (Chapter 2) identifies the main scholarly efforts to date to make sense of judicial activism and restraint in comparative perspective. The chapter addresses the complexity of activism as a contested concept and the importance of having conceptual and methodological clarity at the start of any study of it. The chapter suggests a need to promote innovative measurement approaches and think critically about their leverage and limitations across different contexts. Finally, it proposes the need to promote strong causal research on the topic, building on the excellent descriptive and theoretical work in comparative law and politics on judicial activism. Staton's thought-provoking contribution provided an integral part of the conceptual framework of this volume, with the subsequent chapters implicitly or explicitly engaging with the chapter's key tenets and discussions.

Common Law Legal Jurisdictions

The next section of the book includes case studies, exploring the concept of judicial activism in the contexts of Common Law systems in three Western established democracies: the United States, the United Kingdom, and Canada. Our contributors' discussions in these countries focus on these nations' high courts, i.e., courts of last resort. As these chapters elaborate, in all three cases we witness high courts using their institutional prerogatives to engage in political and policy-making questions, protect rights, and issue transformative case-law in ways that have been, at times, branded judicial activism. Yet, at the same time, they exhibit remarkable differences in terms of their roles, prominence and instances of activism.

We begin this section with the country that has been the primary focus of judicial activism discussion: the United States. Chapter 3 focuses on the U.S. Supreme Court, with Richard Pacelle examining an institution where judicial activism has been a relevant claim and phenomena at different points in its history. There is no question of the policy-making relevance of the U.S. Supreme Court, particularly since the 1950s. But the Court does not always enjoy the latitude to engage in activism and can also face contexts that elicit judicial restraint. Using Supreme Court decisions in the 1953–2017 terms, Pacelle analyzes when the Court is free to exert activism, and when it feels constrained to adopt judicial restraint. He argues the two concepts are complementary principles and balance between them is necessary "to preserve the legitimacy and viability of the institution." His chapter is critical to highlight the importance of questioning analyses that fail to consider the variety of incentives judges face, as political actors, to decide as they deem appropriate.

Next, Chapter 4 focuses on the United Kingdom, and illustrates the uses (and abuses) of the concept of judicial activism. Monica Lineberger explains that, much like the concept of 'fake news', judicial activism has become a rallying cry for governments to rely upon when courts produce decisions counter to their policy preferences. But what does the data show? The chapter seeks to explore whether, and to what degree, it is fair to say that the U.K.'s Supreme Court can be considered an 'activist' institution. There are several notable contributions in this chapter, including a survey of the literature on judicial activism focused on the U.K. judicial system; a discussion on how to conceptualize judicial activism and restraint within the U.K., and an analysis of how different understandings and measures of activism can help elucidate different aspects of judicial decision-making in the U.K. context. Lineberger's analysis helps us understand the institutional developments and differences that impact activism. Once again, this chapter's intention is to integrate the U.K. experience to a comparative framework, helping us to think about judicial activism in a theoretical sense, one that is transportable across countries.

In the final chapter of the section, Chapter 5, we turn our attention to the Canadian case, where there has been a significant growth in the prominence of courts in the political landscape and as a guarantor of rights following the adoption of the Charter of Rights and Freedoms (Hausegger et al., 2009; Songer, 2008; Songer et al., 2012). Riddell, Hausegger and Scott seek to illustrate the complexity of defining activism and determining which behavior qualifies as, in fact, activist when the traditional U.S. definitions might not fit. They begin with a brief review of the history of judicial activism in Canada, before moving on to discuss what activism means in Canadian courts and the different ways of measuring it. Although these analyses owe a great deal to the U.S. literature, the existence of a limitations clause and a "notwithstanding" clause in Canada, coupled with academic and judicial discussions about the possibility of "dialogue" between courts and elected officials, leads to some interesting points of departure from the U.S. and other jurisdictions. Finally, the chapter discusses a possible rising trend of not following (i.e., overturning) precedent as a form of activism, and starts developing an investigation into the impact of a pathway to 'approved activism': the Canadian Supreme Court's articulation of a framework by which trial judges can depart from established precedents.

Latin American Civil Law Jurisdictions

Following our discussions of these three cases in Common Law jurisdictions located in established democracies, we turn our attention to a selection of Latin American countries where the concept of judicial activism has also been employed in different ways. Here, judicial activism often describes instances where courts have transcended their assigned role, usually by engaging in jurisprudential innovations involving open confrontations with other branches of power in contexts of democratization and institutional reform. These contributions connect well with recent conversations that try to update the debate about the role of courts in contemporary Latin American democracies (and else, e.g., Botero et al., 2022; Albert et al., 2019; Uprimny, 2011). They acknowledge, and build upon, the substantial work that has been done in the field to advance studies of judicial politics and constitutional rights protection in Latin America (Kapiszewski and Taylor, 2008; Helmke and Ríos-Figueroa, 2011), whilst also contributing to a growing conversation about the dimensions, consequences, and normative desirability of activist courts in a region where major concerns about judicial performance, independence, access and other aspects of the judicial function remain.

We divide the section on Latin American cases in two different groups. In the first, we look at countries that have characteristically been identified (and assessed) as assertive and independent judiciaries: Colombia, Costa Rica, and Brazil. Their strong institutional role has been characterized as activist in the past, so we wanted to have a closer look at their experiences, but we also encouraged our contributors to engage critically with judicial activism as a conceptual tool. In the case of Colombia—which has one of the most powerful constitutional courts in the region—Benitez, Pulido Ortiz and Rivas Robledo make a strong contribution, not only to our understanding of the experience of judicial activism in Colombia, but most importantly to our thinking about how to make theoretical choices in judicial activism research for analytical purposes in specific contexts. The chapter interrogates the concept of judicial activism setting aside conceptions that equate activism with judicial outcomes, their effects, or their moral content. Instead, it claims that judicial activism is better understood as the improper use of previously established judicial prerogatives. The authors then proceed to examine the Colombian Constitutional Court's case law on judicial review of constitutional amendments, looking into the 'replacement theory' as an activist doctrine. This discussion seeks to show judicial activism as a sort of 'weapon' that the Colombian Court activates or deactivates strategically depending on the political context, the potential repercussions of its rulings, and the degree with which judicial activism hinders or furthers the Court's agenda. Notice how, once again, understanding judges as judicial actors reckoning with a socio-political context is key.

Next, Bruce Wilson looks into another powerful constitutional court—the Costa Rican Constitutional Chamber of the Supreme Court (also known as the *Sala Cuarta*, or 'fourth chamber'). Like other apex courts in the region, the Costa Rican Supreme Court was traditionally a deferential court that failed to use its prerogatives to control the government or protect rights. This changed in 1989 with the creation of the Constitutional Chamber. The court immediately began actively seeking and quickly resolving a wide range of cases of alleged constitutional rights violations by public and private actors alike. The chapter chronicles the creation of the Chamber and its subsequent emergence as a powerful court, with an emphasis on its accountability function; its transformative jurisprudence on economic, social and cultural rights, and its reliance on the Inter-American Court of Human Rights' precedents to protect the rights of marginalized groups like LGBTI communities. Wilson argues that in this context decision making characterized as activist is often required for protecting rights, and that a deferential court is one actively supporting the status quo of elites. Consulting these two chapters back-to-back will afford readers with a very good knowledge of two countries where the judiciary has managed to retain a strong position in the political system over the course of several decades—despite being considered 'activist' by political opponents and other critics.

Together with Colombia and Costa Rica, the most distinctive example of a powerful judicial institution in the region is Brazil's Federal Supreme Tribunal. This is also an emblematic example of a court that became powerful against the backdrop of a democratizing country that transitioned from a military regime during the Third Wave of democracy, in the late 1980s/early 1990s. Whilst Costa Rica and Colombia were democratic regimes with particular strengths and shortcomings (with the Colombian case being afflicted by a decades-long bloody armed conflict); the Brazilian case represents a successful transition to democracy. Yet, a critical question in this transition and the subsequent threats it has faced in recent years—including rising corruption, and the surge of Bolsonaro's populist authoritarian rule in the 2019–2023 presidential term—has been the role of courts and legal interpretation in holding elected leaders to account and effect socio-economic policy (Kapiszewski, 2012). Against this backdrop, Meyer and Bustamante analyze judicial activism in Brazil, subjecting to scrutiny calls for an activist judiciary in Brazil and highlighting the risks this represents for the rule of law. The Brazilian case showcases the risks associated with courts becoming visible political actors and striking a balance between challenging other political actors and interpreting the law in consistent fashion.

In the second group of Latin American cases, we look at three examples of courts and instances of 'judicial activism' in the context of Latin American countries with judiciaries that have traditionally been considered less powerful, but which have had significantly different trajectories in recent times. This includes Venezuela, a country where, regrettably, the judiciary became a key institutional player in the country's context of democratic deterioration and autocratic consolidation; Paraguay, a country with very interesting lessons to offer about the limits of judicial empowerment in weakly institutionalized democracies; and Mexico, a country where the Supreme Court has become an important political actor in the past decades (*see* Castagnola and Noriega, 2016). Interestingly, in two of these countries—Mexico and Paraguay—the judiciary operated in an increasingly fragmented political environment in democracy, after emerging from authoritarian systems with party hegemony (the PRI in Mexico, and the Colorado Party in Paraguay). Meanwhile, in Venezuela the judiciary has operated in recent years in the opposite trajectory, i.e., a system controlled by President Nicolás Maduro and the United Socialist Party (PSUV).

In Chapter 9, Sanchez Urribarri explores judicial activism in the context of democratic backsliding in Venezuela after the arrival of Hugo Chávez in power and throughout the consolidation of the Bolivarian Revolution (1999–Current). The Venezuelan Supreme Tribunal (TSJ) was endowed with major constitutional review prerogatives in the 1999 Constitution but failed to fulfill an accountability role against an increasingly authoritarian regime in a polarized political environment. Moreover, over time, it became an enthusiastic defender of the regime against the political opposition, engaging in an expansive interpretation of its own powers vis-à-vis the rest of the judiciary and state actors, and the creative use of these prerogatives to protect and advance regime interests. This included the complete obstruction of the opposition-controlled National Assembly (2015–2020). Thus, the Tribunal was an 'activist' judicial institution in more than one sense, displaying a particular kind of regressive activism on behalf of a consolidating autocracy. Both the Brazilian and Venezuelan cases are great examples of problematic instances of judicial activism. As much as we can hope for courts to become activist and defend democracy, there are potential dangers in terms of their legitimacy, and their capacity to survive political pressures in adverse environments.

On the other hand, Paraguay offers a very interesting case to study the role of constitutional justice in a context of past party hegemony. Castagnola, Bonzi, Franco and Pérez-Liñán assess the role of the Constitutional Chamber of the Paraguayan Supreme Court, exploring how the Court, despite failing to become assertive versus elected leaders and prominent politicians, nonetheless manages to exercise its authority quite frequently against the President and Congress. This interesting trend is empirically assessed using original data of unconstitutional actions against laws and decrees between 1995 and 2015, and discussing how the Court intervenes to protect rights in key cases described as activist. Strong party hegemony and a long tradition lacking judicial independence, traditionally lead scholars to expect deference from a Court. This is not the case in Paraguay although the Court does appear to limit the areas of its activity—areas away from ruling elites.

In the last chapter of the section, Rebecca Reid evaluates the Mexican Supreme Court's use of conventionality control—a mechanism created by the

Inter-American Court of Human Rights that requires states to conform domestic legislation to the Court's precedents, by empowering and obliging domestic judges to disregard laws that fail to conform to their jurisprudential standards. This power shifts the domestic separation of powers dynamic, with civil law courts gaining strength versus the executive and legislative branches of power. Occasionally, some of these invitations to use their powers can offer the opportunity to exercise their authority in a way that can be catalogued as judicial activism. Reid's chapter offers a comprehensive overview of this important development in Mexican judicial politics.

Finally, following the discussion of these case studies, we offer two different contributions that engage in cross-national analyses of judicial activism, contributing to the theoretical and methodological debates advanced in the single-country case studies. Both authors wrestle with the subdimensions of the concept of activism directly. First, Lee Walker looks at the aspect of legitimacy as a key part of the story of judicial activism, linked to how a court's preoccupation with its own legitimacy can help explain instances where it engages in judicial activism against the government. Walker's piece offers a thorough assessment of judicial legitimacy by using different measurements of the concept. Interestingly, he finds that different approaches to judicial legitimacy successfully influence court decisions on whether presidents can seek re-election—an area where courts across different Latin American countries have the potential to engage in 'activist' rulings.

Susan Achury, on the other hand, closes out our selections by looking at the connection between legitimacy and judicial activism, dealing with the normative difficulty to distinguish between legitimate and inappropriate exercises of judicial prerogatives, and the challenges to identify standards for cross-national analyses. Achury's study thus conceptualizes activism as the breach of the expected intervention of the court derived from its formal prerogatives. As she claims in her chapter, "a priori comparisons of assertive decisions, even if substantially equivalent, cannot be used as examples of activism without qualifying whether the courts were legitimated to intervene." By using formal powers as a proxy to measure these expectations, Achury helps to understand one of the themes of the book: that assessments of activism are sensitive to specific institutional contexts. She argues effectively that any comparison should reckon with this variation in order to have a better idea of when, and under what conditions, a specific court is engaging in judicial activism.

With this volume, we have sought to contribute to current debates on a major topic in comparative law and courts research that, despite its importance in and outside the scholarly world, has been relatively neglected in the field. In addition to addressing the specialized academic audience interested in comparative law and courts, it is deliberately intended to provide a useful volume for students, teachers, and researchers in variety of disciplines. We hope this is the case, and the book opens new pathways to learning, discussing, and doing research on judicial activism cross-nationally.

References

Albert, R., Bernal Pulido, C., & Benvindo, J. Z. (Eds.). (2019). *Constitutional change and transformation in Latin America*. Bloomsbury Publishing.

Belov, M. (Ed.). (2021). *Courts and judicial activism under crisis conditions: Policy making in a time of illiberalism and emergency constitutionalism*. Routledge.

Botero, S., Brinks, D. M., & Gonzalez-Ocantos, E. A. (Eds.). (2022). *The limits of judicialization: From progress to backlash in Latin America*. Cambridge University Press.

Canon, B. C. (1982). Defining the dimensions of judicial activism. *Judicature*, 66, 236.

Castagnola, A., & Noriega, S. L. (Eds.). (2016). *Judicial politics in Mexico: The Supreme Court and the transition to democracy*. Routledge.

Cohn, M., & Kremnitzer, M. (2005). Judicial activism: A multidimensional model. *Canadian Journal of Law & Jurisprudence*, *18*(2), 333–356.

Coutinho, L. P., La Torre, M., & Smith, S. D. (Eds.). (2015). *Judicial activism: An interdisciplinary approach to the American and European experiences*. Springer.

De Witte, B., Muir, E., & Dawson, M. (Eds.). (2013). *Judicial activism at the European Court of Justice*. Edward Elgar Publishing.

Dickson, B. (2007). *Judicial activism in common law supreme courts*. Oxford University Press.

Epp, C. R. (1998). *The rights revolution: Lawyers, activists, and supreme courts in comparative perspective*. University of Chicago Press.

García García, J. F., & Verdugo Ramírez, S. I. (2013). *Activismo judicial en Chile ¿Hacia el gobierno de los jueces?* Santiago: Ediciones LYD.

Green, C. (2009). An intellectual history of judicial activism. *Emory Law Journal*, 58(5), 1195–1264.

Hausegger, L., Hennigar, M., & Riddell, T. (2009). *Canadian courts: Law, politics, and process*. Oxford University Press.

Helmke, G., & Ríos-Figueroa, J. (Eds.). (2011). *Courts in Latin America*. Cambridge University Press.

Hirschl, R. (2008). The judicialization of mega-politics and the rise of political courts. *Annual Review of Political Science*, *11*, 93–118.

Holland, K. M. (Ed.). (1991). *Judicial activism in comparative perspective*. Springer.

Josev, T. (2017). The nursery years of 'judicial activism': From A historian's shorthand to media catchphrase 1947–1962. *Studies in Law, Politics, and Society*, 72, 53–80.

Kapiszewski, D. (2012). *High courts and economic governance in Argentina and Brazil.* Cambridge University Press.

Kapiszewski, D., & Taylor, M. M. (2008). Doing courts justice? Studying judicial politics in Latin America. *Perspectives on Politics*, 6(4), 741–767.

Kmiec, K. D. (2004). The origin and current meanings of "judicial activism". *California Law Review*, 92(5), 1441–1477.

Lindqquist, S., & Cross, F. (2009). *Measuring judicial activism.* Oxford University Press.

Petersen, N. (2017). *Proportionality and judicial activism: Fundamental rights adjudication in Canada, Germany and South Africa.* Cambridge University Press.

Rodia, T. (2022). What defines judicial activism? Not being an activist, says Kermit Roosevelt. *Penn Today*, July 15. Downloaded at: https://penntoday.upenn.edu/news/what-defines-judicial-activism-not-being-activist-says-kermit-roosevelt on December 8, 2022.

Roosevelt, K. (2008). *The myth of judicial activism: Making sense of Supreme Court decisions.* Yale University Press.

Roux, T. (2021). Judicial activism. *Elgar Encyclopedia on Comparative Law.* Downloaded at: https://papers.ssrn.com/sol3/papers.cfm?abstract_id=3923921 on August 8, 2022.

Schlesinger Jr., A. M. (1947). The Supreme Court: 1947. *Fortune*, Jan. 1947, p. 73.

Sherry, S. (2013). *A summary of why we need more judicial activism.* Downloaded on December 12, 2022, at: https://law.vanderbilt.edu/news/a-summary-of-why-we-need-more-judicial-activism/

Songer, D. R. (2008). *The transformation of the Supreme Court of Canada: An empirical examination.* University of Toronto Press.

Songer, D. R., Ostberg, C. L., Johnson, S. W., & Wetstein, M. E. (2012). *Law, ideology, and collegiality: Judicial behaviour in the Supreme Court of Canada.* McGill-Queen's Press-MQUP.

Tate, C. N., & Vallinder, T. (1995). *The global expansion of judicial power.* New York University Press.

Uprimny, R. (2011). The recent transformation of constitutional law in Latin America: Trends and challenges. *Texas Law Review*, 89, 1587.

Waller, J., & Sterling, G. (2020). *What is judicial activism? A debate on legal and political philosophy.* Bloomsbury.

· 2 ·

JUDICIAL ACTIVISM IN COMPARATIVE LAW AND POLITICS

Jeffrey K. Staton

Twenty years ago, I presented research about the Supreme Court of Mexico at a U.S. university. The study I discussed developed conditions under which the Supreme Court would find unconstitutional a policy challenged before it (e.g., an act of Congress, a presidential decree, an administrative order, a state law, etc.). The outcome measure in the paper was a binary indicator tracking whether the Court found that the policy under consideration violated some portion of the Mexican constitution, for any reason. I viewed this indicator as a measure of a form of judicial activism.

The study emerged within the context of a general concern in the field of comparative politics for understanding how constitutional reform empowering courts in the late 20th century affected political processes in the democratizing world (e.g., Ginsburg, 2003; Finkel, 2008). It was certainly undeniable that courts across the globe were addressing a series of salient political questions, questions whose resolutions had historically been left to governments acting alone (Tate, Vallinder et al., 1995; Epp, 1998). The twin processes of constitutional reform and the judicialization of politics raised questions about whether formal promises to protect individual rights and liberties found in countless constitutions and international treaties, and more deeply, promises for limited government, might become a practical reality via the constitutional review powers of judiciaries (Cepeda, 2009; Domingo, 2000).

At the end of the presentation, a member of the audience, a scholar of law and politics in the United States, whose opinion I greatly valued, approached me. As I remember it, the professor said something like, "That was just the oddest take on the concept of judicial activism." The professor then exited the seminar room, leaving me processing all the things that could have gone wrong. I wondered if the professor meant something about the theoretical argument I had presented. Was somehow the logic I offered for why the Supreme Court exercised its powers of constitutional review invalid or unsound? I had been, to be fair, talking about the Supreme Court's media relations strategy as a key element of its constitutional review work, which was admittedly a bit strange. Were the inferences I derived confounded or otherwise wrong? Was it clear how the Mexican case spoke to the experiences of other countries?

The truth is that any (or all) of these critiques could have been levied against my work, I suppose as is true of any piece of scholarship. Reflecting on the experience two decades later, what I believe the professor likely was saying was, quite validly, that my study was not so much wrong as missing a critical element that makes judicial activism a meaningful concept.

What was missing was an explicit normative statement about why the invalidations of policy I was studying were in some way normatively appropriate or inappropriate. For this reason, it was just hard to know what to make of the key theoretical claims, the measures, much less the results. There was, of course, an implicit normative claim in the study, grounded in the literature on the transition to democracy. Invalidating a policy was far from a violation of the proper judicial role in a democratic society. Indeed, in the political context I was considering, Mexico during its transition to democracy, invalidating an act of Congress or a Presidential decree was to be expected if the Supreme Court was properly fulfilling its constitutional role. Under those conditions, judicial activism was something of a good thing. Juxtaposed against a century of use in the United States, in which judicial activism commonly described a court's failure to stick within its proper role, my presentation would have surely appeared odd.

The exchange captures the central challenge that scholars of law and politics confront when making use of the concept of judicial activism. Judicial activism is an *essentially contested concept* (Gallie, 1955). Essentially contested concepts are those "the proper use of which inevitably involves endless disputes about their proper uses on the part of their users" (p. 169). Like democracy, the rule of law, and judicial independence, judicial activism is the subject of frequent definition-giving. Every twenty years or so, scholars set about taking stock of research on the subject, and much of the effort is about characterizing basic meanings (Mason, 1969; Canon, 1982; Young, 2002; Cohn and Kremnitzer, 2005). Complicating matters is the fact that judicial activism is used in popular discussions of politics (Gerhardt, 2001), in ways that seem to merely reflect differences of political orientation. This fact suggests the stakes of getting the concept well-defined. Writing about the rule of law, another contested concept used in non-academic political discussions, Waldron (2017) writes:

> Philosophical analysis of an important term cannot afford to distance itself too much from the use of that term on the streets: otherwise, the analysis is not the analysis of anything interesting, from a political point of view. On the other hand, if street-level use is completely confused, we may have no alternative but to pronounce the term meaningless. That is, it may turn out to be impossible to say what any use of the term implies or is implied by, or what it presupposes or is presupposed by; its protean usage may make it nothing more than a site for equivocation. At that stage, the best we could do would be to substitute for it a well-defined technical term, which will serve us for analytic and theoretical purposes (p. 138).

The conceptual status of judicial activism matters because scientific progress happens in a community. Groups of scholars decide what questions are important to ask, what research designs are credible, what results are worth discussing, and ultimately what implications we ought to draw from studies for broader concerns about the world and the welfare of the people who inhabit it. Because science happens in a community, essentially contested concepts present critical challenges. It is one thing for legal philosophers to engage in an ongoing conceptual debate of the meaning of judicial activism. In that discipline, developing compelling definitions of concepts is often the entire point of the exercise. Social scientists, on the other hand, build models of politics, and disagreements over conceptual definitions present special risks for us. We use concepts in these models, which often interact in complicated ways. Disagreements about any one of these concepts propagate through the entire model or explanation. We also evaluate empirical implications of our models against data, and our conceptual disagreements create fundamental problems of measurement.

The risks are especially true for comparative law and politics. Comparative politics scholars are commonly divided by region, often by country, and sometimes by sub-region of a state. Institutions vary considerably across these contexts. The precise questions that drive us, from trying to understand the origins of social change to the ability of judges to promote democracy, are salient in different locations. Variation in institutions and political context can separate us. They create challenges for building a coherent, dense network of studies. If we also do not agree on a key concept that we use in each of these different settings, we risk basically working outside the context of a true scientific community. Yet, empirically oriented social scientists frequently work with essentially contested concepts. Most obviously, there are deep empirical literatures about the determinants and consequences of democracy (e.g. Beck et al., 2007; Teorell and Lindstedt, 2010; Golder, 2005; Munck and Verkuilen, 2002; Bollen, 1980; Treier and Jackman, 2008; Marshall et al., 2002; Pemstein, Meserve and Melton, 2010; Przeworski et al., 1996; Bernhard, Nordstrom and Reenock, 2001) and the rule of law (e.g. Haggard and Tiede, 2011; Carlin, 2012; Skaaning, 2010; Gutmann and Voigt, 2018; Andrews and Montinola, 2004). And, of course, there are rich literatures in law and politics that combine these concepts in various ways (Sanchez Urribarri, 2011; Ríos-Figueroa, 2016; Staton, Reenock and Holsinger, 2022; Hausegger and Riddell, 2004; Gibson, Caldeira and Baird, 1998). These literatures involve conceptual debates, to be sure, but they also move forward addressing important political questions.

A critical question for law and politics scholars, then, is whether judicial activism can be used effectively even if it is essentially contested. This is the primary question I take up in this chapter. In what follows, I first review features of the concept, which I believe imply that it is most certainly essentially contested. I then suggest two ways of moving forward fruitfully with empirical social science despite the contest.

Judicial Activism as Essentially Contested

Essentially contested concepts have several key features. First and foremost, they are characterized by normativity. To say that a court has engaged in judicial activism is to make a normative claim about the behavior under analysis. Activism should be avoided (or welcomed) depending on one's view, say, of the proper role of a court in a democratic society. Essentially contested concepts are also complex. They consist of multiple features which can be combined, or aggregated, in different ways to result at very different conclusions about the same object. This is to say that the same decision, or better, the same series of decisions, might be characterized by different users of the term as highly or minimally activist. The conclusion depends on how one orders or weights the different elements of activism. Further, the mechanism through which the combination of features is aggregated should be vague so that it is not entirely clear how the same user of the concept, applying the same concept, will aggregate identical features in different cases. And finally, it is nevertheless true that users of distinct versions of the concept are aware of and quite readily understand how other users of alternative uses of the concept.

Waldron (2017) summarizes these features writing "The key to Gallie's idea of essential contestability seems to be a combination of normativity and complexity: only normative concepts with a certain internal complexity are capable of being essentially contested" (p. 150). Judicial activism is characterized by the combination of these two key traits. Waldron writes further that disagreements about essentially contested concepts are defined by their "location." The contest is "at the core, not just at the borderlines or penumbra of a concept (p. 149)." We are not disagreeing about small things or boundary cases. We are disagreeing about paradigmatic cases. Antonin Scalia (U.S.) and Aharon Barak (Israel) are classic examples of activist judges; or maybe they are far from it. Scalia could be a paradigm of judicial restraint. Barak could simply have been fulfilling his role as a protector of core democratic commitments. One's perspective on the classification turns importantly on the concept applied.

Normativity

Scholars have defined judicial activism as a court intervening and striking down an act of the legislature (Posner, 1996). This definition has also been persuasively critiqued through simple examples. They all take the following form. Suppose that a legislature enacted a policy that contradicted a clear constitutional prohibition (e.g., the creation of a national religion in a state that prohibits it, a change to a constitutionally imposed electoral calendar). We would not find it inappropriate for a court endowed with constitutional review powers to strike down such an act. Therefore, it cannot be that all interventions that invalidate acts of a legislature are activist. Notice that we have slipped in a hidden normative premise in this argument. It surely could be that all invalidations of statutes are forms of activism. This is just a matter of definition. But such a rigid definition is considered problematic by many scholars. This is because we have implicitly assumed that courts acting appropriately should strike down some statutes and not others. Of course, to make sense of this kind of concept we would have to say more. We would have to say which kinds of statutes ought to be struck down and why. This type of work is entirely normative.

Scholars have also defined judicial activism as striking down policies that do not unambiguously violate the constitution (Easterbrook, 2002). When constitutional principles are unclear or when policies do not clearly violate clear principles, it is appropriate for courts to defer to the judgment of other branches of government. Of course, the normative work here is done by the clarity of the violation. The proper role of a court is to strike down only the clearest violations of the constitution, leaving hard cases to debate among elected officials. This definition, too, has a standard critique. Reasonable people will differ about what kinds of policies unambiguously violate a constitution. Indeed, nearly all important legal conflicts that involve a matter of constitutionality present difficult questions. They require interpretation in light of well-understood ambiguities. How this ought to be done will naturally be guided by normative principles. Cross and Lindquist (2006) put the matter succinctly, claiming that activism is characterized by the Court's failure to act like a judiciary. What it means to act like a judiciary is clearly subject to reasonable differences of opinion, grounded in one's view of a normatively appropriate political regime.

On the other hand, Cohn and Kremnitzer's (2005) concept of judicial activism demonstrates how judicial activism can be developed with respect to multiple views of the proper role of a judiciary. Specifically, they consider three plausible visions of courts in a democratic system: "Firstly, judiciaries are allotted the power to settle legal disputes under law. Secondly, the judiciary should not be viewed as supreme decision maker and final arbiter of social conflict. Finally, supreme courts in constitutionalist frameworks are entrusted with the role of active participation in the protection of core values (Cohn and Kremnitzer, 2005, p. 340)."

Each of these visions reflects a normative judgment about the role of the judiciary. The first vision tracks a traditional understanding of the role of courts. Under this view, the function of courts is to resolve legal conflicts. They should attempt to do no more and no less than seek the right answer to clearly presented legal questions. Ordinarily, this presents few challenges; however, when the resolution of a case requires that a policy be judged considering constitutional requirements, judges confront the familiar "counter-majoritarian difficulty." Judicial activism means managing the difficulty in a way that is inappropriate in light of a series of norms of judicial interpretation meant to minimize the extent to which judges substitute their judgment for that of the majority.

The second vision derives from a different understanding of the role of courts in a democratic society. Courts ought not to be understood as the only institutional actors endowed with the responsibility and authority to interpret a constitution's meaning. Instead, it is more useful to understand courts as part of a network of actors engaged in a process of "constitutional dialogue" designed to uncover constitutional meaning (Hogg and Bushell, 1997; Meuwese and Snel, 2013). From this perspective, judicial activism means judicial activity that is largely out of touch with the understandings of other political actors and the public at large.

The third vision derives from a view of courts as defenders of core or thin constitutional principles, e.g., equality, democratic freedom embodied in free speech rights, etc. A judiciary's function here is to ensure that a constitution's core is respected, and this may very well require the frequent substitution of a judge's view for that of a legislature. Quite obviously, if elected officials take actions that violate core principles, then courts are not only encouraged, but obligated under this vision to set these actions aside.

The bottom line is that no matter the concept of activism, scholars must take a normative position on the role of courts in a democratic society. In so far as there are multiple, valid positions on this role, we ought to expect contests over meaning. The second feature of judicial activism, its complexity, makes these contests inevitable.

Complexity

The complexity of judicial activism derives from three features. The first is that the concept, no matter the normative principle guiding it, is multidimensional. Figure 2.1 summarizes lists of forms of judicial activism under the concepts developed by Canon (1982), Young (2002), and Cohn and Kremnitzer (2005). Careful inspection of the lists suggests some commonalities, especially if we restrict ourselves to the first of Cohn and Kremnitzer's visions. The lists suggest that the invalidation of public policies is a form of activism. Similarly, they each highlight two types of interpretative behaviors: the failure to adhere to precedent and departures from the clear text of a constitution or from its original intent. Both are understood to reflect a form of activism. Cohn and Kremntizer's list is clearly longer. For example, they highlight the use of broad, non-legal rhetorical styles and the degree of obiter dicta in an opinion as important indicators of judicial activism.

Two additional features of the concept increase its complexity. The first is the absence of clear rules of aggregation. Whether considered from the perspective of a single decision or a series of decisions, it is simply unclear how to order or weight the dimensions. A simple ranking of the dimensions will require further normative statements about which features matter more than others. If we imagine an effort to construct quantitative scores aimed at producing an aggregated whole, we confront the possibility that there are infinite ways to weight the individual scores. This is always true, but the lack of a conceptual structure guiding the weighting further encourages debate.

The second additional feature is that there can be clear tensions between the individual subdimensions. The most obvious one involves the tension between fidelity to precedent and the avoidance of negating public policies. Young offers a particularly prescient hypothetical, which clearly illustrates the point.

> For a more familiar example, consider a hypothetical decision by the currentSupreme Court to overrule Roe v. Wade and Planned Parenthood v. Casey. Surely such a decision would be criticized by supporters of Roe and Casey as activist; in fact, fear of such criticism seems to have been a powerful part of the Court's stare decisis analysis in Casey. But it was Roe and Casey that struck down legislative acts; a decision overruling those decisions would amount to a refusal to invalidate legislative restrictions on the right to an abortion (Young, 2002, p. 1166).

There are multiple ways to manage this tension. One could simply ignore either the adherence to precedent or avoidance of the negation of policies criteria. One could weight one dimension more than the other. One could treat them equally and let them effectively cancel each other out in an aggregation. The basic point is that to arrive at an evaluation of judicial activism using a multidimensional construct requires some kind of ordering across sub-dimensions of the concept, which can be themselves in direct tension with each other.

It is important to notice that normative judgments guide conceptual efforts at multiple levels. Each sub-dimension of activism requires a normative argument about why the subdimension reflects appropriate judicial behavior. Including one set of sub-dimensions relative to others left to the side requires normative judgment. An effort to aggregate the subdimensions we select requires a normative argument about the relative importance of the subdimensions to the aggregated concept of judicial activism. This is precisely the kind of normativity combined with complexity that makes a concept essentially contested.

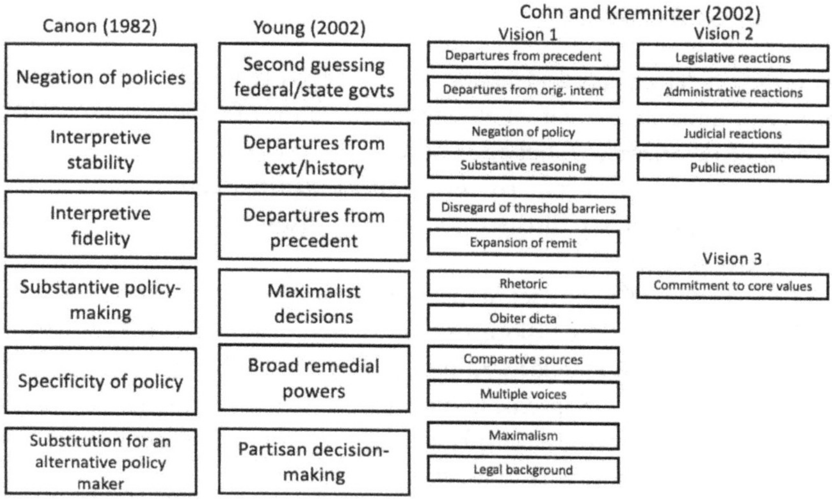

Figure 2.1: Three concepts of judicial activism

Fruitful Uses of an Essentially Contested Concept

The complexity and normativity of judicial activism clearly suggests that setting the concept to the side is a reasonable possibility. A first alternative to moving forward with it, is to focus on the individual concepts that seem to make up what people call activism. An empirical scholarship of forms of constitutional interpretation or the quality of judicial work would surely involve wrestling with Canon's sub-dimensions (e.g. Basabe-Serrano, 2016; Anderson IV, 2011). Similarly, the scholarship on judicial impact deals quite explicitly with a court's "broad remedial powers" (e.g. Spriggs, 1997; Gauri and Brinks, 2008). It might very well be best to simply stop using this term altogether so that scholars can focus more precisely on what judges do, removed at least to some degree from what they *should* do.

Of course, judicial activism is far from the only essentially contested concept with which social scientists work. Most obviously, political science, sociology, and economics have all developed innovative and important literatures on the concept of democracy. Democracy research might prove instructive as a means of structuring the kind of empirical research that might be profitably done even though the concept is contested.

Varieties of Activism

Literatures on democracy and democratization have developed effectively in the presence of multiple indicators of democracy, many of which measure distinct concepts of democracy (Coppedge et al., 2011). The Varieties of Democracy Project (V-Dem) quite explicitly set about measuring features of democracies that are relevant for six distinct conceptions. Research on judicial activism could take this form.

The Cohn and Kremnitzer model suggests a way of proceeding with respect to at least three different visions of judicial activism, each tied to a vision of the proper role of the judiciary. Khosla (2009) has applied this model to three decisions of the Indian Supreme Court and shows clearly how decisions can be sensibly described as activist with respect to one concept while simultaneously failing to appear activist with respect to another.

Cross and Lindquist offer a second possibility. The authors generate scores of judicial activism for United States Supreme Court justices on the Burger and Rehnquist Courts. The scores are probably best thought of as measures of Young's conception of activism. The most basic indicator is simply the proportion of times in which a justice voted to invalidate a federal or state law in cases presenting a constitutional challenge to such a law. They compare rankings of justices using this simple metric to a ranking derived from a procedure meant to capture the degree to which invalidations were likely to be legally justified. To do so, they consider whether justice votes are likely to be independent of the ideological consequences of the validation, independent of the Solicitor General's position if they took one, and likely to be part of a relatively large or small coalition of other justices.

Cross and Lindquist show that while there are some justices whose ranking on their distinct activism scales is captured similarly by both approaches, there are other justices whose ranking changes once they consider legally justifiable rationales for invalidating a policy.

A Minimal Core?

Another important aspect of democracy research has been its ability to identify a conceptual minimal core, which nearly all users of the term will agree to. The contest over the meaning of democracy does not end because of this core, but at the very least, there are a sufficient set of interlocutors who agree that the core is a meaningful component of democracy.

Although there are multiple conceptual definitions of democracy, there is consensus that democracy requires, at its core, a commitment to the use of free and fair elections for the selection of governments. Scholars reasonably differ over whether democracy requires more than this. Liberal democracy implies that leaders selected via free and fair elections ought to be nevertheless limited in their capacity to govern by clearly articulated rights. Deliberative concepts of democracy, in contrast, require that regimes are committed not only to peaceful transfer of power via elections, but reasoned, clear, public deliberation over alternative policy choices. Participatory concepts of democracy not only envision regimes in which parties compete for power via electoral processes, but that citizens are engaged actively in multiple aspects of the civic space.

Democracy means something different in each of these cases. All of them will involve some kind of aggregation of information from potentially many sub-dimensions. Yet all of them envision elections as central to democracy. A state in which policies are discussed openly or in which the government's use of power is constrained, potentially by the state's courts (Barros, 2002), would not be considered democratic if the government were not selected via electoral processes. Elections are the core of democracy, and this core has guided many empirical strategies for measurement as well as important studies on the determinants of democratic states.

The question is whether there is a minimal core of judicial activism. One is naturally drawn to the simplest of elements of activism—the invalidation of policies or departures from precedent. Yet I am skeptical that this could be the core, for reasons summarized above and developed elsewhere in considerable depth. What makes elections core to democracy is that it is hard to argue that systems in which leaders are not elected freely and fairly are democratic. They may be egalitarian, liberal, or participatory, but they are not democratic. Elections are in this way necessary conditions for democracy. Adherence to precedent or failure to invalidate policies, per se, are not necessary conditions for judicial restraint. This follows from recognizing that in some cases, under some concepts of activism, we want judges to overrule precedent and to invalidate laws.

Another possibility, anticipated by Young and Cross and Lindquist is the prohibition against partisan decision-making. This criterion does suggest a possible minimal core. Judges may vary in their approaches to constitutional interpretation, but it is unclear that any scholar would accept as appropriate an approach that was explicitly partisan.

Indeed, one way of understanding the literature on judicial behavior, with its focus on ideological and partisan influences on judging, is that it has very much always been about judicial activism, understood in this way. From this perspective, social scientists have already developed and continue to build upon a quite advanced literature on this essentially contested concept.

References

Anderson IV, R. (2011). Distinguishing judges: An empirical ranking of judicial quality in the United States Court of Appeals. *Mo. L. Rev.*, *76*, 315.

Andrews, J. T., & Montinola, G. R. (2004). Veto players and the rule of law in emerging democracies. *Comparative Political Studies*, *37*(1), 55–87.

Barros, R. (2002). *Constitutionalism and dictatorship: Pinochet, the Junta, and the 1980 constitution* (Vol. 4). Cambridge University Press.

Basabe-Serrano, S. (2016). The quality of judicial decisions in supreme courts: A conceptual definition and index applied to eleven Latin American countries. *Justice System Journal*, *37*(4), 331–347.

Beck, T., Keefer, P. E., Clarke, G. R., Walsh, P., & Groff, A. (2007). DPI 2006 database of political institutios. *Development Research Group. The World Bank.*

Bernhard, M., Nordstrom, T., & Reenock, C. (2001). Economic performance, institutional intermediation and democratic survival. *Journal of Politics*, 63, 775–803.

Bollen, K. A. (1980). Issues in the comparative measurement of political democracy. *American Sociological Review*, 370–390.

Canon, B. C. (1982). *A framework for the analysis of judicial activism.*

Carlin, R. E. (2012). Rule-of-law typologies in contemporary societies. *Justice System Journal*, *33*(2), 154–173.

Cepeda, M. J. (2009). The constitutional protection of IDPs in Colombia. *Judicial Protection of Internally Displaced Persons: The Colombian Experience.*

Cohn, M., & Kremnitzer, M. (2005). Judicial activism: A multidimensional model. *Canadian Journal of Law & Jurisprudence*, *18*(2), 333–356.

Coppedge, M., Gerring, J., Altman, D., Bernhard, M., Fish, S., Hicken, A., Kroenig, M., Lindberg, S. I., McMann, K., Paxton, P., et al. (2011). Conceptualizing and measuring democracy: A new approach. *Perspectives on Politics*, 9(2), 247–267.

Cross, F. B., & Lindquist, S. I. (2006). The scientific study of judicial activism. *Minn. L. Rev.*, *91*, 1752.

Domingo, P. (2000). Judicial independence: The politics of the Supreme Court in Mexico. *Journal of Latin American Studies*, *32*(3), 705–735.

Easterbrook, F. H. (2002). Do liberals and conservatives differ in judicial activism. *U. Colo. L. Rev. 73*, 1401.

Epp, C. R. (1998). *The rights revolution: Lawyers, activists, and supreme courts in comparative perspective.* Chicago: University of Chicago Press.

Finkel, J. S. (2008). *Judicial reform as political insurance: Argentina, Peru, and Mexico in the 1990s*. South Bend, IN: University of Notre Dame Press.

Gallie, W. B. (1955). Essentially contested concepts. In *Proceedings of the Aristotelian society* (Vol. 56, pp. 167–198). JSTOR.

Gauri, V., & Brinks, D. M. (2008). Introduction: The elements of legalization and the triangular shape of social and economic rights. In Varun Gauri & Daniel M. Brinks (Eds.), *Courting social justice: Judicial enforcement of social and economic rights in the developing world* (pp. 1–37). Cambridge University Press.

Gerhardt, M. J. (2001). The rhetoric of judicial critique: From judicial restraint to the virtual bill of rights. *Wm. & Mary Bill Rts. J.*, *10*, 585.

Gibson, J. L., Caldeira, G. A., & Baird, V. A. (1998). On the legitimacy of national high courts. *American Political Science Review*, *92*(2), 343–358.

Ginsburg, T. (2003). *Judicial review in new democracies: Constitutional courts in Asian cases*. New York: Cambridge University Press.

Golder, M. (2005). Democratic electoral systems around the world, 1946–2000. *Electoral Studies*, *24*(1), 103–121.

Gutmann, J., & Voigt, S. (2018). The rule of law: Measurement and deep roots. *European Journal of Political Economy*, *54*, 68–82.

Haggard, S., & Tiede, L. (2011). The rule of law and economic growth: Where are we? *World development*, *39*(5), 673–685.

Hausegger, L., & Riddell, T. (2004). The changing nature of public support for the Supreme Court of Canada. *Canadian Journal of Political Science*, *37*(1), 23–50.

Hogg, P. W., & Bushell, A. A. (1997). The charter dialogue between courts and legislatures, the (or perhaps the charter of rights isn't such a bad thing after all). *Osgoode Hall LJ*, *35*, 75.

Khosla, M. (2009). Addressing judicial activism in the Indian Supreme Court: Towards an evolved debate. *Hastings Int'l & Comp. L. Rev.*, *32*, 55.

Marshall, M., Gurr, T. R., Davenport, C., & Jaggers, K. (2002). Polity IV, 1800–1999: Comments on Munck and Verkuilen. *Comparative Political Studies*, *35*(1), 40–45.

Mason, A. T. (1969). Judicial activism: Old and new. *Va. L. Rev.*, *55*, 385.

Meuwese, A., & Snel, M. (2013). "Constitutional Dialogue": An overview. *Utrecht Law Review*, 9(2), 123–140.

Munck, G., & Verkuilen, J. (2002). Conceptualizing and measuring democracy: Evaluating alternative indices. *Comparative Political Studies*, *35*(1), 5–35.

Pemstein, D., Meserve, S. A., & Melton, J. (2010). Democratic compromise: A latent variable analysis of ten measures of regime type. *Political Analysis*, 18(4), 426–449.

Posner, R. A. (1996). *The federal courts: Challenge and reform* (Revised edition). Harvard University Press.

Przeworski, A., Alvarez, M., Cheibub, J. A., & Limongi, F. (1996). What makes democracies endure?. *Journal of Democracy*, *7*(1), 31–55.

R´ıos-Figueroa, J. (2016). *Constitutional courts as mediators: Armed conflict, civil-military relations, and the rule of law in Latin America*. Cambridge University Press.

Sanchez Urribarri, R. A. (2011). Courts between democracy and hybrid authoritarianism: Evidence from the Venezuelan Supreme Court. *Law amp; Social Inquiry*, *36*(4), 854–884.

Skaaning, S. E. (2010). Measuring the rule of law. *Political Research Quarterly*, *63*(2), 449–460.

Spriggs, J. F. (1997). Explaining federal bureaucratic compliance with supreme court opinions. *Political Research Quarterly*, *50*(3), 567.

Staton, J. K., Reenock, C., & Holsinger, J. (2022). *Can courts be bulwarks of democracy?: Judges and the politics of prudence*. Cambridge University Press.

Tate, C. N., Vallinder, T., et al. (1995). *The global expansion of judicial power*. NYU Press.

Teorell, J., & Lindstedt, C. (2010). Measuring electoral systems. *Political Research Quarterly*, *63*(2), 434–448.

Treier, S., & Jackman, S. (2008). Democracy as a latent variable. *American Journal of Political Science*, *52*(1), 201–217.

Waldron, J. (2017). Is the rule of law an essentially contested concept (in Florida)? In *The rule of law and the separation of powers* (pp. 117–144). Routledge.

Young, E. A. (2002). Judicial activism and conservative politics. *U. Colo. L. rev.*, *73*, 1139.

· 3 ·

THE COMPLEMENTARY USE OF JUDICIAL ACTIVISM AND RESTRAINT IN THE UNITED STATES SUPREME COURT

Richard L. Pacelle, Jr.

Roe v. Wade was a textbook example of judicial activism. The Supreme Court created the right to privacy out of the shadows and penumbras cast by a number of amendments. It was a controversial decision creating a right that would become a core issue in American politics for half a century. The demise of *Roe* had been forecast for decades, but in 2020 it seemed imminent. The death of Ruth Bader Ginsburg and the ideological leanings of her successor (Amy Coney Barrett) pushed the Court further to the right. Still, for decades, courts dominated by Republican appointees had ample opportunities to relegate *Roe* to the dustbin and did not exercise them. The most serious previous threat to *Roe* was blunted by Justices Sandra Day O'Connor, Anthony Kennedy, and David Souter (all appointed by Republicans).[1] Their plurality opinion in *Planned Parenthood v. Casey* a full 30 years before *Dobbs v. Jackson Women's Health Organization* is the textbook definition of judicial restraint and saved *Roe* from the brink.

Chief Justice John Roberts has been criticized by Republicans for failing to cast the tie breaking vote to dismantle policies like the Affordable Care

1 They were joined by Justices John Stevens and Harry Blackmun (Republican appointees) to uphold *Roe*. Indeed, the one justice who was willing to overturn *Roe*, Byron White, was appointed by a Democrat.

Act. In the *Dobbs* case, Roberts was apparently trying to save *Roe* from being overturned. The *Dobbs* decision had two acts: a prequel when the vote was leaked early, and the main act, when the Court's released decision overruled *Roe v. Wade*. It is not often that the Court explicitly overrules a precedent. But Justice Samuel Alito's majority opinion did not mince any words when he did just that.

Dobbs was a lightning rod, of course, but it was far from the only decision the Court announced during the waning days of the October 2021 term. If Chief Justice Roberts was trying to preserve doctrine and keep the Court from flexing its power, he was unsuccessful. Cases involving school prayer, gun rights, and immigration would have been in the first paragraph of a synopsis of the 2021 term. Instead, they seemed to be afterthoughts as focus turned to *Dobbs*. At the end of a term when the Court empties the inbox, the last decisions tend to be very important. Indeed, the final decision on the final day was below the radar of most but consequential, nonetheless. *West Virginia v. Environmental Protection Agency* trimmed the authority of the EPA. Along with *Dobbs*, it may be among the most important decisions of the decade. Like *Dobbs*, the *EPA* case may be a portent of major changes in judicial activism and impact the Court's legitimacy.

This chapter examines the practical dimensions of judicial activism and restraint in the Supreme Court of the United States. The modern Supreme Court has thrust itself into the middle of policy making. The Court has alternated between activist and very activist. But buried below the fold have been rumors of willful judicial restraint. We think of judicial activism and judicial restraint as ends of a continuum or as competing principles. But what if they are complementary and necessary to protect and preserve the legitimacy and viability of the institution?

Alexander Hamilton wrote that the judiciary was the "least dangerous branch of government." It was not difficult to see why. The institutional design of the judiciary and the lack of judicial review did not augur for a strong Supreme Court. Indeed, Hamilton wrote that the Court lacked "the sword and the purse." Its decisions would need the support of the other branches of government. It was the perfect recipe for judicial restraint. No one would argue that the current judiciary is the least powerful branch of government. Still given the fragile nature of its power, even the current judiciary needs to protect its legitimacy (Pacelle, 2002).

The modern Court is intimately involved in the doctrinal construction of every important issue. The Court is shrouded in a mystique that starts with its "marble palace." Justices wear robes and maintain the fiction/illusion that their decisions are grounded on a higher authority. The judicial branch has a quasi-religious aura, complete with the Constitution as its bible. Traditionally, the Court has enjoyed diffuse support from a public that is hazy on how it operates. To not know the Supreme Court is to love the Supreme Court (Pacelle, 2015). The Court's legitimacy buffers it from approbation. The Court normally treats its legitimacy as a precious, finite resource. The power the Court has is extensive, but to wield the power too often is to risk depleting it (Caldeira and Gibson, 1992; Gibson and Nelson, 2015). The Court is expected to be circumspect and show judicial self-restraint. Occasionally, the temptation is too great, and the Court cannot resist the impulse to become more deeply involved.

Words and phrases carry power and can be used for framing issues. They can also be weaponized. One hardy perennial has been the term "judicial activism." There are few terms that carry the pejorative weight of judicial activism. To label someone a "judicial activist" is to cast the worst aspersion on a justice, a nominee, or a court decision (Keck, 2014). On the other hand, it is a hoary generalization supported by office holders, politicians, and even academics to say that judicial restraint is the normative ideal and what we want from unelected judges and their courts, but that judicial activism is much closer to empirical reality. Defining "judicial activism" is difficult. Perhaps, it is like beauty, in the eye of the beholder. But it also may be like obscenity, it cannot be precisely defined, but "I know it when I see it."

As you read through this volume, you will see some common themes connected to judicial activism and restraint. But the book and its authors make clear that there are contextual differences between forms of judicial activism and the nations and courts that use or eschew it. In this chapter, I examine the plural meanings of judicial activism in the United States and consider the conditions that make judicial restraint (and activism) more or less likely (Engel, 2011). Before I define my notions of the dimensions of activism and restraint, let me start with what it is not. Judicial activism and restraint are not ideological. The ultra-liberal Warren Court was a venue of wanton judicial activism (Schwartz, 1983; Powe, 2000). The conservative Rehnquist Court was also an activist body (Keck, 2004). The 2021 term may rival others for the depth and breadth of activism. I advance the argument that there is a safety net (forged in judicial restraint) for judicial activism and the Roberts Court may be operating without that net. After exploring this argument and its connections to different determinants of judicial decision making, I test my argument using economic and civil liberties cases decided by the Supreme Court between 1953 and 2016.

Judicial Activism and Restraint

At the fundamental core, activism and restraint often come down to policy making (Lemieux and Watkins, 2018). A willingness to make policy reflects an activist bent. Reticence to engage in policy making is the province of judicial restraint. The argument that judges should opt for restraint has normative and empirical dimensions. Judicial activism is anti-democratic. Unelected judges should not be legislating from the bench (Wolfe 1997). Under the system of checks and balances that is the work of the other branches. A court that is willing to ignore boundaries and push forward "making the law" could risk its legitimacy as an institution. Donald Horowitz (1977) and Gerald Rosenberg (2008) argue that the courts lack the capacity to build coherent policy, enforce their decisions, and cannot be the engines of social and political change.

Figure 3.1 shows the multiple dimensions of judicial activism and restraint. The traditional view of judicial activism is that unelected judges are willing to substitute their judgment for the elected branches of government. Judicial activism is manifested in the use of judicial review to declare the work of

	Judicial Role	
Activity	Restraint	Activism
Precedent	Adhere/Defer to Existing Precedent	Overturn/Distinguish Existing Precedent
Judicial Review	Uphold Legislation Defer to Elected Branches	Overturn Legislation
Statutory Interpretation	Fill Gaps Consistent with Legislative Intent	Rewrite/Expand/Contract Statutory Provisions
Constitutional Interpretation	Narrow/Consistent with Broad Principles Judicial Interpretation	Broad Interpretation Rewrite Provisions Judicial Legislation

Figure 3.1: The dimensions of judicial activism and restraint

the elected branches unconstitutional. To exercise restraint is to defer to the elected branches and not override the initiatives of Congress and the president through use of judicial review (Pacelle, 2002; Lemieux and Watkins, 2018). An example of judicial activism would be the Court's decision striking down the Defense of Marriage Act. The Roberts Court's refusal to overturn the Affordable Care Act was an exercise in judicial restraint.

Another traditional form of activism and restraint regards the Court's use of precedent. An activist court would not hesitate to overrule a precedent to get to a preferred decision (Ball, 1978; Pacelle, 2002). Proponents of restraint would respect precedents even if they considered them wrongly decided (Kozel, 2017).[2] Typically, precedents meet their demise at the hands of the Supreme Court only after several decades (Hansford and Spriggs, 2006). *Brown* marked the end of *Plessy v. Ferguson*, issued 58 years earlier. But more recently, the Court's decision in *Agostini v. Felton* overruled *Aguilar v. Felton*, a decision barely a decade old (Wood and Petko, 2000).

Since *Cooper v, Aaron* (1958), the Court has claimed hegemony over interpreting the Constitution (Powe, 2000). The scope of an activist decision would be very different from one exercising judicial restraint. The former would be broader in scope and would, in essence, have the Court "rewrite" the provisions of the Constitution. Judicial activism is, in effect, "judicial legislation." The activist Court based *Roe* on the judicially created right to privacy. Proponents of judicial restraint would adhere to the language of the Constitution more closely and issue narrow decisions based on shared and consistent principles (Pacelle, 2002).

Many of the cases before the Court involve statutory interpretation and once again there are a range of possible approaches. The Court would narrowly construe statutes and give the elected branches leeway if it adopted judicial restraint. By contrast, the activist Court might sharply narrow the scope of the statute or broaden it beyond the legislature's original intent. The Court and Congress wrestled for close to a decade with language in civil rights legislation whether Title VI, Title IX, or other provisions. The Court would take a narrow construction and Congress would come back and pass a civil rights restoration package (Eskridge, 1991, 1994).

The late flurry of the Supreme Court decisions in the recent 2021 term was defined by a wide range of judicial activism. If judicial activism is marked by

2 Justice Scalia developed a corollary: "the two wrongs make a right" exception. Scalia argued that if the Court overturned a bad precedent that was, in effect, using activism to cancel an activist precedent was tantamount to judicial restraint (Strauss, 1990–1991).

decisions that overrule precedents, substitute the judgment of unelected judges for that of elected officials or expert agencies, issue sweeping decisions, and act outside the bounds of the Constitution by reading its provisions very broadly, the Roberts Court exercised the full panoply. In *Dobbs*, the Court overturned a precedent approaching its 50th anniversary. In *New York State Rifle and Pistol Association v. Bruen*, the unelected justices ruled a state gun safety law was unconstitutional, ignoring the elected officials and the voters who sent them to Albany. And in the EPA case, the Court ignored the experts and limited the agency's authority.

Justices want to pursue their policy goals in as many cases as possible, moving doctrine close to their sincere policy preferences. Exercising judicial activism can accomplish short term goals. But being too aggressive can take a toll on the institution and invite reaction. Most justices realize that broadly exercised activism is going to be difficult, and they need to temper those impulses by attending to precedent. They need to respect previous decisions, the so-called "golden rule of precedent," so that their colleagues will respect their precedents. Otherwise, they risk harming the institution and their decisions would not carry the imprimatur of legitimacy.

How does the Court protect its prerogatives while accomplishing its collective policy goals and protecting its legitimacy? One recipe is to mix healthy doses of judicial restraint with limited portions of activism. To embark on a path dominated by activism and short on restraint is to risk legitimacy. This is a particularly dangerous brand of judicial activism. In a sense, it represents judicial activism without a safety net. Is the Court too greedily consuming its most important recourse, its legitimacy? This chapter starts with the premise that judicial activism and restraint are complementary, and the latter is a necessary ingredient of the former. The two acting together might be the blueprint for achieving preferences while maintaining legitimacy.

Activism and Restraint in "Abnormal" Times

We measure epochs of the Supreme Court in three ways. They may carry the name of the Chief Justice, the titular head of the Court. The Warren Court, as noted, was an activist tribunal. If a president is fortunate to win judicial roulette and has the opportunity to make a number of appointments and those selections move the median, then we may know the Court by their name. The Roosevelt Court was birthed during the early days of the New Deal. The Reagan Court reinforced the Nixon Court (Abraham, 2008). Donald Trump may also be viewed as such a transformational president able to park justices who remain long after his tenure is over.

There is a third possibility. The Court may come to be known for a major landmark decision, whether exemplary or ignominious. The *Dred Scott* (*v. Sanford*) Court was a reference to the latter. The *Lochner* (*v. New York*) Court was famous for sharply limiting regulations (Gillman, 1993). The *Brown* (*v. Board of Education*) Court or the *Roe v. Wade* Court reflect the significance of those decisions (Clark, 2019). It is not surprising that courts are designated by a major landmark reflecting judicial activism. Judicial restraint decisions need not apply. The *Dobbs* Court is likely to be an enduring sobriquet. And it likely will be the first sentence in the historical narrative of the Roberts Court.

There are times when the Court throws itself into the maelstrom without external support or with an apparent disregard for its legitimacy risking a self-inflicted wound. The Court announces a decision that is out of touch with elite and public opinion, and it may harm the institution. Perhaps the best example is *Dred Scott v. Sanford* (1857) when the activist Court invalidated the Missouri Compromise and pushed the nation closer to the Civil War. The Court was vilified and weakened for decades (McCloskey, 1960). Its rulings were ignored, and the other branches first increased and then decreased the size of the Court as a show of their disdain (Clark, 2019, p. 155). *Dred Scott* was the kind of decision that earns judicial activism its negative connotations.

In 1937, the Supreme Court was in a similar situation. The nation, mired in the Great Depression, gave the Democrats the keys to the White House and both chambers of Congress. This period was widely described as a "partisan realignment" (Sundquist, 1983). The immediate consequences of such a realignment often erupt in political conflict (Funston, 1978). Voters give the reins of power to a new party. But the old party retains an important base of power. In this case, it was burrowed into the judiciary. The question is whether the Court from the old coalition will follow the voters and elected officials and adopt judicial restraint or exercise activism and incur the wrath of the other branches and the public. History tells us that the Court Roosevelt "inherited" tried to reinstate the old order, striking down components of the New Deal. It would turn out to be another self-inflicted wound (McKenna, 2002; Clark, 2011).

Roosevelt bided his time until he was re-elected and then launched a multi-faceted attack on the Court. He tried to demean the Court by nominating Senator Hugo Black and then proposed the Court Reorganization Plan, designed to pack the Court with up to six new justices to build a majority that would sustain his agenda (Shesol, 2010; Clark, 2011). The bullying seemed to work. The Court appeared to blink when Justice Owen Roberts began voting to uphold the New Deal, the so-called "switch in time that saved nine" (but see Ross, 2007; Clark, 2019).

The *Dobbs* decision was not aligned with public opinion. The decision seemed to confirm the charge that the Court was simply a naked power organ and a group of legislators in robes. Will the *Dobbs* case be the next self-inflicted wound? How could the Court parry this to maintain (or reclaim) its rightful place in the separation of powers domain?

In the wake of the threat from Roosevelt, the Court astutely pivoted and redefined its institutional role, avoiding a long-term damaging self-inflicted wound. Justice Harlan Fiske Stone advocated the adoption of a "double standard" (Mason, 1956). In the famous "Footnote Four" in his majority opinion in *United States v. Carolene Products* (1938), Stone argued that in economic regulation cases (the issues that got the justices in trouble), the Court should exercise judicial restraint showing deference to the elected branches and their agents and uphold legislation unless it was clearly unconstitutional. But when the dispute involved civil rights or civil liberties cases, the burden fell on the government to justify the need for the restriction (Pacelle, 1991). Thus, civil rights and individual liberties were to enjoy a "preferred position." And the Court should use activism to protect those rights. In a broader sense, the different issues were linked: activism and restraint were not competing approaches but might be viewed as complementary and perhaps even mutually reinforcing.

Decisions like *Brown*, *Mapp v. Ohio* (1961), *Miranda v. Arizona* (1966), and *Roe* get the lion's share of public, elite, and scholarly attention. We have a good idea theoretically and empirically how we expect justices to decide those cases (Pacelle, Curry, and Marshall 2011). So do the presidents that nominate and the Senators who confirm them. But what of the other cases on the Court's plenary docket? These cases are important enough to survive a *certiorari* process that eliminates over 90% of the petitions, but not important enough to have their decisions posted like banners on the front page of *The New York Times* (Epstein and Segal, 2000).

This study examines the exercise of judicial activism and restraint using a data set that includes economic issues which are close to 180 degrees different from the rights and liberties cases that dominate attention. The economic cases are overwhelmingly decided on statutory grounds rather than based on provisions in the Constitution. The former requires a simple majority in Congress to overturn; the latter require an extraordinary majority. The Court has different goals to fulfill in deciding these cases (Baum, 1997, 2006; Pacelle, 1991; Perry, 1991). The literature strongly suggests the notion that the Court has used judicial activism in deciding constitutional law cases. The goal was to exert leadership on issues of civil rights and liberties. The goal in economic cases, by contrast, was to let others take leadership and to prepare the Court to exit from these issues and leave them to lower courts, agencies, and the elected branches (Pacelle, 2009).

What does this have to say about the relationship between judicial activism and restraint? If the Court's goals in individual liberties and civil rights are different from those in economic cases, it stands to reason, the factors influencing decision making will be apportioned differently. Do the determinants of decision making in economic cases reflect restraint and depart from the perceived activism of the higher profile rights and liberties cases?

Determinants of Decision Making on the Modern Supreme Court

Justices, presidents, members of Congress, and experts in agencies are purposive actors with complex goals that start with a desire to see their policy preferences reflected in the law. But their goal hierarchy also includes institutional objectives and protecting their legitimate authority. The so-called agenda cases and the potential landmark decisions attract everyone's attention and given their constitutional bases, provide limited opportunity for overturning odious decisions (but see Harvey and Friedman, 2006; Martin, 2006). The statutory cases are a different matter in scope, grounds, and visibility. Do they appear on the radar of the various actors?

There is consensus on the factors that influence Supreme Court decision making (Gibson, 1983). There is decidedly less consensus over the relative weight of the influences (Segal and Spaeth, 2002; Bailey and Maltzman, 2011; Pacelle, Curry, and Marshall, 2011; Epstein and Knight, 1997; Hammond, Bonneau, and Sheehan, 2005). The factors fall into three categories: legal, attitudinal, and strategic. The relative weight of these influences is complex and conditional.

At one end of the spectrum is the attitudinal model, a reflection of judicial activism. The importance of filling a Supreme Court vacancy certainly suggests that the sincere policy preferences of the justices are the most important factor in decision making (Epstein and Segal, 2005; Abraham 2008). Presidents spend finite political capital to get their selections confirmed (Krehbiel, 2007).

Justices have lifetime appointments, are at the pinnacles of their careers, and are seldom if ever reversed (Segal and Spaeth, 2002). This presumably gives them freedom to ignore precedent and follow their sincere policy preferences. But the "naïve attitudinal model," which holds that sincere preferences are the sole determinant of decisions, has been rejected (Cross and Nelson, 2001; Songer and Lindquist, 1996).

While the individual policy preferences of the justices are critical determinants of decision-making, they pursue other goals, particularly in economic and statutory cases (Baum, 1997; Hall, 2018; Epstein and Knight, 1997). Legal factors should play an important role in these cases. Justices care about the law, precedent, and institutional legitimacy. Justices want to standardize the law. They may subscribe to the "Golden Rule of Precedent": you respect precedents authored by others and in turn expect them to respect your precedents (Gerhardt, 2008).

The legal model is associated with judicial restraint. *Stare decisis* or attention to precedent is considered a critical (and normative) component of judicial decision making (Aldesert, 1990; Gerhardt, 2008; Hansford and Spriggs, 2006). To follow precedent is to impose consistency on the law, make the law predictable and guide behavior. Horizontal precedent guides the justices. Vertical precedent connects the courts throughout the judicial hierarchy (Clark and Kastellec, 2013; Westerland et al., 2010; Corley, Collins, and Calvin, 2011; Songer, Segal, and Cameron, 1994).

Precedent starts with the premise that often it is more important that something is settled than that it settled correctly (Kozel, 2017). Precedent is more likely to survive when it is relatively new, when it has not been repeatedly challenged, in cases involving statutory interpretation (Hansford and Spriggs, 2006), when it is strong, and when its scope is not too broad (Kozel, 2017). Those conditions are more likely to be found in statutory economic cases than in constitutional civil rights and liberties cases. Kritzer and Richards (2003, 2005) and Richards and Kritzer (2002) argue that decisions are structured by a "jurisprudential regime" which is akin to a core decision or precedent.

While *stare decisis* and precedent are not inviolate, they are respected by all actors (Hansford and Spriggs, 2006; Bailey and Maltzman, 2011; Epstein and Knight, 1997). The Supreme Court has the goal of policing the judicial hierarchy. Controlling precedents may constrain justices who seek to excise them. The notion that justices will slavishly adhere to the law or that they simply check their personal policy preferences at the door when they don the robes is what Cross and Nelson (2001) refer to as the "naïve legal model," an unattainable normative ideal. In addition, precedents are not carved in stone. Justices and the Court may diverge from the script. They may also strip the viability of a precedent while leaving the skeleton as a display (Spriggs and Hansford, 2001).

Somewhere between these naïve models are the strategic or "separation of powers" models. Checks and balances impose constraints on the Court (Bailey and Maltzman, 2011). The president and Congress possess sanctions that can be levied on the judiciary. Some scholars argue that the Court will act strategically to avoid retaliation from its institutional rivals (Clark, 2011; Bartels and Johnston, 2020).[3] The Court will tailor decisions to avoid attacks from the other branches (Epstein and Knight, 1997).[4] There are elements of activism in that justices want to pursue their policy goals though they understand that they have to concede a bit. These models also suggest elements of judicial restraint in that justices would defer to some extent to the elected branches to avoid court curbing measures and issue narrow decisions tailored to the facts of the individual cases (Ulmer, 1982).[5]

Presidents can influence decisions in direct and indirect ways. Presidents can move the Court median when they have an opportunity pulling the Court closer to their preferred policy positions (Krehbiel, 2007). In addition to their constitutional checks, presidents can also work through their political appointees in the agencies (Wood and Waterman, 1991) and the Solicitor General (SG) to advance their policy goals (Scigliano, 1971; Curry, Pacelle and Marshall, 2008; Black and Owens, 2012; Bailey, Kamoie, and Maltzman, 2005;

3 Strategic behavior is not limited to justices of the Supreme Court. Presidents will swallow riders to get legislation they support. Members of Congress will allocate precious resources to "home style" to buy themselves leeway to spend on significant legislation. Lower court judges follow precedent and defer to higher courts in most cases to preserve the ability to defect when they find a case they really care about.

4 The empirical results are decidedly mixed as to whether the Court acts strategically (Segal, 1997; Spiller and Gely, 1992; Spiller and Spitzer, 1992; Bergara, Richman, and Spiller, 2003; Gely and Spiller, 1990; Hansford and Damore, 2000; Sala and Spriggs, 2004; Pacelle, Curry and Marshall, 2011).

5 A Court can exercise "issue expansion" or "issue suppression" (Ulmer 1982; Pacelle 1991; McGuire and Palmer 1995). The latter is judicial restraint and might take the form of addressing only one of the questions presented by the litigants or narrowing the consideration or impact of the issue. Litigants may argue that a case raises constitutional questions, but the Court may confine the decision to statutory grounds. By contrast, litigants might think statutory grounds are most favorable, only to have the Court reframe the issue as constitutional, a display of activism (King, 2007).

Wohlfarth, 2009; Pacelle, 2018). They may also try to mobilize mass or elite opinion by, in effect, "going public" (Collins and Eshbaugh-Sosa, 2019).

Presidents certainly care about the so-called agenda issues. They are the primary basis for their Supreme Court nominations. But a president's ability to get reelected and write their pages of history will also be influenced by the health of the economy during their term(s). The assessment of a presidency is shaped, in part, on the chief executive's ability to navigate separation of powers and checks and balances. Presidents increasingly use the Office of the Solicitor General (OSG) to pursue their legal goals (Pacelle, 2018; Black and Owen, 2012; Lee, 1986; Salokar, 1992; Meinhold and Shull, 1998; Wohlfarth, 2009). Issues such as regulation and taxes will grab the attention of the executive branch. Still when presidents nominate prospective justices, they seldom dwell on their economic and regulation decisions on lower courts.

Similarly, we expect members of Congress to care about such issues. At the most basic level, members of Congress are primarily concerned with re-election (Mayhew, 1974). The economic cases are overwhelmingly statutory, giving members of Congress the ability to overrule a Court decision by a simple majority. Congress can retaliate by using one of its numerous checks to keep the Court in line.[6] But normally the interplay between the branches is not hostile but designed at getting the "correct" interpretation (Hausegger and Baum, 1999). The best conditions for Congressional influence are statutory cases and issues that do not involve rights and liberties (Pacelle, Curry, and Marshall, 2011). Committees, as agents of Congress, can alert the leadership, the president, or interest groups through "fire alarms" (McCubbins and Schwartz, 1984; Maltzman, 1997). Strategic decision making might encourage the Court to preempt opposition by aligning close to the median position in Congress. But it is no secret that Congress has a collective action problem and may lack the institutional cohesion to hold the Court accountable.

While presidents set the agenda and the House and Senate deliberate on potential legislation, the locus of power is often the administrative agency. Agencies promulgate rules and regulations to implement or apply legislative and executive initiatives. Executive departments and legislative committees

6 Among the checks Congress can bring to bear against the Court are tampering with the Court's jurisdiction (Marshall, Curry, and Pacelle 2014), cutting its budget (Toma, 1991), as well as overturning decisions or trying the imposing and bulky amendment process. And while it is difficult to see the justices genuinely feeling threatened, Clark (2011) argues the Court will pull in the reins itself at the first sign of trouble and not wait for Congress to react and engage public approbation.

have delegated plenary authority to the agencies (Lowi, 1969). Agencies sit organizationally on the executive side of the ledger and need to work through the OSG in the Department of Justice. But the agencies are often more closely aligned with interest groups and congressional committees by virtue of similar tenure clocks and the budget process.

Judicial support of the position of the agency is another form of deference. The justices are generalists asked to review the handiwork and priorities of the experts in the agencies. The agencies are at the mercy of the Office of the Solicitor General, which must agree to appeal the case to the Supreme Court, making the OSG the gatekeeper of *certiorari* (Perry, 1991). The Solicitor General is a critical actor in cases involving the U.S. government as a party and arguably the most important actor in federal economic cases (Pacelle, 2018).

There are good reasons to think public opinion might influence the Court. That influence could come indirectly through Congress or the president or through the briefs of litigants and *amici*. At the same time, the independence of the Court provides insulation that would appear to limit the effect of public opinion. Not surprisingly, the literature does not yield a clear conclusion (Devins and Baum, 2019; McGuire and Stimson, 2004; Giles, Blackstone, and Vining, 2008).

The facts of the case also play a significant role in decision making. The attitudinal literature (Schubert, 1965, 1974; Rohde and Spaeth, 1976; Segal and Spaeth, 2002) and fact-pattern analysis (Kort, 1957; Segal, 1986; Ignagni, 1993, 1994; Pacelle, 2009; Kritzer and Richard, 2003, 2005) examine how issues evolve and become more complex over time (Baum, 1988, 1992; Schauer, 1985; Pacelle and Pyle, 2020). These studies demonstrate that differing fact situations have a significant impact on the decisions of individual justices and the Court as a whole. As the facts in a case get more difficult, justices become less inclined to favor the defendant in criminal cases, groups seeking liberties and rights, and the government in regulation cases (Pacelle, 2009; Pacelle and Pyle, 2020; Segal, 1984, 1986; Kritzer and Richards 2003, 2005; Richards and Kritzer, 2002).[7]

7 For instance, if police break into a house without a warrant and with no exigent circumstances, that is an easy case to decide in favor of the suspect. Contrast that with police catching a fleeing gun man in a crowded area and not properly *Mirandizing* the suspect in the heat of the moment.

Judging the Supreme Court

How can different Courts be adjudged? A Court might exercise judicial restraint across the board. That Court would uphold precedents, show deference to the elected branches, issue narrow decisions, and try to remain within the confines of the provisions in the Constitution or in statutes. Such a Court would not spend its legitimacy (unless it was depleted due to the unwillingness to exercise its potential power). At the other end of the spectrum is a Supreme Court that flexes its institutional muscle at numerous junctures: overturning precedents, wielding judicial review, ignoring the elected branches of government, issuing sweeping decisions, and treating the Constitution as a suggestion rather than a mandate. Justices could throw away the metaphorical robes and simply legislate from the bench. Whenever one justice is replaced by another, it would be open season on precedents and doctrine would change as the balance tipped. Such a Court would invite public approbation, lower court recalcitrance, and attack from the other branches. The cost would be borne in decreased legitimacy. And that is why there are few examples of such widespread activism. The idea is that restraint as a normative ideal can be used to fuel activism safely.

Justices (and collectively the Supreme Court) would like to read their personal values into the decisions and legal doctrine. But at the same time, they want the institution to be respected. It is logical to think that the justices must choose their battles. A careful mixture of activism and restraint lets the Court push the boundaries in some issue areas while respecting the law and showing restraints in other areas. We expect that the Court will treat its legitimacy as a finite resource. The Court would want to exercise its prerogatives, but not incur the wrath of the public or the other branches and retain the respect of the lower courts. What utility would be gained by making decisions that would be ignored?

If the Court tempers its occasional activism with large dosages of restraint, it protects its institutional integrity. There are indications that the Court is aware of this dynamic. Studies of the *certiorari* process and case selection argue that the Court has a bifurcated agenda with exigent and volitional cases (Pacelle, 1991). Some cases are accepted as part of what Perry (1991) called the jurisprudential mode (exigent agenda) to standardize the law, while others are accepted as part of the outcome mode (volitional agenda) more concerned with policy goals.

No matter how far left or how far to the right the Court may be, some justices in the middle tend to act as thermostats. Conservative Courts issue liberal decisions and vice versa (Bartels and Johnson, 2020). Regardless of the ideological fissures on the Court, more than a third of the decisions each term are unanimous. These are not accidental or randomly distributed. Conventional wisdom suggests that economic cases, particularly statutory cases, tend to be accepted to resolve circuit conflicts, and the decisions are often unanimous. Some are decided in the liberal direction, and some yield a conservative result. They are often circumscribed cases (the case may have three issues and the Court may only address one) with narrow opinions that do not spawn any concurring or dissenting opinions. On the other hand, the civil rights and individual liberties disputes that find their way to the Supreme Court are much more likely to be decided on constitutional grounds and to split the justices ideologically. Justices who agree with the result may nonetheless decide to author a concurring opinion. The decisions are issued with one or more dissenting opinions.

Even though these economic cases may be less visible than the rights and liberties disputes, they raise important issues about regulation and policies across a vast array of areas. Justices will care about the results, but the need to attend to precedent and defer to the relevant governmental agencies may reduce the impact of their sincere policy preferences.[8]

Are the determinants of decision making weighted differently in the "less salient" cases? In simple terms, does the Court exercise judicial restraint in the economic cases? If so, the preferences of the justices (attitudinal variable) should be subordinated to other determinants of decision making. Evidence that the attitudinal variable had a statistically significant impact on the Court's decisions would constitute a *prima facie* case for judicial activism. The absence of such a significant impact would suggest some elements of judicial restraint, particularly if the Court's decisions were responsive to precedent and *stare decisis*, the agency, and the elected branches (particularly Congress).

I expect the Court in these economic cases to follow precedent, stabilize the law, and show deference to the agencies and perhaps to the other branches. The goal of the Court is to resolve these disputes and set standards to allow lower courts to monitor the field. The Court can then reallocate agenda space to rights and liberties cases (Pacelle, 1991). In the following analysis, I compare

8 Studies of individual decision making in economic areas show a change over time. Early cases were decided on ideological grounds, but that changed during the Warren and Burger Courts. The decisions turned more on deference and federalism grounds rather than ideological position (Dudley and Ducat, 1986; Ducat and Dudley, 1987; Hagle and Spaeth, 1992, 1993).

civil rights and liberties decisions, thought to invite judicial activism in the 1953–2016 terms, to economic cases (decided with restraint). Further I consider the resulting relationships between judicial activism and restraint.[9]

Research Design

There are no direct measures of activism and restraint. Rather, the goal of this chapter is to identify which determinants dominate the decision making of the Supreme Court and most importantly whether they differ by issue, grounds, and salience. I start with proxies for legal, attitudinal, and strategic variables and expect to see that decision making in one set of issues (constitutional civil liberties and rights) will be dominated by the attitudinal variable while other issues (statutory economic) will be governed by legal considerations. If the sincere preferences of the justices crowd out the other factors, those decisions likely represent judicial activism. If the Court relies on the law and precedent, then restraint comes to the fore.

To examine the relative influences of attitudinal, strategic, and legal factors, I use the ideological direction of the decision of the Supreme Court as the dependent variable. I examine the potential influence of factors like precedent and the difficulty of the issue as well as the ideological position of the president, House, and Senate, and public opinion. The unit of analysis is the cases involving economic issues and regulatory authority in the 1953–2016 terms (N = 2212). Using the same model, I examine the civil rights and individual liberties over the same period (N = 1721). The dependent variable is dichotomous, so I estimate the models using logistic regression.

As proxies for the three branches, I use the Common Space measures for the Court and the president (Epstein et al., 2007), and the NOMINATE scores for the House and Senate (Poole and Rosenthal, 1997). I include a variable for public opinion, the Stimson Mood variable (with a year lag).[10] Finally,

9 Some argue that the Court has rejected the double standard. Others argue the Court still has a double standard but has inverted it putting economic issues in a preferred position. Some landmark decisions support that conclusion, but the aggregate numbers do not.

10 While the Supreme Court is theoretically independent of the winds of political change and the justices are unelected with lifetime tenure, studies show that public opinion has some impact on judicial decision making (Casillas, Enns, and Wohlfarth, 2011; McGuire and Stimson, 2004; Giles, Blackstone, and Vining, 2008), That impact may be direct (Mishler and Sheehan, 1996) or indirect (Clark, 2011; Marshall, Curry, and Pacelle, 2014), As the attorney for the United States, a representative of the president and an agent of Congress, the OSG may need to concern itself with public opinion as well.

I add variables for precedent and issue evolution to gain purchase on legal factors. The variable for precedent uses the most important precedent cited in the instant cases, gathered from the Syllabus of the individual decisions (see Benesh and Spaeth, 2001; Pacelle, Curry, and Marshall, 2011).[11] The issue evolution variable measures the difficulty of the issue before the Court (Pacelle, 2009; Pacelle, Curry, and Marshall, 2011).[12] The more difficult the issue, the harder is for the Court to deliver a liberal decision.

The variables are proxies for extant precedents, the "difficulty" of the facts of the cases, and the ideology of the three branches in the instant case. But there is one additional step. My interest is in whether the Court practiced judicial restraint in the economic cases. There is no specific variable for "judicial restraint" or "judicial activism." There are a few dimensions to judicial restraint. It can be defined as justices putting aside their personal preferences, showing deference to the agency and/or the elected branches, and following precedent. Thus, there are three possible avenues to judicial restraint: most directly, the attitudinal variable must have no impact on the decisions. I can infer restraint if the elected branches and/or the agencies exert a positive impact on decisions and/or precedent has a positive effect.

By contrast if the influence of the attitudinal variable is statistically significant and positive, that suggests judicial activism. The expectation is that the legal and strategic variables that represent restraint will primarily be manifested in the economic cases. By contrast, presidents use the civil rights and liberties issues as their litmus tests. The expectation is that the liberal and conservative justices will follow their sincere preferences in deciding cases and not be constrained by Congress or precedent. In other words, they will exhibit judicial activism.

11 Precedent and predictability have always had a strong normative imperative. But there is also an empirical component incorporated into models of decision making (Aldisert, 1990; Bailey and Maltzman, 2008, 2011: Baum, 1997; George and Epstein, 1992; Gerhardt, 2008; Gibson, 1983; Hansford and Spriggs, 2006; Pacelle, Marshall, and Curry, 2007; Songer and Lindquist, 1996). The main precedent, identified in the Syllabus of the cases, is coded 1 for a liberal precedent, -1 for a conservative precedent, and 0 if there is no precedent in that area. It is used in models as an independent variable to explain either the position of the SG or the ideological direction of the Court's decision. It is important to note that for the former, precedent is gleaned from the decision of the case. In the vast preponderance of the cases, the central precedent is clear whether the Court follows it or not.

12 Issue evolution is similar to judicial regime theory (Kritzer and Richards, 2003, 2005; Richards and Kritzer, 2002, but see Bartels and O'Geen, 2015), but it allows for comparison across issue areas.

Results

In trying to understand the relationship between these issues, there are two empirical questions. First, what is the relative weight of the relevant factors in decision making? Second, do they vary across different issues? And the empirical results beg a third question what are the implications for activism and restraint and the role of the Supreme Court?

Because there is no direct measure of judicial activism or restraint, the results are not conclusive. But they are suggestive. There are clear differences between the factors than animate decision making in civil rights and liberties as opposed to economic cases. Cross and Nelson (2001) rejected the naïve legal model and naïve attitudinal model and these results support that conclusion.

The baseline for the study is the constitutional civil rights and individual liberties decisions. The table compares decision making across the two policy domains. The results of this analysis are consistent with virtually every other study of decision making. The sincere preferences of the justices (the attitudinal variable) exert a strong positive influence on decision making in civil rights and civil liberties (Segal and Spaeth, 2002; Maltzman, Spriggs, and Wahlbeck, 2000; Pacelle, Marshall, and Curry, 2007). The president also has a statistically significant positive effect, which might reflect the prowess of the Solicitor General, the ability of the president to move the median justice with appointments, and public opinion (Curry, Pacelle, and Marshall, 2008; Yates 2002; Collins and Eshbaugh-Sosa, 2019). Given that presidents since Nixon have clearly used civil rights and liberties (the agenda cases) as litmus tests (Epstein and Segal, 2005; Krehbiel, 2007), they are apparently getting what they desire (but see Epstein et al 1998).

To be sure, the Court also appears to respond to the difficulty of the issue as well as to precedent (Bailey and Maltzman, 2008, 2011; Pacelle, Curry, and Marshall, 2011). And because these decisions are constitutional in scope, the chances of overturning them are remote. The result might be a tempered version of judicial activism. The Court makes decisions that are consistent with their collective policy preferences, restrained slightly by the complexity of the case and precedent.

The economic decisions have little of the nuance of the rights and liberties cases. Justices apparently put aside their policy preferences to achieve other goals in economic and regulatory cases (Bailey and Maltzman, 2011; Pacelle, Curry, and Marshall, 2011). The influence of the attitudinal variable (median justice) is completely absent in the economic cases. Similarly, none of the elected branches exerts a positive statistically significant effect on decisions. The ideology of the president does not influence these decisions even though the cases involve executive agencies. And the same holds for Congress. Neither the ideology of the House nor the Senate (measured by the median member) affects the Court's decisions in these cases. Rather, the dominant impact comes from precedent.

That is not to say there is no restraint motivated deference. Pacelle (2018), using the same Supreme Court terms, but a slightly different set of cases, found that the position of the Solicitor General has the strongest impact on economic decisions. The addition of a variable for the Office of the Solicitor General (OSG) makes the case even more compelling. The position of the OSG muscles every other variable aside. It weakens the impact of precedent though it remains statistically significant and in the correct direction. The OSG is arguing the case on behalf of the agency and for the Court to rely overwhelmingly on precedent and the position of the Solicitor General is to suggest deference to the agency and the law. It is a strong statement of judicial restraint that the Court follows the recommendation of the Solicitor General who wants to standardize the law and precedent. Both have an independent impact as well as a shared one.

Besides issue difficulty, nothing else rises to the level of statistical significant. The difficulty of the facts of the case, as expected, is negative. Elections come and go (and this was a volatile period), but the results do not disturb or alter the decision-making calculus. While none of these "political" factors has an influence, public opinion has a positive and statistically significant, but limited, impact. This is consistent with the literature.

So, what tentative conclusions can be drawn? Court activism is tempered at the margins even in constitutional rights and liberties cases. Economic decisions show little tempering. The Court treats them as we hope courts will act: attention to precedent and policy preferences left outside the conference room. And as a result, the Court creates good will and builds a reserve that it can borrow against when it wishes to exercise judicial activism or decide cases that are particularly salient. The process of selective activism and a reserve of restraint appears to protect the Court. The Roberts Court might be tampering with this formula, though. The decision to strip the EPA of authority could move the Court into a more activist role on what are typically safety net issues. Certainly, the Burger and Rehnquist Courts trespassed on economic issues, but they were normally constitutionally based issues. If every case, or even the lion's share of them, were subjected to a review dominated by the attitudinal

Table 3.1: Influence of political and legal factors on Supreme Court decision making, 1953–2016 terms constitutional rights and liberties and statutory economic cases

Independent Variable	Constitutional Civil Rights and Liberties Θ (S.E.)	Statutory Economic Cases Θ (S.E.)
Supreme Court Ideology	**2.714**** **(.409)**	.467 (.354)
Presidential Ideology	**.391**** **(.134)**	.117 (1.23)
House Ideology	-.069 (.431)	.234 (3.27)
Senate Ideology	.341 (.713)	-.819 (.576)
Precedent	**.425**** **(.056)**	**.870**** **(.049)**
Issue Evolution	**-.509**** **(.083)**	**-.297**** **(.067)**
Public Mood	**.034*** **(.015)**	**.038*** **(017)**
Constant	-.599 (.784)	-1.201 (.679)
	χ^2= 215.52	χ^2 = 382.72
	P < .0000	P < .0000
	N = 1721	N = 2212

Note: (*) = *p*≤*.05, and* (**) = *p*≤*.01.*

variable, the Court would be outed as a political organ. The Court's precious legitimacy would dissipate rather rapidly.

The results explain institutional decision-making by the Court and have the virtue of being consistent with what we know about individual decision-making in statutory economic cases. Many of these decisions are unanimous regardless of the ideological composition of the Court (Pacelle, 1991). Justices vote in ways that belie their apparent sincere policy preferences (Dudley and Ducat, 1986). Justices observe judicial restraint to achieve institutional goals. The Court takes these cases to resolve lower court conflicts or to tidy up an area of law (Ulmer, 1984). Pacelle (1991) refers to these as "exigent" cases and Perry (1991) describes decision making as "jurisprudential." The Court exercises issue suppression in limiting the scope of review (Ulmer, 1982, McGuire and Palmer, 1995). In addition, the Court systematically reduced the percentage of agenda space allocated to these issues, fulfilling the promise of fleshing out the expanding civil rights and liberties agenda (Pacelle, 1991).

By contrast, in civil rights and individual liberties cases, the Court grants the writ of *certiorari* to deal with "the important questions." Pacelle (1991) considers these issues as part of the Court's volitional agenda. Perry (1991) argues that these issues are subject to the outcome mode of decision making. The Court is much more likely to exercise judicial expansion in civil rights and liberties cases. The Court can transform a case like *Mapp v. Ohio* from a narrow question on the First Amendment to a landmark decision on search and seizure (Pacelle, 1991). Further, in many issue areas, the position of the US government, filtered through the Office of the Solicitor General is consistent regardless of the tenant in the White House. In regulatory cases, the OSG normally supports the agency; in federalism cases, the OSG supports the central government. And in criminal cases, they strive to keep the bad guys locked up. The OSG is the most successful litigant and litigates strategically (Pacelle, 2003; Perry, 1991). In doing so, and being faithful to the law and consistent, the government and the Solicitor General earn the leeway to take a few gambols in more controversial cases often through *amicus curiae* briefs.

Concluding Remarks: Striking a Balance

The massive expansion of the administrative state ushered in by the New Deal response to the Great Depression precipitated a pitched political battle. The president and Congress were pitted against the Court. The double standard was a means of resuscitating the Court and buttressing the regulatory state. The Court took the lifeline, built a new reserve of institutional legitimacy, and became a protector of rights and liberties (McCloskey, 1960; Casper, 1976). The Roberts Court has been a conservative tribunal, but it limited its use of judicial activism at least until recently. With its super majority, the Roberts Court appears free to exercise its prerogatives. How much risk will it be willing to incur? The recent 2021 term suggests a transition to enhanced activism. Additional activism may earn the Court some enmity. If the Court transfers that activism to other issues that were formerly governed by restraint, it could transform the environment.

There are some broader implications revealed about decision making on the modern Supreme Court. The time-period of this study is bounded by the end of *de jure* discrimination and the recognition of same sex marriage. The period begins with the most liberal Court initiating a constitutional revolution

(Schwartz, 1983) and ends with what Keck (2004) calls the most activist conservative Court. Years of Republican control of the White House created profound changes in the ideology of the Court. Republican presidents have appointed 15 of the last 19 justices. Yet despite this migration from liberal activism to conservative activism, in at least one subset of cases consistency and predictability were not victims of wholesale ideological change. The Court used the statutory cases to settle conflicts, monitor the system, police the bureaucracy, and limit the scope of review. The Court applied the brakes and followed the law. And that had numerous benefits. First, this helps lower the temperature that comes from the bold decisions in the civil rights and individual liberties cases. Despite the divisions on the Court, almost a third of the decisions were unanimous. And regardless of how far the Court leaned left or right, the outnumbered justices still won a share of cases (Bartels and Johnston, 2020). The Court abides by precedent to make the law predictable for agencies, lower courts, and citizens. The decisions were consistent with public opinion thus not raising the ire of elected officials. We see a glimpse of the normative ideal of judicial decisions.

The results may be surprising in one respect. We think of the Supreme Court as a major actor in the construction of public policy. That is not the surprising part. The results suggest the Court may not be as activist as we think. In one area of law, economic regulation, the institution shows restraint and fills an interstitial role. While the justices are free to choose their own interpretive lenses in constitutional decisions, they are tethered to the law by precedent to some degree.

The Roosevelt Court advocated and the Warren Court presided over a revolution, expanded pluralism to its greatest level, and protected minority rights (Pacelle, 1991; Casper, 1976). The constitutional civil rights and individual liberties cases shared finite agenda space with statutory economic regulations cases. Those statutory cases pale by comparison to the constitutional rights and liberties decisions. But these economic cases remain important in their own right. They purchased the Court goodwill that could be borrowed against in the more controversial rights and liberties cases Further they helped the Court protect and enhance its finite legitimacy so that resource could be spent elsewhere. And that suggests that we need to look at activism and restraint not as polar opposites but as complementary approaches. A Court that was strictly activist would soon deplete its legitimacy. A Court that adhered just to judicial restraint would forfeit its reason for existence. Better to strike a balance: investing and withdrawing.

References

Abraham, H. J. (2008). *Justices, presidents, and senators: A history of the U.S. Supreme Court appointments from Washington to Bush II* (5th ed.). Lanham, MD: Rowman & Littlefield.

Aldisert, R. (1990). Precedent: What it is and what it isn't; when do we kiss it and when do we kill it?. *Pepperdine Law Review, 17*, 605–636.

Bailey, M., Kamoie, B., & Maltzman, F. (2005). Signals from the tenth justice: The political role of the Solicitor General in Supreme Court decision making. *American Journal of Political Science, 49*, 72–85.

Bailey, M., & Maltzman, F. (2011). *The constrained court: Law, politics, and the decisions justices make*. Princeton: Princeton University Press.

Bailey, M., & Maltzman, F. (2008). Does legal doctrine matter? Unpacking law and policy preferences on the U.S. Supreme Court. *American Political Science Review, 102*, 369–384.

Ball, H. (1978). *Judicial craftsmanship or fiat? Direct overturn by the United States Supreme Court*. Westport, CT: Praeger.

Bartels, B., & Johnston, C. (2020). *Curbing the court: Why the public constrains judicial independence*. New York: Cambridge.

Bartels, B., & O'Geen, A. (2015). The nature of legal change on the U.S. Supreme Court: Jurisprudential regimes theory and its alternatives. *American Journal of Political Science, 59*, 880–895.

Baum, L. (2006). *Judges and their audiences*. Princeton: Princeton University Press.

Baum, L. (1997). *The puzzle of judicial behavior*. Ann Arbor: University of Michigan Press.

Baum, L. (1992). Membership change and collective voting change in the United States Supreme Court. *Journal of Politics, 54*, 3–24.

Baum, L. (1988). Measuring policy change in the U.S. Supreme Court. *American Political Science Review, 82*, 905–912.

Benesh, S. C., & Spaeth, H. J. (2001). Salient to whom? A potential measure of salience to the justices. *Paper presented at the American Political Science Association Meetings*, San Francisco.

Bergara, M., Richman, B., & Spiller, P. T. (2003). Modeling Supreme Court strategic decision making: The congressional constraints. *Legislative Studies Quarterly, 28*, 247–280.

Black, R., & Owens, R. (2012). *The Solicitor General and the United States Supreme Court: Executive branch influence and judicial decision making*. New York: Cambridge.

Caldeira, G. A., & Gibson, J. L. (1992). The etiology of public support for the Supreme Court. *American Journal of Political Science, 36*, 635–664.

Casillas, C., Enns, P., & Wohlfarth, P. (2011). How public opinion constrains the U.S. Supreme Court. *American Journal of Political Science, 55*, 74–88.

Casper, J. D. (1976). The Supreme Court and national policy making. *American Political Science Review, 70*, 50–63.

Clark, T. (2019). *The Supreme Court: An analytical history of constitutional decision-making*. New York: Cambridge.

Clark, T. (2011). *The limits of judicial independence*. New York: Cambridge.

Clark, T., & Kastellec, J. (2013). The Supreme Court and percolation in the lower courts. *Journal of Politics, 75*, 150–168.

Collins, P., & Eshbaugh-Sosa, M. (2019). *The president and the Supreme Court: Going public on judicial decisions from Washington to Trump*. New York: Cambridge.

Corley, P., Collins, P., & Calvin, B. (2011). Lower court influences on U.S. Supreme Court opinions. *Journal of Politics, 73*, 31–44.

Cross, F. B., & Nelson, B. J. (2001). Strategic institutional effects on Supreme Court decision-making. *Northwestern University Law Review, 95*, 1437–1493.

Curry, B. W., Pacelle Jr., R. L., and Marshall, B. W. (2008). An "Informal and Limited Alliance": The president and the Supreme Court. *Presidential Studies Quarterly, 38*, 223–247.

Devins, N., & Baum, L. (2019). *The company they keep: How partisan divisions came to the Supreme Court*. New York: Oxford.

Ducat, C., & Dudley, R. (1987). Dimensions underlying economic policymaking in the early and later Burger court. *Journal of Politics, 49*, 521–539.

Dudley, R., & Ducat, C. (1986). The Burger court and economic liberalism. *Political Research Quarterly, 39*, 236–249.

Engel, S. (2011). *American politicians confront the court: Opposition politics and changing responses to judicial power*. New York: Cambridge.

Epstein, L., Hoekstra, V., Segal, J., & Spaeth, H. (1998). Do political preferences change? A longitudinal study of U.S. Supreme Court justices. *Journal of Politics, 60*, 801–818.

Epstein, L., & Knight, J. (1997). *The choices justices make*. Washington, D.C.: CQ Press.

Epstein, L., Martin, A. D., Segal, J. A., & Westerland, C. (2007). The judicial common space. *Journal of Law, Economics, & Organization, 23*, 303–325.

Epstein, L., & Segal, J. (2005). *Advice and consent: The politics of judicial appointments*. New York: Oxford University Press.

Epstein, L., & Segal, J. (2000). Measuring issue salience. *American Journal of Political Science, 44*, 66–83.

Eskridge, W. N., Jr. (1994). *Dynamic statutory interpretation*. Cambridge: Harvard University Press.

Eskridge, W. N., Jr. (1991). Overriding Supreme Court statutory interpretation decisions. *Yale Law Journal, 101*, 331–417.

Funston, R. (1978). *A vital national seminar: The Supreme Court in American national politics*. Palo Alto: Mayfield.

Gely, R., & Spiller, P. (1990). A rational choice theory of Supreme Court statutory decisions with applications to the *State Farm* and *Grove City* cases. *Journal of Law, Economics, and Organization*, 6, 263–300.

George, T., & Epstein, L. (1992). On the nature of Supreme Court decision making. *American Political Science Review, 86*, 323–337.

Gerhardt, M. (2008). *The power of precedent*. New York: Oxford University Press.

Gibson, J. L. (1983). From simplicity to complexity: The development of theory in the study of judicial behavior. *Political Behavior, 5*, 7–49.

Gibson, J., & Nelson, M. (2015). Is the Supreme Court's legitimacy grounded in performance satisfaction and ideology? *American Journal of Political Science, 59*, 162–174.

Giles, M. W., Blackstone, B., & Vining, R. L. Jr. (2008). The Supreme Court in American democracy: Unraveling the linkages between public opinion and judicial decision making. *Journal of Politics, 70*, 293–306.

Gillman, H. (1993). *The constitution besieged: The rise and demise of Lochner era police powers jurisprudence*. Durham: Duke University Press.

Hagle, T., & Spaeth, H. (1993). Ideological patterns in the justices' voting in the Burger court's business cases. *Journal of Politics, 55*, 492–505.

Hagle, T., & Spaeth, H. (1992). The emergence of a new ideology: The business decisions of the Burger court. *Journal of Politics, 54*, 120–134.

Hall, M. (2018). *What justices want: Goals and personality on the U.S. Supreme Court.* New York: Cambridge University Press.

Hammond, T., Bonneau, C., & Sheehan, R. (2005). *Strategic behavior on the U.S. Supreme Court*. Stanford: Stanford University Press.

Hansford, T. G., & Damore, D. F. (2000). Congressional preferences, perceptions of threat, and Supreme Court decision making. *American Politics Quarterly, 28*, 512–532.

Hansford, T. G., & Spriggs II, J. F. (2006). *The politics of precedent on the U.S. Supreme Court*. Princeton: Princeton University Press.

Harvey, A., & Friedman, B. (2006). Pulling punches: Congressional constraints on the Supreme Court's constitutional rulings, 1987–2000. *Legislative Studies Quarterly, 31*, 533–562.

Hausegger, L., & Baum, L. (1999). Inviting congressional action: A study of Supreme Court motivations in statutory interpretation. *American Journal of Political Science, 43*, 162–183.

Horowitz, D. (1977). *The courts and social policy*. Washington, DC: Brookings Institute.

Ignagni, J. (1994). Explaining and predicting Supreme Court decision making: The Burger court's establishment clause decisions. *Journal of Church and State, 36*, 301–327.

Ignagni, J. (1993). U.S. Supreme Court decision making and the free exercise clause. *Review of Politics, 55*, 511–529.

Keck, T. (2014). *Judicial politics in polarized times*. Chicago: University of Chicago Press.

Keck, T. M. (2004). *The most activist Supreme Court in history: The road to modern judicial conservatism*. Chicago: University of Chicago Press.

King, C. (2007). Strategic selection of legal instruments on the U.S. Supreme Court. *American Politics Research, 35*, 621–642.

Kort, F. (1957). Predicting Supreme Court decisions mathematically: A quantitative analysis of right to counsel cases. *American Political Science Review, 51*, 1–12.

Kozel, R. (2017). *Settled versus right: A theory of precedent*. New York: Cambridge,

Krehbiel, K. (2007). Supreme Court appointments as a move-the-median game. *American Journal of Political Science, 51*, 231–240.

Kritzer, H., & Richards, M. (2005). The influence of law in the Supreme Court's search-and-seizure jurisprudence. *American Politics Research, 33*, 33–55.

Kritzer, H., & Richards, M. (2003). Jurisprudential regimes and Supreme Court decision making: The *Lemon* regime and establishment clause cases. *Law & Society Review, 37*, 827–840.

Lee, R. (1986). Lawyering for the government: Politics, polemics & principle. *Ohio State Law Journal, 47*, 595–601.

Lemieux, S., & Watkins, D. (2018). *Judicial review and contemporary democratic theory: Power, domination, and the courts*. New York: Routledge.

Lowi, T. J. (1969). *The end of liberalism: Ideology, policy, and the crisis of public authority*. New York: W.W. Norton & Company.

Maltzman, F. (1997). *Competing principals: Committees, parties, and the organization of Congress*. Ann Arbor: University of Michigan Press.

Maltzman, F., Spriggs II, J. F., & Wahlbeck, P. J. (2000). *Crafting law on the Supreme Court: The collegial game*. New York: Cambridge University Press.

Marshall, B., Curry, B. W., & Pacelle, R. L. Jr. (2014). Preserving institutional power: The Supreme Court and strategic decision making in the separation of powers. *Politics & Policy, 44*, 37–76.

Martin, A. D. (2006). Statutory battles and constitutional wars: Congress and the Supreme Court. In J. Rogers, R. Flemming, & J. Bond (Eds.), *Institutional games and the U.S. Supreme Court* (pp. 3–23). Charlottesville: University of Virginia Press.

Mason, A. T. (1956). *Harlan Fiske Stone: Pillar of the law*. New York: Viking.

Mayhew, D. R. (1974). *Congress: The electoral connection*. New Haven: Yale University Press.

McCloskey, R. (1960). *The American Supreme Court*. Chicago: University of Chicago Press.

McCubbins, M., & Schwartz, T. (1984). Congressional oversight overlooked: Police patrols versus fire alarms. *American Journal of Political Science, 28*, 165–179.

McGuire, K., & Palmer, B. (1995). Issue fluidity on the U.S. Supreme Court. *American Political Science Review, 89*, 691–702.

McGuire, K. T., & Stimson, J. A. (2004). The least dangerous branch revisited: New evidence on Supreme Court responsiveness to public preferences. *The Journal of Politics, 66*, 1018–1035.

McKenna, M. C. (2002). *Franklin Roosevelt and the great constitutional war: The court-packing crisis of 1937*. New York: Fordham University Press.

Meinhold, S., & Shull, S. (1998). Policy congruence between the president and the Solicitor General. *Political Research Quarterly, 51*, 527–537.

Mishler, W., & Sheehan, R. S. (1996). Public opinion, the attitudinal model, and Supreme Court decision making: a micro-analytic perspective. *Journal of Politics, 58*, 169–200.

Pacelle, R. L., Jr. (2018). Of political principles and legal principals: The Solicitor General of the United States. In R. Howard & K. Randazzo (Eds.), *The handbook of judicial behavior*. New York: Routledge.

Pacelle, R. L., Jr. (2015). *The Supreme Court in a system of separation of powers: The nation's balance wheel*. New York: Routledge.

Pacelle, R. L., Jr. (2009). The emergence and evolution of Supreme Court Policy. In M. Miller (Ed.), *Rethinking U.S. judicial politics*. New York: Oxford University Press.

Pacelle, R. L., Jr. (2003). *Between law and politics: The Solicitor General and the structuring of race, gender, and reproductive rights litigation*. College Station: Texas A&M University Press.

Pacelle, R. L., Jr. (2002). *The role of the Supreme Court in American politics: The least dangerous branch?* Boulder: Westview Press.

Pacelle, R. L., Jr. (1991). *The transformation of the Supreme Court's agenda: From the New Deal to the Reagan administration*. Boulder: Westview Press.

Pacelle, R. L., Jr., Curry, B. W., & Marshall, B. W. (2011). *Decision making by the Modern Supreme Court*. Cambridge: Cambridge University Press.

Pacelle, R. L., Jr., Marshall, B. W., & Curry, B. W. (2007). Keepers of the covenant or Platonic guardians? Decision making on the United States Supreme Court. *American Politics Research, 35*, 694–724.

Pacelle, R. L., Jr. & Pyle, B. W. (2020). Issue emergence and evolution in the US Supreme Court. In R. Spill Solberg, J. Segal Diasco, & E. J. Waltenburg (Eds.), *Open judicial politics*. Corvallis: Oregon State University Press.

Perry, H. W., Jr. (1991). *Deciding to decide: Agenda setting in the U.S. Supreme Court*. Cambridge: Harvard University Press.

Poole, K., & Rosenthal, H. (1997). *Congress: A political-economic history of roll call voting*. New York: Oxford University Press.

Powe, L. A., Jr. (2000). *The Warren Court and American politics*. Cambridge: Belknap Press.

Richards, M. J., & Kritzer, H. M. (2002). Jurisprudential regimes in Supreme Court decision making. *American Political Science Review*, 96, 305–320.

Rohde, D., & Spaeth, H. (1976). *Supreme Court decision making*. San Francisco: Freeman.

Rosenberg, G. (2008). *The Hollow hope: Can courts bring about social change?* Chicago: University of Chicago Press.

Ross, W. (2007). *The chief justiceship of Charles Evans Hughes, 1930–1941*. Columbia: South Carolina Press.

Sala, B. R., & Spriggs II, J. F. (2004). Designing tests of the Supreme Court and the separation of powers. *Political Research Quarterly, 57*, 197–208.

Salokar, R. M. (1992). *The Solicitor General: The politics of law*. Philadelphia: Temple University Press.

Schauer, F. (1985). Easy cases. *Southern California Law Review*, 58, 399–440.

Schubert, G. (1974). *The judicial mind revisited*. New York: Oxford University Press.

Schubert, G. (1965). *The judicial mind*. Evanston, IL: Northwestern University Press.

Schwartz, B. (1983). *Super chief: Earl Warren and his Supreme Court—A judicial biography*. New York: New York University Press.

Scigliano, R. (1971). *The Supreme Court and the presidency*. New York: Free Press.

Segal, J. (1997). Separation-of-powers games in the positive theory of Congress and the courts. *American Political Science Review*, 91, 28–42.

Segal, J. (1986). Supreme Court justices as human decision makers: an individual level analysis of search and seizure cases. *Journal of Politics*, 48, 938–955.

Segal, J. (1984). Predicting Supreme Court cases probabilistically: The search and seizure cases, 1962–1981. *American Political Science Review*, 78, 891–900.

Segal, J., & Spaeth, H. (2002). *The Supreme Court and the attitudinal model revisited*. New York: Cambridge University Press.

Shesol, J. (2010). *Supreme power: Franklin Roosevelt and the Supreme Court*. New York: W.W. Norton.

Songer, D., & Lindquist, S. (1996). Not the whole story: The impact of justices' values on Supreme Court decision making. *American Journal of Political Science*, 40, 1049–1063.

Songer, D., Segal, J., & Cameron, C. (1994). The hierarchy of justice: Testing a principal-agent model of Supreme Court-Circuit Court interactions. *American Journal of Political Science, 38*, 673–696.

Spiller, P., & Gely, R. (1992). Congressional control or judicial independence: The determinants of U.S. Supreme Court labor decisions, 1949–1988. *RAND Journal of Economics, 23*, 463–492.

Spiller, P. T., & Spitzer, M. L. (1992). Judicial choice of legal doctrines. *Journal of Law, Economics, and Organization*, 8, 8–46.

Spriggs, J. F., II & Hansford, T. G. (2001). Explaining the overruling of U.S. Supreme Court precedent. *Journal of Politics, 63*, 1091–1111.

Strauss, D. (1990–91). Tradition, precedent, and Justice Scalia. *Cardozo Law Review, 12*, 1699–1716.

Sundquist, J. (1983). *Dynamics of the party system: Alignment and realignment of political parties in the United States* (Revised edition). Washington, D.C.: Brookings Institution.

Toma, E. (1991). Congressional influence and the Supreme Court: The budget as a signaling device. *Journal of Legal Studies, 20*, 131–146.

Ulmer, S. S. (1984). The Supreme Court's Certiorari decisions: Conflict as a predictive variable. *American Political Science Review, 78*, 901–911.

Ulmer, S. S. (1982). Issue fluidity in the United States Supreme Court. In S. Halpern & C. Lamb (Eds.), *Supreme Court activism and restraint* (pp. 319–359). Lexington: Heath.

Westerland, C., Segal, J., Epstein, L., Cameron, C., & Comparato, S. (2010). Strategic defiance and compliance in the U.S. Courts of Appeals. *American Journal of Political Science, 54*, 891–905.

Wohlfarth, P. C. (2009). The tenth justice? Consequences of politicization in the Solicitor General's Office. *Journal of Politics*, 71, 224–237.

Wolfe, C. (1997). *Judicial activism: Bulwark of freedom or precarious security?* Lanham, MD: Rowman & Littlefield.

Wood, B. Dan., & Waterman, R. W. (1991). The dynamics of political control of the bureaucracy. *American Political Science Review, 85*, 801–828.

Wood, R. C., & Petko, M. C. (2000). Assessing *Agostini v. Felton* in light of *Lemon v. Kurtzman*: The coming of age in the debate between religious affiliated schools and state aid. *Brigham Young University Education & Law Journal*, 1–16.

Yates, J. (2002). *Popular justice: Presidential prestige and executive success in the Supreme Court.* Albany: State University of New York Press.

· 4 ·

IF YOU GIVE A MOUSE A COOKIE, HE MIGHT WANT A GLASS OF MILK: JUDICIAL ACTIVISM IN THE UNITED KINGDOM

Monica Lineberger

In June 2017 I had the privilege to visit the United Kingdom's highest court, the Supreme Court,[1] and listen to the justices deliberate a case concerning European Union law. In discussing whether or not to refer the case to the European court, the justices jovially joked that this may be the last instance they ever send a case up to the European Court of Justice.[2] The year prior, in a closely-decided referendum, the people of the United Kingdom voted to leave the European Union. The formal negotiations on how to leave the European Union commenced days before I entered the courtroom in 2017.

Fast-forward to 2019 and the logistical, political, and legal quagmire of the British exit (Brexit) from the European Union had still not been determined. The political maneuverings of Prime Minister Boris Johnson in September

1 The Supreme Court of the United Kingdom is the court of last resort for civil cases coming from England, Wales, Northern Ireland, and Scotland. It is the court of last resort for criminal cases from England, Wales, and Northern Ireland. For the most part, a criminal case cannot be appealed from Scotland's Court of Criminal Appeal to the U.K. Supreme Court unless the case involves a question emanating from the Human Rights Act of 1998 or an issue with devolution (see Section 288ZA of Scotland's Criminal Procedure Act 1995).

2 Under Article 267 of the Treaty of the Functioning of the European Union, member states can ask the European Court of Justice for assistance in interpreting EU law.

of that year would soon provide the U.K. Supreme Court the opportunity to weigh in on the issue of Brexit once again.[3] After the elections of July 2019 and the selection of the new Prime Minister Boris Johnson, Johnson called for a prorogation of Parliament, which is typically a week-long legislative break to provide the new government time to focus on a legislative agenda. However, the prorogation of 2019 happened to be five weeks long and would have ended days before Parliament had to vote on a Withdrawal Agreement; the opposition was quick to critique the irregularity of this move and subsequently petition the judiciary for relief. By a unanimous court on the 24th of September, eleven Justices voted that the prorogation of Parliament in the days before the Brexit deadline was unlawful (*R (Miller) v. The Prime Minister* and *Cherry v. Advocate General for Scotland*, 2019). Outrage at the ruling extended from the Prime Minister's office throughout the Conservative Party. Some Tories vilified the institution by saying that the Supreme Court behaved in a political manner. The politicians further noted that this ruling was indicative of a larger pattern where judges rely upon their own opinions to decide cases, instead of the intentions and sovereignty of Parliament. Suella Braverman, a Brexit minister, aptly summarized the Conservative Party's issue with the ruling when she said:

> We have a principle called judicial deference, which means that our courts and our judges generally stay out of politics . . . it is for the politicians to make political decisions not for judges. There has been a sense since the prorogation decision of the Supreme Court that our judges have been pulled into this political sphere. That has been worrying and concerning (Watt, 2019).

After the Court's decision in *Cherry*, politicians circulated ideas for judicial reforms, such as adding in parliamentary scrutiny to the appointment process. In response, the outgoing Chief Justice Brenda Hale of the Supreme Court, highlighted the rising tension between the Court and Parliament. Lady Hale cautioned the government against implementing reforms that would politicize the appointment of judges. Her comment that "[the court does] not want to turn into the Supreme Court of the United States, whether in powers or in process of appointment," is a reaction to criticisms by Conservatives and the media that the Court acted as the enemy of the people (Hale, 2019). In an attempt to quell fears, Lady Hale noted that "we don't decide political

3 The Court first heard a case dealing with Brexit in 2017 where it ruled that then-Prime Minister Theresa May had to acquire Parliament's approval prior to triggering Article 50, the formal process to leave the European Union, in *R (Miller) v. Secretary of State for Exiting the European Union* [2017] UKSC 5.

questions, we decide legal questions. And in any event, parliament always has the last word" (Hale, 2019).

The leaders of the Conservative party's critiques of the Court's actions and the attempts by Lady Hale to distinguish the UK Supreme Court from its U.S. counterpart indicate the fear of growing judicial activism in the U.K. Whether or not the whispers of parliamentary oversight of judicial appointments would actually yield less 'political' justices on the Supreme Court, the idea of strengthening parliamentary control was central to the election that provided Boris Johnson's government a commanding lead in Parliament. The slogan that played a prominent role in Johnson's manifesto was 'taking back control'. This seemed to be primarily directed at the European Union, but it also had an important domestic meaning tied to how courts have used European Union law to 'disapply' English law.[4] The Conservative Party's ire, under Prime Minister Johnson's leadership, thus seemed directed at the Courts for overly-political behavior. In other words, the judges were being targeted for perceived judicial activism.

However, is the perception of judicial activism warranted? How do we know if courts, or individual justices, are engaging in judicial activism? Much like the concept of 'fake news', judicial activism has become a rallying cry for governments to rely upon when courts produce decisions contrary to their policy preferences. The goal of this chapter is threefold: (1) to understand the institutional developments that propelled activism or restraint within the UK judiciary; (2) to demonstrate the importance of institutional differences across countries and courts when creating concepts; and (3) to offer a conceptual framework of activism and restraint portable across judicial environments. In pursuit of these goals, I first discuss various definitions of activism and restraint within and outside of the U.K. judicial system. Next, I trace key developments in the U.K. judiciary that allowed for the growth of activism. I then highlight my own ideas about how activism and restraint can be conceptualized and measured within the U.K.'s judicial system. I end with a discussion about how scholars can define concepts in ways that can be used comparatively.

4 Interestingly, the provisions within the Human Rights Act, 1998, which provided the legal justification for justices to disapply the law, were passed under a similar slogan: "Bringing rights home."

What Is Judicial Activism?

The tensions between Parliament and the Supreme Court surrounding the so-ruled unlawful prorogation of Parliament provide insight into the debate on the role of courts within a democracy. Elected legislators pass bills that represent the will of the majority, which are formally recognized as law by an executive.[5] Challenges to those laws are then decided upon by an unelected judiciary. At what point do justices reviewing the validity of laws or actions by the elected branches of government cross the threshold into creating laws? Scholars and political commentators acknowledge that once judges write legislation within their judgments, the judiciary has engaged in judicial activism.

Identifying when that bridge has been crossed can be difficult and subjective. In the public realm, politicians have used judicial activism more as a rallying cry to rile up voters than as a useful concept to identify aberrant judicial behavior. The popular definition of judicial activism connotes a "decision inconsistent with the speaker's politics" (Roosevelt, 2008), or even an insult, evident in both comments by Suella Braverman and Lady Brenda Hale.[6] On the other hand, among scholars there is no consensus on what judicial activism is or how we can recognize it. This is true within a country's judiciary (e.g. within the U.S. judiciary) and when comparing courts across countries (e.g. the U.S. and U.K.'s judiciaries). The basic theme across most definitions involves the idea that the judiciary acts outside of its proper judicial role, yet the difficult issue involves identifying what this means in practice. At its most basic definition, judicial activism is "any occasion where a court intervenes and strikes down a piece of duly enacted legislation" (Jones, 2001, p. 143) or a willingness to act "contrary to the will of the other branches of government." (Posner 1999, p. 320). The common way that studies measure whether or not courts have engaged in judicial activism is to investigate the frequency with which courts invalidated legislation (Ringhand, 2007; Howard & Segal, 2004; Segal & Spaeth, 2002). Not only do we see this definition being used in other works focused on the United States, but comparative studies have adopted this definition as well (e.g., see Weiden, 2011; Wenzel, Bowler & Lanoue, 1997).

Defining activism by striking down statutes does not translate to the case of the United Kingdom. Judicial review, the power to declare statutes unconstitutional, does not exist in the U.K. Initial discussions of judicial activism in

5 Called 'Royal Assent' in the U.K. and is pro forma.

6 Though directed at different courts, the U.K. Supreme Court and the U.S. Supreme Court, respectively.

the U.K. examined the structure of the Human Rights Act (HRA), the history of growing review of administrative decisions, and discussed hypothetical paths of the British constitutional arrangement (Stevens, 1999; Young, 2002; McCleave, 2008; Bonner, Fenwick & Harris-Short, 2003). These early forays into examining judicial activism outlined neither a conceptual framework nor a methodology by which scholars could determine activist behavior. For the most part, these studies relied upon imported definitions of judicial activism. Scholars, at times, explicitly relied upon work developed in the U.S. context to define judicial activism as "the subordination of precedents, statutes, and deference to the judge's personal attitudes, values, and goals" (Cahill-O'Callaghan, 2013); or understood activism to play the role of 'unelected legislators' (McCleave, 2008). However, defining activism as any instance where the court invalidates legislation by an elected branch ignores an essential function of the court, which is to be an impartial adjudicator. Cross and Lindquist rightly critique the unidimensional conceptualization of activism within the U.S. context as well. By limiting the court's interpretive capabilities, activism would "fail to account for the possibility that the exercise of judicial review is justified on legal grounds" (Cross and Lindquist, 2006).[7]

Cohn and Kremnitzer (2005) made the first step in filling this need by outlining a multidimensional model (as shown in Figure 2.1 of Chapter 2), placing judicial decisions on a spectrum of restrained to activist. They identified three categories of activism: traditional vision; deviation from social equilibrium, and protection of core values. Each category could be further defined with one (1) to twelve (12) parameters. This model's goal was to reflect the complexity of judicial decision-making. However, it is not clear whether the model captures specifically judicial activism or a mixture of related concepts. Conversely, Dickson presents a simpler model of judicial activism by surveying the degree to which: (1) Justices departed from precedents, (2) Interpreted legislation in unanticipated ways, (3) Rejected the government's position on matters of social economic or foreign policy, and (4) Developed the common law (Dickson, 2015). Yet, though more manageable, Dickson's approach calls into question what scholars should mean when they use the term 'activism'. In the Practice Statement of 1966, the Law Lords acknowledged that there are moments that need a departure from precedent in order to avoid an injustice (Practice Statement, 1966). If we take a literal approach to activism (such as Dickson's), all instances of a court departing from precedent would be considered activist.

7 A classic example of this would be when the U.S. Supreme Court overturned the separate but equal doctrine of *Plessy v. Ferguson* when deciding *Brown v. Board of Education.*

However, overruling or distinguishing precedent may arise for other legitimate reasons.

Judicial Restraint

Defining activism as a 'willingness to act outside of the proper judicial role' presents scholars with the necessity of defining judicial restraint. In an attempt to define a restrained judge, U.S. Supreme Court Justice Stevens referred to the doctrine of judicial restraint as a guide for "judges to focus their attention on the issue that must be addressed in order to decide the case or controversy between the specific litigants before the Court" (Stevens, 1985, p. 452). Justice Powell similarly remarked that judicial restraint "means . . . the court should focus specifically on the particular facts of the case and the questions properly presented" (Powell, 1990, p. 281). In the Justices' definitions, 'restraint' does not appear altogether different from everyday judge-craft. Other scholars like Thayer highlighted that their definition lacks deference to an externality. Thayer proposed that judicial restraint imparts the ability for the people, not the courts, to interpret the Constitution (Thayer, 1893). A similar component of externality resides in Justice Scalia's definition of restraint when he prescribed the "Court to ground its decisions in some source of authority *external* to the judge's will" (Manning, 2017, p. 749). Diedrich makes Scalia's externality explicit. He accredits the elected branches as the authority the Court should respect in order to conform to principles of judicial restraint (Diedrich, 2019). One criticism with the preceding definitions lies with the role of apex courts in upholding the rule of law. Courts would *not* be engaging in their proper role if they deferred to an elected branch of government that acted outside the plain meaning of the constitution.

Some scholars have attempted to define judicial restraint in other ways. Analyzing judicial restraint in the U.K. and Hong Kong, Chng defined restraint as "minimizing intrusion into the merits of decision-making as the doctrine as applied to the facts" and "insuring that an application of the doctrine strikes a proper balance between securing justice for individual applicants and the broader public good" (Chng, 2021). Roosevelt takes a binary approach to studying judicial behavior by examining whether doctrine allows for the court to defer (or not) to another governmental actor. Thus, the authors incorporate a discussion of activism and restraint, deference, and doctrine (Roosevelt, 2008). Most definitions tend to define activism and restraint as opposite from one another.

If we believe that judicial restraint is the obverse of judicial activism, then the U.K.'s Judiciary Committee of the House of Lords pre-1950 could be considered the paragon of judicial restraint. Scholars characterize the judiciary in the early 20th century as a deferent body that was not considered an active part of political culture. However, studies on judicial restraint during this era are essentially non-existent. We could attribute this to the fact that scholars did not see the judiciary as an important political player. Waltman notes that British political textbooks from this time did not even mention the judiciary (Waltman, 1991).

Despite its reputation for judicial restraint, much of the scholarly literature on restraint at the U.K. Supreme Court was published *after* politicians began focusing on the court's perceived activism. Those studies claim that the Supreme Court is still a 'restrained' court (Dickson, 2015; King, 2008; Edwards, 2002). Dickson, defining restraint as the opposite of judicial activism, came to this conclusion by analyzing a number of recent U.K. Supreme Court decisions. While it is unclear how he devises his ranking, he places justices on an activist-restrained scale. Of the twelve justices on the court, he determines that six of them should be considered 'restrained', four as willing to engage in activism but consistently hesitant in the follow-through, and two justices as firmly 'activist' (Dickson, 2015). Cahill-O'Callaghan, on the other hand, presents the most systematic examination of judicial restraint, though in her theoretical framework she discusses the concept through the lens of personal values. In her account, 'traditional' values closely relate to what other scholars identify as judicial restraint. When analyzing decisions, she discovers that this traditional approach to decision-making is an important influence on the Supreme Court. Other authors take a normative slant on defining restraint, outlining guidance on how the Supreme Court can adopt a principled approach to deferring to the executive (Edwards, 2002). Some discuss the value of judicial restraint, especially when the court is weighing important institutional considerations in a case (Kavanagh, 2010). What is clear from the current scholarly discussion of judicial restraint in the U.K. is the dearth of consistent empirical measures for determining the extent to which judicial restraint exists.

Activism and Restraint in the U.K.: A Sleepy Court Awakens

Twenty years ago, Malleson observed "the English judiciary is not generally regarded as an institution that welcomes radical change" (Malleson, 2016, p. 1).

These words ring especially true when looking back at some of the major principles and developments within the judiciary and constitutional law. Institutional structures and legal culture slowly changed in a way that was conducive to the development of a more 'activist' judiciary. Thirty years ago, Waltman (1991) outlined four areas of institutional barriers that stalled the development of activism within the British legal system: (1) parliamentary sovereignty, (2) judicial background, (3) adherence to *stare decisis*, and (4) an unwritten constitution. Incremental changes within each of these strands carved a path for activism to emerge.

Parliamentary Sovereignty

Parliamentary sovereignty places politics, and the direction of those politics, within the grasp of the people by uplifting legislation passed by Parliament as superior to regulations or judicial rulings.[8] For this reason, the judiciary never developed an authority to strike down legislation as unconstitutional. This principle in the U.K.'s political system is, perhaps, the largest barrier to activism as seen within other apex courts. It could also be cited as a primary reason for long-standing judicial restraint within the courts and a judicial philosophy that venerates deference.

The principle of parliamentary sovereignty does not totally constrain the ability of justices to review statutes or the actions of public authorities. In order to understand what powers judges hold with respect to judicial review, it is necessary to discuss the role of primary and secondary legislation. Primary legislation refers to the main laws passed by the legislatures of the U.K. (acts of the U.K. Parliament, Scottish Parliament, Welsh Parliament, and Northern Ireland Assembly), and the acts passed by historical Parliaments. Secondary legislation or 'subordinate legislation' is made by a person or body acting on behalf of primary legislation. For example, the Secretary of State has the ability under subordinate legislation to make regulations giving employees shared parental leave if they meet certain conditions. There have been two major shifts within the principle of parliamentary sovereignty that have relaxed strict judicial deference to Parliament. The first occurred within judicial review of secondary legislation in the 1980s. The second shift occurred when the Human Rights Act imbibed the courts with the ability to review primary legislation. I discuss

8 For the classic definition of parliamentary sovereignty, see Dicey (1897).

the first transformation within this section, and the second within the section "Unwritten Constitution".

Under the doctrine of *ultra vires,* the court can declare actions of administrators (secondary legislation) unlawful. In essence, the court can declare that a person has acted outside of the law, by interpreting what Parliament intended for the law to be when it was passed. Scholars cite the doctrine of *ultra vires* as one of the primary factors in the transformation of administrative law (e.g., Waltman, 1991; Elliott, 1999; Drewry, 1992; Griffith, 2001; Schwartz, 1987). Beginning in the 1980s, progress in administrative law opened the doors for judges to engage in policy making and for scholars to turn their attention to the judiciary (Griffith, 2001). Tracing the history and development of judicial activism, Waltman noted the pattern of English judges to first establish precedents with minimal reach, and then later rely upon those precedents to uphold procedural fairness with public authorities. Drewry's analysis of the decisions of the British courts provides evidence that in reviewing administrative actions, judges influence policy making (1992). And, almost a decade before it occurs, he observes that a written bill of rights would further attract judges into engaging with political issues.

Background of the Judiciary

It is no secret that the U.K.'s higher courts *presently* lack diversity, including racial, ethnic, gender, educational background, and cognitive diversity (Malleson, 2022). This was ubiquitous but not necessarily controversial during the first half (or longer) of the 20th century. The judges' homogeneity throughout the 19th and 20th century shaped the judiciary's values, norms, and doctrines. Overwhelmingly, during this time period, judges tended to be white men, appointed at middle age, who had studied at Oxford or Cambridge. It was also understood that judges would have independent means to practice for the first few years after becoming a barrister. Usually, once called to the Bar, barristers initiated a 12-month pupillage. Only afterward were they able to practice independently (self-employed). During the pupillage, barristers must build up contacts to gain clients and eventually make profit. Thus, the background of most legal professionals in the early 20th century came from the upper strata of society.

The commentary on the background of judges is important to understand how judicial activism was suppressed during the early history of the Appellate Committee of the House of Lords. Conservatism, both political and philosophical, was not just the norm within the judiciary, but nearly the rule. Lord Chancellor Jowitt (in office 1945–1951), took pride in appointing judges from the Conservative Party (Stevens, 2002). The entrenchment of conservative (non-political) values about the law certainly had an impact upon the way in which judge-craft was performed. Strong norms about how judges should work together created pressure for unanimity in judgments. This is evidenced by judges' statements[9] and validated by research.[10] Even after the judiciary began to diversify (in some categories) in the 1970s and 1980s, the norms of socialization and precedents with a conservative (non-political) style of thinking remained.

As can be said about any development within the judiciary, the 'shock' of added diversity to the legal profession and the bench came gradually. The High Court gained its first woman judge in 1965, the Court of Appeal earned it in 1988, and the first woman appointed to the Appellate Committee of the House of Lords occurred in 2004. Other 'shocks' to the conservative norms came with the appointment of reforming law lords. As an example, Lord Reid in the 1960s focused on procedural due process. Particularly during the 1980s and 1990s, the perception of the role of judges changed. The changing attitudes within the judiciary reflected a larger cultural shift within the U.K. (Waltman, 1991, *see* also Malleson, 2016; Stevens, 2002). Shifts within the backgrounds of aspiring judges and legal professionals thus have a tremendous impact upon the flow and direction of judging. Changes in the types of judges being appointed have particular impact within a judiciary known for consensus and teamwork decision-making.[11]

Adherence to Stare Decisis

While the norm of adhering to *stare decisis* had always been a robust tenet of the common law, it was not until 1898 that, while hearing a case about accounting principles, the Lord Chancellor stated "nothing but an Act of

9 "You follow precedent because it is your duty—that is why you are a judge . . . This duty is socialized into you." (Masood and Lineberger, 2020, 716).

10 For example, Masood and Lineberger (2020) find that professionalization of judges plays a key role in the frequency of dissent. Cahill-O'Callaghan (2020) finds that institutional constraints and judicial norms limit the ability for a justice to express their values.

11 For example, Thomas Poole and Sangeeta Shah discuss decision making behavior in their 2011 article on the law lords and human rights. For a more recent discussion, see Alan Paterson's examination of Lord Neuberger's legacy on collective judicial decision making (2021).

Parliament can set right that which is alleged to be wrong in a judgment of this House" (*London Tramways Co v. London County Council*, 1898, p. 381). For the better half of a century this rigid rule stood as a firm normative guide to judicial decision-making. It was only in 1966 that the House of Lords acknowledged the utility of overturning its own precedents in a speech called the Practice Statement, —one of the institution's first radical departures from its staunch conservatism.[12] Oddly, there was a lack of clear motivation for the statement, as "there was no pending case that raised the issue . . . the judges and their reforming Lord Chancellor simply got together and decided to make the change" (Lewis, 1966).

To demonstrate the strong norm and practice of adhering to precedent, I graph every instance in which the court treats their own precedents. Figure 4.1 below presents data from the U.K.'s House of Lords treatment of its own precedents (1970–2013).[13] This encompasses the newly created Supreme Court in 2009, with the blue line distinguishing between these two institutions. Clearly the Practice Statement of 1966 did not impact judicial behavior immediately. In fact, the only instance in the data in which the Law Lords explicitly overruled a precedent occurred in 2008. The other negative treatments of previous precedents combine instances where the Court distinguished, did not follow, or doubted those prior judicial pronouncements. Additionally, the substance of such precedents rarely lends itself to be categorized as 'broad' or 'maximalist'. Scholars frequently note how the "traditionally British incremental approach as building on developments and trends in common law, rather than as something wholly new," is the status quo for judicial pronouncements (Bonner, Fenwick and Harris-Short, 2003, p. 585).

Unwritten Constitution

Waltman identifies an unwritten constitution as the last major barrier to the growth of judicial activism within the U.K. judiciary. There is no written constitution in the U.K. embodied in a singular document named the "Constitution." However, the written statutes passed by Parliament do serve as a constitution.

12 The text reads, "Their Lordships nevertheless recognize that too rigid adherence to precedent may lead to injustice in a particular case and also unduly restrict the proper development of the law. They propose, therefore, to modify their present practice and, while treating former decisions of this House as normally binding, to depart from a previous decision when it appears right to do so." [1966] 1 W.L.R. 1234 (H.L.).

13 This data comes from Masood and Lineberger (2020).

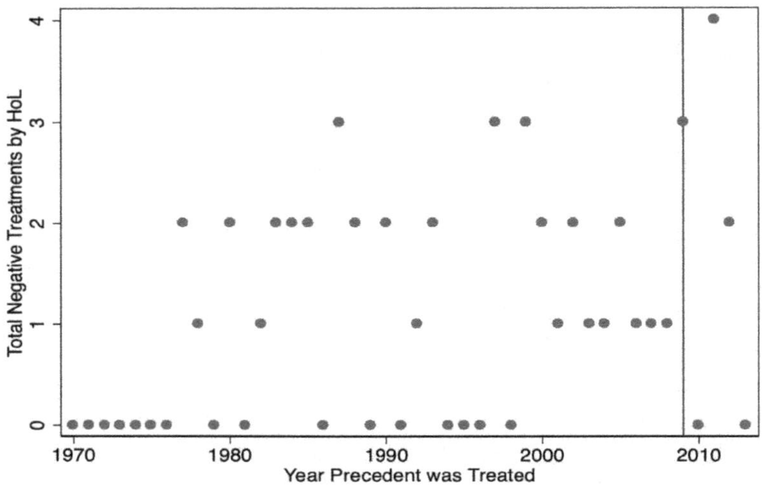

Figure 4.1 : Treatment of precedent 1970–2013

Many describe this constitutional format as 'partly written and wholly uncodified' (e.g., see Budge, Mckay, Newton and Bartle, 2013). Combine this political feature with the principle of parliamentary sovereignty and it becomes clear why judges have no authority to describe a law as 'unconstitutional'. With the entrance into and exit from the European Union, the adoption of the Human Rights Act, and the supremacy of the European Court of Justice, this previous barrier to activism has transformed into its conduit. Two supranational bodies provided the mechanisms for judges to engage in an activist style of judicial review: the Council of Europe and the European Union.

The Council of Europe

The U.K. was a founding member of the Council of Europe in 1949, created after World War II as a forum to uphold human rights and democracy in Europe. The Council of Europe quickly ratified the European Convention of Human Rights (ECHR), a document that outlined the human rights and political freedoms that citizens within member states enjoy. The Convention also established the European Court of Human Rights (ECtHR) where citizens within member states could petition the supranational court if they believed one of their Convention rights had been violated. If the ECtHR found that the U.K. had violated one of the Convention rights, then the person could be entitled to compensation. Importantly, judges in the U.K. were not obliged to use those rulings as binding precedents in future cases. Judges could 'take account' of the ruling by the European Court, but it would not affect U.K. domestic law.

A major shift in the relationship between U.K. domestic law, judicial review, and human rights occurred when Parliament adopted the Human Rights Act of 1998 (HRA). The HRA is an ordinary statute that, nonetheless, provided judges with an abundance of new judicial power. It requires that "public authorities in Great Britain observe the civil and political rights enumerated in the European Convention of Human Rights" (Maiman, 2005, pp. 410–411). To ensure that public authorities remain accountable to this duty, the HRA allowed for judges to declare primary and secondary legislation, as well as the actions of public authorities, as 'incompatible' with the ECHR (Human Rights Act 1998, 4:2). A declaration of incompatibility does not automatically strike down the law. In fact, Parliament is not required to amend the legislation. In most instances where the court declares a law incompatible with the Convention, Parliament remedies the statute. These declarations of incompatibility have been used sparingly, averaging about two (2) per year from 2000 to 2017 (Hanretty, 2020).

Section 3 of the HRA provides an alternative mechanism that has truly paved the way for increased judicial creativity, and as a consequence, potential judicial activism. Section 3 calls for judges to read and to give effect to primary and subordinate legislation "in a way which is compatible with the Convention rights" (Human Rights Act, 1998, 3:1). Hoffman and Rowe (2010) suggest that judges have three common methods for interpreting legislation with respect to Section 3: reading in, reading out, and reading down. Declarations of incompatibility and "reading in" methods for interpreting primary and secondary legislation have provided judges with more opportunities to engage in activism. After the (formal) completion of the Brexit process in 2020, the ruling Conservative party has begun to discuss reforms, and even the potential repeal, of the HRA. A recent proposal, put forth by Justice Secretary Dominic Raab, is a Bill of Rights that would replace the HRA. It would empower judges to ignore rulings by the ECtHR and introduce a "permission stage" to human rights cases that would require courts to evaluate whether significant disadvantage was suffered by the claimant before proceeding with a case. These proposals, if implemented by Parliament, could significantly curb the power of the judiciary.

The European Union

The U.K.'s entrance into the European Union, and its subsequent withdrawal, will have a lasting impact upon the way in which judges interpret domestic law. Unlike the relationship between the U.K. and the Council of Europe, when the U.K. joined the European Union in January of 1973 the legal and judicial systems began to absorb EU law immediately. As the judges interpreted domestic law in light of EU law, they decided precedents that disapplied or set aside domestic law when it conflicted with EU Law.[14] Such precedents of judges absorbing EU law accumulated for nearly 50 years until the U.K. left the European Union in 2020. The concerning question now is, how should courts treat their previous precedents that incorporated EU law domestically?

Hameed (2022) examines the treatment of EU law norms on the judicial system in a post-Brexit world. In exploring the text and nature of the European Union Withdrawal Agreement (EUWA), he argues that the "options for diverging in future from relevant retained EU norms are legally more constrained than hitherto anticipated" (Hameed, 2022, p. 754). Partly, this stems from the duty within the Withdrawal agreement that courts interpret "the validity, meaning or effect of any retained EU law . . . in accordance with any retained case law" (European Union Withdrawal Agreement 2020, Section 6:3). Initial interpretations of the EUWA appear to conclude that the courts will certainly hear cases that require reconciliation of past retained case law and future enactments. The fact that the EUWA leaves the subject and direction of that interpretation up to the courts indicates that, for now, the withdrawal from the European Union will not directly curb judicial activism. As it currently stands, the Withdrawal agreement appears to allow for judges to engage in either activism or restraint.

Conceptual Framework of Activism and Restraint in the U.K.

Now, what does judicial activism and restraint mean in the context of the U.K.? Key problems repeatedly discussed in this chapter, such as parliamentary sovereignty, the lack of a written constitution, and the judiciary's penchant for legal conservatism distinguish it from its U.S. counterpart, but other judicial systems share such qualities. Therefore, in constructing a conceptualization that could capture both activism and restraint in a simplified manner, my goal is to also create a framework that may be easily adapted to jurisdictions with similar features. Here, I develop a conceptual framework that categorizes two types of activism and two types of restraint: procedural activism, substantive activism, procedural restraint, and substantive restraint. This categorization

14 See *Regina v. Secretary of State for Transport ex parte Factortame Limited*. Case C-213/89, 1989 E.C.R. 1-1029.

provides a framework where scholars can substitute in (or out) the powers that the studied judiciary retains. By not defining activism or restraint by one institutional feature, the framework seeks to provide scholars more flexibility across different contexts.

The starting point is that, on a scale from 'restrained' to 'neutral' to 'activist' judge-craft, most judicial output should fall within the 'neutral' category. At the heart of this belief is that there are certain *anchors*, or constraints, on the judicial decision-making process. These *anchors* represent the vital resources of judge-craft, such as norms, precedents, doctrines, and legislation. The anchors ground the judging process, allowing for a certain radius of movement—or, in this case, judicial interpretation, —while ultimately preventing the boat from drifting too far away. Judicial activism and judicial restraint occur when they move beyond the radius of what anchored their previous decisions. The difference between activism and restraint is the direction of change. Judicial activism occurs in any instance where the court inserts itself into deciding a question, issue, or policy where it was unnecessary, unexpected or not predicted to do so. Judicial restraint is the obverse. It occurs when the court limits its own ability to decide questions, issues, or policies when there is an opportunity to engage in activism.

This conceptualization of restraint departs from previous definitions in important ways. For example, Holland defines restraint as "confining the judiciary to the task of applying to the specific cases laws and regulations made by the political branches of government." Edwards notes that a judge acts restrained when they "declare the substance of a case non-justiciable." However, these conceptualizations describe 'neutral' judicial behavior: behavior that cannot be labeled as activist or restrained. In the decisional process, judges must rely upon certain constraints, certain anchors, that inform their decision-making process in a given case. The previous definitions capture instances where judges are both constrained and restrained; this is an instance of observational equivalence. However, judicial behavior is not always restrained. A restraint is a force or influence that keeps someone within limits. In the judicial realm, when judges behave in a restrained manner, they are imposing self-control upon their own decisions in moments when they could have gone beyond the normal judicial function.

The dimension of 'restrained', 'neutral', and 'activist' judicial behavior can be further sub-categorized by whether or not the question or issue decided is procedural or substantive in nature. 'Procedural' questions decided by the court are those that relate to the court's process: the boundaries of a court's jurisdiction, the types of cases that can be appropriately resolved by the court, or the rules surrounding how cases move up the judicial hierarchy (e.g., leapfrogging). When the public or politicians accuse the court of activism, it is usually in reference to 'substantive activism'. Substantive, as a subcategory of judicial behavior along the restrained-activist scale, refers to when the court inserts itself into the policy realm. 'Substantive' issues decided by the court relate to the policy scope of the decision, the use of precedent, and the interpretation of legal documents (statutes, the constitution, regulatory schemes).

Using this central motif as a guide, I posit that there are two areas in which the court can go 'beyond' its normal role. The first occurs when courts expand or contract the boundaries that separate the judicial realm from legislative and executive functions. This procedural activism does not affect the content of policy; rather it modifies the scope of issues that fall under these respective institutions. Thus, this conceptualization of activism, will be useful for scholars who are examining the dynamic relationship between the judiciary, legislature, and executive, or the institutional change of the judicial system over time. On the other hand, the second type of activism relates to the widely used definition that identifies when the courts engage in policy-making, i.e., when courts engage in developing public policy, moving beyond deciding the case based on the facts or its legal determinants, and beginning to discuss the meaning of that policy. In this discussion, courts can be identified as being substantively active when the discussion leads them to include additional categories or qualifications of a statute or broaden the factual situations to which the statute applies (See Figure 4.2).

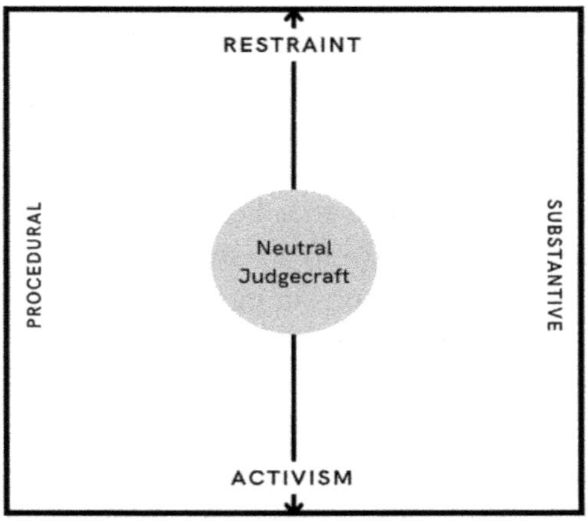

Figure 4.2: My conceptualization of judicial activism and restraint

In the United Kingdom, it is easier to identify instances of an activist court rather than a restrained one. This is because the characteristics of the English judicial system lend themselves to foster adherence to the norms of an already conservative legal culture. The problem, then, in measuring restraint will be to determine when a court is actually practicing judicial restraint versus operating in a 'neutral' way. I believe there is a distinction between these 'neutral' decisions and instances where the court is purposefully behaving in a restrained manner. I posit that judicial restraint exists when the opportunity to employ activism occurs, but judges choose not to engage in either procedural or substantive activism.

There is an immediate concern with this conceptualization of judicial restraint. How can scholars identify when the opportunity to engage in activism exists? Scholars could surely argue that in almost any case there is an opportunity for a judge to engage in activism. However, this critique also highlights the benefit of defining restraint this way. If we define judicial restraint solely by the times in which a court was *not active*, such as not invalidating a provision of the legislature or not overturning precedent, scholars capture both instances of restraint and judicially 'neutral' moments. The benefit of examining judicial restraint as when justices choose not to engage in activism, is that it provides leverage for scholars to understand the determinants of a justice's preference for activism or restraint. The drawback to this definition of restraint, is that it becomes a pivot from activism, rather than a concept that can be identified on its own.

Procedural and substantive restraint are the definitional opposites of procedural and substantive activism. Procedural restraint exists when the court makes an explicit decision that either keeps the political boundaries at their equilibrium or when the court contracts its own areas of judicial review. Substantive restraint occurs when the court explicitly decides not to engage in the development of public policy. Substantive judicial restraint can include when the court decides not to read into the meaning of statutes, and when the court creates additional requirements or burdens upon itself in order to decide these public policy issues. Creating additional restrictions to engage in the development of public policy is a positive instance of the court restricting its own ability to behave as an 'unelected legislator'.

Illustrative Examples of the Restraint-Activist Dimension

Separating instances of procedural activism or restraint from substantive activism or restraint is conceptually and operationally useful. Modifying the process of judicial review often occurs for different motivations than substantive judicial decision-making. Substantive activism or restraint typically centers around modifying (or deciding against modifying) a policy outcome. Procedural activism or restraint can be connected with a judge's or a court's philosophy on the powers of the judiciary relative to the elected branches of government. Or it can be tied to larger beliefs about judging in certain political moments. Within this section, I will examine four cases decided by the Supreme Court or the House of Lords that illustrate each of the categories of judicial behavior offered above.

Procedural Activism

Anisminic Ltd. v. Foreign Compensation Commission is a classic example of procedural activism. Decided in 1968, the case represented one of the first instances of the Law Lords breaking away from strict deference to the legislature. Just two years prior, the Law Lords acknowledged that they could overturn wrongly-decided precedents. Additionally, *Anisminic* created the opportunity for future judges to engage in substantive activism by stating that errors in law made by public bodies are subject to judicial scrutiny even when ouster clauses are present.[15]

In order for a judgment of the court to be considered as an instance of 'procedural activism', certain elements have to exist within the judgment. First, there have to be certain anchors within the law that provide a guide to understanding the radius of expected decision making. Second, the judgment has to augment the ability of the court to weigh in on cases that were not under the scope of review prior to the case. The norms of judicial practice at the time of the decision, parliamentary sovereignty, and precedent of the court provide helpful anchors in determining if the decision of *Anisminic* went beyond neutral judicial behavior. While parliamentary sovereignty certainly looms in the background of all cases decided by any level of court, it is particularly relevant

15 An ouster clause is a clause within legislation that excludes judicial review of specified actions.

in a case where a statute prescribes that "[T]he determination by the commission of any application made to them under this Act shall not be called in question in any court of law" (Foreign Compensation Act, 1950, section 4:4).

To understand why deviating from this statute is a moment of procedural activism, it is necessary to contextualize how decisions were made in English law before *Anisminic*. Tribunals constituted by Parliament commonly made decisions when enacting policy passed by Parliament. Often these tribunals were protected by ouster clauses as referenced above. Before *Anisminic*, if a tribunal made an erroneous decision, the courts would not grant *certiorari* as a way to defer to Parliament.[16] Pre-*Anisminic*, judicial review of tribunal decisions when an ouster clause existed was limited to questions of jurisdiction (i.e., did the tribunal have the authority to hear the case?). Moreover, in addition to the constitutional norms of parliamentary sovereignty, previously decided decisions should act as binding authority. In 1956, the House of Lords examined a similar ouster clause to the one present in *Anisminic* and held ouster clauses excluded all judicial review "even where the administrative act was challenged on the ground that it had been made 'wrongfully' and 'in bad faith'" (*Smith v. East Elloe Rural District Council*, 1956, p. 750).

Judicial practice, parliamentary sovereignty, and norms seemingly would direct the court to conclude that the plain language of the ouster clause removed judicial review in this instance. However, the majority of the justices, even those who dissented, agreed that the courts were able to judicially review cases where tribunals make errors in law that exceed their jurisdiction. On the issue of precedent, Lord Reid did not "regard this case as a binding authority" (*Smith v. East Elloe Rural District Council*, 1956, par.14), and Lord Pearce suggested that even if it were binding authority, the Law Lords should rely upon the dissenting opinions (one of whom was Lord Reid).

With the precedential case put aside easily, parliamentary sovereignty still controlled how statutes were to be treated in court. While the court regarded the language of the ouster clause in *Smith v. East Elloe* as "plain", the ouster clause of *Anisminic* was determined to be vague by many of the justices. Contemplating on what Parliament had intended with the clause, Lord Reid "expected to find something much more specific than the bald statement that a determination shall not be called in question in any court of law" (*Smith v. Elloe Rural District Council*, 1956, par. 13). However, the intentions of Parliament could have been gleaned from the fact that the Tribunals and Inquiries

16 However, there were cases where the court believed a tribunal acted outside of its authority, which prompted the court to interfere (McInnes, 1977, p. 37).

Act 1958 repealed many preclusion clauses that ousted the judiciary's jurisdiction to hear appeals from tribunal. One of the few ouster clauses that remained in statute was present in the *Anisminic* case. Lord Pearce addressed Parliament's repeal of other ouster clauses by stating it "cannot have any bearing on the construction of the Foreign Compensation Act 1950" (*Smith v. Elloe Rural District Council*, 1956). The Law Lords disregarded Parliamentary intent to not remove the ouster clause of the Foreign Compensation Act as irrelevant.

What makes *Anisminic* both a landmark case and classifies it as an instance of procedural activism is the majority's idea that the Commission had exceeded its jurisdiction by asking a question it had no right to consider. Additionally, Lord Reid provided a list of situations, such as acting in bad faith, non-compliance with natural justice, misconstruing provisions of statutes, and not considering relevant factors in a decision, to be instances when tribunals exceed their jurisdiction and are subject to judicial review, even when Parliament precluded review. These errors of law were wide-ranging enough to cover any situation. In effect, this provided a large area for courts to review cases that would have otherwise been outside of their own jurisdiction. *Anisminic* changed the court's ability from reviewing cases based only on jurisdiction to being able to review actions by public bodies that potentially made an error of law.

Procedural Restraint

Judges engage in procedural restraint the least often of the four subcategories that classify judicial behavior. Procedural activism supplements judicial power, substantive activism results in preferred policy preferences or legal outcomes, and substantive restraint can insulate the court from political backlash. While procedural restraint can offer benefits, manipulating the powers of the judiciary with respect to jurisdiction and justiciability can result in years-long limitation of the court's scope of power. Part of the opinion of *AXA General Insurance Ltd. v. HM Advocate*, decided by the Supreme Court in 2011, represents an instance of procedural restraint.

AXA raised a few important issues, though the pertinent one as an example of procedural restraint concerns the relationship between the devolved Scottish Parliament and Westminster. The reason for appeal also reveals a central 'anchor' in this case: *Rothwell v. Chemical & Insulating Co. Ltd* (2007). In *Rothwell*, the House of Lords held that the presence of pleural plaques in a person's lungs "did not constitute an injury which was capable of giving rise to a claim for damages" (*AXA General Insurance Ltd. & Ors v. Lord Advocate & Ors*, 2011, par. 2). After this ruling in 2007, the Scottish Parliament passed the Damages Act 2009 with the intent to specifically reverse the decision of *Rothwell* and provide the ability for claimants to seek damages based upon the presence of pleural plaques. A Scottish insurance company that would be liable for these claims sought review from the U.K. Supreme Court on the basis that the legislation is open to judicial review by the Court as an unreasonable, irrational, and arbitrary exercise of legislative authority.[17]

In the *AXA* case, the court had an opportunity to engage in procedural activism by classifying acts of the Scottish Parliament as 'secondary' legislation which would have allowed courts to strike down legislation of the Scottish Parliament as 'unreasonable'. If the Court were to have taken this approach, the Scottish Parliament would have been placed on the same level, and would have been under the same constraints and limitations, as administrative bodies (like the tribunal in consideration in *Anisminic*). Nevertheless, the justices sidestepped the classification of Scottish legislation; Lord Reed and Lord Hope instead focused on the Constitutional responsibilities of courts and legislatures. In their respective discussions, the Law Lords pointed to the role of courts in protecting individuals against abuses and excesses of powerful executives. However, "judges could not go against the will of Parliament" (*AXA General Insurance Ltd. & Ors v. Lord Advocate & Ors*, 2011, note 72, par. 50) and courts "must be careful to respect the sphere of action of the other" (*AXA General Insurance Ltd. & Ors v. Lord Advocate & Ors*, 2011, note 72, par. 148). Relying upon parliamentary sovereignty and principles of democracy, the Court held that they had no power of review over Acts of Scottish Parliament. Lord Hope opined that it would be "quite wrong for the judges to substitute their views on these issues for the considered judgment of a democratically elected legislature" (*AXA General Insurance Ltd. & Ors v. Lord Advocate & Ors*, 2011, note 72, par. 52).

As for the precedent of *Rothwell*, the justices concluded that Parliament's responsibility to create social policy outweighs adherence to precedent. Lord Hope noted that "this was a social problem that the Scottish Parliament ought to address" (*AXA General Insurance Ltd. & Ors v. Lord Advocate & Ors*, 2011, note 72, par. 29). Even Lord Brown, who thought the legislation "ill-judged" and created an 'extreme' departure from the common law position put forth in *Rothwell*, still believed that the "democratically elected body determining

17 These represent grounds for judicial review of administrative decisions. Lord Diplock summarized these in *Council of Civil Service Unions v. Minister for the Civil Service* [1985] AC 374.

the public interest by reference . . . to political, economic, and social considerations" outweighed his personal concerns and consistency within the common law.

AXA General Insurance Ltd. v. HM Advocate demonstrates an instance of justices engaging in procedural restraint. The nature of the case created an opportunity for the justices to engage in procedural activism: a recently-decided precedent would be overturned, personal dislike of the legislation was evident, and the courts would have slightly augmented their review powers vis-a-vis devolved legislatures. However, the justices consistently referenced principles of democracy, deference to Parliament, and the vital importance of the rule of law as their justification for restraining themselves on the procedural issue at hand.

Substantive Judicial Activism

Instances of substantive activism surged after the HRA came into force in 2000. This increase can be traced back to the judges' ability to interpret both primary and secondary legislation to be compatible with the European Convention on Human Rights. The common ways that judges engage in activism in these instances are by 'reading in', 'reading out', or 'reading down'. This is in tension with the principle of parliamentary sovereignty because theoretically the absence or presence of any words within a statute was by design. When judges interpret through 'reading in' or 'reading out' parts of statutes, they contradict the intention of Parliament when it left out or added those specific words.

An illustrative example of this type of activism (and restraint) can be found in *Ghaidan v. Godin-Mendoza* (2004). The case involves a homosexual couple (Godin-Mendoza) who had lived together from 1983 to 2001. Godin-Mendoza's partner passed away in 2001 and the landlord, Ghaidan, claimed possession of the apartment. Under the Rent Act of 1977, a surviving spouse is allowed to continue as the statutory tenant. The landlord argued the Rent Act of 1977 did not include homosexual relationships as it explicitly mentions "spouse" and "wife or husband" (sched. 1, par, 2:2). I will examine the judgments in the majority and the dissenting opinion by Lord Millett as examples of substantive activism and substantive restraint, respectively.

There are two components to the definition of substantive activism that must be identified within a case in order to label the behavior as such. First, the judgment must alter the outcome of a public policy or precedent. Second, the behavior must occur in a moment when it was not necessary, expected, or predicted to occur. In other words, there must be some departure from the expected behavior of the judges. The statements by the judges in the majority opinion of this case contain both of those elements.

The first component of substantive activism would not be difficult to prove, and is likely uncontroversial. The Rent Act of 1977 provided:

> 2(1) The surviving spouse (if any) of the original tenant, if residing in the dwelling-house immediately before the death of the original tenant, shall after the death be the statutory tenant if and so long as he or she occupies the dwelling-house as his or her residence.
> (2) for the purposes of this paragraph, a person who was living with the original tenant as his or her wife or husband shall be treated as the spouse of the original tenant.
> 3(1) Where paragraph 2 above does not apply, but a person who was a member of the original tenant's family was residing with him in the dwelling-house at the time of and for the period of 2 years immediately before his death then, after his death, that person or if there is more than one such person such one of them as may be decided by agreement, or in default of agreement by the county court, shall be entitled to an assured tenancy of the dwelling-house by succession (Rent Act 1977, sched. 1, par. 2: 1–2 to par. 3:1).

In 1999, the House of Lords decided *Fitzpatrick v. Sterling Housing Association* (1999), a case with similar circumstances to the *Ghaidan v. Godin-Mendoza*. In *Fitzpatrick*, the Law Lords decided that a homosexual relationship does not qualify under section 2 of the Rent Act, but it would qualify as a 'family' and the surviving person in the relationship would be provided assured tenancy as given in section 3 of the Rent Act. *Fitzpatrick* is important on multiple accounts. First, it demonstrates that the judgment issued in *Ghaidan v. Godin-Mendoza* should be considered a change in policy. *Fitzpatrick* determined that homosexual relationships were not spousal relationships and surviving partners were entitled to assured tenancy. *Ghaidan v. Godin-Mendoza* classified homosexual relationships as "spousal relationships" that would be subject to statutory tenancy as provided for in paragraph 2(2) of the Rent Act. Second, *Fitzpatrick* is important because it provides us with an anchor that (1) occurred before the implementation of the HRA and (2) should act as a binding precedent upon the court. The first point matters because it provides insight into how the justices interpreted the Rent Act without the ability to determine its compatibility with the HRA. It demonstrates how the justices would have examined the statute under previous judicial rules. There is an additional benefit that *Fitzpatrick* was decided only a few years prior to *Ghaidan*. We can infer that the culture or preferences of the court did not change abruptly over this time. Moreover, one justice, Lord Nicholls of Birkenhead, issued a judgment in both *Fitzpatrick* and in *Ghaidan*. Second, as discussed throughout this chapter, the judicial system is still highly deferential to *stare decisis* (Masood and Lineberger, 2020).

Given our anchor of *Fitzpatrick*, the norm of *stare decisis*, and the fact that one of the justices in the majority of *Fitzpatrick* also issued a judgment in *Ghaidan*, the expectation that the outcome of *Ghaidan* would be the same should be high. However, 'all else equal' does not ring true in this instance. Four of the five law lords in *Ghaidan* decided that Section 3 of the HRA requires the court to "read and give effect to" legislation in a way that makes it compatible with the ECHR. To do this, the law lords interpreted the use of Section 3 of the Human Rights Act in order to arrive at the determination that the judges can interpret "as his or her wife or husband" to include cohabiting homosexual partners. Lord Nicholls of Birkenhead noted the various methods of interpreting section 3 of the HRA, but ultimately opting for the "unusual and far-reaching character" of interpretation obliged by the section. In contemplating 'how far' the court is able to go, Lord Nicholls opines:

> Section 3 enables language to be interpreted restrictively or expansively. But section 3 goes further than this. It is also apt to require a court to read in words which change the meaning of the enacted legislation, so as to make it Convention-compliant. In other words, the intention of Parliament in enacting section 3 was that, to an extent bounded only by what is 'possible', a court can modify the meaning and hence the effect, of primary and secondary legislation.

Lord Steyn puts this interpretive method into action. Lord Steyn observes that the ECHR prohibits discrimination based upon sexual orientation and that the Rent Act violates that prohibition. The 'prime remedial remedy' resides in the interpretation under section 3(1) of the HRA, rather than section 4, which should be considered a last resort. Lord Steyn concludes by modifying "as his or her wife or husband" in the Rent Act to read "*as if they were* his wife or husband" (*Ghaidan v. Godin-Mendoza*, 2004, par. 51). With three seemingly trivial words, the House of Lords subsequently protected an entire class of people who may have had to appeal to Strasbourg (ECtHR) to gain relief.

Clear factors were present in this case that should have led the justices to conclude that Godin-Mendoza, the tenant, was entitled to assured tenancy as a 'family' member of the deceased tenant. In fact, it seemed that all the factors pointed to such a conclusion. The Court had determined the same facts in *Fitzpatrick*, the court has an obligation to defer to parliamentary sovereignty, justices deciding *Fitzpatrick* also issued judgment in *Ghaidan*, there was no clear prohibition against discrimination based on sexual orientation within the European Convention of Human Rights, and how to apply section 3 of the HRA was still being debated. Yet, the majority of justices in this case significantly changed a public policy and progressed LGBTQ+ rights a few steps forward. The discussion about how to use section 3 of the HRA that occurs in *Ghaidan* becomes an important precedent that judges later rely upon when reading in cases under section 3 of the HRA (van Zyl Smit, 2007).

Substantive Judicial Restraint

Lord Millett's dissent in this case provides an excellent example of substantive restraint by adhering to the principles of *stare decisis* and parliamentary sovereignty. He acknowledges that:

> As this House decided in *Fitzpatrick v. Sterling Housing Association Ltd* [2001] 1 AC 27, an ordinary reading of paragraph 2(2) the survivor of two persons of the opposite sex living together as man and wife in a dwelling house which is subject to the Rent Acts has a statutory right to succeed to the statutory tenancy of the deceased tenant; but the survivor of two persons of the same sex living together in similar circumstances has no such right (*Ghaidan v.Gozin-Mendoza*, 2004, par. 54).

There are a few components of Lord Millet's dissent that are of particular importance to the discussion of substantive restraint. One is that Lord Millett was sympathetic to the concerns of the defendant, Godin-Mendoza. He believed that "such discriminatory treatment of homosexual couples is incompatible with their Convention rights and cannot be justified by any identifiable legitimate aim" (*Ghaidan v. Gozin-Mendoza*, 2004, par. 55). His commentary shows motivation to engage in judicial activism and the HRA provided its mechanism.

Lord Millett, despite being motivated by a personal belief, nevertheless outlines why both the language of the HRA and parliamentary sovereignty forbid reading into the case as the majority did. First, Lord Millett draws attention to the language used within Section 3 of the HRA: legislation must be "read and given effect to." Reading, Lord Millett believes, means interpretating, not legislating. If Parliament had intended for the Court to modify the words of the statute, it would have expressly provided the authority for the court to perform that function. Additionally, the language of Section 3 calls for the court to "read legislation in a way which is compatible with the Convention only '*so far as it is possible to do so*' (*Ghaidan v. Gozin-Mendoza*, 2004, p. 66). Millett believes that this section directs the court, via an interpretative process only, to read legislation in a way that could be compatible with the Convention. Here, the justice even notes that section 3 may "require" that the statute be given a different meaning by reading in or reading down. The restriction that Section 3 places, is that it cannot give an impossible meaning to the statute. Lord Millett believes that adding in the language to the Rent Act of 1977 changed the meaning to be inconsistent with the original and fundamental feature of the legislation.

To support his point, he goes through a series of examples about what Section 3 of the HRA allows for and does not allow for. He states:

> 'red, blue or green' cannot be read as meaning 'red, blue, green, or yellow'; the specification of the three only of the four primary colours indicates a deliberate omission of the fourth ... Section 3 cannot be used to supply the missing colour, for this would be not to interpret the statutory language but to contradict it (*Ghaidan v. Gozin-Mendoza*, 2004, par. 71).

Lord Millett demonstrates, through discussion of the legislative history and debates surrounding the Rent Acts, that Parliament did not intend to include homosexual relationships, for they had specific opportunities to include these relationships within the statute but decided against it. Second, he specifically mentions the tensions that will arise between Parliament and the judiciary, as well as Parliament and the European Court of Human Rights. He believes that the majority, by reading in, employs a "quasi-legislative power, not a purely interpretive one" (*Ghaidan v. Gozin-Mendoza*, 2004, par. 64). Lord Millett highlights a number of consequences that will stem from the majority's decision that should be left to Parliament to legislate. For example, he asks when does the 'law' change to allow for homosexual couples to be considered as spouses vis-à-vis the law. If the Court were to decide this question, they "would be usurping the function of Parliament" (*Ghaidan v. Gozin-Mendoza*, 2004, par. 99). Finally, Lord Millett concludes by critiquing the court's decision with that ever-common popular idea of what judicial activism is. He states that "these questions are essentially questions of social policy which should be left to Parliament" (*Ghaidan v. Gozin-Mendoza*, 2004, par. 101). Lord Millett's dissent is, I believe, an emblematic example of substantive restraint. He explicitly acknowledges both the opportunity and motivation to judicially decide that the Rent Act of 1977 applies to homosexual relationships. Yet his decision is a resolute endorsement of judicial deference to Parliament made via references to precedent and the role of parliamentary sovereignty.

Discussion and Future Direction

The legal system of the United Kingdom has transformed over the past seventy years. The culture, background, and beliefs of the Law Lords have diversified. Justices began to assert themselves into judicial control of administrative law. The HRA allowed for judges to declare statutes as incompatible with laws passed by Parliament. Within that time frame the U.K. entered and exited from membership within the European Union. Despite the numerous shifts within the British judiciary that created opportunities for activism, the institutional features of the system constrain judges. The transformation has been slow, with incremental steps creating space for further changes. The accumulation of these minor changes in the process and substance of judicial outputs has led to calls for judicial reforms. With Brexit complete, the next potential target is the HRA. If this law were to be repealed, the judiciary would lose an invaluable tool in its ability to engage in activism.

This chapter has explained the status of the judiciary's proclivity or hesitation to insert itself into policy and procedural decisions. The unique position of the United Kingdom's Supreme Court in the constitutional structure makes it difficult to import U.S.-designed measures of judicial activism. I have outlined a framework for what activism and restraint could mean in the British context. I posit that activism and restraint can both be divided into two subcategories: procedural and substantive. Procedural activism and restraint are useful for studies seeking to explain the changing boundaries between the judicial, legislative, and executive institutions. On the other hand, substantive activism and restraint could be useful concepts for those scholars interested in jurisprudence, judicial behavior, and policy development. By distinguishing between procedural and substantive activism and restraint, scholars can simplify conceptually muddy measures.

To demonstrate the conceptual boundaries of the framework, I examine four cases decided by either the House of Lords or the Supreme Court. The conceptual framework emphasizes the importance of 'anchors' within judicial decision-making. I discuss what anchors each case and what scholars would expect to observe. In analyzing the relationship between the anchors, legal reasoning, and outcome of each case, I identify the decision as procedural activism, procedural restraint, substantive activism, or substantive restraint. This comparative analysis demonstrates how the conceptualizations of activism and restraint can be expanded upon and measured on a restraint-neutral-activist scale. Further work using text analysis would provide scholars leverage to study a judiciary's propensity to engage in activism or restraint without having to measure it by how many times a court declared a law unconstitutional. This chapter's framework should be useful to comparative judicial scholars, though I believe the measure could also be applied as successfully in the U.S. context.

References

AXA General Insurance Ltd. & Ors v. Lord Advocate & Ors. (2011) UKSC 46.

Bonner, D., Fenwick, H., & Harris-Short, S. (2003). Judicial approaches to the human rights act. *I.C.L.Q.*, *52*, 549.

Budge, I., Mckay, D., Newton, K., & Bartle, J. (2013). *The new British politics*. Routledge.

Cahill-O'Callaghan, R. (2013). The influence of personal values on legal judgments. *Journal of Law and Society*, *40*(4), 596–623.

Cahill-O'Callaghan, R. (2020). *Values in the Supreme Court: Divisions, division and diversity*. Bloomsbury Publishing.

Chng, W. Y. (2021). An analysis of judicial restraint in the doctrine of substantive legitimate expectations in the UK and Hong Kong. *Hong Kong Law Journal*, *51*(2), 467–490.

Cohn, M., & Kremnitzer, M. (2005). Judicial activism: A multidimensional model. *Canadian Journal of Law & Jurisprudence*, *18*(2), 333–356.

Council of Civil Service Unions v. Minister for the Civil Service. (1985) AC 374.

Cross, F. B., & Lindquist, S. A. (2006). The scientific study of judicial activism. *Minn. L. Rev.*, *91*, 1752, 1760.

Dicey, A. V. (1897). *Introduction to the study of the law of the constitution.*

Dickson, B. (2015). Activism and restraint within the UK Supreme Court. *European Journal of Current Legal Issues*, *21*(1).

Diedrich, J. S. (2019). Article III, judicial restraint, and this Supreme Court. *SMU L. Rev.*, *72*, 235.

Drewry, G. (1992). Judicial politics in Britain: Patrolling the boundaries. *West European Politics*, *15*(3), 9–28.

Edwards, R. A. (2002). Judicial deference under the Human Rights Act. *The Modern Law Review*, *65*(6), 859–882.

Elliott, M. (1999). The *Ultra Vires* doctrine in a constitutional setting: Still the central principle of administrative law. *The Cambridge Law Journal*, *58*(1), 129–158.

Fitzpatrick v. Sterling Housing Association. (1999) UKHL 42.

Ghaidan v. Godin-Mendoza. (2004) UKHL 30.

Griffith, J. A. G. (2001). The common law and the political constitution. *L.Q.R.*, *117*, 42.

Hale, B. (2019). Interviewed by Nick Robinson and Justin Webb. *Best of Today*. BBC Radio 4. 27 December. Available at: https://www.bbc.co.uk/sounds/play/p07z0fhq

Hameed, A. (2022). UK withdrawal from the EU: Supremacy, indirect effect and retained EU law. *The Modern Law Review, 85*, 726–754.

Hanretty, C. (2020). *A court of specialists: Judicial behavior on the UK Supreme Court*. New York, NY USA: Oxford University Press.

Hoffman, D., & Rowe, J. (2010). *Human Rights in the UK: An introduction to the Human Rights Act 1998*. Pearson Education.

Howard, R. M., & Segal, J. A. (2004). *A preference for deference? The Supreme Court and judicial review. Pol. Res. Q., 57*, 131.

Jones, G. (2001). Proper judicial activism. *Regent U.L. Rev., 14*, 141, 143.

Kavanagh, A. (2010). Judicial restraint in the pursuit of justice. *University of Toronto Law Journal*, 60(1), 23–40.

King, J. A. (2008). Institutional approaches to judicial restraint. *Oxford Journal of Legal Studies, 28*(3), 409–441.

Lewis, A. (1966, July 31). *The law: Britain breaks with precedent*. N.Y. Times.

London Tramways Co v. London County Council. (1898) A.C.

Maiman, R. J (2005). Asylum law practice in the United Kingdom after the Human Rights Act. *The World Cause Lawyers Make: Structure and Agency in Legal Practice*, 410–424.

Malleson, K. (2016). *The new judiciary: The effects of expansion and activism*. Routledge.

Malleson, K. (2022). *Values diversity in the United Kingdom Supreme Court: Abandoning the 'Don't-Ask-Don't-Tell' policy. Journal of Law and Society*, 49(1), 2022.

Manning, J. F. (2017). Justice Scalia and the idea of judicial restraint. *Mich. L. Rev., 115*, 747–782.

Masood, A. S., & Lineberger, M. E. (2020). United Kingdom, United Courts? Hierarchical interactions and attention to precedent in the British judiciary. *Political Research Quarterly, 73*(3), 714–726.

McCleave, T. (2008). Judicial discretion versus restraint in the realm of Human Rights: A contextual approach to the UK Human Rights Act 1998. *Trinity CL Rev., 11*, 102.

McInnes, R. D. (1977). Jurisdiction review after anisminic. *Victoria U. Wellington L. Rev.*, 9.

Paterson, A. (2021). Creating a group oriented Supreme Court-Lord Neuberger's legacy. *International Journal of the Legal Profession, 28*(1), 107–126.

Posner, R. A. (1999). *The federal courts: Challenge and reform*. Harvard University Press.

Powell Jr., L. F. (1990). Stare decisis and judicial restraint. *Wash. & Lee L. Rev., 47*, 281.

Practice Statement of 1966. (1966) 1 W.L.R. 1234 (H.L.).

R (Miller) v. Secretary of State for Exiting the European Union. (2017) UKSC 5.

R (Miller) v. The Prime Minister and *Cherry v. Advocate General for Scotland*. (2019) UKSC 41.

Rent Act 1977.

Ringhand, L. A. (2007). *Judicial activism: An empirical examination of voting behavior on the rehnquist natural court*. Const. Comment.

Roosevelt, K. (2008). *The myth of judicial activism: Making sense of Supreme Court decisions*. New Haven, CT: Yale University Press,

Rothwell v. Chemical & Insulating Co. Ltd. (2007) UKHL 39.

Schwartz, B. (1987). *Lions over the throne—the judicial revolution in English administrative law*. New York University Press.

Segal, J. A., & Spaeth, H. J. (2002). *The Supreme Court and the attitudinal model revisited*. Cambridge University Press.

Shah, S., & Poole, T. M. (2011). The law lords and Human Rights. *The Modern Law Review*, *74*(1), 79–105.

Smith v. East Elloe Rural District Council. (1956) A.C. 736.

Stevens, J. P. (1985). Judicial restraint. *San Diego L. Rev.*, *22*, 437.

Stevens, R. (1999). A loss of innocence?: Judicial independence and the separation of powers. *Oxford Journal of Legal Studies*, *19*(3), 365–402.

Stevens, R. (2002). *The English judges: Their role in the changing constitution*. Bloomsbury Publishing.

Thayer, J. B. (1893). *The origin and scope of the American doctrine of constitutional law*. Little, Brown.

van Zyl Smit, J. (2007). *The new purposive interpretation for statutes: HRA Section 3 after Ghaidan v. Godin-Mendoza*. *The Modern Law Review*, *70*(2), 294–317.

Waltman, J. L. (1991). Judicial activism in England. In *Judicial activism in comparative perspective* (pp. 33–52). London: Palgrave Macmillan.

Watt, N. (2019, December 20). Scaling back the Supreme Court. *BBC News*. https://www.bbc.com/news/uk-politics-50863138

Weiden, D. L. (2011). Judicial politicization, ideology, and activism at the high courts of the United States, Canada, and Australia. *Political Research Quarterly*, *64*(2), 335–247.

Wenzel, J. P., Bowler, S., & Lanoue, D. (1997). Legislating from the state bench: A comparative analysis of judicial activism. *American Politics Quarterly*, *25*(3), 363–379.

Young, E. A. (2002). *Judicial activism and conservative politics*. *U. Colo. L. Rev.*, *73*, 1139, 1141.

· 5 ·

JUDICIAL ACTIVISM IN CANADA: OVERTURNING PRECEDENT AT THE LOWER COURT LEVEL

Troy Riddell, Lori Hausegger and Nicole Scott

In October 2012, Gerard Comeau traveled from his home in New Brunswick to buy beer at cheaper rates in the neighboring province of Quebec. Unfortunately for Mr. Comeau, the Royal Canadian Mounted Police (RCMP) were trying to curtail this practice and he was caught in a sting operation as he crossed the border back into New Brunswick. He was charged with violating New Brunswick's *Liquor Control Act*. Mr. Comeau contested this charge arguing that the New Brunswick law violated s. 121 of the *Constitution Act, 1867*: "All Articles of the Growth, Produce, or Manufacture of any one of the Provinces shall, from and after the Union, be admitted free into each of the other Provinces." The trial judge sided with Comeau. His decision relied heavily on a historian's testimony that s. 121 was meant to create a strong economic union in Canada—a conclusion contrary to how s. 121 had been interpreted in leading precedents. Departing from precedent was justified, the trial judge argued, as it followed a framework that the Supreme Court of Canada had articulated in two leading *Charter of Rights and Freedoms* cases (*Bedford* and *Carter*) for lower courts to override precedent.

On appeal, the Supreme Court of Canada disappointed many Canadians searching for cheaper beer and overturned the trial judge. In its decision, in what became known as the "Free the Beer" case, the Supreme Court took issue with the trial judge's interpretation of s. 121 and argued that he misapplied the analytical framework for overriding vertical precedents. The case attracted significant attention with one prominent commentator suggesting that "It's the pitch-perfect case for why judicial deference to a legislature can still be inappropriately political, even activist" (Macfarlane, 2018).[1] According to this argument the Court gave a credulous interpretation to s. 121, and did not overrule a likely wrongly decided precedent, based on the calculation that the Court needed to intervene to save Canada from the massive economic uncertainty that would have been generated by striking down New Brunswick's law (Macfarlane, 2018). This conclusion is in line with an argument that the courts practice "activist judicial restraint" when they improperly resist striking down a statute or overturning illegitimate precedents (see Cross and Lindquist, 2007, p. 1760).

The *Comeau* decision, and the response it generated, illustrate the complexity of judicial activism. Was the trial judge being activist for overriding a precedent and striking down a law—although using the "original intent" of the framers and Supreme Court precedent to do so? Or was the Supreme Court being "activist" for following precedent but using dubious interpretations of seemingly clear constitutional wording to do so and delivering what appeared to be a politically motivated decision? In turn, these questions raise broader ones about conceptualizing and measuring activism. Does "activism" describe modes of interpretation and decision-making and, if so, which types (not following the text or original understanding of the text, not following precedent, making a decision based on political considerations, etc.)? Or is it more of an outcome-based concept (does the court require a change to a legal rule)? How does the Supreme Court's invitation to trial judges to overturn higher court precedent under certain conditions fit into the analysis? In Canada, these types of animated controversies over the role of courts have happened more frequently with the addition of the *Charter of Rights and Freedoms* to the Canadian Constitution in 1982. The *Charter* gave courts the power to strike down or alter policy even when a government was acting within its sphere of jurisdiction. When the Supreme Court began to strike down federal and provincial laws, debates about judicial activism arose, many of which paralleled those heard in the United States.

This paper explores judicial activism in Canada—first in broad terms and later by taking an empirical look at a specific type of activism. We begin with a

1 In his more recent work, Emmett Macfarlane (2022) argues that "undue deference" is not the same thing as activism but can still be political.

brief review of the history of activism in the country, before moving on to discuss what activism means in Canadian courts and the different ways of measuring it. Although these analyses owe a great deal to the U.S. literature, the existence in Canada of a limitations clause and a "notwithstanding" clause, coupled with academic and judicial discussions about the possibility of "dialogue" between Canada's courts and its elected officials, leads to some interesting points of departure from the U.S. and other jurisdictions.

The paper then turns to focus on one articulation of activism which has been generating more attention in Canada in the last few years: the decision not to follow precedent. While there has been much written on the propriety of the Supreme Court's rulings on overturning precedent—from *Bedford* to *Comeau*—scholars have yet to conduct an in-depth empirical study of the impact of these decisions. Here we begin to fill this gap. We investigate the impact of what some might call a pathway to approved activism: the Supreme Court's recent articulation of a framework by which trial judges can depart from established precedents. Conceptually, how does this fit into a framework for analyzing activism? Empirically, have Canadian courts adopted this form of activism in a significant way? How often have lower courts grappled with deciding whether to overturn a precedent and how many precedents have been overturned? When precedents are overturned, is the outcome activist as well? We address these questions as a lens through which to examine Canadian judicial activism in comparative perspective.

The History of Activism and Restraint in Canada

Pre-Charter Activism

Prior to the introduction of the *Charter of Rights and Freedoms* in 1982, the Supreme Court of Canada was described by one commentator as the "quiet Court in an unquiet country" (Cheffins, 1966). Some of its federalism decisions were important to political and legal elites, but rarely did they garner much public attention. Even in its decisions under the 1960 *Bill of Rights*,[2] the Court struck down only one law. It was the model of restraint. Laws that were upheld under the 1960 *Bill of Rights*, often with judges using a narrow reading of rights

2 The *Bill of Rights* was a federal statute (not a constitutional document) that applied only to the federal government.

and judicial authority, included abortion restrictions, Sunday closing laws, and laws allowing the unequal treatment of Indigenous women.

Dissatisfaction with the Court's approach under the *Bill of Rights* was one of the factors that led to calls for an entrenched constitutional rights document. And certainly s. 52 of the *Constitution Act of 1982* and s. 24 of the *Charter of Rights and Freedoms* are thought to give the Canadian courts a more explicit power of judicial review and to encourage a more active Court. However, when the *Charter* was being proposed, those who were worried about U.S.-style judicial "activism" demanded certain concessions. The most important was the s. 33 notwithstanding clause, which allows the federal Parliament or provincial legislatures to pass a law in which it is declared that the law will operate for five years "notwithstanding" certain rights in the *Charter* (fundamental freedoms such as free speech and religion, legal rights, and equality rights).[3]

In addition to the notwithstanding clause, the *Charter* also contains a general limitations clause (s. 1): "the *Canadian Charter of Rights and Freedoms* guarantees the rights and freedoms set out in it subject only to such reasonable limits prescribed by law as can be demonstrably justified in a free and democratic society." The drafters of the *Charter* also used the phrase "principles of fundamental justice" in s. 7 of the *Charter* (protecting life, liberty, and security of the person) rather than "due process of law" as a hedge against substantive due process being used by courts under the Charter. Thus, the document includes several provisions that potentially dampen how actively Canadian courts exercise their powers of judicial review.

Charter Activism

With these potential limiting tools in place, it remained an open question as to how the Supreme Court would interpret and apply the *Charter* when it came into effect in Spring 1982. Interestingly, the Court quickly rejected its *Bill of Rights* jurisprudence in favor of a "large and purposive" approach to rights adjudication. Two landmark decisions in 1988 highlighted the Court's new role under the *Charter* and generated considerable criticism about an "activist court." In its *Morgentaler* (1988) decision, the Supreme Court struck down (by a 5-2 vote) the *Criminal Code* provisions around abortion. Although it was a complex decision with three separate judgments making up the majority, all the judges in the majority decided that the abortion law did not meet

3 The declaration of notwithstanding lasts for five years and can be renewed with the passage of another resolution by Parliament or the provincial legislature that used it originally.

the justification required under the s.1 limitations clause. The two dissenting judges countered that the framers of the *Charter* had stated clearly that the abortion question was to be dealt with by Parliament and not the courts.

In *Ford v. Quebec* (AG) (1988), the Court struck down Quebec's French only sign law as violating free expression. In its s. 1 analysis, the Court indicated that requiring non-French language to be half the size of the French language on signs could be justified. However, that was not enough to placate an angry Quebec provincial government which subsequently passed a blanket s. 33 declaration that all its laws were to operate "notwithstanding" the *Charter*. That move contributed to the perception in Canada that the use of s. 33 was illegitimate and made other governments very reluctant to invoke it. This development has dismayed Charter critics and effectively weakened one deliberately placed check on judicial activism.

After the passage of the Charter the Court also adopted a "living tree" approach to interpret rights broadly and imposed numerous constitutional obligations around police investigations (eg. *Hunter v. Southam*, 1984; *R. v. Therens*, 1985); to require provinces to establish official minority-language school boards where the numbers warranted (*Mahe v. Alberta*, 1990); and to read-in "sexual orientation" as a prohibited ground in Alberta's Human Rights Code (*Vriend v. Alberta*, 1998). Of course, not all rights claimants achieved victory at the Supreme Court, but the 30% success rate in the Charter era was much higher than it had been under the *Bill of Rights* (five wins out of 34 cases from 1960 to 1982) and involved the Court in a number of controversial policy areas.

In a development that would have been unimaginable previously, the Court became the focus of attention in the media, political, and academic arenas. The newly established Reform Party made attacks on judicial activism a key part of its platform in the 1990s. There was considerable attention paid in the media to individual decisions, and commentary was written attacking and defending the Court's Charter jurisprudence. Legal academics and political scientists wrote on the issue. Even judges themselves began to comment on activism in public forums (Wilson, 2001) and in their decisions (*Newfoundland (Treasury Board) v. Newfoundland Association of Public Employees*, 2004).

These debates over activism in Canada would be very familiar to those acquainted with debates over judicial power in the United States. Critics charged that unelected judges were too frequently overturning legislation by elected officials and that these judges lacked the democratic legitimacy, policy-making expertise, or philosophical wisdom to make decisions about hotly contested social and political issues over which reasonable people could disagree (Manfredi, 2001; Knopff and Morton, 1992; Mandel, 1994). Judges were also accused of not following the original meaning of the *Charter* and instead using a living constitutional approach to reach policy outcomes that they, and allies in the legal intelligentsia, favored (Morton and Knopff, 2000).

Defenders argued that the democratic process in Canada was flawed. Legislatures often did not want to decide controversial issues or did not adequately protect the rights of disadvantaged groups. They also reminded critics that elected politicians explicitly gave judges the power of judicial review under the Charter. Judges needed to read rights broadly to avoid the "frozen rights" approach that resulted in injustices under the 1960 *Bill of Rights*. Moreover, proponents of a more activist approach argued that the explosion of interveners (amicus) that occurred after the Charter—and the Court's liberal policy that produced it—allowed judges to hear a wide range of opinion and expertise on an issue, which would help democratize the process (Hein, 2001).

The Meaning and Measurement of Judicial Activism in Canada

Perhaps because a concrete definition of "activism" had proved elusive in the United States (see, for example, Canon, 1983), Canadian literature on Supreme Court decision-making tended not to try to explicitly measure dimensions of activism. Instead, an outcome-oriented measure tended to be adopted as literature would refer to the success rates of rights claimants or the number of laws struck down by the Court in the context of discussing activism (see Morton and Knopff, 2000, p. 15; Manfredi, 2001).

Choudhry and Hunter (2003) tried to fill this gap by adopting an explicitly "counter-majoritarian" definition of activism to study. They examined how often the Court struck down primary legislation under the Charter; whether the rate increased or decreased over time; if legislation most often failed at the s. 1 reasonable limits stage; and whether the Court become more activist after the unpopular use of s. 33 (and in cases in which s. 33 did not apply). They found an overall rate of striking down laws of 38%—the rate did not increase over time, and it did not appear that the real or perceived availability of governments to use s. 33 had an impact on trends. Whether the government won or lost at the s. 1 stage was linked with the rights at issue.[4]

4 Manfredi and Kelly, two political scientists, chastise Choudhry and Hunter, two legal scholars, for fabricating a strawman argument falsely claiming that political scientists were

A much different approach to measuring activism was employed by Murchison and Jochelson (2015; see also Murchison, 2017) who adapted Cohn and Kremnitzer's (2005) model using 17 different parameters to assess activism. These ranged from more traditional measures such as does the Court change established law or create new legal tests, to measures that include interpretive techniques, the extent of the decision, the use of "core" constitutional values, the use of obiter and so on (Murchison and Jochelson, 2015; Cohn and Kremnitzer, 2005).[5] Muttart (2011) proposed a mixed quantitative and qualitative model that included eight criteria ranging from "whether legislation or government action was struck down" to "modes and types of tests used to determine issues." Meanwhile, Riddell (2016) argued for a more outcome-based approach to defining "activism" with judicial interpretive choices (for example, defining rights) analyzed along a scale from more "adjudicative" approaches to more "policy-making" ones.

Despite the best intentions of these scholars to more explicitly define and measure activism, this research gained little traction in the wider debates about judicial power in Canada. Instead, a paper by prominent legal academic Peter Hogg and his collaborator Allison Bushell (later Bushell Thornton) shifted the ground of the debate to analyze the possibility of "dialogue" between the Supreme Court and legislatures. This effort drew considerable academic attention (from both law professors and political scientists) and was even invoked in Supreme Court decisions. We review this rather unique Canadian contribution to the debate over judicial power in the next section.

Canadian Debate: Dialogue and Its Critics

Hogg and Bushell state that where "a judicial decision is open to legislative reversal, modification, or avoidance, then it is meaningful to regard the relationship between the Court and the competent legislative body as a dialogue"

arguing that activism was continually increasing. After taking issue with the case selection and analysis of the results, Manfredi and Kelly conclude that it is clear that the Court is more activist compared to the pre-Charter era (whether that is "undue" activism or not remains an open question). They also suggest that political scientists tend to emphasize the Court is a political institution in which judicial policymaking is not an accidental by-product of legal decision-making and activism "is simply one dimension of the response to entrenched rights" (Manfredi and Kelly, 2004, p. 763).

5 Unfortunately, the use of so many variables, coupled with difficulties in coding, make interpretation of their conclusions more difficult (see Riddell, 2016, and the subsequent discussion back and forth between each set of authors).

(1997). According to Hogg and Bushell, "concern about the legitimacy of judicial review is greatly diminished" when dialogue occurs. Two key features of Canada's *Charter* encourage dialogue—the s. 33 "notwithstanding" clause and the s. 1 "reasonable limits" clause. The use of s. 33 in this regard is fairly self-evident, though commentators have pointed out that if provincial legislatures or the federal Parliament use the section pre-emptively then that scuttles opportunity for dialogue between the branches. As for s. 1, Hogg and Bushell claim that because the Supreme Court rarely fails legislation under the first part of the s.1 test—whether the "legislation has a pressing and substantial objective"—elected officials are usually free to pursue their policy goals through other means that are more respectful of Charter rights as outlined by the Court. Hogg and Bushell traced the number of instances in which "a judicial decision striking down a law on Charter grounds is followed by some action by the competent legislative body" and found this occurred in 66% of cases.

Their article generated considerable attention within Canada and also became a reference point for scholars interested in the "Commonwealth model" of judicial review comparing Australia, New Zealand, Great Britain and Canada (King, 2018). Critics, particularly political scientists, contended that Hogg and Bushell's definition of "dialogue" was so broad that it included many instances where a legislative body either simply repealed a law or altered it to precisely match the Court's decision—the latter was described as "ventriloquism" rather than "dialogue" (see Manfredi and Kelly, 1999; Morton, 2001; Macfarlane, 2012).[6] In Macfarlane's updated coding—which counted genuine dialogue as those instances in which a legislature positively responds to a Supreme Court decision with a creative new element or some, at least partial, disagreement—only 17.4% of cases met that criteria (Macfarlane, 2012, p. 47).

Other skeptical scholars pointed out that Hogg and Bushell underestimate the difficulties that legislatures have in responding to Supreme Court decisions. Not only does s. 33 not apply to all sections of the Charter, but politicians are also wary of being seen as "overriding" Charter rights, especially after its use by Quebec (Tushnet, 2003; Dixon, 2009). More generally, risk-averse politicians and bureaucrats often find it is easier to do nothing after a Court decision or to reformulate the law along the lines indicated by the Court (Macfarlene, 2012). And, adhering to the "means" articulated by the Court may make it harder to

6 Manfredi and Kelly, and Manfredi, noted that Hogg and Bushell were not consistent in how they defined dialogue in their 1997 article, particularly as to whether their needed to be "action" or whether "avoidance" was also considered dialogue.

fully achieve the government's original objectives, contrary to Hogg and Bushell's assumption (Manfredi and Kelly, 1999).

Questions were also raised about the normative commitments in the article, which were somewhat ambiguous (King, 2018). Some used the dialogue metaphor to bolster justification for judicial review (see Roach, 2001). In a symposium ten years after the original paper was published, however, Hogg, Thornton and Wright (2007) emphasized the empirical dimensions of the metaphor—showing statistically that the courts did not have as much influence as feared—while locating the justification for judicial review in more traditional arguments, such as the need for interpretive finality. According to King (2018), this discussion had the effect of reassuring no one. The justification of judicial review reinforced the skepticism of critics who saw Hogg and his co-authors as supporters of judicial supremacy, while the argument that legislatures can easily respond to court decisions caused concern for those who worried about the fragility of judicial enforcement of rights.

"Second Look" Cases

These alternative viewpoints were acutely revealed in debates over the question of how the Court should react in "second look" cases where a legislative body reacts to a judicial decision in a way that does not completely comport with the decision and the Court is asked to review the new or modified legislation. One group of commentators argued that in these situations the Court should tend towards deference if it appears that the legislature acted within a reasonable interpretation of Charter rights (Dixon, 2009). Certain scholars justified this view by arguing explicitly that the executive and legislative branches had a coordinate role with the courts in interpreting the constitution (Baker, 2010; Knopff et al., 2017). However, others—such as Peter Hogg and Kent Roach—maintained that the Court should not approach second look cases any differently and prioritized the Court's role in defining the parameters of Charter rights.

Interestingly, these different perspectives found expression in decisions by the Supreme Court in which judges in the majority and dissent both referenced the dialogue model to justify their positions.[7] As Haig and Sobkin note, likely the "most hostile use of the metaphor" came in the 2002 case of *Sauvé v. Canada (Chief Electoral Officer)* which was a second-look case about whether

7 For a full list of cases in which the dialogue metaphor was used by the Supreme Court and lower courts up to 2007 see Haigh and Sobkin (2007).

prisoners had the right to vote in federal elections (2007, p. 80). In its original *Sauvé* decision, the Court issued a short judgment striking down a complete ban on prisoner voting as being an unreasonable limit on the right to vote without providing guidance as to what a Charter-compliant law might look like.[8] Parliament responded by enacting a law that disenfranchised voters who were sentenced to a period of incarceration of two years or more and Sauvé challenged the law again.

The Court was badly split in striking down the rewritten law. The dissenting judgment written by Justice Gonthier argued that since "this case is about evaluating choices regarding social or political philosophies and about shaping and giving practical application to values, especially values that may lie outside the *Charter* but are of fundamental importance to Canadians, the 'dialogue' between courts and Parliament is of particular importance." Gonthier argued that this does not mean that the s.1 standard for justification is lowered; rather, courts should scrutinize laws to ensure that a legislature has acted reasonably without preferring an outcome based on a particular social or political philosophy. Chief Justice McLachlin for the majority countered that the "healthy and important promotion of a dialogue between the legislature and the courts should not be debased to a rule of 'if at first you don't succeed, try, try again'" and that Parliament must ensure that "whatever law it passes, at whatever stage of the process, conforms to the Constitution" (Sauvé no. 2, 2002).

A leading skeptic of judicial power, Christopher Manfredi, proclaimed that *Sauvé II* represented "the day dialogue died" (2007). Among other things, Manfredi suggested that Chief Justice McLachlin's argument that s. 3 voting rights needed to be vigorously defended as they are not subject to the s. 33 notwithstanding clause in the *Charter* could be turned on its head in that judges should be cautious in cases where a legislature has no recourse through the notwithstanding clause.

Activism and Recent Court Decisions

Ironically, however, by the time of Manfredi's article in 2007 the debate over judicial activism and dialogue had died down, in part because the Court under Chief Justice McLachlin was deciding fewer high-profile cases and acting in

8 Knopff, Baker and LeRoy (2009) speculate that the Court's very brief original Sauvé decision masked disagreements over what, if any, limits could be placed on prisoner voting which were later revealed in the split Sauvé II decision.

a more restrained fashion than demonstrated in *Sauvé II*. One book declared that it was "The End of the Charter Revolution" (McCormick, 2015).

Some very prominent decisions starting in late 2013, however, suggested that such a pronouncement was premature and reignited the debate over judicial activism. The Court struck down laws prohibiting prostitution (*Bedford* 2013) and physician-assisted suicide (*Carter* 2015), enshrined the right to strike in the *Charter* (*Saskatchewan Federation of Labour* 2015), and struck down a number of mandatory-minimum penalties in the Criminal Code (*Nur* 2015, *Lloyd* 2016). In a number of these cases the Court altered its previous interpretation of the *Charter* and struck down laws that it had previously upheld.

In the wake of these decisions a number of media commentators and politicians accused the Court of ignoring precedent, rewriting the constitution, writing law rather than just applying it, having almost unlimited and unaccountable control over the meaning of the Charter, and becoming "the greatest threat to our democracy" (for a review see Macfarlane, 2015). Academics, meanwhile, have not only revisited the dialogue debates but have also taken the research in a number of interesting directions (see Sigalet, Webber & Dixon, 2019). Some have tried to analyze and explain different levels and conceptions of dialogue between Canada and other countries, particularly the US, the UK, Australia, and New Zealand (King, 2018, Schor, 2017). Others have tried to assess whether the relationship between the Supreme Court and the government under Conservative Prime Minister Stephen Harper was different than in previous eras. Was the Court more "activist" and less deferential towards the Harper government (see Macfarlane, 2018; Manfredi, 2015; Hennigar, 2017)?

In the next section of the chapter, we focus on one dimension of the Supreme Court's more recent decisions: the Court's pronouncement that precedent can be overturned, even by lower courts, if there has been a sufficient change in social context or the law. Thus far, this has received attention from law professors primarily from a normative perspective without the necessary empirical data to assess the legal and political significance of the Court's pronouncement. After a brief review of the decisions that produced the Court's framework, the next section lays out our approach to collecting and analyzing the necessary data to fill the empirical gap.

Another Type of Activism: Overturning Vertical Precedent

The Supreme Court Builds a Path to Overturn Precedent

The cases in which the Supreme Court struck down Canada's laws prohibiting prostitution (*Bedford*), and physician-assisted suicide (*Carter*), began with trial judges striking down those laws—laws that had been explicitly upheld in previous (and relatively recent) Supreme Court decisions (*Prostitution Reference*, 1990, and *Rodriguez*, 1997, respectively). In both instances, the intermediate provincial courts of appeal overturned the trial judges for failing to follow Supreme Court precedent. The Supreme Court, however, upheld the trial judges' decisions to strike the laws down and in doing so created a set of conditions under which lower court judges could depart from the precedents of higher courts, including the Supreme Court itself. In *Carter*, the Supreme Court stated that trial courts "may reconsider settled rulings of higher courts in two situations: (1) where a new legal issue is raised; and (2) where there is a change in the circumstances or evidence that 'fundamentally shifts the parameters of the debate'" (at para 44). The Court, though, also noted that "lower courts are not entitled to ignore binding precedent, and the threshold for revisiting a matter is not an easy one to reach" (*Bedford* at para 44).

Although the wording of the framework is a little ambiguous, it appears that lower courts only have to meet one of the requirements in order to depart from precedent (Newman, 2015). In *Bedford* and *Carter* both conditions were met. Both cases centered around the right to "life, liberty, and security of the person" and the right "not to be deprived thereof except in the accordance with the principles of fundamental justice" in s. 7 of the *Charter*. The Supreme Court argued that its s. 7 jurisprudence had evolved over time to include the concepts of "overbreadth" and "gross disproportionality" when assessing whether a law that limits "life, liberty and security of the person" does so in accordance with the "principles of fundamental justice."

In *Bedford*, the Court argued that, while prostitution itself was not criminalized, the Criminal Code's prohibitions on keeping a bawdy house, communicating in public for the purpose of prostitution, and living off the avails of prostitution infringed on sex workers' "security of the person" in ways that were grossly disproportionate to the legislative goals of preventing public nuisance and the exploitation of prostitutes. For instance, a law could make "pimping" illegal while allowing for bodyguards, receptionists, and accountants to be hired by sex workers. The Court also held that the trial judges' use of social facts—particularly research that highlighted the increased safety risk of not being able to engage in sex work from a (known) fixed location—not only highlighted how social context had changed since the precedent but the findings were also entitled to deference. Finally, the Court held that the violations of s. 7 of the *Charter* could not be saved under the s. 1 "reasonable limits" test.

In *Carter*, the Court held that the Criminal Code's blanket prohibition on medical-assistance in dying was "overbroad" and "grossly disproportionate"—the two concepts introduced into s. 7 reasoning since the Court (narrowly) upheld the law in its 1997 *Rodriguez* decision. Moreover, the Court accepted the trial judge's findings that the social and political context surrounding assisted suicide had changed since *Rodriguez* in that more jurisdictions were allowing the practice and that studies had shown that there could be effective legal safeguards to protect vulnerable people when assisted dying was legalized.

The response to the *Bedford/Carter* framework has been mixed with some commentators applauding the Court's willingness to allow justice to prevail over simply adhering to precedent, while others argue that the framework is too permissive and will undermine the rule of law in favor of the rule of judges (Newman, 2015, Souter, 2015). Despite these debates about the appropriateness of the Court's framework, very little empirical work has been done to assess what is happening in the lower courts.

Parkes (2016) analyzed seven cases where courts sought to reconsider vertical precedent using the *Carter* test, in no cases was the threshold met. Judges rejected claims that precedent should be revisited in cases involving extradition, using cell phones to contact counsel, protesting around abortion clinics, printing Alberta's legislation in French and English, and disclosing records relating to breathalyzer machines. Parkes does not indicate though whether she did a comprehensive search for cases and her study was conducted in 2016, which limited the availability of the dataset due to its close proximity to the *Bedford/Carter* decisions themselves. Thus, there is a need for more empirical work.

An Empirical Analysis of Overturning Precedent

As noted above, there are different ways of defining activism, from not following the original intent of the law (particularly the Constitution), to generously interpreting rights, to not following precedent, to overturning government law or policy. Arguably, *Bedford* and *Carter* are "activist" under all of these definitions, particularly if one is convinced that the *Charter* was worded in such a way as to preclude "substantive due process" under s. 7. However, because it is often difficult to clearly locate and define "framers' intent," and reasonable people can disagree over what a "generous" interpretation of rights are, here we stick to measuring two components of activism that can be measured more easily: (1) how often have lower courts used the *Bedford/Carter* framework to overturn established precedent; and (2) in cases where precedent has been overturned has this led to a change in common law, statutory interpretation, or the constitutional striking down of a law (or another constitutional remedy)? Investigating these empirical questions can help inform the normative debate about activism and corollary debates about precedent.

We used *QuickLaw* to search for cases decided up to June 2021 in which the *Bedford/Carter* framework was invoked in provincial courts (trial courts and appellate courts administered by the province).[9] Seventy cases mentioned the *Carter* test, but it was only applied in 43 of those cases. We took a strict definition of applied and only included those 43 cases in our analysis.[10]

Roughly two thirds of these cases (67%) occur at the trial court level. Public law cases dominate in our sample (74%), and there are more Charter Criminal Code cases than any other. However, several of our incidents occur in contract law, federalism, torts, and administrative law cases. Indeed, as Table 5.A1 of the Appendix illustrates, our cases are spread across issue areas, years, and courts.

The threshold for revisiting precedent was met in 30% of the 43 cases (see Appendix 1). Given our small numbers it is probably not surprising that we do not find significantly different patterns for the cases meeting the threshold. These cases were also spread across years, and issue areas. However, they were more likely to occur in Courts of Appeal—69% of cases meeting the threshold were decided at the Court of Appeal level.

9 In the lower courts administered by the provinces, the judges are appointed by the provincial government. In the superior trial courts and provincial appellate courts in the provinces the federal government appoints the judges even though the courts are administered by the provinces.

10 We should note that at this point of the project only the lower court decisions are in our database. Federal courts in Canada are administered by the federal government and the judges are appointed by the federal government. The docket of the Federal Court of Canada and the Federal Court of Appeal is dominated by cases involving federal regulatory agencies such as the Canadian Immigration and Refugee Board. The Supreme Court of Canada is a general appellate court for both federal and provincial law and the Court has considerable control over its docket.

Perhaps most importantly for our purposes here, it appears that, in general, the judges in these cases refrained from overturning precedent in favor of extending or modifying the law. Indeed, only two cases in our sample period overturned precedent: *R. v. Comeau* (2016) and *Cabana v. Newfoundland and Labrador* (2016). In *Cabana*, the Newfoundland and Labrador Court of Appeal reconsidered *Franey* (1997) which had refused compensation to self-represented litigants who did not have counsel costs. Justice Green overturned precedent and declared costs awarded to successful self-represented litigants based on time, effort, and cost (para 36). In *Comeau*, as noted in the introduction, the trial judge used expert evidence from a historian to argue that s. 121 of the Constitution had been misapplied in precedents that upheld provincial regulations interfering with interprovincial trade.[11]

In other instances, the *Bedford/Carter* test was found to be met but this finding was used in more of a supplemental fashion to provide additional justification when not adhering to precedent. These cases, although raising interesting legal questions, have not been the kind of high-profile cases discussed above. Moreover, the judges in these cases likely would have avoided precedent by distinguishing, or otherwise parsing, the ratio of the case from the obiter. Legal change nevertheless resulted in such cases. In *Duggan*, for example, a case about whether liability and damages could be bifurcated in civil litigation, the trial judge avoided the arguably binding authority (*Bondy-Rafael*) by establishing that the obiter in that decision did not apply to the instant case. However, the trial judge did go further to suggest that if his obiter analysis was mistaken the *Carter* threshold was met for not upholding a precedent. The trial judge argued that the SCC case *Hryniak (2014)*, represented a fundamental shift in law that justified deviating from *Bondy-Rafael* (para. 63).

Similarly, the *Bedford/Carter* framework has been used by judges to bolster decisions to distinguish cases from precedent. In *York v Tomovski (2018)*, for example, Justice McInnis first distinguished the instant case—involving a provincial highway traffic act offence—from *R v Jordan (2016)*, a SCC decision

11 Of course, as mentioned in the introduction, the Supreme Court criticized the trial judges' approach to the *Carter* test finding expert opinion and historical accounts not sufficient to reconsider precedent. The Court clarified that "for a binding precedent from a higher court to be cast aside on the basis of new evidence, the new evidence must 'fundamentally shif[t]' how jurists understand the legal question at issue. It is not enough to find that an alternate perspective on existing evidence might change how jurists would answer the same legal question" (at para 34). There has to be "profound social change" based on "evolving legislative and social facts."

that set a new framework for assessing s.11b Charter claims of unreasonable delay in criminal trials. *Jordan* established an 18-month presumptive ceiling for criminal cases tried in provincial courts. The presumptive ceiling was determined based on criminal proceedings; therefore, McInnis reasoned the current case could determine new presumptive ceilings for minor infractions dealt with under the *Provincial Offences Act*. Once the case was distinguished, McInnis J. was free to decide the instant case without referencing the *Carter* test. Nevertheless, his decision employed the *Carter* test. The different procedural and substantive context between criminal and Provincial Offences proceedings fundamentally shifted the parameters of the debate in *Jordan* (para. 147). His decision suggested a ceiling of 13–15-month delay is better suited for Part I provincial offences and applied a 14-month ceiling to the appeal. Justice McInnis restricted the impact of the decision by declining to set presumptive ceiling for Provincial Offences in general, deferring to higher courts to set broad legal principles.

Of course, in the majority of decisions in our database, the threshold of *Bedford/Carter* is found not to have been met. The result is that there was no change in law. For example, in *R. v. Caswell* (2015), there was disagreement on the Alberta Court of Appeal about the possibility of an important change to police procedures under the *Charter*, but ultimately a restrained outcome prevailed. One judge in dissent held that the court should reconsider a 20-year old precedent of the court, which followed a Supreme Court decision holding that violation of the right to counsel during roadside sobriety tests was a "reasonable limit" under s.1 of the Charter. The dissenter argued that changes in technology (the availability of cellphones to phone a lawyer) and changes in the law (such as immediate roadside suspensions) indicated the need to overturn precedent. The majority, though, disagreed and indicated that the threshold for overturning a precedent established in *Bedford* should be applied strictly (also see Parkes, 2016: 156).

This initial analysis suggests that the permission the Supreme Court gave to lower court judges in *Bedford/Carter* to overturn precedent under certain conditions has not resulted in trial judges actively diverting from precedent as often as critics feared. Indeed, if we consider the more traditional debate around activism—are courts striking down legislation under the Charter—cases in our database suggest this is instead occurring in cases where obvious precedent does not exist (for example, did a law limiting the credit at sentencing for time served pre-trial violate the Charter). In a number of these cases judges mentioned the Bedford/Carter test as they questioned whether they were bound by other courts at their level or by appellate courts in other provinces. However, the crux of the matter was really law in development responding to multiple Charter challenges of a new law rather than an application of Bedford/Carter per se. Thus, we do not see rampant activism in our sample as a result of the *Bedford/Carter* directive. Nevertheless, the 30% of cases in which the threshold was found to be met suggests that it does have the potential to have a significant effect.

Conclusions

This preliminary study may underestimate the potential for activism that *Bedford/Carter* generated. First, given the pace of litigation, especially complex Charter-litigation, we are still relatively close in time to the *Bedford/Carter* decisions by the Supreme Court. We will likely see more activity in coming years as cases make their way through the system. Lower courts may be emboldened, not only by *Bedford/Carter* itself, but also by the Supreme Court's support for lower courts overturning precedent in cases.[12] It will also be worth tracing whether intermediate appellate courts, which have often struck down attempts by trial judges to override precedent, will tend to uphold such decisions more frequently in the future.

Second, it is possible that courts are performing their normal duties of updating common law or statutory rules without explicit recourse to the *Bedford/Carter* test—these decisions would not be captured in our analysis. And

12 For example, the majority of the Supreme Court argued the *Bedford/Carter* framework applied to the *Saskatchewan Federation of Labour* (2015) case (despite the fact the trial judge had decided the case before the *Bedford/Carter* jurisprudence had been established). This case involved Saskatchewan legislation that limited the ability of public sector workers responsible for essential services to strike. Foreshadowing *Bedford/Carter*, the trial judge had argued that changes in jurisprudence around the "freedom of association" in s. 2(d) of the *Charter* suggested the section encompassed the right to strike. The Supreme Court majority, applying *Bedford/Carter*, agreed. In doing so they overturned the Saskatchewan Court of Appeal and provoked an objection from their colleague Justice Rothstein, who (despite signing on to *Bedford* and *Carter*), wrote a strong dissent arguing for the importance of stare decisis and encouraging deference in the context of labor negotiations (see Parkes, 2016: 145–148). Of course, since our database only includes decisions from lower provincial courts this case is not included, but it is worth remembering for the signal it provides to lower courts that the Supreme Court is in fact open to them overturning precedent.

we do have some cases in our broader database where *Bedford/Carter* is only "mentioned" (not applied) that do feature modest legal changes.[13]

However, we do not believe this will result in missing significant legal changes, particularly under the Charter, since judges addressing important Charter issues—in which they are revisiting an established precedent—would likely specifically apply the *Bedford/Carter* test. Also, appellate courts may invoke the *Bedford/Carter* test even when trial judges fail to do so. This happened in *Nova Scotia (Community Services) v. Nova Scotia (Attorney General)* (2017) where the trial judge raised a constitutional question on his own about whether Nova Scotia's *Children and Family Service's Act* was unconstitutional because it did not automatically include a biological father in the definition of a "parent." The appellate court issued an "unusually blunt rebuke" to the trial judge indicating that there was a precedent directly on this issue and that the *Bedford/Carter* test, which the trial judge did not reference, was not met (Bundale, 2017). According to the Court, "hypothetical musing on the part of the hearing judge does not, in our view, justify turning a blind eye to the principle of stare decisis." Although we would have missed the trial court decision in this case, the Court of Appeal's mention of *Bedford/Carter* would ensure its inclusion in the database.

Aside from methodological issues, there remains the tricky question of defining activism. When the *Bedford/Carter* threshold is met, it is possible that there will be some change in precedent and an outcome that changes government policy (such as the striking down of a law or government action in a Charter case). However, changes in precedent and outcome might not always work in tandem in an "activist" direction. This issue is particularly relevant in second-look cases. Dixon (2009), for instance, argues that if a legislature responds to a Charter decision within reason the Court should be deferential and perhaps cast its original decision more narrowly to uphold the legislation. Put differently, some advocates of dialogue argue that there should be a deviation from precedent in second-look cases which would produce a restrained result. For instance, will the Supreme Court depart from its precedent in *Bedford* and uphold the Conservative government's legislative response? The new law decriminalizes sex work and allows sex workers to hire non-exploitative third-parties; however, it criminalizes the purchase of sexual services, which critics argue continues to make sex work very dangerous. Or, will the Court apply *Bedford* in such a way as to strike down the new law for violating the

13 These would typically not fall under most definitions of activism, or at least the definitions that are focused on significant policy change initiated by judges.

right to "security of the person adhering to precedent in this situation could be argued to be a more activist approach.

There is also the question of whether judges who overturn precedent because they believe a law (perhaps the constitution itself) was incorrectly interpreted are acting in an activist manner if indeed their decision more closely adheres to the original law. We will need to wrestle more with these conceptual issues.

A better approach might be to distinguish between outcomes—does law or policy change as a result of a court decision (activism or restraint)—and interpretive approaches. An adjudicatory approach to rules is one in which there is only "interstitial" rulemaking whereas a more policy-making approach is one in which courts are more likely to make or change existing rules (Weiler, 1968; Hausegger, Hennigar and Riddell, 2015). A policy-making approach may correlate with more "activism" and vice-versa, but they should be treated as distinct categories. Studies that try to create indices of activism by combining interpretive choices and outcomes often create muddled results. And, of course, either interpretive approach (adjudication or policymaking) or outcome (activist or restrained) could reflect either more liberal or more conservative ideological positions depending on the nature of the case.

Our next steps in this research are to refine our database and results to include such variables as how the *Bedford/Carter* test is being used (relied upon to make a decision or in a more secondary way), the level of court, and the date of the precedent or law being considered (since some argue striking down older precedents and laws is more a matter of housekeeping than activism). We are also interested in more systematically determining the outcome of the decision—the changes that occur (both statutory and constitutional) when a court overturns a precedent. Analyzing these questions will allow us to determine the impact of the Supreme Court's (perhaps unusual) decision to lay out a pathway for lower courts to actively overturn precedent. This in turn should provide some insight into how judicial activism in Canada (its form, its use and acceptability) compares to activism in other countries.

References

Baker, D. (2010). *Not quite supreme: The courts and coordinate constitutional interpretation*. Montreal and Kingston: McGill-Queen's University Press.

Bundale, B. (2017). Judge put adoptive parents in "unnecessary turmoil," appeal court rules. *CBC News* (Aug 24). https://www.cbc.ca/news/canada/nova-scotia/adoption-hearing-delayed-appeal-court-ruling-1.4260116

Canon, B. (1983). Defining the dimensions of judicial activism. *Judicature, 66*, 236–247.

Cheffins, R. (1966). The Supreme Court of Canada: The quiet court in an Unquiet Country. *Osgoode Hall Law Journal, 4*, 259–275.

Choudhry, S., & Hunter, C. (2003). Measuring judicial activism on the Supreme Court of Canada: A comment on Newfoundland (Treasury Board) v. NAPE. *McGill Law Journal, 48*, 525–558.

Cohn, M., & Kremnitzer, M. (2005). Judicial activism: A multidimensional model. *Canadian Journal of Law and Jurisprudence, 18*, 333–356.

Cross, F., & Lindquist, S. (2007). The scientific study of judicial activism. *Minnesota Law Review, 91*, 1752–1784.

Dixon. R. (2009). The Supreme Court of Canada, charter dialogue and deference. *Osgoode Hall Law Journal, 47*(2), 235–286.

Haigh, R., & Sobkin, M. (2007). Does the observer have an effect? An analysis of the use of the dialogue metaphor in Canada's courts. *Osgoode Hall Law Journal, 45*, 67–90.

Hausegger, L., Hennigar, M., & Riddell, T. (2015). *Canadian courts* (2nd ed.). Toronto: Oxford University Press.

Hein, Gregory. (2001). Interest group litigation and Canadian democracy. In Paul Howe & Peter H. Russell (Eds.), *Judicial power and Canadian democracy* (pp. 214–254). Montreal: Published for the Institute for Research on Public Policy by McGill-Queen's University Press.

Hennigar, M. (2017). Unreasonable disagreement?: Judicial-executive exchanges about charter reasonableness in the Harper era. *Osgoode Hall Law Journal, 54*(4), 1245–1273.

Hogg, P. W., & Bushell, A. (1997). The charter dialogue between courts and legislatures (or perhaps the charter of rights isn't such a bad thing after all). *Osgood Hall Law Journal, 35*(1), 75–124.

Hogg, P. W., Bushell Thorton, A., & Wright, W. (2007). Charter dialogue revisited—or "Much Ado About Metaphors." *Osgoode Hall Law Journal, 45*, 1–65.

King, J. (2018). Dialogue, finality and legality. In Rosalind Dixon, Jeffrey Sigalet, & Gregoire Webber (Eds.), *Constitutional dialogue: Democracy, rights, institutions*. Cambridge: Cambridge University Press.

Knopff, R., Evans, R., Baker, D., & Snow, D. (2017). Dialogue: Clarified and reconsidered. *Osgoode Hall Law Journal, 54*(2), 609–644.

Knopff, R., Baker,D., & LeRoy,S. (2009). Courting controversy: Strategic judicial decision making. In James Kelly & Christopher Manfredi (Eds.), *Contested constitutionalism: reflections on the Canadian Charter of Rights and Freedoms*. Vancouver: UBC Press.

Knopff, R., & Morton, F. L. (1992). *Charter politics*. Toronto: Nelson Canada.

Macfarlane, E. (2012). Dialogue or compliance? Measuring legislatures' policy responses to court rulings on rights. *International Political Science Review, 34*(1), 39–56.

Macfarlane, E. (2015). What we're talking about when we talk about "judicial activism": Has the Supreme Court gone too far?. *MacLean's Magazine*, Feb. 25.

Macfarlane, E. (2018). 'You Can't Always Get What You Want': Regime politics, the Supreme Court of Canada, and the Harper government. *Canadian Journal of Political Science, 51*, 1–21.

Macfarlane, E. (2022). Revisiting judicial activism. In Kate Puddister & Emmett Macfarlane (Eds.), *Constitutional Crossroads: Reflections on charter rights, reconciliation, and change.* Vancouver: UBC Press.

Mandel, M. (1994). *The Charter of Rights and the legalization of politics in Canada.* Toronto: Thompson Educational.

Manfredi, C. (2001). *Judicial power and the charter: Canada and the paradoxes of liberal constitutionalism* (2nd ed.). Toronto: Oxford University Press.

Manfredi, C. (2007). The day the dialogue died: A comment on *Sauvé v. Canada. Osgoode Hall Law Journal, 45*, 105–122.

Manfredi, C. (2015). Conservatives, the Supreme Court of Canada, and the constitution: Judicial-government relations, 2006–2015. *Osgoode Hall Law Journal, 52*(3), 951–983.

Manfredi, C., & Kelly, J. B. (1999). Six degrees of dialogue: A response to Hogg and Bushell. *Osgoode Hall Law Journal, 37*(3), 513–527.

McCormick, P. (2015). *The end of the charter revolution: Looking back from the new normal.* Toronto: University of Toronto Press.

Morton, F. L. (2001). Dialogue or monologue?. In Paul Howe & Peter H. Russell (Eds.), *Judicial power and Canadian democracy* (pp. 111–1117). Montreal and Kingston: McGill-Queen's University Press.

Morton, F. L., & Knopff, R. (2000). *The charter revolution and the court party.* Peterborough: Broadview Press.

Murchison, M. (2017). Making numbers count: An empirical analysis of judicial activism in Canada. *Manitoba Law Journal, 40*, 425–503.

Murchison, M., & Jochelson, R. (2015). Canadian exclusion of evidence under section 24(2) of the charter: An empirical model of judicial discourse. *Canadian Journal of Criminology and Criminal Justice, 57*, 115–152.

Muttart, D. (2011). One step forward, one step back: Measuring activism in the Supreme Court of Canada. *Social Science Research Network Working Paper.*

Newman, D. (2015). Judicial method and three gaps in the Supreme Court of Canada's assisted suicide judgment in Carter. *Saskatchewan Law Review, 78*(2), 217–224.

Parkes, D. (2016). Precedent revisited: Carter v. Canada (AG) and the contemporary practice of precedent. *McGill Journal of Law and Health, 10*, s123–s158.

Riddell, T. (2016)."Measuring activism and restraint: An alternative perspective on the Supreme Court of Canada's exclusion of evidence decisions under section 24(2) of the charter. *Canadian Journal of Criminology and Criminal Justice*, 58, 87–111.

Roach, K. (2001). *The Supreme Court on trial: Judicial activism or democratic dialogue.* Toronto: Irwin Law.

Schor, M. (2017). Constitutional dialogue and judicial supremacy. In Gary Jacobsohn & Miguel Schor (Eds.), *Comparative constitutional theory.* Northhampton, MA: Elgar Press.

Sigalet, Geoff, Grégoire Webber and Rosalind Dixon. (2019). *Constitutional dialogue: Rights, democracy, and institutions.* Cambridge: Cambridge University Press.

Souter, J. (2015). "Clearly the arc bends": Stare decisis and Saskatchewan federation of Labour v. Saskatchewan. *Saskatchewan Law Review, 78*(2), 397–410.

Tushnet, M. (2003). New forms of judicial review and the persistence of rights—and democracy-based worries. *Wake Forest Law Review, 38*, 813–838.

Weiler, P. (1968). Two models of judicial decision making. *Canadian Bar Review, 46*, 406–471.

Wilson, B. (2001). We didn't volunteer. In Paul Howe & Peter H. Russell (Eds.), *Judicial power and Canadian democracy* (pp. 73–79). Montreal and Kingston: McGill-Queen's University Press.

Cases Cited

Bondy-Rafael v. Potrebic (2015) ONSC 3655

Cabana v. Newfoundland and Labrador et al. (2016) NLCA 75

Canada (AG) v. Bedford (2013) 3 SCR 1101

Carter v. Canada (Attorney General) (2015) 1 SCR. 331

Duggan v. Durham Region Non-Profit Housing Corporation (2018) ONSC 1811

Ford v, Quebec (1988) 2 SCR 712

Franey v. Franey (1997) 148 NFLD. & P.E.I.R. 181

Hryniak v. Maudlin (2014) 1 SCR 87

Hunter v. Southam (1984) 2 SCR 145

Mahe v. Alberta (1990) 1 SCR 342

Newfoundland (Treasury Board) v Newfoundland Association of Public Employees (2004) 3 SCR 381

Nova Scotia (Community Services) v. Nova Scotia (AG) (2017) NSJ No. 333

Reference re ss. 193 & 195.1 (1)(c) of Criminal Code (Canada) (the Prostitution Reference) (1990) 1 SCR 1123

R. v. Caswell (2015) ABCA 97

R, v, Comeau (2016) NBPC 3

R. v. Comeau (2018) 1 SCR 342

R. v. Jordan (2016) 1SCR 631

R. v. Lloyd (2016) 1 SCR 130

R. v. Morgentaler (1988) 1 SCR 30

R. v. Nur (2015) 1 SCR 773

R. v. Therens (1985) 1 SCR 613

Rodriguez v. British Columbia (AG) (1993) 3 SCR 519

Saskatchewan Federation of Labour v. Saskatchewan (2015) 1 SCR 245

Sauvé v. Canada (Attorney General) (1993) 2 SCR 438

Sauvé v. Canada (Chief Electoral Officer), Sauvé II (2002) 3 SCR 519

Vriend v. Alberta (1998) 1 SCR 493

York v. Tomovski (2017) OJ 6073

Appendix

Table 5.A1: Cases applying Bedford/Carter 2013–2021

Case Name	Court, Year	Threshold Met? Yes (Y), No (N)	Precedent Overturned? Yes (Y), No (N), Other	Outcome?	Type of Case
R. v. Caron	Ct App, 2014	N	N	No Change	Public Law, Charter
R. v. Junek	Trial Ct, 2014	N	N	No Change	Public Law, Charter
US v. Fraser	Trial Ct, 2014	N	N	No Change	Public Law, Administrative Law
R. v. Hersi	Trial Ct, 2014	N	N	No Change	Public Law, Charter/ Criminal Code
R. v. Proctor	Trial Ct, 2015	N	N	No Change	Public Law, Charter
R. v. Oland	Trial Ct, 2015	N	N	No Change	Public Law, Criminal Code
Trinity Western University v. NS Barristers' Society	Trial Ct, 2015	N	N	No Change	Public Law, Criminal Code
R. v. Fitts	Trial Ct, 2015	N	N	No Change	Public Law, Charter/ Criminal Code
R. v. Wagner	Trial Ct, 2015	N	N	No Change	Public Law, Charter/ Criminal Code
Cabana v. Newfoundland and Labrador	Ct. App, 2016	Y	Y	Change in Judicial Process	Judicial Process
R. v. M.B.	Ct App, 2016	Y	N	New Trial	Public Law, Charter/ Criminal Code
R. v. H.S.S.	Trial Ct, 2016	Y	Precedent Extended	Declared Unconstitutional	Public Law, Charter/ Criminal Code
R. v. Ejigu	Trial Ct, 2016	N	N	No Change	Public Law, Charter/ Criminal Code
R. v. Comeau	Trial Ct, 2016	Y	Precedent Overturned	Change in Interpretation	Public Law, Federalism
R. v. Hair	Trial Ct, 2016	N	N	No Change	Public Law, Federalism
R. v. Al-Isawi	Ct App, 2017	N	N	No Change	Public Law, Charter
Fengyun v. He	Trial Ct, 2017	N	N	No Change	Private Law, Contract Law
R. v. Topham	Trial Ct, 2017	N	N	No Change	Public Law, Charter/ Criminal Code

(*Continued*)

Table 5.A1: *Continued*

Case Name	Court, Year	Threshold Met? Yes (Y), No (N)	Precedent Overturned? Yes (Y), No (N), Other	Outcome?	Type of Case
Arseneau v. O'Brien	Trial Ct, 2017	Y	Conflicting Precedents Sorted	Change to Common Law	Private Law, Torts
NS (Minister of Community Services) v. NS (AG)	Ct App, 2017	N	N	No Change	Private Law, Family Law
Black v. Owen	Ct App, 2017	N	N	No Change	Private Law, Contract Law
Robson v. Law Society of Upper Canada	Ct App, 2017	N	N	No Change	Public Law, Administrative Law
York (Regional Municipality) v. Tomovski	Ct App, 2017	Y	Precedent Distinguished	Principle Common Law Extended	Public Law, Charter
Sliwin v. College of Physicians & Surgeons of Ontario	Trial Ct, 2017	N	N	No Change	Public Law, Administrative Law
Shah v. LG Chem. Ltd	Trial Ct, 2017	N	N	No Change	Private Law, Contract Law
Duggan(Litigation Guardian of) v. Durham Region Non-Profit Housing Corp.	Ct App, 2018	Y	Precedent Distinguished	Change in Judicial Process	Judicial Process
Rosas v. Toca	Ct App, 2018	Y	Precedent Extended	Change to Common Law	Private Law, Contract Law
R. v. Catling	Trial Ct, 2018	N	N	No Change	Public Law, Charter
R. v. Harrisson	Trial Ct, 2018	N	N	No Change	Public Law, Charter/ Criminal Code
R. v. McCaw	Trial Ct, 2018	N	N	No Change	Public Law, Charter/ Criminal Code
R. v. Savoie	Trial Ct, 2018	N	N	No Change	Public Law, Charter
Panther Sports Medicine and Rehabilitation Centres Inc. v. Adrian G. Anderton Professional Corp.	Ct App, 2019	Y	Conflicting Precedents Sorted	Principle Common Law Extended	Private Law, Contract Law

Table 5.A1: *Continued*

Case Name	Court, Year	Threshold Met? Yes (Y), No (N)	Precedent Overturned? Yes (Y), No (N), Other	Outcome?	Type of Case
Collins Family Trust v. Canada (AG)	Trial Ct, 2019	N	N	No Change	Public Law, Federalism
R. v. Sanghera	Trial Ct, 2019	N	N	No Change	Public Law, Charter/ Criminal Law
R. v. Lutz	Trial Ct, 2019	N	Precedent Distinguished	Change in Judicial Process	Public Law, Criminal Code
R. v. Gorman	Trial Ct, 2019	N	N	No Change	Public Law, Criminal Code
Zaugg v. Ontaro (AG)	Trial Ct, 2019	N	N	No Change	Public Law, Charter
R. v. Amarelo-Gemus	Ct App, 2019	Y	Precedent Extended	Change in Judicial Process	Public Law, Charter/ Criminal Code
R. v. Craig	Trial Ct, 2019	Y			
R. v. Canfield	Ct App, 2020	Y	Precedent Extended	Change in Interpretation, Declare Unconstitutional	Public Law, Charter
Lanfer v. Eilers	Ct App, 2021	Y	Conflicting Precedents Sorted	Change to Common Law	Private Law, Contract Law
R. v. Chheng	Trial Ct, 2021	N	N	No Change	Public Law, Criminal Code
De Facendis v. Toronto Parking Authority	Trial Ct, 2021	N	N	No Change	Private Law, Torts

N = 43 cases applied Carter/Bedford

· 6 ·

JUDICIAL ACTIVISM AS THE (IM)PROPER USE OF JUDICIAL POWERS: A LOOK AT THE COLOMBIAN CONSTITUTIONAL COURT

Vicente F. Benítez-R., Fabio Enrique Pulido-Ortiz and Pablo Rivas-Robledo

Judicial activism is, without doubt, a key problem in contemporary jurisprudence and the practice of law. Despite its relevance being almost universally recognized, there is a persistent disagreement about the definition of judicial activism. As we will see, this is in part because researchers have been focused on studying particular manifestations of judicial activism, rather than the concept itself. Furthermore, studies on the matter are normally limited by the legal and political system the author comes from. This ultimately leads them to take some U.S. examples or manifestations of judicial activism as universal examples of judicial activism, just because they would be considered as judicial activism in the U.S. at some point in time. Surprisingly, some of these examples would be considered everyday judicial practice in systems that belong to the Civil Law tradition.

For example, some instances of judicial review are almost universally accepted as prime examples of judicial activism from a U.S. point of view. This has led some to conclude that judicial review is a paradigmatic instance of judicial activism. Nevertheless, those who write from the different perspective of a different legal system (as we do) find this perplexing and disagree with such a statement given that judicial review, in Colombia, has been recognized as a valid exercise of judicial power for over a hundred years. Thus, it would be wrong to call Colombian judges activists just because they exercise their prerogatives.

Therefore, we think there is a conceptual problem in the following sense: there is no definition of judicial activism that can account for its different manifestations on a global scale. In this chapter we want to address this problem from a theoretical and practical point of view: we want to offer a proper definition of judicial activism that encompasses all its possible manifestations and then apply it to specific cases. To that end, we want to first offer a conceptualization or definition of judicial activism, and then analyze how it can travel well across different countries and legal systems. Thus, we claim that judicial activism can be explained in terms of *norms of competence*, and then test the soundness of this definition in various landmark cases. We argue that judicial activism is the judge's modification of competences by her decisions (i.e., (im)proper use of powers). This concept allows us to avoid false positives and false negatives when analyzing judicial activism, as demonstrated by examining two paradigmatic decisions by the Colombian Constitutional Court.

We have divided the chapter in two main sections. The first section aims to provide a notion of judicial activism capable of improving upon conventional accounts of judicial activism. To reach this goal, this first section is composed of three subsections. In the first subsection, we summarize the main theories of judicial activism and point out how many of them use local manifestations of judicial activism to try to define it. In contrast, we offer our own definition of judicial activism, i.e., norms of competence, constitutive rules, and their relation. In the second subsection we make a case against previous theories of judicial activism. In the third, we contend that the best way to understand judicial activism is as the judge's modification of his competences through his decisions. We call this the (im)proper use of competences. Thus, presenting activist judges as those who go beyond the valid use of their powers (either by expanding them or by limiting them) but who act as if they were within a valid use of those powers, thus the (im)proper. Finally, in this subsection we show how the definition proposed here has clear advantages over those discussed previously, overcoming the critiques formulated against previous definitions.

The second part of the chapter constitutes the empirical section where we assess the performance of our conceptual framework. Relying on two decisions by the Colombian Constitutional Court on constitutional amendments, we show that extant approaches to judicial activism are unable to capture actual instances of judicial non-activism and of judicial activism in Colombia. We also find that, in contrast, our conception accurately distinguishes activist judgments from those who are not.

Defining Judicial Activism

Judicial Activism, Constitutive Rules, and Norms of Competence

The purpose of this subsection is to provide a framework for our subsequent analysis. First, we survey the main theories of judicial activism. We highlight how many of them prioritize distinct manifestations of judicial activism over the concept itself. Then, in the second part, we present the concepts necessary to develop our theory of judicial activism. We explain the concept of *norms of competence*, and Eugenio Bulygin's theory of norms of competence as constitutive rules.

Judicial Activism from Schlesinger to Zarbiyev

More than 70 years ago, Arthur Schlesinger coined the term *judicial activism* for the first time. In 1947 he used the term in a somewhat derogatory fashion to talk about judges who, in their rulings, went beyond the self-restraint that is expected from them (Schlesinger, 1947, pp. 73–74, 201–204). This original sense may have contributed to the fact that, even today in legal practice, judicial activism tends to be associated with judges that go beyond their roles or usurp the roles of other bodies.[1]

In addition, Schlesinger was the first to notice the close relationship that exists between judicial activism, decision-making, and politics (Schlesinger, 1947, p. 78). He did not only mean that every decision by judges has political motivations or political consequences. He also thought that courts with a higher hierarchy have a far greater political power than any other courts and this, in turn, makes higher courts (such as the United States Supreme Court) drift away from the self-restraint that is expected from them (Schlesinger, 1947, pp. 78, 202).

Schlesinger's work has been very influential. It basically gave birth to a whole wave of scholarship on the subject that quotes his original piece

1 Vestiges of Schelesinger's proto-definition can also be found in more recent scholarship, see (Kmiec, 2004; Pulido Ortiz, 2019; Saffon and García-Villegas, 2011; Terpan and Saurugger, 2018; Waltman, 2015).

extensively. Normally, studies on judicial activism can be divided into two categories. The first one comprises works that presuppose the concept of judicial activism and focus on judicial activism's impact and justification, disregarding any theoretical consideration. For some scholars, this impact is positive for it promotes social rights and strives towards morally acceptable results (Gómez Pinto, 2012; Landau, 2010; Lozada, 2018; Rodríguez, 2005; Saffon and García-Villegas, 2011; Smith, 2015; Terpan and Saurugger, 2018). Others, however, think that this impact is negative because it affects institutions and, more generally, the rule of law (Escobar Torres et al., 2013; Pulido Ortiz, 2019; Stone, 2011; Waltman, 2015).

A second category includes works that list certain activities that are paradigmatic examples of the activism of courts, that is, manifestations of judicial activism (Canon, 1983; Harwood, 1992; Itoh, 1990, 1991; Kmiec, 2004; Maraniello, 2012; Schubert, 1965; Zarbiyev, 2012). For example, for Kmiec the following manifestations are expressions of judicial activism: (1) striking down constitutional actions of other branches, (2) ignoring precedent, (3) crafting judicial legislation, (4) departing from the accepted interpretive methodology, and (5) injecting moral result-oriented contents to judicial outcomes (Kmiec, 2004, p. 1444). According to Harwood, typical manifestations of judicial activism occur when the judge (1) refuses to take an attitude of judicial deference for legislative or executive, (2) relaxes requirements for justiciability, (3) breaks precedent; and (4) loosely or controversially construes the law, contained in either constitutions, statutes or precedent (Harwood, 1992, pp. 2, cited in Zarbiyev, 2012, pp. 249–250).

Lastly, it is important to talk about Canon's theory which is not widely read today, but that inspired contemporary accounts that understand judicial activism from the perspective of its manifestations (Kmiec, 2004; Marshall, 2002; Young, 2010). For Canon, judicial activism has six dimensions or degrees. The more salient these dimensions are in a court's judgments, the more activist it is. The dimensions are (1) the extent to which judgments strike down or make void public policy adopted by democratic bodies, normally via judicial review; (2) the degree to which judgments modify precedent, legal doctrine or interpretations of the law; (3) the degree to which judgments interpret dispositions against their ordinary meaning; (4) the extent to which judgments introduce public policy that distort democracy; (5) the degree in which judgments establish how to implement public policy, usurping the role of state agencies; and (6) the degree to which judgments replace arguably constitutional decisions and actions by other branches (Canon, 1983).

Canon's most interesting contribution is that he proposes there are two practices that, if followed, lead to judicial activism, namely, the creation, modification or elimination of public policy, and the improper use of judicial powers (Canon, 1983, pp. 238–239). As we examine later, this last point is particularly useful to develop a definition of judicial activism because it separates judicial activism from some indigenous manifestations of activism, and makes explicit reference to the powers that judges have within legal frameworks. It is undeniable that Canon's work made a great impact in subsequent jurisprudence from the U.S., an analysis of the theories inspired by Canon reveals that they are limited, geographically speaking. Canon, who is an American scholar, treats these dimensions in a derogatory manner. Those who followed him saw in these dimensions some negative aspects of the American legal system and from them proposed a concept of judicial activism based on its manifestations in the U.S.

This brings into the spotlight a common pitfall of building concepts based specifically on a particular legal reality, where one is led into wrongly condemning or praising a particular manifestation of the concept, based on whether it fits the concept in that context. In this case, the concept is judicial activism; but the fact that in the U.S. the implementation of public policy is taken as a manifestation of judicial activism should not be taken as an absolute truth, since it may be the case that in other jurisdictions/legal systems, the introduction of public policy falls within the judge's competences or prerogatives.

On the other hand, even in the light of complaints that there is no uniform understanding of judicial activism, it is surprising that there is little scholarship on conceptual aspects of judicial activism besides exploring its dimensions.[2] We do find definitions is in texts such as *Black's Law Dictionary* (BLD) or, in the Spanish-speaking context, in the *Panhispanic Dictionary of Legal Spanish* (Diccionario Panhispánico del español jurídico, DPEJ). The former claims that judicial activism is "[a] philosophy of judicial decision-making whereby judges allow their personal views about public policy, among other factors, to guide their decisions, with the suggestion that adherents of this philosophy tend to find constitutional violations and are willing to ignore precedent" ("Judicial Activism," 1999). The DPEJ holds that judicial activism is a "particularly

2 There is a small group of works that, even if they are not trying to provide a definition of activism, propose terms or variables that can be used to define it. In this sense, La Torre (2015) holds that a definition of judicial activism can be offered from the concepts of constitution, reasoning and Law; whilst de Almeida Ribeiro (2015) prefers powers (in the sense of separation of powers) and adjudication.

creative position of judges and courts, by which they interpret available sources of law or they cover legal lacunae" ("Activismo Judicial," 2017). Both definitions reduce activism to some manifestations: BLD cites two, while the DPEJ cites two others.

As we can see, many of the theories presented here only point to some manifestations of judicial activism, and always do it with a sense of resentment, because judges are not supposed to act in this or that way that is considered activist. Therefore, there is a common feature in all the theories that has been overlooked: they depend precisely on a proper understanding of judicial powers. And so, to understand what judicial activism is, we need to first understand what is for a judge to have the power to do something. That is why before we can discuss and criticize the theories of judicial activism referred to so far it is necessary to introduce the concept of norms of competence, that is, the norms that establish the extent of the powers that authorities have in a legal system.

Constitutive Rules and Norms of Competence: Searle and Bulygin[3]

As Schlesinger first noticed, the concept of judicial activism is linked to what judges are supposed to do. To make this explicit, it is beneficial to understand this in terms of norms of competence. In our view, what defines judicial activism is the fact that judges rewire the norms of competence that define the powers of judicial bodies through their own acts. To elaborate, we first present the notion of competence and norm of competence, and in a different subsection we explain how judicial activism is the judge's modification of competences by her decisions.[4]

The debate over the nature of the norms of competence is an ongoing discussion. Nonetheless, nowadays it is possible to say that there is some consensus on some general issues. In particular, on how we can use the concept of constitutive rules to explain the nature of norms of competence, a theory championed by Bulygin (1992) and followed by others (Alexy, 1986; Ferrer Beltrán, 2000; Spaak, 2003, 2009; Villa Rosas, 2018).

Norms of competence are those that establish what powers individuals and legal bodies are entitled to exercise in a given legal system. For example,

3 Here *rule* and *norm* are not synonyms. For the purpose of this chapter, norms are legal dispositions, rules are dispositions that regulate an agent's behavior, whether legal or not.

4 As far as we know, there are no previous attempts to define judicial activism based on the concept of norms of competence. Villalobos (2015) is probably the only one that has noticed the relationship between judicial activism and judicial powers, but he does not elaborate.

presidential regimes usually have a norm that establishes the actions that the president is entitled to do as a public official; for instance, appointing ministers. In this sense, we understand that the president has the competence—the power—to appoint ministers.

The role that norms of competence play in legal systems is crucial, as they allow institutions and all other participants to know what actions are permissible for them in a particular legal system. In other words, the president's norm of competence or the norms of competence of a ministry endow these offices with certain powers or the 'competence' to act in a certain way.

With judges and courts something similar happens. Take, for example, these three dispositions of a legal system 'C':

- Judges of the criminal jurisdiction may decide over all the matters brought by district attorneys.
- The Constitutional Court has to decide over claims of unconstitutionality against constitutional amendments.
- The Court will choose its own Chief Justice.

The way these norms are written may confuse us. It seems like the first says that criminal judges *may* decide over some matters, that the Constitutional Court *has* to decide over other issues, and that the Chief Justice of the Court *will* be appointed by the Court's members. Despite these differences, these three norms provide that said courts or judges have the power to bring upon certain acts. Thus, they are not requiring or permitting any conduct, but rather establishing the limits of what these judges are entitled to do (Bulygin, 1992, secs. 3–6).

To explain norms of competence in this fashion, Bulygin and those who follow him have used the concept of constitutive rule, developed in John Searle's work. In social ontology it is common to draw a distinction between two types of rules, regulative and constitutive. Searle has used this distinction through his opus continuously with a myriad of different purposes, including how social institutions such as law, money and government are created and maintained thanks to human collective actions. According to Searle, most institutions are systems of constitutive rules, and they have the following structure: 'X counts as Y in C' (Searle, 1969, 1995, 2010, 2018).[5]

5 For instance, 'moving the king one block to the right (X) counts as a valid movement for the king (Y) in chess (C)'. Thus, the set of constitutive rules that states what counts as what in chess constitutes the totality of chess. This allows us to tell institutions and sets of

These rules are definitional in that they do not demand any behavior from the recipients of the rules, contrary to what regulative rules do (Placani, 2017, p. 60; Searle, 2010, pp. 9–10, 2018, p. 52). What constitutive rules do is to take facts and assign them an institutional interpretation that otherwise it would not have. It is because of this that it is claimed that in the absence of a constitutive rule, the action that it is constituted would not exist: there would be no king's movement in chess if there wasn't a constitutive rule that defines how the thing is to be moved (Searle, 2010, p. 10, 2018, p. 53).

According to those who consider norms of competence as a kind of constitutive rules, norms of competence have the same structure ('*X* counts as *Y* in *C*'), such that we need to interpret them as *X* being the action an official must do to bring about *Y* in C. In terms that will be more familiar, the norm of competence according to which the president can appoint ministers can be restated as 'the appointment of someone as the head of an administrative sector by the president (X) counts as the appointment of a minister (Y) in Colombia (C)', and it is, therefore, conferring the president the power to appoint ministers. The very same analysis can be carried out with the examples provided earlier: cases brought up by district attorneys count as matters to be decided by criminal judges in C, and so on. We will follow this proposal in the next subsections to advance our notion of judicial activism.

Against Previous Theories of Judicial Activism

Theories such as Canon's (and those of scholars who follow him) are usually posited from a U.S. based perspective, and frequently make use of U.S. examples to elaborate. And even when this is not the case, this methodology is often replicated elsewhere, changing the examples. Hence, these accounts are limited by the legal systems they write from. Briefly stated, they mix judicial activism with the manifestations that it can have across systems. This hinders any possible conceptualization of judicial activism as it only points out some limited examples of judicial activism for a system at a given point in time. Perhaps the most ironical case of this problem can be found in the book *Judicial Activism in Comparative Perspective*, edited by Kenneth Holland. In the introduction, the editor claims that judicial activism occurs when the judge creates public policy (Holland, 1991, p. 1). Nevertheless, this book collects other accounts of judicial activism from places other than the US., and it is notorious

rules from one another (for example, chess from sudoku). And this is precisely what Bulygin would later apply to norms of competence.

that in several of these countries creating public policy is not considered as judicial activism. For example, in Jacobsohn's contribution, it is claimed that there is judicial activism when the judge takes a pedagogical role with both parties of a legal dispute, as happens in Israel, for instance (Jacobsohn, 1991).

And even conceding for the sake of discussion that judicial activism entails the creation of public policy, in places like Colombia that is hardly the case. Colombian judges have the power to create, modify or even eliminate policies when solving issues in which social rights are at stake (Gómez Pinto, 2012). Consequently, if judges in Colombia are endowed with the power to create, modify, or eliminate public policy, are they really activist judges? It is safe to answer this question in the negative. To see this point more clearly, note we would only consider this judicial activism precisely because in the U.S. that would be the case. We have no reason to extend this reasoning to the Colombian context, or any other, since in those jurisdictions they are granted the competence to do so. Consequently, it is not possible to define activism as a function of some examples from the U.S. legal system, or from some current examples of judicial activism in that jurisdiction. A definition based exclusively on that system would be pointless, as legal systems constantly change (and even disappear),so what could be considered activism at one point in time may not be regarded as so in a short time. Thus, for comparative purposes, we need a definition of activism that can comprise all or at least most of the manifestations at a global level, at any point in time.

On the other hand, the definitions by the BLD and the DPEJ also lead to false positives. Let's imagine a very conservative judge that pronounces a judgment that agrees with her moral principles but also with applicable law. This would be activist according to the BLD's definition because the judgment reflects the judge's personal opinion, but it is not against the law. For the DPEJ's definition, on the other hand, a judge that uses the analogy to fill a lacuna would be an activist judge, even when analogy is normally permitted across legal systems (except in criminal law). Is filling lacunae really an activist conduct? Precisely because the analogy is even considered as a source of law, in general we are inclined to say no.

So, What Is Judicial Activism?

Inspired in Schlesinger's own take, we hold that activism not only implies to do things outside judges' own norms of competence, but to perform as if they were within their legally conferred powers. In our view, judicial activism is the judge's modification of competences by her decision. Thus, the activist judge is the one who goes beyond the exercise of her competences, extending or reducing them, but acting as if she was within the scope of the powers defined in the rule of competence, i.e., she issues orders as if she could do so in these cases. In what follows, let us look at a case on how a court can be considered activist.

For example, *Siri* and *Kot* are two cases labeled as activist judgments by Argentinian scholarship (Laise, 2020, pp. 163–164; Maraniello, 2012, p. 55; Racimo, 2015, pp. 136–137). And in the light of this definition, they indeed are. In these cases, the Argentinian Supreme Court established that a *habeas corpus* could now be filed against violations to any constitutional right, despite the fact that the Constitution was clear that it could only be filed against violations to the right of personal freedom (*Samuel, Kot S.R.L*, 1958; *Siri, Ángel*, 1957). It is important to note that the Supreme Court had no bearing on the nature of the *habeas corpus*, as it was a writ established in the Constitution, and the Court did not have the competence to modify the Constitution either. Judicial activism? From the point of view of our definition, yes. The Supreme Court not only decided over an *habeas corpus* despite it not being appealed, it also changed the way it worked, which was probably something worthy of a constitutional amendment. Here, the Supreme Court was acting precisely as if it could decide over these cases despite the fact that (1) it had no jurisdiction over an unappealed *habeas corpus* and (2) could not change the Constitution.

Judicial activism, therefore, consists of issuing an order on which the court does not have jurisdiction and of making it pass as if the court had the power to do so. To better understand this, remember that the norms that confer legal powers to courts have the structure "*X* counts as *Y* in C" where *X* is a fact and *Y* is its interpretation. Consequently, when a judge passes down an activist decision it is taking another fact, *Z*, which is not accepted as valid use of powers and making it look as *Y*. In the previous example, *Z* is either deciding over non-appealed *habeas corpus* or changing the nature of the *habeas corpus*.

Therefore, we are starting from a *count as* (the norm of competence) and moving to an *as if* (the activist decision itself). Activist judges are those who make invalid uses of power, as if they were otherwise. The way in which judicial activism manifests varies not only from country to country, but also from court to court (according to their jurisdiction and the definition of their powers). Consequently, it is important to underscore that although we can provide a definition of judicial activism, its manifestations change depending on the country the court in question operates in, and on the period when it renders its decision. In a few words, instantiations of activism are context-dependent. This indeed opens the possibility for further research in comparative legal systems in which the *tertium comparationis* is the different manifestations of judicial activism throughout a particular time and legal system. Three logical combinations are possible: comparing manifestations in (i) different systems at different points in time (i.e., Japan in 1946 and Germany in 1992), (ii) different systems at the same point in time (i.e., Japan and Germany in 1992), and (iii) the same system at the different points in time (i.e. Japan in 1946 and in 1992). Of these, we consider the second and third options the most interesting for our purposes.

In sum, we can discern whether a particular decision is activist by looking at judges' norms of competence and by judging if the decision went beyond these norms. Therefore, definitions of activism such as Kmiec's or Harwood's (who list a series of behaviors that they conceive of as activism) can be accepted, as long as we keep in mind that their breadth is limited: Without further explanation, these are just examples of activism from the U.S. at a particular point in time.

This notion of judicial activism overcomes the critiques raised against the two types of theories examined earlier. By interpreting judicial activism as a concept (and not as the sum of its manifestations) in the U.S. legal system, we avoid the criticism that we cannot generalize the concept of judicial activism just from its local manifestations. Moreover, it does not suffer from the problems that undermine the BLD's and DPEJ's definitions (existence of false positives and false negatives). More specifically, a conservative judge whose decisions follow the rule of law is not activist and a judge that fills lacunae is not activist either, provided that they have the competence to do so. In the next section, we further discuss how our framework successfully prevents the existence of false positives and false negatives in the Colombian context.

Judicial Activism in the Colombian Constitutional Court

This second section will test the previous conceptual considerations using, as case studies, two decisions rendered by the Colombian Constitutional Court after reviewing the constitutionality of constitutional amendments. The main contention we will advance in this section is that extant approaches to judicial activism are not accurate enough to capture real instances of judicial activism because they are prone to, both, yield false positives (i.e., incorrectly labeling certain non-activist decisions as activist judgments) and false negatives (i.e., missing the identification of actual activist decisions). At the same time, we show that an understanding of judicial activism associated with whether the court in question has (im)properly made use of its powers by modifying its own competences, overcomes the problems of inaccuracy that riddle some of the traditional accounts.

Before delving into the analysis of specific decisions, it is appropriate to say a few words about case selection. The two cases we picked to conduct our examination dealt with two consequential amendments. These amendments were not only heavily endorsed by the president's office (the most powerful office of government) and its congressional coalition, but they also significantly restricted key fundamental rights and enlarged the orbit of influence granted to the President by the 1991 Constitution. In addition to their political relevance, these two cases on amendments clearly illustrate how, if we follow traditional approaches advanced in the literature that embrace a U.S. perspective, we can very well miss the mark when determining whether a particular ruling was, indeed, activist. Thus, in what follows, we first address a case that under a conventional approach would be erroneously categorized as a manifestation of judicial activism. Afterwards, we study a second Constitutional Court's decision that, prima facie, does not constitute judicial activism but that, upon closer inspection, is an activist judgment.

Decision on the 'Anti-Terrorist' Amendment (Decision C-816/2004): A False Positive

Álvaro Uribe was elected as president in 2002 during a severe public-order crisis triggered by the presence of far-right and far-left armed groups across the country and the correlative weakness of the government in many regions. From day one, Uribe made clear that the main political goal of his administration would be the military destruction of guerrilla groups and, most prominently, of the Revolutionary Armed Forces of Colombia (*Fuerzas Armadas Revolucionarias de Colombia*, FARC) (Gamboa, 2017, pp. 459, 463; Mayka, 2016, p. 139). According to Uribe, it was necessary to amend the Constitution to accomplish that end. His government proposed an amendment bill that, among others, dramatically restricted some fundamental rights, such as the right to hold private communications, and loosened some of the constitutional guarantees of individuals under criminal prosecution. Namely, the amendment proposal authorized the interception of private communications, police raids in private domiciles, and arrests of suspected criminals without a judicial warrant (Acto Legislativo 2, 2003, arts. 1 and 3).

Despite the outcry such a proposal provoked, Uribe's legislative coalition passed the amendment in late 2003. This amendment's constitutionality was challenged before the Constitutional Court. The petitioners advanced two different arguments. First, they argued that the amendment implied a replacement of the Constitution, as it destroyed essential constitutional principles that, in turn, were part of the identity of the 1991 Constitution. Second, and from a procedural standpoint, the claimants maintained that a majority of members of one of the committees of Congress had rejected the amendment bill, but the chairman of the committee dismissed such a vote and adjourned until next day when, finally, the amendment was passed by the required majority. As a consequence, the plaintiffs asserted that there had been a procedural irregularity that breached the Constitution (*Decision C-816*, 2004).

In Decision C-816/2004, the Constitutional Court struck the amendment down based on the procedural allegation. For the Court, the strategic postponement of the discussion amounted to a manipulation of the will of the committee's members who, when the deliberation was being held, were ready to shelve the amendment bill. Since the will of Congress was manipulated and the bill did not reach the required absolute majority for its adoption, the Court held that the amendment was not passed in conformity with the Constitution. Although the Court could have given the opportunity to Congress to rectify this procedural mistake by holding another vote, it observed that the irregularity was so important that this was not an option. Once the amendment was quashed, the Court decided not to tackle the substantive allegation brought by the claimants (*Decision C-816*, 2004, paras. 8–12).

Now, if we read this judgment through the prism of Kmiec's, Hardwood's and Canon's manifestations of judicial activism, or the BLD's and DPEJ's definitions of activism, we could interpret this decision as activist. For a start, the Court invalidated a constitutional amendment, that is, a constitutional rule supported by an important number of congress members and, probably, the people at large. This was the first time, after the enactment of the 1991 Constitution, that an entire amendment was nullified. By the same token, the Court imposed its political-moral views on how constitutional amendments ought to be approved by Congress and, thus, showed no deference to the elected branches. As a matter of fact, one congressman declared that the Court's decision-making in this case had been guided by political, not legal, criteria (Redacción El Tiempo, 2004a). In some sense, the message sent by the Court was that modifying the Constitution, even if it was motivated by such an important objective such as public-order maintenance, was a rule-oriented enterprise that should follow all the procedural steps enshrined in the constitutional text.

However, this was not, by any means, an activist decision. As a descriptive matter, no single Colombian scholar nor political actor at the time (except for the one peculiar congress member already mentioned) regarded this decision as an activist exercise of judicial power. On one hand, in Colombian legal academia judicial review of amendments on procedural grounds was a settled discussion (Cepeda Espinosa and Landau, 2017, pp. 327–328; Quinche Ramírez, 2009, p. 581). The constitutional text made very clear that the Court had the power to assess the constitutional soundness of amendments from a procedural vantage point (Constitución Política de Colombia, 1991, arts. 241.1, 241.2 and 379). No scholar saw this decision as an improper use of judicial power.[6] Of course, there were some disagreements about whether the alleged manipulation had, indeed, occurred, but no one suggested that the Court had gone beyond the boundaries of its power. Procedural review of amendments was a common feature of the Colombian constitutional landscape since 1978, and striking down a constitutional change, in and of itself, was not viewed as something akin to the Court imposing its views on congressional majorities or a lack of judicial deference (*Sentencia del 5 de mayo de 1978*, 1978). This might come as a baffling assertion to, say, an American scholarly audience—an unconstitutional amendment is something unconceivable; it's a political question beyond the province of the judiciary (*Coleman v. Miller*, 1939). However, this is precisely the point we are trying to make: U.S.-oriented determinations of activism based on its purported manifestations do not work well in other realities.

Now, regarding the political reactions, no consequential political player opined that the decision was activist. It is true that they disagreed with the decision, and asked the Court to reconsider its verdict, but they never indicated that an amendment being invalidated due to procedural reasons represented judicial activism. For example, although President Uribe expressed some preoccupations about the future of his security-laden agenda, he ultimately abided

6 There is one point in our account that warrants further elaboration. There might be situations where there are mixed signals or disagreements within the legal and political communities as to whether a specific action counts as the (im)proper use of judicial power. After all, the (constitutional) law is indeterminate, subject to different (and opposing) interpretations and prone to the inclusion of moral and political arguments. In this type of scenarios, the application of our notion would find some obstacles in the application. Nevertheless, we think we have made some progress by advancing a definition of judicial activism that works well in many other cases where there is a stable consensus on the respective court's powers. The examples explored in this chapter are a good illustration of this.

by the decision (Redacción El Tiempo, 2004a). Some members of his legislative coalition, on their part, acknowledged that the ruling was a valid exercise of judicial review of amendments, and announced they were planning to work hard to pass, according to the procedural rules, another amendment to tackle the rising spiral of violence in the country (Redacción El Tiempo, 2004b).

Why was this decision widely regarded as non-activist? We submit that the main factor behind all these reactions is the notion of (im)proper use of competence. The procedural scrutiny of amendments and a potential decision voiding them, is an appropriate use of the Colombian Constitutional Court's powers. It was consistent not only with the precedent of the Court but, more importantly, with the rules of competence laid out in the Constitution.[7] On the contrary, the decision that comes next evinces how the examination of improper use of judicial powers opens a promising path for a better comprehension of judicial activism.

The First 'Fast Track' Peace Amendment (Sentencia C-699/2016): A False Negative

Uribe's military approach radically changed under the administration of his successor in the presidential office, Juan Manuel Santos. Santos initiated a series of peace talks with FARC that led to a far-reaching peace agreement ('the Pact') signed between the parties in September 2016. However, the legal implementation of some of the Pact's contents required the adoption of some constitutional amendments. To secure a smooth and quick implementation, Santos proposed, and Congress passed, a constitutional amendment that reduced the procedural strictures established in the Constitution's amendment clauses to modify the Constitution (Durán Smela and Cruz Gutiérrez, 2021, pp. 14–18). To be specific, this amendment—known as the 'Fast Track' amendment (hereinafter, FT)—lowered the number of hearings or readings required to modify the Constitution and prohibited congress members' from altering the content

7 It is important to highlight that the cases under analysis do not exhaust the possibilities of judicial activism, to wit, the (im)proper use of judicial powers. There are, at least, two additional possibilities. First, there is judicial activism when a court does not make use of the prerogatives endowed by the constitution. This is an interesting example of judicial activism that, in principle, is counterintuitive in light of extant notions that usually highlight just positive traits in activist decision-making. Second, a judge can also be activist when she suddenly interprets her powers in a radical different manner vis-à-vis the prior and stable interpretation the court had adopted through its precedents, and does not offer acceptable reasons for such a departure from the settled precedent.

of the bills introduced by the government unless the government itself greenlighted such proposals (Acto Legislativo 1, 2016). The rationale of FT was that the implementation of the peace pact through amendments required a faster amendment track than the one required for any other kind of constitutional modifications.

Now, since the amendment reduced the constitutional rigidity to amend the Constitution, the government feared that the Constitutional Court might very well quash FT. In 2003 the Court created a doctrine (known as the replacement doctrine) according to which a congressional amendment that destroys essential aspects of tenets of the Constitution, is tantamount to a constitutional replacement. Such an amendment, for the Court, would be *ultra vires* because Congress does not have the power to replace the Constitution (just the people themselves can do it) (Roznai, 2017, pp. 65–67; *Sentencia C-551/03*, 2003). To reduce this risk and to invite the Court to deploy a gentler scrutiny, the government organized a plebiscite, asked the people to vote for or against the peace accord, and introduced a provision in FT saying that this abbreviated amendment procedure could be activated only if there was a 'popular endorsement'. The people's support for the agreement would make the Court think twice before nullifying FT (González-Jácome, 2016).

In October 2016, a slim majority of voters rejected the peace agreement (Cobb and Casey, 2016). Hence, one of the main questions in the air was whether FT could be activated. Santos pointed out that the popular endorsement to activate FT could be supplied by Congress as the institution that represents the people's will (Casey, 2016). His opponents, led by former President Uribe, stated that this was a constitutional mockery and that a second popular vote was required given that the Constitution's amendment requirements had been considerably lowered. This issue was brought before the Constitutional Court. More specifically, the Court had to determine whether 'popular endorsement' could also be understood as a Congressional endorsement so as to trigger FT, and whether lowering the amendment's procedures passed constitutional muster.

In this context, the Court issued the Sentencia C-699/2016 and upheld the amendment. The Court held that FT did not destroy the rigid nature of the Constitution. Colombia was going through a transitional process towards peace and this end justified relaxing some of the procedural steps to amend the Constitution. With respect to FT's activation, the Court deferred this issue to the legislature—Congress had the duty to decide whether its endorsement was enough to trigger FT. Nonetheless, the Court ruled that if Congress were to endorse the pact, this endorsement should be the product of a democratic process with ample popular participation and with enough spaces of deliberation (*Decision* C-699/16, 2016).

At first glance, this would not count as an activist decision. To begin with, the Court was certainly deferential to the elected branches. Besides the fact that the amendment was upheld thanks to the application of a more lenient scrutiny, the court was not an obstacle in the road for the implementation of a public policy (the peace agreement) backed by the elected branches. The President and Congress made a decision with a clear moral-political orientation and the Court did not interfere with it. This is what the standard view of judicial activism that we have questioned would say about this case. But, once again, this appreciation is inexact. Equating decisions striking down legislation (or, in this event, amendments) to judicial activism is not right. Courts can be tremendously activist institutions even when upholding governmental decisions. And Decision C-699/2016 is a case in point.

Let us begin by noting that the Court made an improper use of its competence. Even though the very same Court in 2003 created for itself the new power to assess the substantive validity of constitutional amendments, and consistently applied it in a strict fashion in several cases, it strategically abandoned such a rigorous stance in this judgment (Cajas-Sarria, 2017, p. 272; Garcia-Jaramillo and Currea-Moncada, 2020, pp. 17–21). As a result, the Court did not expand its powers. Quite the opposite: it limited its own jurisdiction. Thus, the Court basically established an exception to the standard it had used, up until that point, to examine an amendment—from that moment onwards, amendments aimed at attaining the goal of a transition to peace should be reviewed more softly to facilitate reconciliation between warring groups. As two of us have argued elsewhere, this justification was relatively weak, at least in light of the competences granted to the Court by the Constitution (Pulido-Ortíz, 2017; Pulido-Ortíz and Rivas-Robledo, 2017). There were some other equally important areas (such as amendments to the judiciary) where the Court carried out a particularly strict vigilance.[8]

This legal perspective is echoed by many political figures that reacted to the judgment at that time. First, the political opposition expressed that, with this decision, the Court had relinquished its constitutional duty to protect the Constitution against amendments that enlarged the presidential power's influence on the amendment power ("Las Seis Críticas Del Uribismo al Fallo

8 See (*Sentencia C-285/16*, 2016; *Sentencia C-373/16*, 2016).

Del Fast Track," 2016). Apparently, the need for peace prevailed over any consideration linked to the enhanced powers of the President in FT. Secondly, even sympathizers of the peace agreement (most notably the government) would eventually and indirectly criticize some of the contents of this decision, particularly the deliberative, democratic and participatory principles that, in the Court's interpretation, should inform the FT's popular endorsement. The Decision C-699/2016 laid the groundwork for a subsequent ruling (Decision C-332/2017) in which the Court limited the presidential prerogatives in the FT amendment process. In this second ruling, the Court found that the way in which the peace negotiations took place and how FT had been used to pass peace amendments, were far from being deliberative, democratic, and participatory. Therefore, it struck down, among others, the prohibition for Congress to autonomously (i.e., without governmental authorization) introduce modifications to the amendment bills tabled by the government (*Sentencia C-332/17*, 2017). The government's reaction was somewhat harsh—a governmental peace negotiator suggested that the Court could have misused its powers (Peña, 2017). Likewise, one of the judges of the Court—known for his unwavering support to the Pact—filed a dissenting opinion and claimed that the Court's enforcement of the principles set forth in Decision C-699/2016 (deliberation, democracy and participation) was the exemplar of an activist decision (*Dissenting vote of Justice Antonio Lizarazo to Sentencia C-332/2017*, 2017).

The gist of all of this is that Decision C-699/2016 was an activist decision because of how the Court deployed its powers, i.e., used their competencies (rather than whether the judgment did fit into one of the manifestations of judicial activism put forward by some scholars and dictionaries). In the political opposition's eyes, the Court gave up its mission to protect constitutional supremacy by applying a deferential scrutiny to FT. In those of the government and of a member of the Court, establishing a set of principles that should permeate the whole implementation of the Pact and that would be later enforced in another decision, went beyond the scope of the Constitutional Court's powers.

In spite of this, it could be argued that Decision C-699/2016 is not an activist decision but, quite the contrary, a deferential one. Yet, categorizing this ruling as such is problematic because the Court did more than simply defer to the government's agenda. While it is true that it employed a softer scrutiny, it also set a series of conditions that ought to be met for the FT to be activated and used. Even more, assuming that the Court had not introduced these conditions and had rendered just a deferential decision, this deference is just the flip side of the same coin—the improper use of legal competences and, hence, judicial activism as well. Despite first-impression perceptions that would signal the absence of activism, these reasons explain why this ruling was regarded as an activist by many consequential actors.

Conclusions

The main motivation behind this chapter was to refine our grasp on judicial activism. After surveying the most popular approaches to this phenomenon, a key finding of our research was that they are inaccurate because they can produce false positives and false negatives. Hence, we proposed a revamped notion of judicial activism that could overcome these issues. Judicial activism is better understood as the (im)proper use, in judicial decisions, of the powers vested on a court. One direct consequence of understanding judicial activism in this way is the fact that these types of judicial decisions are not valid. However, the fact that judicial rulings from lower judges tend to be overruled while judicial decisions from higher courts not only become precedent but also landmark cases, speaks volumes about the political power of the latter.

To test the practical implications of this conceptual conclusion, we conducted an analysis of two prominent decisions rendered by one of the most activist courts in the world and in an area of the law amenable to judicial activism—judicial review of constitutional amendments by the Colombian Constitutional Court. The results of this analysis are clear: extant notions of judicial activism are not sensitive enough to detect actual instances of activist decisions. *Decision* C-816/2004, which is widely regarded as an example of a non-activist decision, is incorrectly interpreted as an activist judgment under traditional criteria. Furthermore, *Decision* C-699/2016, which pursuant to standard conceptions should be a non-activist ruling, is, as a matter of fact, an activist judgment.

From these general considerations we can derive some other specific conclusions. First, our study was geared towards the conceptual clarification of a contested concept such as judicial activism. Although our definition of activism as 'improper' use of powers might have some normative content, our chapter's aim was neither normative nor explanatory. However, this conceptual clarification might open the door to hold more productive normative and explanatory conversations. Understanding the phenomenon we are seeking to evaluate and explain is a necessary step to determine the desirability of activist or non-activist courts as well as the sources thereof. From this follows that judicial activism is not necessarily a judicial vice, nor judicial self-restraint inevitably a judicial virtue. This is a pending discussion that presupposes the existence of sound and accurate conceptions like the one we hope we provided in this chapter.

Second, one of the main implications of the practical analysis is that decisions invalidating constitutional changes cannot be equated to judicial activism. Conversely, rulings endorsing amendments should not necessarily be conceived of as non-judicial activism. Striking down or upholding pieces of legislation—and criteria related to it like (not)replacing decisions made by the elected branches or (lack of) deference—are over inclusive indicators that not always capture cases of judicial activism and non-activism, respectively (Hein, 2020, pp. 198–199). Even more, the existence of a judicial judgment is not a prerequisite to talk about judicial (non)activism. As Hein has aptly shown in the European context, there have been cases of judicial activism when courts have refrained from adjudicating on amendments when they are supposed to do so and, similarly, examples of non-activism in those events in which courts have properly decided not to intervene in amendment-related cases (Hein, 2020, pp. 197–199). Judicial activism in the absence of a ruling on the merits, is an intriguing new avenue of research that compels us to rethink prevailing ideas of judicial activism.

References

Activismo Judicial. (2017). In S. Muñoz Machado (Ed.), *Diccionario panhispánico del español jurídico: Vol. 1 A-F.* Santillana.

Acto Legislativo 1. (2016).

Acto Legislativo 2. (2003).

Alexy, R. (1986). *Theorie der Grundrechte.* Suhrkamp.

Bulygin, E. (1992). On norms of competence. In C. Bernal, C. Huerta, T. Mazzarese, J. J. Moreos, P. E. Navarro, & S. L. Paulson (Eds.), *Essays in legal philosophy*. Oxford University Press (Publicado originalmente en 1992).

Cajas-Sarria, M. A. (2017). Judicial review of constitutional amendments in Colombia: A political and historical perspective, 1955–2016. *The Theory and Practice of Legislation*, 5(3), 245–275. https://doi.org/10.1080/20508840.2017.1407397

Canon, B. C. (1983). Defining the dimensions of judicial activism. *Judicature*, 66(5), 236–247.

Casey, N. (2016, November 24). Colombia and FARC sign new peace deal, this time skipping voters. *The New York Times.* https://www.nytimes.com/2016/11/24/world/americas/colombia-juan-manuel-santos-peace-deal-farc.html

Cepeda Espinosa, M. J., & Landau, D. (2017). *Colombian constitutional law: Leading cases* (1st ed.). Oxford University Press.

Cobb, J. S., & Casey, N. (2016, October 2). Colombia peace deal is defeated, leaving a nation in shock. *The New York Times*. https://www.nytimes.com/2016/10/03/world/colombia-peace-deal-defeat.html

Coleman v. Miller, 307 U.S. 433 (Supreme Court of the United States 1939).

Constitución Política de Colombia. (1991). http://www.secretariasenado.gov.co/senado/basedoc/constitucion_politica_1991.html

de Almeida Ribeiro, G. (2015). Judicial activism and fidelity to law. In L. P. Coutinho, M. La Torre, & S. D. Smith (Eds.), *Judicial activism: An interdisciplinary approach to the American and European experiences* (pp. 31–46). Springer International Publishing. https://doi.org/10.1007/978-3-319-18549-1_4

Dissenting vote of Justice Antonio Lizarazo to Sentencia C-332/2017, (Corte Constitucional de Colombia 2017).

Durán Smela, D., & Cruz Gutiérrez, D. (2021). El "fast track": ¿un mecanismo de flexibilización de la Constitución de 1991? *Revista Derecho del Estado*, *48*, 3–29. https://doi.org/10.18601/01229893.n48.01

Escobar Torres, S., Hernández Vargas, L. M., & Salcedo Franco, C. M. (2013). El juez constitucional como garante de los derechos sociales en Colombia una mirada crítica al activismo judicial de la Corte Constitucional Colombiana. *Universitas Estudiantes*, *10*, 121–151.

Ferrer Beltrán, J. (2000). *Las normas de competencia. Un aspecto de la dinámica jurídica*. Boletín Oficial del Estado – Centro de Estudios Políticos y Constitucionales.

Gamboa, L. (2017). Opposition at the margins: Strategies against the Erosion of democracy in Colombia and Venezuela. *Comparative Politics*, 49(4), 457–477.

Garcia-Jaramillo, S., & Currea-Moncada, D. (2020). The Colombian tale of two legal revolutions. *Cornell International Law Journal*, *53*, 1–24.

Gómez Pinto, L. R. (2012). *El juez de las políticas públicas*. Pontificia Universidad Javeriana – Ibáñez.

González-Jácome, J. (2016). Courts and public opinion: The Colombian peace process and the substitution of the constitution doctrine. *I·CONnect. Blog of the International Journal of Constitutional Law*. http://www.iconnectblog.com/courts-and-public-opinion-the-colombian-peace-process-and-the-substitution-of-the-constitution-doctrine/

Harwood, S. (1992). *Judicial activism: A restrained defense* [PhD Thesis]. Cornell University.

Hein, M. (2020). The least dangerous branch?: Constitutional review of constitutional amendments in Europe. In M. Belov (Ed.), *Courts, politics and constitutional law: Judicialization of politics and politicization of the judiciary* (pp. 187–205). Routledge. https://www.taylorfrancis.com/chapters/edit/10.4324/9780429297069-11/least-dangerous-branch-michael-hein

Holland, K. M. (1991). Introduction. In K. M. Holland (Ed.), *Judicial activism in comparative perspective* (pp. 1–11). Palgrave Macmillan UK. https://doi.org/10.1007/978-1-349-11774-1_1

Itoh, H. (1990). Judicial review and judicial activism in Japan the constitution of Japan – the fifth decade: III. Judicial review. *Law and Contemporary Problems*, 53(1), 169–180.

Itoh, H. (1991). Judicial activism in Japan. In K. M. Holland (Ed.), *Judicial activism in comparative perspective* (pp. 189–201). Palgrave Macmillan UK. https://doi.org/10.1007/978-1-349-11774-1_11

Jacobsohn, G. J. (1991). Judicial activism in Israel. In K. M. Holland (Ed.), *Judicial activism in comparative perspective* (pp. 90–116). Palgrave Macmillan UK. https://doi.org/10.1007/978-1-349-11774-1_6

Judicial Activism. (1999). In B. A. Garner (Ed.), *Black's law dictionary* (7th ed.). West Group.

Kmiec, K. D. (2004). The origin and current meanings of "Judicial Activism." *California Law Review, 92*(5), 1441–1478. https://doi.org/10.2307/3481421

La Torre, M. (2015). Between nightmare and noble dream: Judicial activism and legal theory. In L. P. Coutinho, M. La Torre, & S. D. Smith (Eds.), *Judicial activism: An interdisciplinary approach to the American and European experiences* (pp. 3–13). Springer International Publishing. https://doi.org/10.1007/978-3-319-18549-1_1

Laise, L. D. (2020). ¿Puede la expansión del derecho al acceso a la justicia potenciar al activismo judicial? *Anuario Iberoamericano de Justicia Constitucional, 24*(1), 147–173. https://doi.org/10.18042/cepc/aijc24.05

Landau, D. (2010). Political institutions and judicial role in comparative constitutional law. *Harvard International Law Journal.* https://ssrn.com/abstract=1774915

Las Seis Críticas del Uribismo al Fallo del Fast Track. (2016, December 15). *Semana.* https://www.semana.com/nacion/articulo/centro-democratico-critica-fallo-de-la-corte-constitucional/509609/

Lozada, A. (2018). Activismo judicial y derechos sociales: Un enfoque postpositivista. *Doxa. Cuadernos de Filosofía del Derecho, 41*, 211–226. https://doi.org/10.14198/DOXA2018.41.11

Maraniello, P. A. (2012). El activismo judicial, una herramienta de protección constitucional. *Tla-melaua: revista de ciencias sociales*, 5(32), 46–83.

Marshall, W. P. (2002). Conservatives and the seven sins of judicial activism. *University of Colorado Law Review, 73*, 1217.

Mayka, L. R. (2016). Delegative democracy revisited: Colombia's surprising resilience. *Journal of Democracy, 27*(3), 139–147. https://doi.org/10.1353/jod.2016.0050

Peña, E. (2017, May 22). 'La Corte Constitucional puso en jaque el acuerdo de paz': De la Calle. *El Tiempo.* https://www.eltiempo.com/politica/proceso-de-paz/humberto-de-la-calle-dice-que-corte-constitucional-puso-en-jaque-el-acuerdo-de-paz-90528

Placani, A. (2017). Constitutive and regulative rules: A dispute and a resolution. *Phenomenology and Mind, 13*, 56–62. https://doi.org/10.13128/Phe_Mi-22429

Pulido-Ortíz, F. E. (2017). La validez de los procedimientos de reforma constitucional fast track. *International Law: Revista Colombiana de Derecho Internacional, 15*(30), 151–184. https://doi.org/10.11144/Javeriana.il15-30.vprc

Pulido Ortiz, F. E. (2019). 'Rule of law' y activismo judicial. *Ámbito Jurídico.* https://www.ambitojuridico.com/noticias/analisis/constitucional-y-derechos-humanos/rule-law-y-activismo-judicial

Pulido-Ortiz, F. E., & Rivas-Robledo, P. (2017). La Rigidez Constitucional como Condición de Validez en el Derecho Colombiano. In J. A. Escobar Solano (Ed.), *Acciones Legislativas: Una Aproximación Multivalente del Papel del Legislativo Frente a los Desafíos de Colombia* (Vol. 4). CAEL (Centro de Altos Estudios Legislativos). https://www.researchgate.net/publication/331699406_La_rigidez_constitucional_como_condicion_de_validez_en_el_derecho_colombiano

Quinche Ramírez, M. F. (2009). *Derecho constitucional colombiano de la Carta de 1991 y sus reformas* (3rd ed.). Editorial Universidad del Rosario.

Racimo, F. M. (2015). El Activismo Judicial sus Orígenes y su Recepción en la Doctrina Nacional. *Revista Jurídica de La Universidad de San Andrés, 2*, 101–181.

Redacción El Tiempo. (2004a, April 9). Piden Anular Fallo de Estatuto. *El Tiempo*. https://www.eltiempo.com/archivo/documento/MAM-1542079

Redacción El Tiempo. (2004b, August 31). Corte Tumbó Paquete Antiterrorista. *El Tiempo*. https://www.eltiempo.com/archivo/documento/MAM-1550906

Rodríguez, M. (2005). *Minorías, acción pública de inconstitucionalidad y democracia deliberativa*. Universidad Externado de Colombia.

Roznai, Y. (2017). *Unconstitutional constitutional amendments: The limits of amendment powers* (1st ed.). Oxford University Press.

Saffon, M., & García-Villegas, M. (2011). Derechos sociales y activismo judicial: La dimensión fáctica del activismo judicial en derechos sociales en Colombia. *Estudios Socio-Jurídicos, 13*(1), 75–107.

Samuel, Kot S. R. L., Fallos241:291 (Corte Suprema de Justicia de la Nación Argentina 1958).

Schlesinger, A. M. (1947, January). The Supreme Court. *Fortune, XXXV*(1), 73–204.

Schubert, G. (1965). Judicial policy making: The political role of courts. In D. F. Forte (Ed.), *The Supreme Court in American politics: Judicial activism vs. Judicial restraint (Problems in political science)* (pp. 131–135). Heath.

Searle, J. R. (1969). *Speech acts: An essay in the philosophy of language*. Cambridge University Press.

Searle, J. R. (1995). *The construction of social reality*. The Free Press. A Division of Simon & Schuster Inc.

Searle, J. R. (2010). *Making the social world: The structure of human civilization*. Oxford University Press.

Searle, J. R. (2018). Constitutive rules. *Argumenta – Journal of Analytic Philosophy, 4*(1), 51–54. https://doi.org/10.14275/2465-2334/20187.sea

Sentencia C-285/16 (Corte Constitucional de Colombia 2016).

Sentencia C-332/17 (Corte Constitucional de Colombia 2017).

Sentencia C-373/16 (Corte Constitucional de Colombia 2016).

Sentencia C-551/03 (Corte Constitucional de Colombia 2003).

Sentencia C-699/16 (Corte Constitucional de Colombia 2016).

Sentencia C-816 (Corte Constitucional de Colombia 2004).

Sentencia del 5 de mayo de 1978 (Corte Suprema de Justicia de Colombia 1978).

Siri, Ángel, Fallos 239:459 (Corte Suprema de Justicia de la Nación Argentina 1957).

Smith, S. D. (2015). Judicial activism and "Reason." In L. P. Coutinho, M. La Torre, & S. D. Smith (Eds.), *Judicial activism: An interdisciplinary approach to the American and European experiences* (pp. 21–30). Springer International Publishing. https://doi.org/10.1007/978-3-319-18549-1_3

Spaak, T. (2003). *Norms that confer competence*. Social Science Research Network. https://papers.ssrn.com/abstract=411186

Spaak, T. (2009). Explicating the concept of legal competence. In J. C. Hage & D. von der Pfordten (Eds.), *Concepts in law* (pp. 67–80). Springer Netherlands. https://doi.org/10.1007/978-90-481-2982-9_5

Stone, G. R. (2011). Selective judicial activism. *Texas Law Review*, 89, 1423–1431.

Terpan, F., & Saurugger, S. (2018). Assessing judicial activism of the CJEU the case of the court's defence procurement rulings. *Journal of European Integration*, 1–19. https://doi.org/10.1080/07036337.2018.1537268

Villa Rosas, G. (2018). Prescribir y definir. Cuatro tesis para una teoría de la competencia jurídica. *Revus. Journal for Constitutional Theory and Philosophy of Law/Revija za ustavno teorijo in filozofijo prava*, 36, 111–141. https://doi.org/10.4000/revus.4950

Villalobos, M. F. (2015). El nuevo protagonismo de los jueces: Una propuesta para el análisis del activismo judicial. *Revista de Derecho Universidad Católica Del Norte*, 22(2), 173–198.

Waltman, J. (2015). *Principled judicial restraint: A case against activism*. Palgrave Pivot. https://doi.org/10.1057/9781137486967

Young, K. G. (2010). A typology of economic and social rights adjudication: Exploring the catalytic function of judicial review. *International Journal of Constitutional Law*, 8(3), 385–420. https://doi.org/10.1093/icon/moq029

Zarbiyev, F. (2012). Judicial activism in international law—A conceptual framework for analysis. *Journal of International Dispute Settlement*, 3(2), 247–278. https://doi.org/10.1093/jnlids/ids005

· 7 ·

ACCOUNTABILITY FUNCTION AND RIGHTS REALIZATION: AN EXAMINATION OF COSTA RICA'S ASSERTIVE APEX COURT

Bruce M. Wilson

In 2010, the Constitutional Chamber of the Costa Rican Supreme Court ('Sala Constitucional' or 'Sala IV') faced considerable backlash when it ruled unconstitutional a certified petition to mandate a national referendum to amend Article 52 of the constitution to ban same sex-marriage (Resolution 2010-013313).[1] Criticism of the court's decision included accusations that it was "legislating from the bench," abdicating its proper role as a "neutral conflict-adjudicator," and thus engaging in "judicial activism." This, though, was not the first time that the court had ruled in a manner that appeared to contradict popular opinion or appeared to " privilege" an unpopular minority group.[2] Rather, it was like many other cases in which the court was called

1 The referendum was initiated through a popular petition that garnered certified signatures from over five (5) percent of electoral register. Support for same sex marriage in the country was very low, thus the court's decision was seen as overturning the popular will of the electorate and more generally of popular opinion on the matter (Madrigal, 2017).

2 A 2010 poll showed that 68% of Costa Ricans surveyed believed that the Sala IV needed to be reformed to limit its ability to routinely overstep its constitutional powers. As well as blocking the Same Sex Marriage referendum, Costa Ricans were unhappy with Sala IV decisions that restricted police powers to search vehicles, annulled parts of state pension plans, strengthened environmental regulations for builders, among others (*Tico Times*, 2010; Wilson, 2011a).

upon to resolve intractable socio-political issues that were historically not part of a rights-dialogue, or failed to be resolved in the political arena.[3] Since its inception in 1989, the Sala IV has quickly become one of the most "activist" apex courts in the Americas (Navia and Ríos-Figueroa, 2005), ending a long-running pattern of judicial inactivity that characterized the pre-reformed Supreme Court.

This chapter details the transformation of Costa Rica's apex court from a moribund, politically insignificant body into an assertive institution that comprehensively fills all aspects of its constitutional mandate. It also reveals that even during the Supreme Court's most dormant periods, its inactivity effectively leaned on the scales of justice to privilege the interests of the dominant political and economic elite. What changed with the creation of the Sala IV was the establishment of a new chamber of the Supreme Court that was willing and able to hold the other branches of government to account, to enforce the constitutional rules for law makers, and protect an expansive range of previously ignored constitutional rights.[4] Here I illustrate the scale and scope of the expansive exercise of judicial power through three short case studies highlighting (1) the court's exercise of its accountability functions in intergovernmental disputes; (2) its constitutional rights creation and protection in health rights cases; and (3) its protection of the rights of marginalized, politically alienated minority groups, previously trampled by political forces and ignored by the pre-reformed court. Without diving too deep into the ongoing debate on the normative question of the relative merits or appropriateness of so called "judicial activism," I argue, and the case studies illustrate, that courts, even when exercising "judicial restraint," are frequently actively supporting a status quo and the interest of political and economic elites through their inaction. Instances of judicial decision-making that are sometimes described as "Judicial Activism" are often required for purposes of protecting rights.

The Costa Rican apex court spent almost 170 years in an inactive slumber during which it abrogated its role as constitutional umpire, allowing political

3 This was the case, for example, for the issue of presidential reelection (Resolution 02771-2003); the North America Free Trade Agreement with Central America (Resolution 9469-07); and the long running disagreement on the legalization of In Vitro Fertilization treatments (Resolution 1323-96). All were hot-button issues that the popularly elected branches had failed to resolve.

4 Indeed, the Sala IV's jurisprudence has constructed new constitutional rights that are not explicitly delineated in the 1949 Constitution, including a right to health that subsequently became one of the most frequently litigated rights (Wilson, 2011b).

elites to adjudicate the constitutionality of their own actions. It also consistently supported a tyranny of the majority in deciding which groups' constitutional rights should be protected, and which groups' rights left unprotected. This long period of inactivity underwent a rapid transformation towards an activist court starting in 1989. In this chapter, a brief overview of Costa Rica's political and economic context is offered, followed by a short history of the courts up to the reforms of the 1980s, which opened the court as a legal opportunity structure (Wilson and Rodriguez, 2006; Wilson and Gianella, 2019). The three case studies then illustrate the reformed court's activity and impact before the chapter's conclusions are presented.

Democracy in Costa Rica

Costa Rica is a small, middle-income country situated on the Central American isthmus between Nicaragua to the north, Panama to the south, and with extensive Caribbean and Pacific coastlines. It was, along with the rest of Central America, a Spanish colonial possession until the early 19th century. Unlike its neighbors, though, its geographic isolation made it a political and commercial backwater that fostered considerable political autonomy and attracted few colonial settlers. In the post-independence period, democracy took root slowly and sporadically, and was finally fully consolidated after the short 1948 civil war and the promulgation of the 1949 Constitution. Since the first post-civil war general election in 1953, presidents and all 57 members elected to the single-chamber legislative assembly have been democratically elected in quadrennial elections that are among the freest and fairest in the Americas (Wilson, 1998). As a result, Costa Rica is generally regarded as one of the most democratic countries in the world and (Freedom House, 2022), is the only "consolidated democracy" in Central America (Bertelsmann Status Index, 2021), a country with "high-performing democratic endurance in a democratically weak subregion" (IDEA, 2020).

Compared to its Central American neighbors, Costa Rica is not just a notable democratic success story, but also "a success story in terms of development," "a global leader for its environmental policies and accomplishments," and a country with "one of the lowest poverty rates in Latin America" (World Bank, 2021). The country's Human Development Index (HDI) rank is consistently and significantly higher than countries at similar level of economic development (UNDP, 2020). Another notable difference is Article 12 of the 1949 Constitution that prohibits the maintenance of a standing army, which freed up resources for the development of one of the most expansive social welfare systems in the Americas (Wilson, 1998). Citizens, for example, enjoy universal access to health care and free mandatory education, which help the country enjoy socio-economic development levels similar to much more developed countries (OECD, 2017; Rodriguez et al., 2018). Finally, good governance, the rule of law, and low levels of corruption,[5] rare in the region, are the norm in Costa Rica as "anticorruption laws are generally well enforced" (Freedom House, 2022).

Legal Foundations

Stotzky (2003, 198–199) notes the "paucity of research on the role courts" in Latin America, which reflects researchers' well-placed lack of interest in courts because they historically played a "minor, if not irrelevant" role in the region (Correa Sutil, 1999, p. 256). Compounding the lack of interest is that historically, superior courts were originally designed to hamper significant economic, political, and social reform and acted as political ciphers with little political independence from the ruling elites (Hirschl, 2004). High levels of deference to the executive and/or legislative branches gave courts little interest in holding those branches to account or ensuring their actions were within the permissible limits imposed by the constitution (Gloppen et al., 2010). Courts, then, were designed as a barrier to the enforcement of rights, and through their jurisprudence they frequently protected existing political economic and social elites' power and interests while "exacerbating the powerlessness of more marginalized social groups" (Wilson 2011b, p. 452). Thus, even though many Latin American constitutions granted courts judicial review powers and accountability functions, those powers remained largely unused, rendering constitutions little more than "parchment barriers, ineffective against political power" (Epp 1998, p. 197).

Latin American constitutions' delineation of expansive individual and collective rights, tended to be viewed as "aspirational" rights that reflect a country's future ambition. Aspirational or "third generation" rights, it is argued, should not be justiciable rights claimable and enforced through litigation because as positive rights they are imprecisely defined, beyond judges' expertise to adjudicate, and expensive to achieve (Trispiotis, 2010). Costa Rica's current 1949 constitution contains many such rights including traditional rights, such

5 It is regularly classified as the third least corrupt country in Latin America behind Chile and Uruguay (Transparency International, 2020; Mungiu-Pippidi and Johnston, 2017).

as freedom from slavery (Article 20), freedom of movement (Article 22), freedom of speech (Article 28), property rights (Article 45), freedom of association (Article 25), freedom of peacefully assemble (Article 26), the protection of life (Article 21), and equal treatment before the law (Article 33). Also, like many Latin American constitutions, Costa Rica's constitution contains many positive rights including social, economic, and cultural rights. Welfare rights (Article 50), protection for mothers, children, elderly, and people with disabilities (Articles 51 and 55), social security rights (Article 73), free education (Article 78), etc. are all defined in the document. But these constitutional rights remained non-justiciable aspirational rights that had little effective impact until the 1989 creation of the constitutional chamber of the Supreme Court.

The Apex Court before and after the Creation of the Sala IV

Gonzalez-Ocantos (2021) notes that "In the aftermath of the third wave of democratization, Latin American courts left behind decades of subservience, conservatism, and irrelevance, to become central political players." Although Costa Rica was already a well-functioning democracy, this description correctly captures Costa Rica's superior court transformation as a consequence of the 1989 judicial reform. The Apex court changed from an inactive, moribund, politically irrelevant institution that declined to hold popularly elected leaders to account and largely ignored claims to enforce trampled constitutional rights. This section presents a brief historical overview of Costa Rican courts and constitutions before examining the creation of the Sala IV, and the metamorphosis of the behavior of the apex court over the last 30 years.

In the mid-1980s, a series of major corruption scandals implicated a Supreme Court magistrate and sparked a congressional investigation in which the final report proposed institutional reforms in the judiciary to create a more effective, up-to-date form of constitutional adjudication (Hernández, 2007).[6] The 1989 reform was a simple amendment of Articles 10, 48, 105, and 128 of the 1949 Constitution, adding a new seven-member constitutional chamber to the Costa Rican Supreme Court's existing three chambers.[7] Alex Solís Fallas,

6 A detailed history of the creation of the Sala IV can be found in Murillo (1994), Hernández (2007, 2009), Wilson (2007, 2011a), and Rodríguez (2011)

7 See Ley No. 7128, Reforma Constitucional (Creación de la Sala Constitucional) [Constitutional Amendment (Creation of the Constitutional Chamber)] (Costa Rica, Aug.

a leading scholar of Costa Rican constitutional law, notes that the creation of the new chamber was a "revolution" and that no one anticipated the "magnitude, the transcendence, the consequences that it [the Sala IV] was going to have on constitutional justice in our country" (quoted in Martinez Barahona 2009, p. 69).

Navia and Rıos-Figueroa (2005, pp. 202–204) also note that the new chamber of the Supreme Court, the Sala IV, was granted more powers than nearly all other Latin American superior courts, including the power to resolve conflicts of competency between government branches and the expansive power of judicial review, where it can review the constitutionality of a bill as it moves through congress, as well as the constitutionality of the bill once it becomes a law. That is, unlike many superior courts, the Sala IV can exercise *a priori* and *a posteriori* constitutional review. The court's holdings are binding *erga omnes* on everyone except the court itself and are unappealable.[8] The Constitutional Chamber of the Supreme Court is widely regarded as one of the most assertive courts in the Americas, exercising its broad accountability function and protecting constitutional rights of individuals (Gloppen et al., 2010; Helmke and Ríos-Figueroa, 2011; Wilson and Rodriguez, 2017). One Sala IV magistrate notes there is "no other tribunal in the world that has the competencies of the Sala IV" (Vizcaıno, 2006). The Sala IV is composed of seven full magistrates elected by a two-thirds super majority of the Legislative Assembly, and a reserve panel of twelve similarly elected *suplente* magistrates who function as replacement when any of the seven full magistrates is unavailable to hear a case.

A major objection to the creation of the Sala IV concerned an apparent lack of need for such an institution. Rubén Hernández Valle (2009, p. 324), a leading legal scholar and one of the main proponents of the constitutional chamber, noted on the twentieth anniversary of the Sala IV that "in 1989 the number of *amparos* did not exceed 10 per month and the number of unconstitutionality cases did not exceed 15 per year." He argued that the Supreme Court "misinterpreted the meaning of the *amparo* and unduly limited it . . ." and by doing so the court routinely rejected *amparos* against government actions that "trample fundamental rights" (quoted in Barker, 1986, p. 264).[9]

18,1989) for the details of the reform, and Ley Orgánica del Poder Judicial [1993], Articles 55 through 57.

8 While its decisions are unappealable and binding in Costa Rica, it is, though, possible to appeal a Sala IV decision at the Inter-American Commission of Human Rights.

9 Amparo is "a summary proceeding designed to discuss claims involving fundamental right breaches (individual and social rights). It provides for an injunction relief except for those

The Supreme Court's 1989 caseload was not an aberration but was typical of the 40 years after the promulgation of the rights-rich 1949 Constitution (Wilson and Rodriguez, 2021) during which the supreme court heard very few cases dealing with constitutional rights and upheld fewer still (Murillo Víquez, 1994). As Barker (1986, 254) notes, every Costa Rican "constitution since 1859 has expressly provided that constitutional norms are superior to other norms, and that all statutes, decrees, and orders of the legislature or the executive which contravene the Constitution are null and void."[10] Despite that and the political and financial independence granted to the judicial branch,[11] the Costa Rican Supreme Court failed to use its constitutional accountability functions and instead displayed high levels of deference to the popularly elected branches. The court "exercised constitutional control with excessive timidity" (Gutierrez, 1999, 49) assuming the "constitutionality for all laws" (Cruz Castro, 2007, 557). This pattern of deference is often explained through those courts' civil law tradition (Merryman, 1985) that fostered a general lack of constitutional culture and little understanding of the importance of constitutional adjudication in a well-functioning democracy (Cruz Castro, 2007: 562). In Civil Law courts, like the Costa Rican court, their decisions only apply to the case in front of the judge; they are generally not considered precedent for future decisions or lower courts. Since the creation of the Sala IV its jurisprudence, in contrast, is frequently treated as precedent that must be followed by all lower courts.

The 1949 Constitution granted the Supreme Court high levels of political independence with all magistrates effectively enjoying life tenure. In 1957, the

rights relating to personal liberty that are protected by the writ of habeas corpus" (Rodríguez, 2011: 250). It is a simple, inexpensive, legal tool that can be used by anyone present in Costa Rica to seek the protection of their constitutional rights. Article 27 provides the "freedom of petition, both collectively and individually, against any public official or official entity and the right to a speedy response." Although the writ of amparo was created in the 1950s it was rarely used before the creation of the Sala IV, currently almost 90% of all cases filed each year take the form of writs of amparo.

10 The earliest constitutional documents did not specify how constitutional supremacy should be enforced; later constitutions allowed congress or the president to decide what was constitutional (Barker 1986, 255; Wilson and Rodriguez, 2021).

11 Constitution, Article 9: "The Government of the Republic is popular, representative, alternative and responsible. It is exercised by three distinct and independent branches: Legislative, Executive, and Judicial. None of these Branches may delegate the exercise of their own functions." Since 1957, the Poder Judicial (Judicial Branch), which is controlled by the supreme court, has been constitutionally guaranteed "no less than six percent of the state's annual budget" (Constitution, Article 177).

country's judicial branch, which includes the Supreme Court, was constitutionally guaranteed "no less than six percent" of the country's annual budget (Constitution Article 117), affording it financial autonomy from the other branches of state. Yet, in the subsequent 40 years, the Supreme Court rarely exercised its constitutionally granted accountability function; nor did it advance and protect individual constitutional rights. The court's inaction, though, was at the same time a clear form of judicial activism where the court was effectively protecting the actions of the popular branches despite the clear unconstitutionality of their actions. For example, in the aftermath of the civil war in 1949, the Supreme Court let stand clear contraventions of constitutionally protected rights of the vanquished forces including the confiscation of property (prohibited by Article 34) trying citizens in the immediate aftermath of the war in special tribunals (prohibited by Article 35), and the exiling of political leaders (prohibited Articles 22 and 32) (Wilson, 2007). While these are quite extreme examples of courts ignoring, and thereby sanctioning through inaction, unconstitutional actions by political leaders, they reflect the extent of the Supreme Court's deference to the other branches of government that failed to stop numerous actions of constitutional abuse during its first 40 years of existence. The court, through its decision not to act, effectively tilted the scales of justice in favor of the state and against the claims of the non-state actors.

Another leading judicial scholar notes the centrality of open access to the Sala IV to protect the constitution and fundamental rights contained in international human rights instruments (Wilson and Rodriguez, 2021). Piza argues that

> The cornerstone of our entire political system resides in the supremacy of the Constitution, which for us is the guarantee of democracy, freedom, the rule of law. So, everything we do should tend toward the constitutionality of the actions of all public authorities and individuals, all that being conducive to getting things done under the Constitution, should be welcomed and everything that harms it must be rejected (quoted in Castillo and Sansonetti, N.D. 334).

This new specialized chamber adjudicates all questions of constitutionality (Article 73) and acts as a court of first instance. The concentrated constitutional review precludes any lower court judge from deciding questions of constitutionality. The chamber is also responsible for all cases of writs of *amparo* (protection of rights), and of *habeas corpus* (the protection against arbitrary arrest) (Article 48) (Wilson and Rodriguez, 2021).

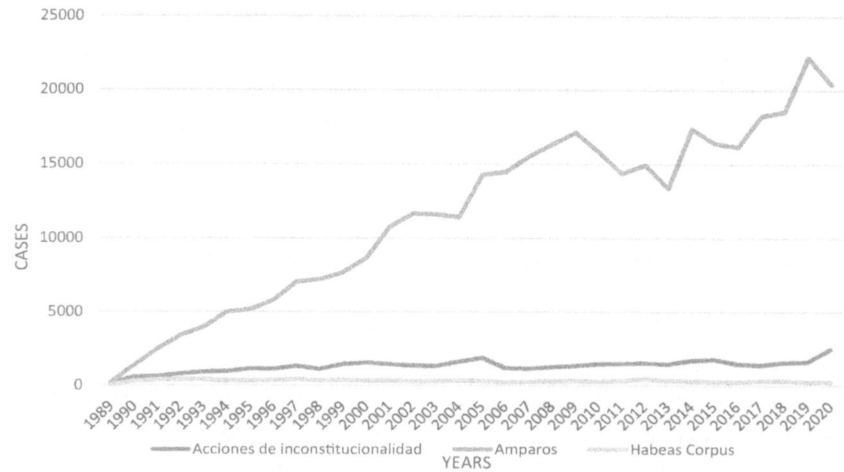

Figure 7.1: Sala IV caseload by type, 1989–2000

Figure 7.1 shows that the number of cases filed with the court rose exponentially before leveling off at approximately 20,000 cases per year in 2018, an enormous increase from the caseload of the pre-reformed Supreme Court. During the Sala IV's first 30 years almost 400,000 cases were filed and resolved by the court: these cases touched nearly every article of the Constitution. As one Sala IV magistrate notes, because of the new constitutional chamber's actions the rights-rich 1949 Constitution was transformed from "a document of formal reference having little consequence . . . into a living body of law with actual application to all levels of Costa Rican society" (Cruz Castro, 2007, p. 559).

Thus, the creation of the Sala IV ended the pre-reformed court's judicial "contempt for the constitution" and ended the Legislative Assembly's ability to pass "unjust discriminatory laws" (Murillo, 1994, 34, 37) that had been facilitated and fostered by the pre-reformed court's deference to the elected branches of government. The new chamber of the Supreme Court quickly became an attractive and effective legal opportunity structure,[12] replacing the tightly controlled access to the constitutional adjudication of the pre-reformed court. The

12 A legal opportunity structure defines a court framework and rules that create a new arena, in which individuals and groups can seek to protect their rights and/or demand private and public officials be held accountable for the constitutionality of their actions (Hilson, 2002; Wilson and Rodríguez, 2006; Wilson and Gianella, 2019).

new court rejected judicial formality,[13] the restricted understanding of amparo, the narrow definition of standing, and its slow judicial process, and replaced the practice that favored the status quo by requiring two-thirds super-majorities of the full court to hold a law unconstitutional, with a simple majority of the seven-member Sala IV (Wilson and Rodriguez, 2021).

Opening Access to the Court

The simplicity of filing a writ of Amparo at the Sala IV stands in stark contrast to the difficulties of filing one under the pre-reformed court. With the creation of the Sala IV anyone in Costa Rica can file a writ of amparo 24 hours a day, seven days a week and without the need for lawyers or legal fees. Amparos can be typed, handwritten, or in braille and do not need to state legal arguments or the specific constitutional issue.[14] Data from 2014, for example, show one-third of all amparo cases are successful,[15] while in some specific areas of litigation, the success rates are significantly higher; for example, in health rights claims the success rate can be as high as 60% (Wilson, 2011b; PEN 2015, 2017).

The creation of the Sala IV and its enabling law, *Ley de la Jurisdicción Constitucional* (Law of Constitutional Jurisdiction)[16] permitted and encouraged[17] people to bring claims to the Sala IV to protect their rights before an effective, efficient apex court whose magistrates see their role as assertive rights protectors. Access to the new constitutional chamber of the supreme court relies on a very broad conceptualization of "standing" that opened the legal avenue to anyone in the country regardless of age, race, nationality, or income; effectively granting an unfettered, very low cost, direct access to the country's apex

13 The Sala IV, unlike the pre-reformed court, takes seriously Constitutional Article 27 that guarantees the "freedom of petition, both collectively and individually, against any public official or official entity and the right to a speedy response."

14 There are even examples of handwritten claims on used bread wrapping paper being accepted and processed by the Sala IV.

15 This includes all cases decided "Con Lugar" or "Con Lugar Parcial."

16 The Sala IV must "guarantee the supremacy of the norms and constitutional principles, international law, and community law in force in the republic, their uniform interpretation and application of fundamental rights and freedoms consecrated in the constitution or in inter-national instruments in force in Costa Rica." (Ley de la Jurisdicción Constitucional, Ley No. 7135, October 11, 1989).

17 The Sala IV outreach and educational programs include websites and plain language videos that show the simple steps needed to file a case at the Constitutional Court (See, for example, https://salaconstitucional.poder-judicial.go.cr/index.php/Prensa)

court. One of the original magistrates of the court, Eduardo Sancho, reveals the changing in the magistrates' thinking on new court when he notes that the Sala IV was not "created to be at the service of the executive branch, but quite the reverse: to protect the rights of people" (Wilson, 2011b, p. 139).

Asserting Court Powers

The following case studies illustrate the scope of the new court and its transition from its historical moribund condition to being one of the most assertive courts in the Americas.

Interbranch Power: Parliament and Executive

The pre-reformed Supreme Court's low caseload and high level of deference to the popularly elected 57-member Legislative Assembly allowed lawmakers to believe their "power to legislate was absolute" (Urcuyo 1995, 3). The reformed court, though, was quick to signal that all branches of government would have to act within the limits of the constitutional document, noting that "public functionaries are representatives of a sovereign nation and not sovereign representative of the nation" (Hernandez, 2007, p. 324). From the start of its operation the reformed court declared its willingness to hear and rule on the constitutionality of actions of the other three other branches of state—legislature, executive, and Elections Tribunal.

In the first full year of operation, the Sala IV heard 129 constitutional challenges; by the end of its first decade the court routinely heard more than 1,400 constitutionality cases each year. Currently, after three decades of operation, it hears approximately 1,600 constitutionality cases per year. In one very early case in 1989, the court ruled against a decree from the Minister of Security demanding the removal of a shaved-ice salesperson from his usual location outside of the Legislative Assembly during a meeting of the heads of state of the Americas in Costa Rica (Resolución No. 75–89). The salesman, popularly known as "don Trino," had plied his trade from a wooden cart outside the congress building over three decades. In deciding against the Minister of Security, the court's decision argued that for don Trino, "the most important thing was to eat and to bring sustenance back to his family" and thus he should be allowed to keep working in his regular location during the meeting. This decision by the court transmitted an important message to the executive branch that the new constitutional chamber was willing to hear cases from even the humblest person even when they were seeking relief from the actions of the most powerful people in the country. This was an early recognition of clear constitutional limits on the actions of state agencies, including the executive branch, when those actions infringed on the constitutional rights of individuals (Wilson, 2007, p. 247).

In subsequent years the court continued to remind the executive branch of the constitutional limits on its actions. In 2002, for example, it ruled President Pacheco's declaration of Costa Rican support for the US-led "War on Terror" to be unconstitutional (2002–2006). Again in 2006 the court twice ruled executive branch foreign policy actions to be unconstitutional: first, the court rejected the executive's action to allow Costa Ricans to march in military parades abroad (2006-15245) and, second, an executive decree permitting the exportation of Costa Rican materials to foreign munitions manufactures was similarly unconstitutional (Executive Decree No. 33240-S). A major impact of these court rulings was a significant reduction of the use of executive decrees (Wilson, 2012, p. 462).

The court used its broad judicial review powers to adjudicate existing law, no matter how old, for constitutional errors during their creation. Organized labor, traditionally very weak in Costa Rica, challenged parts of the Labor Code's strict limits on their right to strike, and won a decision from the court that removed the shackles on their exercise of their economic rights and organizational capacities (Resolution 1998-1317). Similarly, journalists won a right to work case in 1995 when the Sala IV ruled mandatory state licensing of journalists unconstitutional (Resolution 1995-2313).

A major rebuke to Congress came in 2003 (Decision No 2003-2771) when the Sala IV held that Congress did not have the constitutional power to amend some articles of the constitution. The court held that the legislature's ability to amend the constitution did not extend to constitutional reforms that reduce "fundamental rights" (Article 196).[18] In this case, Law No 4349 of 11 July 1969

18 According to the Sala IV holding, the central constitutional principle concerned an unconstitutional reduction of the political right to seek election in the 1949 Constitution as well as international human rights law that Costa Rica was a signatory. Article 7 of the Constitution states, "public treaties, international agreements and concordats duly approved by the Legislative Assembly shall have a higher authority than the laws upon their enactment or from the day that they designate." Article 48 expands the domestic standing of international human rights instruments stating, "Every person has the right to present writs of habeas corpus to guarantee his freedom and personal integrity and writs of amparo to maintain or reestablish the enjoyment of other rights conferred by this Constitution as well as those of fundamental nature established in international instruments on

amended Constitutional Article 132.1 to disqualify presidents who had served a term in office from ever seeking reelection. The original language in the 1949 Constitution allowed presidents to seek reelection after being out of office for two presidential terms (eight years). What was surprising about this ruling was that the amendment had been in effect for over 30 years and had been challenged a few years earlier but was held constitutional. The court, thus, corrected a previous erroneous holding and exercised its constitutionally granted accountability function to highlight and limit the unconstitutional actions of the legislative assembly. While this holding concretely concerned presidential reelection, it was, perhaps indirectly, but more importantly, about limits on the exercise of power of the legislative assembly.

The Tribunal Supremo de Elecciones (Supreme Election Tribunal, TSE), a quasi-fourth branch of state, has similarly not escaped Sala IV jurisprudence that have limited its power. While the TSE's remit is to "to interpret, with exclusive and compulsory effect, all constitutional and legal provisions on electoral matters" (Article 102), the Sala IV has frequently ruled on electoral issues that were historically decided by the TSE. In 2006, for example, the Court ruled unconstitutional the TSE's requirements for political party registration (Article 64 of the Electoral Code). Four years later, a court decision held that a TSE-sanctioned national referendum seeking to ban same-sex marriage (SSM) was unconstitutional and could not proceed (Resolution 2010-013313). The court's majority decision overturned the TSE's previous decision declaring the referendum constitutional.[19] The Sala IV argued in its holding that minority rights "cannot be subjected to a referendum process where majorities rule." The court also recognized that individuals in same-sex relationships are a "disadvantaged group and are the object of discrimination that requires the support of government agencies for the recognition of their constitutional and other rights under the Constitution" (Resolution 2010-013313). If the court had maintained its pre-1989 defense to the other branches of state, the referendum would have gone ahead and very likely constitutionalized a ban on same sex marriage and opened the door for subsequent similar rights restrictions against

human rights, enforceable in the Republic. Both writs shall be within the jurisdiction of the Chamber indicated in Article 10." (As amended by Law No. 7128 of August 18, 1989).

19 In his dissent Magistrate Armijo notes that only the TSE has the competency to rule on electoral questions and that the use of a writ of amparo is inappropriate for such a claim. The Sala IV decision negated a national petition, signed by over 5% of electorate, that should have automatically mandated the TSE to hold a referendum on the question of banning same sex marriage.

other politically powerless, socially unpopular, marginalized minority groups. These short examples illustrate how the pre-reformed court's deference to the other branches of government effectively and actively supported the actions of elected officials even when they acted outside of their constitutional powers. Similarly, the court has acted on questions of economic, social, and cultural (ESC) rights that could be claimed to be "activist" rather than restrained, but that effectively gave life to constitutional rights that were previously ignored by the governing and administrative elites. The next section illustrates how ESC rights were animated by the Sala IV after its creation in 1989.

Health Rights

One area of judicial activism that has been regularly criticized across Latin America is the rise of health rights litigation, where judges became key actors in the allocation of scarce medical resources (Cubillos et al., 2012; WHO, 2014; Rumbold et al., 2017; Navarro Fallas, 2010). Leaders of many national health care systems have pushed back against this "judicialization of health care", claiming court decisions undermine health systems' capacity to follow rational priority setting goals of allocating scarce resources "fairly and accountably" (Luciano and Voorhoeve, 2019). They also argue that the judicialization of health care harms health care systems' financial wellbeing and consequently the health care of the general population (Yamin and Gloppen, 2011; Lamprea, 2017; Solano Carrera, 2007). These criticisms have been frequently leveled at the Costa Rican Constitutional Chamber's expanding health rights caseload and jurisprudence that tends to favor those claimants at much higher levels than any other area of rights litigation (Norheim and Wilson 2014).

The rise of health rights litigation in Costa Rica (Chaves Matamoros, 2010) was surprising for several reasons: first, Costa Rican residents enjoy almost universal access to one of the best performing health care systems in the Americas. Second, unlike many Latin American constitutions (Brewer-Carías, 2009), the Costa Rican constitution contains no explicit right to health. And third, in the early years of the Sala IV's existence, few health rights cases were filed and only a small percentage of those were successful. By the mid-1990s, though, the Sala IV's health jurisprudence created a justiciable "fundamental right" to health that was limited only by perceived budgetary constraints of the Caja Costarricense de Seguros Sociales (Costa Rican Social Security Agency, CCSS, commonly called "Caja"). This played out with the rise of HIV/AIDS and the court's response to claims to antiretroviral medications starting with the first recorded AIDS-related death in 1983. The Caja, which funds and administers the country's health care system, viewed the disease as fatal and incurable and declined to purchase and distribute any medications that might treat the disease. Disregard for AIDS patients was reflected in some Caja doctors who categorically refused to treat them in the state funded clinics and hospitals.[20]

In 1992 the Sala IV unanimously rejected an *amparo* claim from a group of people living with HIV/AIDS who had become chronically ill and who sought to force the Caja to purchase and prescribe azidothymidine to people in their health situation. The court's key concern voiced in its decision was that "the cost of purchasing the drug implies a very large sacrifice for [the Caja], which does not have a budget committed to such ends." The court argued that "to disregard certain other programs to assist those suffering from AIDS, no matter how hard it seems, is not reasonable" (Resolution No. 280-92). After the 1992 HIV/AIDS medication decision, the court gradually and deliberately created an expansive justiciable right to health. The court relied on Constitutional Article 21 (protection of human life), Article 50 (healthy environment), and Article 73 (right to social security protection) as well as a series of international legal instruments[21] that, taken together, created a justiciable right to health.[22]

> These rules significantly strengthen the internal mechanisms available to all citizens to protect their constitutional rights by fully integrating international treaties on human rights into Costa Rican constitutional law. This has the effect of placing human rights . . . . . . as a standard for interpretation of the Constitution itself and of those principles deprived therefrom, naturally affecting the interpretation and

20 In 1997 the Sala IV held that all doctors in all hospitals must treat AIDS patients as they would any other patient (Resolution No. 6761-97).

21 The instruments include the Universal Declaration of Human Rights, the American Declaration of Rights and Duties of Man, the American Convention on Human Rights, the International Pact of Civil and Political Rights and Economic, Social, and Cultural Rights, and the American Convention on Human Rights, all of which contain implied or explicit rights to health.

22 Article 48 gives international human rights treaties ratified by Costa Rica are treated the same domestic law and Article 1 of the Law of the Constitutional Jurisdiction grants the court the power to "regulate the constitutional jurisdiction, with the purpose to guarantee the supremacy of the constitutional provisions and principles, as well as International and Community Law enforceable in the Republic, its uniform interpretation and application, likewise the fundamental rights and liberties enshrined in the Constitution or the international instruments of human rights in force in Costa Rica."

application of secondary legislation with respect to such principles. (Cruz Castro, 2007, p. 559).

Five years later, in response to a second claim for antiretrovirals medications having been filed by three people living with HIV/AIDS, the Sala IV delivered its most expansive expression of its court-created right to health. The court stated, "What good are the rest of the rights and guarantees . . . if a person cannot count on the right to life and health assured?" (Resolution 5934-97). In the decision, the court built on its growing health rights jurisprudence[23] to dismiss the Caja's budgetary constraints arguments. Although there was considerable backlash from some Caja personnel about the financial burden of paying for medications that were deemed not to be a priority, compliance with the decisions was very high (Ávalos, & Méndez, 1999; Hogerzeil et al., 2006, pp. 305–311; Wilson and Rodriguez, 2017).

Studies of the financial impact of the court's decisions repeatedly invalidate the Caja's allegation that costs incurred from compliance with these decisions are bankrupting the health system or causing an unwanted re-equilibration of expenditures. Indeed, a 2009 study sponsored by the Caja itself revealed that the total cost of providing all successfully litigated medications amounted to less than 1% of the institution's medication budget (Zamora, 2010). Similar studies undertaken by other researchers, not affiliated with the Caja, corroborate the Caja's findings. Costa Rica Magistrates have noted in their holdings that their decisions were justified because "administrative inefficiencies or prioritization processes of health services fail to protect an individual's right" and rejected the idea that "access to care should be determined by the price mechanism" (Cubillos et al., 2012, p. 392; Resolution 5934-97).

This decision gave immediate relief to the individuals directly involved in the litigation and ushered in a deluge of health rights cases that currently account for the largest single category of amparos filed with the Sala IV.[24] The 1997 AIDS medication holding "served as a model that has shaped the field of health rights" (Zamora, 2010) and to animate litigation from other sufferers of chronic incurable diseases including liver disease and multiple sclerosis. The 1997 holding also helped create the legal framework for the state to provide

23 In a 2007 decision, the court stated categorically that "eminently economic reasons" for not providing patient's prescriptions would not be accepted by the court (Resolution 2007-00043).

24 In 2018, 44% of amparos cases were claims for health rights, significantly higher than the second most common type of amparo, workers' rights, which constitute 11% of the total (Sala IV, 2021).

very expensive orphan drugs such as the one used to treat Gaucher disease (Norheim and Wilson, 2014, p. 50) as well as the blanket provision of pneumococcus vaccinations (Resolution 2009-8339) to all people over 65 that costs more than US$8 million per year (Avalos, 2008; Ramirez, 2010).

Protecting Marginalized Minorities' Constitutional Rights

As noted above, in one of its earliest decisions the court protected a humble shaved-ice seller's right to earn a living against the deleterious actions of the Minister of Security. In the subsequent years many marginalized groups have successfully filed cases with the Sala IV to protect and/or establish their constitutional rights. Prisoners, for example, successfully sought to end poor, overcrowded conditions in prisons in the early 2000s (Resolution No 2000-7484), while disabled people filed successful claims with the court forcing reluctant private transportation companies and government agencies to improve access to their vehicles and public buildings (Resolution 1996-4576). The full power of the court for marginalized people's claim for their rights is most starkly visible in the case of LGBTQ+ people, whose rights were routinely trampled by public authorities including government agencies, the police, and private employers (see Schifter, 1989, 1999; Wilson 2007, 2009; Wilson and Rodriguez 2006). A series of litigated victories for LGBTQ+ people began in the 1980s including the ending of abuse of power by police (Resolution 1994-4732), conjugal visits in prison in 2011 (Resolution 2011-13800), and in 2017 the court dismissed a constitutional challenge to pro-LGBT presidential decrees from evangelical deputies (Muñoz, 2017), among many other decisions.

The question of same sex marriage (SSM) illustrates that court inaction or action can have significant impacts on an outcome; in the case of ESC rights inaction can deny the realization of powerless minorities' constitutional rights, and concretizing the power of the political and economic elite or the court's action can make constitutional rights real even for the most marginalized members of society. In Costa Rica, when a lawyer wanted to exercise his right to marry his same sex partner, he filed a case with the Sala IV in 2003. At the time, no political party supported same sex marriage and public opinion polls revealed that more than 80% of Costa Ricans opposed to SSM with only 9% in favor (Wilson, 2007, 254). Three years later, in a negative 5-2 split decision, the court ruled that the Family Code's (Código de Familia 1974) definition of marriage as between one man and one woman was constitutional. The court held that the 1949 constitution did not guarantee a right to SSM

(Resolution 2006-07262).[25] The court noted, though, that SSM was a political issue that must be resolved by the popularly elected deputies in the Legislative Assembly rather than by the court (Vizcaíno, 2006). Deputies, though, had little motivation to propose and pass laws to rectify the legal inequality of same sex relationships identified in the court's decision. While some deputies in the popularly elected branches have championed LGBTQ+ rights, little progress was made in codifying same sex relationships into law in the years after the Court's 2006 decision. The popularly elected congress proved a hostile arena for advancing SSM. Anti-LGBTQ deputies, a minority in congress, used parliamentary rules and procedures, including filing hundreds of amendments, to thwart progress on bills to legalize civil unions for same sex couples, even when a majority of congress was in favor.

In 2018, an Inter-American Court of Human Rights (IACtHR) advisory opinion (Opinión Consultiva OC-24/17) noted Costa Rican law on SSM was not in compliance with the Inter-American Human Rights convention. In response, the Sala IV legalized SSM (Resolution 12782-2018). The decision came after 12 years of congressional foot dragging that resulted in a failure to legislate on the legal inequality of same sex couples that the Sala IV had highlighted in its 2006 decision.[26] To overcome the legislative and judicial failure to address the marriage inequality, the executive branch (which was supportive of SSM), requested the consultation from the IACtHR on the Costa Rica marriage law. The IACtHR decision came at the height of the 2018 presidential election, making it one of the major issues of the campaign and again revealing that almost 60% of Costa Ricans opposed to marriage equality (AMPrensa, 2017). This case provides another illustration of the impact of inaction and action by the court: the inaction cemented the status quo that privileged the views of a majority to prevent minorities from enjoying their right to marriage established by the Inter-American Court. The court's decision to push the question to congress without any deadlines or guidance was almost guaranteed to result in the stalemate that transpired and denied the right to marry same sex couples for almost two decades.

25 Marriage is not defined in the Constitution, but the 1974 Family Code Article 14 explicitly notes that marriage is "legally impossible between people of the same sex" and is backed by jail terms ranging from six month to three years for anyone entering into or officiating an "illegal" marriage (Penal Code Article 176).

26 Four different congresses served during this period and in no congress did a SSM bill progress beyond the committee stage.

Concluding Remarks

The short case studies presented in this chapter reveal weakness in even one of the most democratic countries in the Americas, where without the actions of an assertive court, majorities can willfully ride roughshod over the rights of minorities. Similarly, without an assertive court fulfilling its accountability function, elected politicians can ignore constitutional limits on their power and bend the rules to fit their own agenda. The very existence of "inactive" courts does not necessarily make them any less impactful on the polity. As Hirschl (2004) and Couso (2006) note, courts were viewed with suspicion by non-elites because through their inaction they effectively strengthened the status quo and privileged the political, economic, and social elites. That is, when courts hide behind legal formality, marginalized people are denied their access to the courts to defend or seek their constitutionally enumerated rights. Similarly, when courts show high levels of deference to the popularly elected branches, they effectively remove the constitutional harness from those actors and enable already powerful groups to engage actions to protect their privileged position that fall outside of their formal constitutional powers.

Inactive courts are in a weak position to fulfill the role of the third branch of government as their deference to the legislative and executive branches precludes their fulfilling their accountability function. Courts are, by design, not popularly elected and therefore they are in a good position to act with less concern for public opinion than the other branches. There is much debate on whether the impact on democracy is positive or negative or exactly how much oversight supreme courts should provide. While this chapter does not answer this question in full, it contributes to the ongoing debate by illustrating the effects of an activist court compared to its "inactive" predecessor. It shows how by exercising an accountability function, and opening access to the court to even the most marginalized sectors of society, the court merely acknowledges the constitutional rights and can make it easier for all citizens to enjoy those rights. When popularly elected branches of government fail to protect existing rights of minorities or enact laws and decrees that are outside of their constitutionally granted powers, courts play an active role—no matter if they counterbalance those acts or enable them with their inaction.

References

AMPrensa. (2017). Mayoría de ticos se oponen a matrimonio homosexual y legalización de marihuana. January 20, 2017. https://amprensa.com/2017/01/mayoria-ticos-se-oponen-matrimonio-homosexual-legalizacion-marihuana/ [accessed July 24, 2022]

Ávalos, Á. (2008). Sala IV ordena vacunar contra neumococo y rotavirus. *La Nación*. Available at http://wvw.nacion.com/ln_ee/2008/octubre/22/pais1746428.html [accessed July 24, 2022]

Ávalos, Á., & Méndez, W. (1999). Caja y Sala IV chocan por medicinas. *La Nación*, Nov. 29, 1999, available at http://www.nacion.com/ln_ee/1999/noviembre/29/pais1.html [accessed July 24, 2022]

Barker, R. (1986). Constitutional adjudication in Costa Rica: A Latin American model." *The University of Miami Inter-American Law Review*, *17*(2), 249–274. http://www.jstor.org/stable/40176099 [accessed July 24, 2022]

Bertelsmann Foundation (BTI). (2021). *Transformation index*. Available at http://www.bti-project.org/index [accessed July 24, 2022]

Brewer-Carías, A. R. (2009). *Constitutional protection of human rights in Latin America: A comparative study of amparo proceedings*. New York: Cambridge University Press.

Chaves Matamoros, A. (2010). Derecho a la salud pública: papel de la Sala Constitucional. (Escuela de Salud Pública de la Facultad de Medicina de la Universidad de Costa Rica, August 26, 2010);

Código de Familia. (1974). Available at http://www.acnur.org/biblioteca/pdf/2300.pdf [accessed July 24, 2022]

Correa Sutil, J. (1999). Judicial reforms in Latin America: Good news for the underprivileged?. In J. E. Mendez, G. A. O'Donnell, & P. S Pinheiro (Eds.), *The (Un)rule of law and the underprivileged in Latin America*. Notre Dame UP.

Corte Suprema de Justicia, Sala Constitucional. (2021). "Estadísticas." Available at http://www.poder-judicial.go.cr/salaconstitucional/estadisticas.htm [accessed July 24, 2022]

Couso, J. A. (2006). The changing role of law and courts in Latin America: From an obstacle to social change to a tool of social equity. In P. Domingo, R. Gargarella, & T. Roux (Eds.), *Courts and social transformation in new democracies: An institutional voice for the poor?* Routledge.

Cruz Castro, F. (2007). "Costa Rica's constitutional jurisprudence, its political importance and international human rights law: Examination of some decisions. *Duquesne Law Review*, *45*(3), 559.

Cubillos, L., Escobar, M.-L., Pavlovic, S., & Iunes, R. (2012). Universal health coverage and litigation in Latin America. *Journal of Health Organisation and Management*, *26*, 390–406.

Epp, C. (1998). *The rights revolution: Lawyers, activists, and supreme courts in comparative perspective*. Chicago University Press.

Freedom House. (2022). "Freedom in the World 2022: The Global Expansion of Authoritarian Rule." Available at https://freedomhouse.org/report/freedom-world/2022/global-expansion-authoritarian-rule

Gloppen, S., Wilson, B. M., Gargarella, R., Skaar, E., & Kinander, M. (2010). *Courts and power in Latin America and Africa*. New York: Palgrave Macmillan.

Gonzalez-Ocantos, E. (2021). Courts in Latin America. In G. Prevost & H. Vandem (Eds.), *The Oxford encyclopedia of Latin American politics*. New York: Oxford University Press.

Gutiérrez Gutiérrez, C. J. (1999). La constitución 50 años después. In C. J. Gutiérrez Gutiérrez et al. (Eds.), *Temas claves de la constitución política* (pp. 25–52). San José: Investigaciones Jurídicas.

Helmke, G., & Ríos-Figueroa, J. (Eds.). (2011). *Courts in Latin America*. New York: Cambridge University Press.

Hernández Valle, R. (2007). Tribunales Constitucionales y consolidación de la Democracia. La evolución de la justicia constitucional y sus retos en Costa Rica. *Suprema Corte de Justicia de la Nación 2007, 324*. México D.F.

Hernández Valle, R. (2009). La Sala de la Libertad. Available at http://www.poder-judicial.go.cr/salaconstitucional/ARTICULOS%20Y%20CONFERENCIAS/Seminario_20Aniversario/005.pdf [accessed June 12, 2010]

Hilson, C. (2002). New social movements: The role of legal opportunity. *Journal of European Public Policy*, 9, 238–255.

Hirschl, R. (2004). *Towards juristocracy: The origins and consequences of the new constitutionalism*. Cambridge: Harvard University Press.

Hogerzeil, H. V., Samson, M., Casanovas, J. V., & Rahmani-Ocora, L. (2006). Is access to essential medicines as part of the fulfilment of the right to health enforceable through the courts?. *Lancet*, 368/9532.

IDEA. (2020). *The global state of democracy 2019 addressing the ills, reviving the promise*. Available at: https://www.idea.int/publications/catalogue/global-state-of-democracy-2019 [accessed March 1, 2021].

Lamprea, E. (2017). The judicialization of health care: A Global South perspective. *Annual Review of Law and Social Science, 13*. 431–449

Luciano, A., & Voorhoeve, A. (2019). Have reforms reconciled health rights litigation and priority setting in Costa Rica?. *Health and Human Rights Journal*. https://www.hhrjournal.org/2019/11/have-reforms-reconciled-health-rights-litigation-and-priority-setting-in-costa-rica/ [accessed July 24, 2022]

Madrigal, L. (2017). ENCUESTA: Seis de cada diez costarricenses rechazan el matrimonio igualitario. *El Mundo*. Available at https://elmundo.cr/costa-rica/encuesta-seis-de-cada-diez-costarricenses-rechazan-el-matrimonio-igualitario/ [accessed July 24, 2022]

Martinez Barahona, E. (2009). *Seeking the Political Role of the Third Government Branch: A Comparative approach to High Courts in Central America*. Saarbrücken, VDM Verlag.

Merryman, J. (1985). *The civil law tradition: An introduction to the legal systems of Western Europe and Latin America*. Stanford University Press.

Mungiu-Pippidi, A. & Johnston, M. (Eds.). (2017). *Transitions to Good Governance: Creating Virtuous Circles of Anti-Corruption*. Elgar Press.

Muñoz, F. (2017). Sala IV rechaza reclamo de diputados contra decretos sobre "ideología de género." *Monumental (San José)*, November 8. http://www.monumental.co. cr/2017/11/08/sala-iv-rechaza-accion-de-diputados-contra-decretos-sobre-ideologia-de-genero [accessed July 24, 2022]

Murillo Víquez, J. (1994). *La sala constitucional: Una revolución político-jurídica en Costa Rica*. San José, Costa Rica: Editorial Guayacán.

Navarro Fallas, R. A. (2010). *Derecho a la salud: un análisis a la luz del derecho internacional, el ordenamiento jurídico costarricense y la jurisprudencia constitucional*. San José: Editorial Juricentro.

Navia, P., & Ríos-Figueroa, J. (2005). The constitutional adjudication mosaic of Latin America. *Comparative Political Studies*, *38*(2), 189–217.

Norheim, O. F., & Wilson, B. M. (2014). Health rights litigation and access to medicines: Priority classification of successful cases from Costa Rica's Constitutional Chamber of the Supreme Court. *Health and Human Rights*, *16/2*. Available at: https://www.hhrjournal.org/2014/10/health-rights-litigation-and-access-to-medicines-priority-classification-of-successful-cases-from-costa-ricas-constitutional-chamber-of-the-supreme-court/

OECD. (2017). *OECD reviews of labour market and social policies: Costa Rica*. Paris: OECD Publishing, https://dx.doi.org/10.1787/9789264282773-en [accessed July 24, 2022]

PEN. (2015). Judicialización de la Salud. In Programa Estado de la Nación (Ed.), *Primer Informe Estado de la Justicia*. San José, Costa Rica.

PEN. (2017). El control constitucional: patrones de votación de la Sala Constitucional. In Programa Estado de la Nación (Ed.), *Segundo Informe Estado de la Justicia*. San José, Costa Rica.

Ramírez Flores, E.(2010). Ratifican condena contra la CCSS por caso de vacunas. *Seminario Universitario* (June 6, 2010). Available at: https://historico.semanariouniversidad.com/pais/ratifican-condena-contra-la-ccss-por-caso-de-vacunas/ [accessed Sepember 24, 2023]

Rodríguez, O. A. (2011). The Costa Rican constitutional jurisdiction. *Duquesne Law Review*, 49(2), 259.

Rodriguez, O., Morales, S., Norheim, O., & Wilson, B. (2018). Revisiting health rights litigation and access to medications in Costa Rica: Preliminary evidence from the Cochrane collaboration reforms. *Health and Human Rights*, *20*(1), 79–91.

Rumbold, B., Baker, R., Ferraz, O. et al. (2017). Universal health coverage, priority setting, and the human right to health. *Lancet*, *390/10095*, 712–714.

Schifter, J. (1989). *La formación de una contracultura: Homosexualismo y Sida en Costa Rica*. San Jose, Costa Rica: Ediciones Guayacán.

Schifter, J. (1999). *Public sex in Latin society*. Routledge.

Solano Carrera, L. F. (2007). Derecho fundamental a la salud. *Gaceta Médica de Costa Rica*, 9/2, 141–150.

Stotzky, I. (2003) Lessons learned and the way forward, *Democratization*, 10:4, 198–202, DOI: 10.1080/13510340312331294097

Tico Times. (2010). Sala IV rides the waves of public opinion. October 8, 2010. https://ticotimes.net/2010/10/08/sala-iv-rides-the-waves-of-public-opinion [accessed July 27, 2022]

Transparency International. (2020). Exporting corruption report. Costa Rica profile. https://images.transparencycdn.org/images/Costa-Rica.pdf [accessed July 24, 2022]

Trispiotis, I. (2010). Socio-economic rights: Legally enforceable or just aspirational?. *Opticon*, *1826*(8). doi: 10.5334/opt.081007.

UNDP. (2020). Global human development indicators. Available at http://hdr.undp.org/en/content/latest-human-development-index-ranking [accessed July 24, 2022]

Urcuyo Fournier, C. (1995). La Sala Constitucional: Necesarios límites al poder. *Revista Parlamentaria, 3*, 37, 44.

Vizcaino, I. (2006). Sala IV cierra puertas a matrimonio entre homosexuals. *La Nación*, May 24, 2006, available at https://www.nacion.com/el-pais/sala-iv-cierra-puertas-a-matrimonio-entre-homosexuales/4YL35UCAWVDITDK7NVSGJYPEHY/story/

Wilson, B. M. (1998). *Costa Rica: Politics, Economics, and Democracy*, Boulder, CO: Lynne Rienner Publishers Inc.

Wilson, B. M. (2007). Claiming individual rights through a constitutional court: The example of gays in Costa Rica. *I•CON, International Journal of Constitutional Law, 5*, 242–257.

Wilson, B. M. (2009). "Institutional Reform and Rights Revolutions in Latin America: The Cases of Cost Rica and Colombia." Journal of Politics in Latin America, Vol. 1(2):59–85.

Wilson, B. M. (2011a). Enforcing rights and exercising an accountability function: Costa Rica's constitutional court. In G. Helmke & J. Rios-Figueroa (Eds.), *Courts in Latin America* (pp. 55–80). New York: Cambridge University Press.

Wilson, B. M. (2011b). The causes and consequences of health rights litigation in Costa Rica. In A. Yamin & S. Gloppen (Eds), 2011. *Litigating health rights: Can courts bring more justice to health?* Harvard University Press.

Wilson, B. M. (2012). "Constitutional Rights in the Age of Assertive Superior Courts: An Evaluation of Costa Rica's Constitutional Chamber of the Supreme Court." *Willamette Law Review*. Vol. 48 (4): 451–471.

Wilson, B. M., & Gianella, C. (2019). Overcoming the limits of legal opportunity structures: LGBT rights' divergent paths in Costa Rica and Colombia. *Latin American Politics and Society*, *61*(2), 138–163. https://doi.org/10.1017/lap. 2018.76 [accessed July 24, 2022]

Wilson, B. M., & Rodríguez. J. C. 2006. "Legal Opportunity Structures and Social Movements: The Effects of Institutional Change on Costa Rican Politics." *Comparative Political Studies*. 39(3): 325–351.

Wilson, B. M., & Rodríguez, O. (2017). Costa Rica: Understanding variations in compliance. In M. Langford, C. Rodríguez Garavito, & J. Rossi (Eds.), *Social rights judgements and the politics of compliance: Making it stick* (pp. 111–139). Cambridge University Press.

Wilson B. M., & Rodriguez, O. (2021). Costa Rican constitutions. In C. Huebner & R. Gargarella (Eds.), *Oxford handbook of constitutional Law in Latin America*. Oxford U. P.

World Bank. (2021). The world bank in Costa Rica. Available at https://www.worldbank.org/en/country/costarica/overview [accessed July 24, 2022]

World Health Organization (WHO). (2014). *Making fair choices on the path to universal health coverage: Final report of the consultative committee on equity and universal health coverage*. Geneva: World Health Organization.

Zamora Zamora, C. (2010). *Los recursos de amparo y los recursos de constitucionalidad con la Caja de 1989 a 2008*. Caja Costarricense de Seguridad Social, Dirección Actuarial, working paper on file with the author.

· 8 ·

JUDICIAL ACTIVISM AS A THREAT TO THE RULE OF LAW

Thomas R. Bustamante and Emilio Peluso Neder Meyer

This chapter analyzes the advance of judicial activism in Brazil, especially under the influence of the theory of constitutional adjudication defended by Justice Luís Roberto Barroso, from the Federal Supreme Court. We begin by a historical account of judicial activism in Brazil and a profile of the Brazilian judicial system, to explain how judicial activism has become a problem in Brazil. In the second section, we distinguish between two variants of activism: an *epistemic activism*, of the sort supported by Ronald Dworkin, and a *political activism*, of the kind supported by Justice Barroso. We argue in the conclusion that the combination of an epistemic passivism (or intuitionism) and a political activism presents a threat to the rule of law.

An Outlook of Judicial Activism in Brazil

The basic structure of the Brazilian judiciary is inherited from the 1891 Constitution, when Brazil adopted a federal system of government. At the state level, first instance judges were part of a Tribunal of Justice in each of the members of the Federation. At the federal level, federal judges had their rulings reviewed by a Federal Court of Appeals (*Tribunal Federal de Recursos*).

The 1988 Constitution gave rise to a more complex judicial organization. In the states' judiciary, the traditional structure was preserved, although there was an expansion of judicial activity throughout the territory with a view to reach the countryside's populations. Each state continues to have first-degree judges (*juízes de direito*) and an Appellate Court (*Tribunal de Justiça*). At the federal level, the country's territory was divided in six regions encompassing one or more states depending on the number of lawsuits filed. Regional Federal Courts (*Tribunais Regionais Federais*) were created with that purpose in mind. The Superior Court of Justice (*Superior Tribunal de Justiça*) was also created, with the competence to deliver judgments with a uniform interpretation of federal laws. This court is composed of 33 Justices nominated by the President of the Republic with the approval of the Federal Senate. Finally, at the top of the judicial system, with the simultaneous function of an apex court and a constitutional tribunal, the Federal Supreme Court (*Supremo Tribunal Federal*) was preserved by the 1988 Constitution, with 11 Justices also indicated by the President of the Republic with the Federal Senate's approval.

The most important expansion of the activities of the Federal Supreme Court was in its powers to exercise constitutional review. Although the diffuse form of constitutional review was preserved, allowing any judge to deny application of a statute that contradicts the 1988 Constitution, the concentrated form of constitutional review was expanded and became more influential. The Federal Supreme Court can deliver general and abstract decisions holding that a congressional or executive act is null and void, expelling it from the legal system. There are several procedures of abstract judicial review: direct action of unconstitutionality (*ação direta de inconstitucionalidade*); direct action of unconstitutionality by omission (*ação direta de inconstitucionalidade por omissão*); declaratory action of constitutionality (*ação declaratória de constitucionalidade*), which consists of a constitutional action to dispel arguments for unconstitutionality when a disagreement emerges in lower courts; claim of breach of fundamental precept (*arguição de descumprimento de preceito fundamental*), which is a subsidiary remedy for the cases in which a direct action of unconstitutionality is not admissible; and interventive direct action (*ação direta de inconstitucionalidade interventiva*), which refers to requests for federal intervention at the state level. This expansion of procedures for constitutional review was accompanied by remedies that further widened the court's jurisdiction. Binding effects, deferral remedies, prospective rulings, and non-compliance procedures (*reclamações*) strengthened the Federal Supreme Court's role in an unprecedent way.

Although the institutional design mentioned in the previous paragraphs facilitated the expansion of the judicial branch, its impact was felt only a few years after the promulgation of the 1988 Constitution, since it took a while before the current activist judicial mindset replaced the legal culture that prevailed during the military regime. During the 1964–1985 dictatorship, the judicial branch played a predominantly subservient role, with only a few cases of judicial resistance against authoritarian measures in the regime, especially during the first years of the regime (Recondo, 2018). After December of 1968, when the military enacted an Institutional Act to suspend several chapters of the 1967 Constitution and ban judicial review of executive action, the whole of the judicial branch was entirely domesticated by the military regime (Meyer, 2022). After the collapse of the 1964–1985 military dictatorship, this picture would suffer a gradual but significant change. The 1988 Constitution emerges from one of the most democratic moments in Brazil's constitutional history, which embraced a commitment to change the authoritarian practices of the previous regime. To prevent the attacks on judicial autonomy that took place during the military rule, several provisions protect judicial independence and establish effective forms of judicial review of legislative and executive acts. But it took some time for the courts to internalize the principles of the new constitution.

While the Federal Supreme Court adopted minimalist decisions in the aftermath of the enactment of the new constitution—deflecting from the responsibility to render the norms of the 1988 Constitution effective—judges from other courts began, soon after the enactment of the 1988 Constitution, to adopt more proactive forms of judicial review (Benvindo, 2010). The Federal Supreme Court had at its disposal a wide set of instruments to rapidly expand its activities, but it took more than a decade for the tribunal to expand its jurisdiction towards different realms of Brazilian social life. When new nominations (especially the appointment of Justice Gilmar Mendes) were made in the 2000s, the court gained confidence in its legitimacy to adjudicate new forms of rights litigation confronting a conservative and inactive National Congress. At the doctrinal level, this process was fueled by the emergence of constitutional theories heavily focused on methods of constitutional interpretation that attempted to rationalize constitutional review—such as the method of proportionality analysis, which found a large audience in the Brazilian constitutional scholarship (*Ibid*, p. 95). Justice Barroso's influential theory of constitutional 'effectiveness' was also popularized in tandem and with his views on the role of constitutional courts, which explicitly advocates a version of judicial activism. All of this contributed, as explained in previous work, to increase the judicialization of mega-politics in Brazil (Meyer, 2018, see also Hirschl, 2008).

During the 1990s, a conservative Federal Supreme Court (still politically aligned with the executive branch) was partly pushed by an activist judicial branch operating in the inferior courts. Slowly, the Federal Supreme Court embraced the idea that it should expand its powers by making its decisions strictly binding while reducing its caseload. This shift in the court's understanding of its role can be described as a process of 'Germanification' of the system of constitutional review, by which the court took several steps to transform itself in a sort of *de facto* constitutional court, without being initially conceived as one. That transformation, however, was achieved not only through interpretive practices of the courts, but also through a series of legal and constitutional *reforms* adopted by the legislature from 1993 to 2004, which increased the competences of the Federal Supreme Court in order to prioritize the concentrate and abstract forms of constitutional review and reduce the scope of the diffuse forms of constitutional review (Brazil adopts both models, see Benvindo, 2010, p. 99).

In the institutional context that arose from the 1988 Constitution and its subsequent reforms, the rise of judicial activism in Brazil's Federal Supreme Court has both internal motives (the gradual change in attitude of judicial authorities and in the court's interpretation of the separation of powers), and external causes (an institutional design that allows a broad access to the court and a set of legislative reforms aimed at enhancing the concentrated system of constitutional review). Yet, it is not easy to understand how this activism came about. A few years after the 2004 constitutional reform on judicial process, Brinks predicted that the Federal Supreme Court's authority would not change considerably, given the system of binding precedents created by the 2004 constitutional reform (Brinks, 2011). That prediction turned out to be incorrect. Not only has the Federal Supreme Court been able to reduce the high number of appeals and lawsuits it receives annually, but it also engaged in more numerous and more sensitive political matters throughout the 2010s and 2020s. Furthermore, the court pronounced general and abstract rulings in several mass procedures that allowed it to decide more cases in a smaller time frame. Nonetheless, Brinks was right to point out a problem that would become acute in the following years: the absence of parameters for setting the court's docket and the arbitrariness of the Chief Justices in defining it.

An even more serious problem is the strong concentration of powers on individual judges, which undermines the institutional and collegiate aspects of the Federal Supreme Court. As there is no effective control of the injunctions and other sort of decisions pronounced by individual Justices, the Federal Supreme Court's Justices engage on sensitive political matters both for strategic and voluntaristic reasons. Very frequently, single Justices have managed to suspend the efficacy of statutes and even constitutional amendments for several years, without bringing the case to the court's plenary section and making a great impact in ordinary politics.

By the same token, some Chief Justices of the Federal Supreme Court (whose terms last two years) have also applied an extensive interpretation of some the statutory provisions found in Law 8.437 of 1992 (that empowers the Chief Justice, in its Article 4th, to suspend the efficacy of provisional injunctions against the Executive) in order to enable themselves to halt not only judicial decisions from other courts, but also their colleagues' provisional rulings, creating a true war of injunctions inside the court that can only be solved by the full bench (Arguelhes and Ribeiro, 2018; Reis and Meyer, 2021).

Judicial Activism and the Predominant Judicial Mindset

In addition to the incentives to judicial activism provided by the institutional design that resulted from the 1988 Constitution and its subsequent reforms, there are features of judicial *ethos* that played a major role in determining the scope and the character of the existing forms of judicial activism in Brazil. For instance, there is at least one background shared by the lower judges and the Federal Supreme Court Justices: they usually come from the higher levels of economic classes and elites in Brazilian society. According to a recent judicial census from the National Justice Council, they are mostly white (80.3%), 63% are men, 26% were born in the state of São Paulo (the richest one in Brazil), 20% have relatives who are also judges, 57.5% are Catholics, and 51% studied in private universities (Conselho Nacional de Justiça, 2018).

Furthermore, the judicial salaries in Brazil are the largest salaries in public service. As one can observe in the chart below, Brazil is one of the countries with the highest judicial salaries in the world.

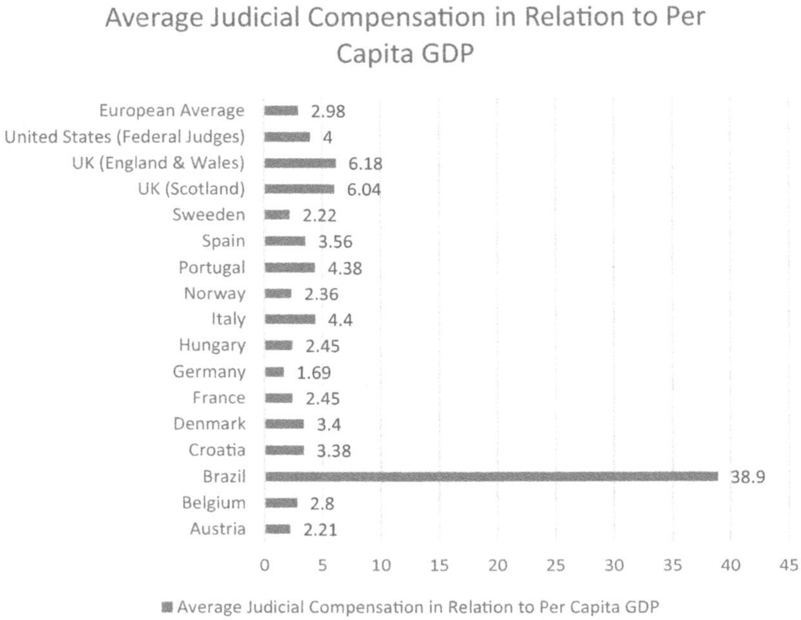

Graphic 8.1 : Judicial compensations in relation to per capita GDP[1]

Such an elitist judicial profile helps explaining the low enforcement of social rights or their inadequate application, and the emergence of a judicial mindset that is roughly equivalent to that of Brazilian economic elites. Furthermore, this elitist profile is replicated in the judicial selection process, which

1 All the data is from the year 2016. The average gross salary (or compensation) of all countries was calculated by the arithmetic mean of the lowest judicial salary and the highest judicial salary in each country. Sources of judicial salaries: For Brazil, Conselho Nacional de Justiça, *Justiça em Números (Ano-Base 2016)*, 2017, p. 60, https://bibliotecadigital.cnj.jus.br/jspui/bitstream/123456789/48/1/Justi%c3%a7a%20em%20n%c3%bameros%202016.pdf; for the USA (federal judges), United States Courts, 'Judicial Compensations', https://www.uscourts.gov/judges-judgeships/judicial-compensation; for all other countries, Council of Europe, CEPEJ Studies No. 26, European Judicial Systems: Efficiency and Quality, 2018, https://rm.coe.int/rapport-avec-couv-18-09-2018-en/16808def9c, at Table 3.20, 123 (for the average gross salary of judges) and Table 1.1., 14 (for the per capita GDP). For the per capita GDP of United States, see IMF Data Mapper, https://www.imf.org/external/datamapper/NGDPDPC@WEO/OEMDC/ADVEC/WEOWORLD/USA. For Brazil's per capita GDP, see: Agência IBGE, *IBGE divulga o rendimento domiciliary per capita de 2016*, https://agenciadenoticias.ibge.gov.br/agencia-sala-de-imprensa/2013-agencia-de-noticias/releases/9865-ibge-divulga-o-rendimento-domiciliar-per-capita-de-2017.

makes it unlikely that a lawyer from the lower economic classes finds a way to a judicial office. The competitive process to these positions tends to select young people with enough free time to spend years studying for a battery of exams that spreads over four different phases, which can take more than a year in every round of applications for judicial positions in each court. The ideology of 'meritocracy' contributes, in addition, to develop a common sense according to which judges are better equipped than traditional politicians to promote social change, which explains the fact that several of these judges consider themselves as protagonist political actors that are especially virtuous, incorruptible, and immune from the pressures of ordinary politics.[2] This is an important part of the explanation for the advancement of judicial activism in Brazil—an ethos that has gradually imposed itself on all spheres of the judicial branch, including, after the turn of the century, the Federal Supreme Court.

When corruption scandals started to tarnish the Workers' Party (*PT, Partido dos Trabalhadores*) government in the mid-2000s, the Federal Supreme Court, pressed by public opinion and by the media outlets' intense coverage of the cases, came to believe that it also had a role in 'cleaning' politics. Until that moment in Brazil's constitutional history, judicial activism mainly affected lower courts and usually concerned health rights and other forms of overseeing public policy decisions (Ferraz, 2020), instead of imposing moral virtues upon the government. The first case that drove judicial activism towards criminal law involving mega-politics was the 'Mensalão' case. It involved bribery and money laundering for buying federal representatives' support to the Workers' Party's political project. At that same time, a lower Federal Judge in the state of Paraná, Sergio Moro, began to adopt a ruthless pragmatism and restrict some procedural rights in the name of fighting corruption in a smaller case called 'Banestado'.

A few years later, in 2014, shortly after thousands of people went to streets all over Brazil to protest against political authorities in the so-called Journeys of June 2013, Judge Moro returned with another, and much more strident case,

2 Perhaps an example can illustrate this point. In a marketing campaign on Facebook during the hey-days of the Car Wash Operation (*Operação Lava Jato*, the huge corruption investigation we will discuss further), an online course addressed to young lawyers aspiring a judicial office posted an advertising material with the *motto*: 'Be a judge or a prosecutor. Be a hero!' ('Seja juiz ou procurador. Seja herói!'), to attract 'students' intending to prepare themselves for the exams. This kind of advertising material mirrors a social ethos that depicts judges as particularly virtuous citizens with a kind of moral or political 'mission', a special kind of legitimacy that entitles them to impose their virtues and their perception of the common good upon elected officials, whose activity is usually portrayed as marked by corruption and compromise.

which came to be known as the 'Car Wash' Operation. Again, the accusations involved the Workers' Party and were leveled at bribery, money laundering, and other crimes to fraud bids promoted by giant oil company Petrobras and other public enterprises. The accusations involved millions of dollars; and, again, media outlets played a decisive role in glorifying former judge Sergio Moro and the prosecutors in their missions against corrupt politics. Following several convictions of businessmen and politicians, former President Lula was included in the investigation and convicted by Moro on accusations of illegally receiving a flat, based on evidence regarded by most legal experts as very weak (See contributions in Proner et al., 2018).

Such scenarios pressed the Federal Supreme Court, which had developed a longstanding case law on criminal guarantees associated to due process of law, to make significant changes in its precedents. Under pressure from supporters of the Car Wash Operation, the Federal Supreme Court reversed its case law on the presumption of innocence,[3] now allowing imprisonment in virtue of criminal convictions pending extraordinary appeals, thus forcing then ex-President Lula da Silva to face imprisonment for more than one year (including during the 2018 presidential elections, when he became ineligible in virtue of Judge Moro's conviction).[4]

The Court would, three years later, change its case law again and allow Lula to leave prison. But this shift occurred under the presidency of Jair Bolsonaro, a politician painted as an outsider who benefitted from the chaotic political and juridical scenario Brazil has experienced since 2014.

The Emergence of Bolsonaro and Judicial Activism

Probably due to the blatant attacks made on the court by Bolsonaro and his supporters, the Court adopted a more textual and direct interpretation of the

3 Decision S.T.F., HC 126292, Relator: Teori Zavascki, 17.02.2016, D.J.e., 07.02.2017.

4 Although the text of the constitution expressly establishes that 'no-one shall be considered guilty' until a criminal conviction becomes *res judicata* (Constituição Federal, art. 5th, par. LVII), the court decided that a person can be arrested immediately after the judgment of an appeal against the sentence of a trial judge. The ruling of the court established not only that the constitution does not prohibit detention without final conviction, which already contradicts the ordinary meaning of the constitutional text. It went further, to say also that not even the legislature can determine, by a statutory enactment, that punishment should wait for an irreversible appeal.

1988 Constitution under his administration: it reversed several of Bolsonaro's most deceitful public policies in order to protect certain minority rights, struck down ideological control in schools,[5] and developed a strong case law on COVID-19 related cases that aimed at controlling the president's lethal policies.[6] In this context, the Federal Supreme Court returned to a more protective interpretation of the right to presumption of innocence.[7] Finally, the court nullified Lula's criminal convictions on the ground that Judge Moro acted ultra vires, acknowledging his partiality and a violation of a series of procedural guarantees, i.e., due process of law.

In Justice Gilmar Mendes's reporting opinion, followed by 7 out of 11 Justices of the Federal Supreme Court, the following grounds were offered to consider the former Judge Sergio Moro a biased and political judge: (1) the illegal seizure and relocation of Lula da Silva, in order to coercively take him to a hearing in advance of any formal communication, and with massive media coverage that created a general impression of guilt; (2) the arbitrary interception of telephone conversations between Lula da Silva, his family members, and even the 25 counselors who have offices in the firm that took over his defence; (3) the disclosure of the recording of a telephone conversation between Lula da Silva and former President Dilma Rousseff, which has been recorded by Judge Moro and leaked to the press in the most decisive moment of an impeachment process, and with the intention to create social conditions favorable to the conviction of Rousseff; (4) The off-duty engagement of former Judge Moro with informal acts and ultra vires pronouncements to interfere in the Federal Police and avoid the release of Lula da Silva, in virtue of an habeas corpus writ granted by a federal judge in July 2018; (5) the fact that Judge Moro's sentence convicting Lula da Silva for corruption was pronounced merely two minutes after the defence presented the final allegations, and made several comments that revealed an animosity between the judge and the barristers responsible for the defence; (6) the fact that, 'in the last week before the first round of the elections', Judge Moro disclosed to the public part of a draft of a plea bargain agreement signed by Lula's former Minister of Revenue (but rejected as unreliable by the prosecutor's office), with the aim of destroying Lula's reputation and interfering in the electoral process; and (7) the fact that

5 S.T.F., ADI 5.537, Relator Roberto Barroso, j. 24.08.2020, D.J.e., 17.09.2020.

6 S.T.F., Case Law Compilation: COVID-19/Brazilian Federal Supreme Court, 2nd edn (Supremo Tribunal Federal 2021). Available at https://portal.stf.jus.br/textos/verTexto.asp?servico=jurisprudenciaInternacional.

7 See S.T.F., ADC's 43, 44 and 54, Rel. Min. Marco Aurélio, j. 7.11.2019.

shortly after convicting Lula da Silva, the judge accepted a position of Minister of Justice under Bolsonaro's presidency.[8]

The Federal Supreme Court's decision was pronounced, however, in a very different context. Leaked conversations between Judge Sergio Moro and the Head Prosecutor in Lula's case had shown that Moro combined procedural tactics with prosecutors, gave advice to prosecutors on appeals, and recommended witnesses to the prosecutors. By the same token, Moro's credibility was shaken by the fact that shortly after the results of the presidential election became public Moro resigned from his judicial office and became Bolsonaro's first Minister of Justice (resigning six months later and accusing the President of trying to capture the Federal Police). Moro's resignation from Bolsonaro's government did not mark, however, the end of his political career. In 2022, after unsuccessfully launching a presidential campaign, Moro was running for Senator as this chapter was being written.

The Federal Supreme Court's annulation of Lula's convictions was an important measure to restore the rule of law in Brazil in the context of Bolsonaro's government. Nonetheless, it does not indicate that judicial activism will disappear, or that the judicial branch has always been a safeguard of the rule of law against the advance of Bolsonaro's illiberalism. As we argued in previous work, the 'general pattern in the relationship between the executive and the judiciary in contemporary illiberalism' can be summarized thus: 'threats to judicial independence usually come by means of external constraints that appear as a result (instead of a cause) of the ascent of illiberal leaders' (Mafei, Bustamante and Meyer, 2021, p. 785). But this pattern is not confirmed in Brazil, either because Bolsonaro 'has not managed to impose a burden on judicial authorities and still lacks the capacity to interfere effectively with judicial autonomy', or because Bolsonarism may be distinguished from other illiberal ideologies because its development was fuelled by judicial activism' (*Ibid.*, p. 785–787).

There are several examples of activist judicial decisions which played an important part to create the social conditions that led to the advancement of Bolsonarism. Perhaps the most striking contribution of the federal judiciary to the impeachment of former President Dilma Rousseff, for instance, was Judge Moro's cautionary decision in the context of the Car Wash Operation to make public an illegal recording of a conversation between Lula and several persons, including the President of the Republic at the time. Given Rousseff's

8 S.T.F., Habeas Corpus 164.493, Rel. p/ acórdão Min. Gilmar Mendes, j. 09.03.2021.

position of President of the Republic, only the Federal Supreme Court could have authorized a recording of such conversation, and any fortuitous recording should be immediately destroyed or sent to the Federal Supreme Court. But the release of the audio to the press was not a mere technical error. As one can read in the holding of the decision, the aim was to cause a popular reaction against the President and interfere in the ongoing impeachment process to manipulate it.[9]

As the Federal Supreme Court would recognize a couple of years later, the judge disclosed to the press the recording with the political aim of inciting the people against the President of the Republic, and creating social and political conditions more favorable to the impeachment process. By the same token, with equal gravity, Justice Gilmar Mendes ignored the case law of the Federal Supreme Court and modified his own precedents in order to grant an injunction to suspend the nomination of Lula da Silva to the office of Chief of Staff of the Presidency of the Republic of Dilma Rousseff, on the basis of the same audio released by Sergio Moro.[10] Although Judge Moro's decision to disclose the audio was later considered illegal by the full bench of the Federal Supreme Court,[11] Justice Gilmar Mendes's decision to remove Lula from office was never sent to the Plenary Session of the Court, and remained in force until the impeachment of President Dilma Rousseff was consummated.

The influence of Moro's activist decisions on the impeachment process (and later in Bolsonaro's election) cannot be underestimated. During the most decisive moments of that process, he was treated as a hero, and sometimes portrayed by his admirers as a contemporary version of 'Superman'.[12]

As we believe to be shown by these events, the corruption scandal of the Operation Car Wash created a propitious scenario for nurturing an *anti-politics sentiment* that would fuel radical far right and populist proposals, such as Bolsonaro's. If we consider the pronouncements and public appearances of the prosecutors that commanded the political corruption investigations, this phenomenon becomes particularly visible. As de Sá e Silva (2022) demonstrated

9 See El País, 'Quebra de sigilo de Sergio Moro é questionada por juristas: entenda', 18/03/2016. Disponível em https://brasil.elpais.com/brasil/2016/03/17/politica/1458183598_880206.html.

10 STF, Medida Cautelar em Mandado de Segurança n. 34.070-DF, Min. Gilmar Mendes, 18/03/2016, http://www.stf.jus.br/arquivo/cms/noticiaNoticiaStf/anexo/ms34070.pdf .

11 STF, Recl. 23.457-PR, MC, j. 31/03/2016, https://portal.stf.jus.br/processos/detalhe.asp?incidente=4951535.

12 Image reproduced at: Guilherme Amado, 'Moro a uma canetada de pedir demissão', O *Globo*, September 12, 2019, available at https://oglobo.globo.com/epoca/guilherme-amado/moro-uma-canetada-de-pedir-demissao-23943676.

in an analysis of posts on social media by notorious prosecutors (and of the comments common people made on these posts), the activist rhetoric of legal officials like public prosecutors and other members of the Operation Car Wash staff played a central role to produce a legal consciousness that gradually crystalized a strong *public sentiment against the rule of law* and institutions such as the National Congress and the Federal Supreme Court. An astonishing number of users of Facebook, in this context, glorified public prosecutors that were portrayed as having a messianic role that is immune to any sort of criticism. In fact, many posts by Deltan Dallagnol, the former chief prosecutor of Operation Car Wash, reflect the same anti-institutional mindset against the National Congress and the Federal Supreme Court that was radicalized by President Bolsonaro, especially during the COVID-19 pandemic and the electoral period of 2022.

It is safe to conclude, given the media strategy adopted by the prosecutors' office, and several judicial decisions that directly targeted the Worker's Party, that the practice of legal activism strengthened and contributed to render viable the political ambitions of Jair Bolsonaro, as the wife of former Judge Moro acknowledged shortly after the outcome of the 2018 presidential elections, when she declared: 'I do not see Bolsonaro, or Sergio Moro. I see Sergio Moro in president Jair Bolsonaro's government: I can only see one thing' (Poder 360, February 16, 2020).

Judicial Resistance to Bolsonarism

Nevertheless, not all judicial decisions with an important impact in electoral politics were harmful to the rule of law. After Bolsonaro's election the impact of judicial decisions in politics changed dramatically, because the Federal Supreme Court was able to offer a powerful resistance to Bolsonaro's attacks against democracy, science, indigenous populations, and the electoral system. Perhaps the most important judicial decision in the past four years was Justice Barroso's injunction to order the Chairman of the Senate to install a Parliamentary Enquiry Commission to investigate Bolsonaro's denialism with regards to COVID-19. However, the judicial resistance against Bolsonarism cannot be confused with the kind of judicial activism described above, since in this case the Court's decisions are normally not infused with the anti-liberal rhetoric and messianic tone characteristic of the Car Wash Operation.

For example, consider the following case that played a central role to resist Bolsonaro's denialist politics adopted with regards to the pandemic of COVID-19. After the breakout of the pandemic, the federal government adopted several measures to undermine state and municipal governments' policies to contain the disease. Moreover, President Bolsonaro campaigned against the use of masks, relucted to acquire vaccines, attempted to achieve herd immunity through intentional exposure of large populations to the virus, and advocated for the use of ineffective and harmful drugs even after a scientific consensus had emerged against their use (Bustamante and Meyer, 2022). Although the National Congress enacted laws to prevent the spread of the disease and conceded social benefits to enable workers to adopt social distancing, the president fiercely resisted these measures and vetoed some important legislative provisions (although most of these vetoes have been reversed in the legislative branch, *see* Bustamante & De Godoi Bustamante, 2022). Further, a minority in the Federal Senate had been able, moreover, to secure 32 signatures in favor of the creation of a Parliamentary Enquiry Commission to investigate the president's mismanagement of the pandemic. According to Article 58, § 3rd, of the Constitution, the minority needed only one third of the house members (27 Senators) to open the enquiry's proceedings. Hence, Justice Barroso ordered the Chairman of the Senate to install the Enquiry Commission, in a decision that played a central role to challenge the government's denialism about COVID-19.

The space for controversy on the legality of Justice Barroso's decision is very narrow: one can easily conclude that the minority has a *legally enforceable prerogative* to install the Parliamentary Commission and open a public enquiry. Yet, the Chairman of the Federal Senate was reluctant to discuss the minority's petition in the House and resisted the creation of the Enquiry Commission on the ground that he, as Chairman of the Legislative House, has discretion to decide whether the Commission shall be installed. This argument did not convince the Federal Supreme Court, given that the wording of the 1988 Constitution is very clear and there is a settled case law on the issue.[13] After consulting his peers and committing to bring this provisional decision to the court in the next session, Justice Barroso granted an injunction to order the Chairman of the Senate to open the procedures urgently, with a view to

13 STF, MS 24.831 and 24.849, Reported by Min. Celso de Mello, judged on 22.06.2005; ADI 3.619, Reported by Min. Eros Grau, judged on 01.08.2006; and MS 26.441, Reported by Min. Celso de Mello, judged on 25.04.2007 (all quoted in Justice Barroso's decision).

protecting the minority's right to investigate Bolsonaro's responsibility for the critical health situation in Brazil.[14]

Although this and other decisions against Bolsonaro cannot be regarded as a form of judicial activism, since they merely applied an uncontroversial provision of the 1988 Constitution, they motivated a fierce attack from the President to the authority of the Federal Supreme Court. Bolsonaro's relationship with Justice Barroso became very tense. The president cursed the judge, made false accusations of paedophilia on him, and distrusted the electronic voting system overseen by Justice Barroso, who served as former President of the Brazilian Electoral Superior Court (Bustamante and Godoi Bustamante, 2021).

According to the President's rhetoric, Justice Barroso and other Justices of the Federal Supreme Court are illegitimately interfering in his presidency, with the sort of activism that leads, in several places across the globe, to the judicialization of mega-politics. It becomes urgent, therefore, to delineate the concept and the forms of judicial behavior generically described as judicial activism—that is, to discriminate, from the perspective of the Brazilian legal order, the judicial behaviors that fall into that category from those that are not subsumed in this general description, despite the fact that they contradict the political interests of the legislature or the executive branch.

Interpreting the Concept of Judicial Activism

The Brazilian Federal Supreme Court (and some of its critics) incorporated in its practices a political vocabulary that makes it difficult to understand its institutional role, especially with regards to its relationship with the legislative and executive branches. Inside and outside the court, decisions are described as 'activists' or 'passivists' according to a *metric* that evaluates them in light of the degree of 'deference', i.e., its capacity to please or defy the legislature, instead of its (dis)conformity with the legal order.

Nevertheless, the metric 'activism versus passivism', instead of the conjunction 'licit versus illicit', is problematic because it *obscures* the *legal* aspects of the of the judgments regarding whether the decision is actually right (or not), thus classifying judicial pronouncements according to their political consequences instead of their legal grounds. In our view, a better conception of the concept

14 Thomas Bustamante and Evanilda Godoi Bustamante, 'Negationism's "Day in Court": Bolsonaro between Legal Defeats and Threats to Judicial Independence', *VerfBlog*, 2021/4/11, https://verfassungsblog.de/negationisms-day-in-court/, DOI: 10.17176/20210411-101033-0.

of 'judicial activism' should offer, instead of this consequentialist account, a more detailed conception of that concept, distinguishing between an *epistemic* concept of 'activism' (which refers to an intellectual attitude required by legal interpreters, regardless of whether they occupy a judicial office), and a *political* concept of 'activism' (which refers to a practical attitude adopted by judicial officials, when they are asked to expand or restrain the competences assigned to a court by the constitution). While epistemic activism is a rationalist attitude that can be described as opposed to intuitionism, political activism is a recommendation to change the law according to a strictly moral or political judgment of the interpreter in question.

Thus, we argue in the next pages that the only kind of activism that is problematic is the "political" form of activism, which is the kind of judicial activism that is practiced and endorsed by Justice Barroso in his academic scholarship and in his practice as a Justice in Brazil's Federal Supreme Court. To this end, we need to elaborate on what epistemic and political activism mean.

Epistemic Judicial Activism

In this sense, judicial activism is merely the kind of epistemological attitude adopted by those who assume there is a correct answer about interpretive questions in law. Ronald Dworkin, for instance, can be regarded as a legal philosopher who endorses this approach, and is consequently strongly opposed to political judicial activism.

Dworkin advocates for a strict separation between the activities of legislation and adjudication based on the kind of judgments that participants in these activities are allowed to make. There are two crucial ideas in Dworkin's jurisprudence that are inconsistent with political activism. First, the distinction between principles and policies, which he employs to delineate the realm of acceptable legal arguments and, second, the thought that the legal system does not attribute discretion (in the strong sense specified below) to the authorities in charge of the judicial application of law.

According to Dworkin's first claim, the province of adjudication is defined by the type of reasons judges are allowed to employ, which should be limited to arguments of principle and avoid any kind of policy consideration in the justification of a legal decision. 'Arguments of policy', Dworkin argues, are those that 'justify a political decision by showing that the decision advances or protects some collective goal of the community as a whole', whereas 'arguments of principle' are only those that 'justify a political decision by showing that the decision respects or secures some individual or group right'. While an argument for or against the concession of a subsidy for aircraft manufacturers is by its nature an argument of policy, an argument 'in favor of anti-discrimination statutes, that a minority has a right to equal respect and concern, is an argument of principle' (Dworkin, 1978, p. 82).

The distinction between principles and policies plays a central role in Dworkin's legal philosophy because it clearly distinguishes his jurisprudence from any sort of *political* form of judicial activism. But there is also another reason for distinguishing between legislation and adjudication. According to Dworkin's second idea, judges lack political legitimacy to change the law, because the law does not give them discretion to make policy judgments about the welfare of a political community or the convenience of a particular goal. To make sense of this claim, Dworkin provides an equally important distinction in his interpretive scheme, between 'weak' and the 'strong' senses of judicial discretion. There are three possible senses for the assertion that a judge 'has discretion' in Dworkin's thought. First, we can say someone has discretion if her duty 'is defined by standards reasonable men can interpret in different ways, as a sergeant has discretion if he is told to take the five most experienced men on patrol'. Second, someone can have discretion in the sense that her decision is final and cannot be reviewed by someone else, as it happens with the referee in a football game. Third, someone can be said to have discretion in a stronger sense, 'when some set of standards which impose duties upon him do not in fact purport to impose any duty as to a particular decision, as when a clause in a lease gives the tenant the option in his discretion to renew' (Ibid, p. 69). According to Dworkin, the law does not leave any discretion to judges in the third sense of the term. In other words, the law does not leave judges in a position analogous to our tenant who can decide whether he exercises the choice to renewal a contract, or, as it often happens, to buy the property at the end of the lease for a previously stipulated price. In this kind of example, the tenant is said to have discretion because the law gives her only a power to decide, without fixing the direction of her decision and establishing a concrete obligation or duty for her to satisfy.

Dworkin is postulating, with this reasoning, a distinction between *indeterminacy* and *uncertainty*. Given the possibility of uncertainty, any interpreter of the law can have discretion in the first sense, because the content of the law (at least in controversial or difficult cases) cannot be established without a judgment or an evaluative assessment of the interpreter. Just like different sergeants may have different assessments about who are the most experienced men in a military staff, different judges can have different interpretations when it comes to the specification of a constitutional value. Nevertheless, the fact of uncertainty does not necessarily imply the absence of a correct decision, and we cannot know whether this is the case before we undertake a serious interpretive effort to determine the right answer to a particular legal case. Although the question 'Who are the five most experienced soldiers in a group?' may turn out to be difficult or disputable, it makes perfectly good sense for the participants in the decision process to assume that, even though we may fail in our assessment of the experience of the men in question, it is very likely that *there is an answer* to this interpretive question. Uncertainty can sometimes make our task difficult, but it cannot be a conclusive reason for indeterminacy or discretion (in a strong sense). Dworkin understands interpretation, thus, as a form of *active thinking*, because he attributes to interpreters a responsibility to construct acceptable judgments in their interpretive endeavors. He assigns to interpreters the burden of rendering their interpretations objective, through a rational and disciplined rational argument.

In an early essay, later incorporated in *Taking Rights Seriously*, Dworkin claimed that this is a sort of 'judicial activism', although he defines that locution in the sense we described as an *epistemic* sense. 'The program of judicial activism', Dworkin argued, holds that courts should '*work out* the principles of legality, equality, and the rest, revise these principles from time to time in the light of what seems to the Court fresh moral insight, and judge the acts of Congress, the states, and the President accordingly' (Ibid, p. 137). Thus, when Dworkin distinguished between principles and policies, he meant to reject judicial activism in the *political* sense. By the same token, when he claimed that judges lack discretion in the strong sense, the aim was, again, to deny to the judges the right to change the legal order, with a view to rejecting judicial activism in that same *political* sense. None of this has to do with Dworkin's endorsement of judicial activism in an *epistemic* sense, because the defense of an epistemic activism is merely a claim about the kind of intellectual responsibility involved in determining the content of controversial legal concepts, while remaining faithful to a commitment to fidelity to the legal practice. Dworkin's point with the idea of 'judicial activism', in this epistemic sense, is a point about the intellectual task that we must take up to remain faithful to the law by reconstructing and applying the principles that the legislators endorsed through the enactment of legislative texts (Dworkin, 1996).

Justice Barroso on Political Activism

A feature of Justice Barroso's theory of adjudication is that it provides an explicit defence of a form of *political* judicial activism. According to Justice Barroso, judicial activism becomes a viable option because of two factual assumptions that he regards as uncontroversial: first, the judicialization of life and, second, the unavoidable need for judicial creation of laws.

By 'judicialization of life' Justice Barroso means that 'relevant political, social, or moral issues are being decided, ultimately, by the judiciary'. (Barroso, 2019, p. 113). The constitutional framework itself is one of the sources of judicialization, inasmuch as the expansion of competences for judicial review implies a transfer of power from the elected branches to the judiciary. This phenomenon of judicialization, for Barroso, should be distinguished from 'judicial activism', which denotes not an observable empirical event but rather a *political attitude* adopted by the judicial branch. While the former is 'an inescapable fact, a circumstance arising from the institutional design adopted by most democratic countries as well as from the dynamics of politics' (Ibid., p. 114), the latter is an *attitude* of judicial authorities, a performance 'associated with a broader and more intense participation of the judiciary in the accomplishment of constitutional values and purposes, with grater interference in the spheres of competences of other branches' (Ibid., p. 115). Judicial activism, therefore, is presented as a *choice* to interpret the constitution, in ways which purport to extend its meaning and scope.

In our view, the thought that judges have the prerogative to make discretionary choices while interpreting the law entails both an endorsement of *political* activism and a denial of *epistemic* activism. In effect, Justice Barroso does *not* make a distinction between 'indeterminacy' and 'uncertainty', and sustains that judges grasp the content of the law relying on the *intuitive meaning* that 'comes naturally' to our mind, through a mix of perceptual mechanisms, emotions, and intuitions. This is *precisely the opposite* of what Dworkin attempted to develop in his legal theory. However, Justice Barroso attempts to justify his views with a metaphor that is similar to Dworkin's aesthetic hypothesis (which holds that judges should 'make' the law the 'best it can be'). Instead of comparing judicial argumentation with a 'chain novel', Justice Barroso compares constitutional interpretation with a musical performance, and refers to the 'Girl from Ipanema', the famous Brazilian song by Antonio Carlos Jobim and Vinicius de Moraes, to explain the plurality of interpretations acceptable for the same melody. The metaphor is described with a hint of philosophical essentialism, but the author contradicts this doctrine in the same sentence and introduces a relativism in the following terms: 'The Girl from Ipanema, in the voice and instruments of different interpreters, retains its essence, the elements which constitute its nature, but it is never the same' (Barroso, 2009, p. 268).

The key to understand the problem of Justice Barroso's activism lies in the answer to the question 'Why is it not the same?'. Barroso's answer shows that the affinity between Dworkin's and his metaphors is only superficial. While Dworkin refers to the authors of the chain novel as engaging, together, in a single enterprise and sharing the duty to write a single novel, undertaking a *collective* responsibility to *figure out* the content implicit in the law, Justice Barroso seems to regard each interpreter as a soloist, who not only plays alone but can also improvise the melody according to his own sensibility, as we can read in the following fragment:

> 'The reason [why the Girl from Ipanema will never be the same] is that in between the work and the public there is a necessary intermediation of the performer. Interpretation is certainly undertaken on the basis of a preexisting work and musical conventions. But it is always subject to the perception and sensibility of the interpreter'. (Ibid.)

We can notice in this picture an important difference between judges and citizens. Barroso places the interpreter as an intermediary between the work and the public. The interpreter plays a creative role, whereas the latter is a spectator or a passive recipient of an interpretive product. This becomes particularly problematic because right after claiming that the judicial interpreter is an intermediary between the constitution and the general public, and that each judge can make her interpretation by herself, Justice Barroso affirms that there are *no right answers* about interpretive questions. Each interpreter has, therefore, an entitlement to her own *intuitive interpretation*. It is precisely this entitlement that Justice Barroso claims when he says, just a few lines after the quotation above, that 'if there is fidelity to the melody and original lyrics, it is not possible to say that one [interpretation] is right and the other wrong. They are only different ways of seeing the same creation'. (Ibid., pp. 268–269)

As we can see, the assumption that there is a *plurality of interpretations* comes not as a skeptical result from a failed interpretive exercise, but as an *a priori* assumption that is postulated at the outset of any interpretive endeavor, which is coupled with another *a priori* transcendental premise that there is always indeterminacy in the law. Instead of assuming that there is a right answer and that the job of the interpreter is to *find* that answer, and then *submit* herself to the law that she finds through that critical judgment, Barroso accepts too easily the conclusion that there are 'gaps' or 'discretionary spaces' in the law, which are coupled with a license to choose by intuition the content the law shall have. Thus, for Justice Barroso, interpretation is always subject to the 'perception and sensibility of the interpreter' (Ibid, p. 268). Justice Barroso explicitly rejects the possibility of objectivity and endorses, therefore, a radical subjectivism. Judicial interpretation is presented as a product of one's sensibility, perception, becoming itself a mysterious mental state.

The notion of constructive interpretation is sometimes ambiguous, and the comparison between Dworkin and Justice Barroso expresses in a clear way this ambiguity: while in Dworkin a constructive interpretation is an interpretation in which one undertakes an effort to show inferential relations between implicit principles and explicit norms, with a view to show that some interpretations cannot be adopted because they contradict other norms that the interpreter cannot deny, in Justice Barroso's theory what defines a constructive interpretation is not the responsibility of showing its rationality (like an epistemic activism would require), but the fact that it is based on the sensibility and the perception of the interpreter (like a passivism in an epistemic sense would require). That is why Justice Barroso rejects the possibility of objectivity in interpretation and defines a decision as 'representative' if it is capable to coincide with the 'social sentiment' of the majority (See Barroso, 2019, pp. 127–133, see also Bustamante, Meyer and Godoi Bustamante, 2022).

Concluding Remarks: The Perils of Political Activism

Justice Barroso's political judicial activism produces very dangerous political consequences. In the last working day before President Bolsonaro took office, Barroso wrote the following words:

> The severe critics of the Supreme Court must have in mind that the country is facing a political, economic, and ethical torment . . .. It would be an illusion to assume that the court could escape unharmed in an environment that is politically polarized and lives the tensions of the substitution of an old order for a new order. In the old order the private appropriation of the state by extractive elites was legitimate, and so were the deviation of public funds for the pocket and the electoral campaigns, the patronage, the nepotism, the overbillings, the moral weakness, and the cronyism. The new order which intends to flourish reflects the immense demand for integrity, idealism

and patriotism that has developed in the Brazilian society. We are trying to change unacceptable paradigms and push history in the right direction." (Barroso, 2018) [15]

Justice Barroso's core submission is that judges should push history forward through a more rigorous application of criminal law (a 'law and order' doctrine). This was not an occasional speech. He usually undertakes this kind of reasoning when the interpretation of criminal law is at stake. Perhaps Justice Barroso's dissenting opinion in ADPF 395, in which the court decided that (barring some exceptions) no person can be seized and forcefully conducted to a court or a police station without previous notice and a refusal to comply with a legal notice, provides an interesting example. One of the most decisive moments in recent Brazilian legal history was Judge Sergio Moro's cautionary restraining order authorizing the police to seize and forcefully conduct ex-president Lula da Silva to testify in an investigation regarding the acquisition of an apartment allegedly funded by a construction company investigated under the Car Wash Operation. This episode marks the beginning of Lula's legal fate, given that he would be formally indicted just a few days later and the massive TV and radio coverage would create not only an irreversible impression of guilt in many persons, but also an open conflict between Lula da Silva and the National Association of Federal Judges (ANAJUFE), which emphatically defended Sergio Moro's decisions.

When the issue finally made to the Federal Supreme Court, after Bolsonaro's election, the Car Wash operation suffered one of its most important defeats. Justice Barroso, however, was among the minority, and made fierce pronouncements against the majority. He claimed that the critics of coercive conductions are against 'a more egalitarian criminal law, instead of against punitivism'. After a long speech about the need for tougher punishment for the rich, he defended the Car Wash operation and Judge Sergio Moro with the following words:

> And now that brave judges breach this oligarchic pact of impunity and immunity and begin to design a less selective criminal law and reach white collar criminals, there is an epidemic of '*garantismo*'. That's evil dressed up as good.[16]

15 Luís Roberto Barroso, 'Retrospectiva 2018: Atravessando a Tempestade em Direção à Nova Ordem', *Conjur*, December 28, 2018, https://www.conjur.com.br/2018-dez-28/luis-roberto-barroso-atravessando-tempestade.

16 The term 'garantismo' refers here to the theory of Italian Professor Luigi Ferrajoli, who developed a theory of criminal law based on the strict observance of the due process of law and a rejection of instrumentalism in the practice of criminal law (See Ferrajoli, 1989). For

Justice Barroso seems to endorse a populist principle according to which judges have a moral mission to make things better through an activist judicial practice in the enforcement of criminal laws, to make politics 'purer', 'cleaner', and 'virtuous'. He provides an influential *justification* for the moralization of criminal law and the Operation Car Wash. We believe that his theory, and the kind of judicial activism it legitimizes, is, at least when coupled with the epistemic passivism to which Barroso also subscribes, a serious threat to the rule of law that can have dramatic consequences for social and political life.

The authors would like to acknowledge the funding from the National Council for Scientific and Technological Development (CNPq), Grants # 306284/2020-0 and # 304139/2021-1, and the Minas Gerais Research Foundation (FAPEMIG), Grants # APQ-02138-22 and # 00272-17.

References

Arguelhes, D., & Ribeiro, L. (2018). The court, it is I? Individual judicial powers in the Brazilian Supreme Court and their implications for constitutional theory. *Global Constitutionalism*, *7*, 236.

Barroso, L. R. (2009). Curso de Direito Constitucional Contemporâneo (Saraiva).

Barroso, L. R. (2018). Retrospectiva 2018: Atravessando a Tempestade em Direção à Nova Ordem. *Conjur*, December 28, 2018, https://www.conjur.com.br/2018-dez-28/luis-roberto-barroso-atravessando-tempestade.

Barroso, L. R. (2019). Countermajoritatian, representative and enlightened: The roles of constitutional courts in democracies. *American Journal of Comparative Law*, *67*, 109,113.

Benvindo, J.Z. (2010). *On the Limits of Constitutional Adjudication: Deconstructing Balancing and Judicial Activism*. Springer. DOI: 10.1007/978-3-642-11434-2

Brinks, D. (2011). *'Faithful Servants of the Regime:* The Brazilian Constitutional Court's Role Under the 1988 Constitution. In G. Helmke and J. Rios-Figueroa (Eds) *Courts in Latin America*. Cambridge University Press, 136.

Bustamante, T., & Bustamante, E. G. (2021). Negationism's "Day in Court": Bolsonaro between legal defeats and threats to judicial independence. *VerfBlog*, 2021/4/11, https://verfassungsblog.de/negationisms-day-in-court/, DOI: 10.17176/20210411-101033-0.

Bustamante, T., & de Godoi Bustamante, E. N. (2022). O enfrentamento do negacionismo pelo Poder Legislativo: Análise das respostas aos vetos do Poder Executivo no enfrentamento da COVID-19. In U. Silvério dos Reis, R. L. Giesta Cabral, & E. Peluso Neder Meyer (Eds.), *Pandemia da COVID-19 e Federação Brasileira* (p. 123). Arraes.

Justice Barroso's dissenting opinion, see S.T.F., ADPF 395, Relator: Gilmar Mendes, D.J.e., 22.05.19 at pp. 93–94.

Bustamante, T., & Neder Meyer, E. P. (2022). Brazil: COVID-19, illiberal politics, and the rule of law. In J. Grogan & A. Donald (Eds.), *Routledge handbook on law and the COVID-19 pandemic* (p. 225). Routledge.

Bustamante, T., Neder Meyer, E. P., & Godoi Bustamante, E. N. (2022). Luís Roberto Barroso's theory of constitutional adjudication: A philosophical reply. *American Journal of Comparative Law*, ahead of print, https://doi.org/10.1093/ajcl/avac006.

Caetano, G, Caetano and M. Ramos (2017)., 'Cursinho preparatório compara juízes federais e procuradores da República a heróis', *Época*, 27 Jan 2017, https://epoca.oglobo.globo.com/politica/expresso/noticia/2017/01/cursinho-preparatorio-compara-juizes-federais-e-procuradores-da-republica-herois.html.

Conselho Nacional de Justiça, Perfil Sócio-Demográfico dos Magistrados Brasileiros (2018). Available at: https://www.cnj.jus.br/wp-content/uploads/2011/02/5d6083ecf7b311a56eb12a6d9b79c625.pdf

de Sá e Silva, F. (2022). Relational legal consciousness and anticorruption: Lava Jato, social media interactions, and the co-production of law's detraction in Brazil (2017–2019). *Law and Society Review, 56*, 344–368.

Dworkin, R. (1978). *Taking rights seriously* (2nd ed., p. 82). Harvard University Press.

Dworkin, R. (1996). Reflections on fidelity. *Fordham Law Review, 65*, 1799, 1815.

Ferrajoli, L. (1989). Diritto e Ragione: Teoria del Garantismo Penale (Laterza).

Ferraz, O. (2020). *Health as a human right*. Cambridge University Press.

Hirschl, R. (2008). 'The Judicialization of Mega-Politics and the Rise of Political Courts'. *Annual Review of Political Science* 11, 93.

Mafei, R., Bustamante, T., & Neder Meyer, E. P. (2021). From Antiestablishmentarianism to Bolsonarism in Brazil. In A. Sajó, R. Uitz, & S. Holmes (Eds.), *Routledge handbook of illiberalism* (pp. 778, 785). Routledge.

Meyer, E. P. N, (2018). 'Judges and Courts Destabilizing Constitutionalism: The Brazilian Judiciary Branch's Political and Authoritarian Character'. *German Law Journal* 19, 727.

Poder 360. Rosângela Moro sobre o marido e Bolsonaro: uma coisa só, 16 Feb 2020, https://www.poder360.com.br/governo/rosangela-moro-sobre-o-marido-e-bolsonaro-uma-coisa-so/.

Proner, C., et al. (Eds.) (2018). *Comments on a notorious verdict: The trial of Lula*. CLACSO. https://doi.org/10.2307/j.ctvn96gjp.

Recondo, F., (2018), *Tanques e Togas: o STF e a Ditadura Militar*. Companhia das Letras.

Reis, U., & Meyer, E. (2021). Ministrocracia e Decisões Individuais Contraditórias No Supremo Tribunal Federal. *Revista Brasileira de Políticas Públicas, 11*, 402.

· 9 ·

AUTHORITARIAN JUDICIAL ACTIVISM: A LOOK AT THE VENEZUELAN CASE UNDER CHAVISMO

Raul A. Sanchez Urribarri

This chapter explores instances of judicial activism in contexts of democratic backsliding, with special reference to the Constitutional Chamber of the Supreme Tribunal of Justice (TSJ) in Venezuela during the Bolivarian Revolution (1999–*Current*). In this article, I use the notion of *authoritarian judicial activism* to describe instances where judicial institutions—especially courts of last resort with constitutional adjudication prerogatives—deliberately interpret constitutional and legal norms in an 'activist' fashion, or otherwise undertake an 'activist' role on behalf of an authoritarian government engaged in dismantling democracy and building an authoritarian regime. The concept of judicial activism is controversial, and refers to many different phenomena at the same time, making it a challenging (and often misguiding) concept for systematic analysis as discussed in the introductory section of this volume (*see also* Kmiec, 2004; Roux, 2021). However, I argue that it is precisely its polysemic nature what makes it useful as a heuristic to identify the different aspects in which a captured judiciary exercises its power to the construction of an autocratic polity, i.e., deliberately engaging in authoritarian practices, routines and institutionalization (Daly, 2017, Ambrosio, 2014).

Like other institutions of constitutional adjudication in the region that were created or reformed during the democratization, pro-human rights era (mid-1980s/1990s), the new Venezuelan Supreme Tribunal contemplated in the 1999 Bolivarian Constitution was endowed with a wide variety of institutional prerogatives—as many, and as generous, as other institutions of constitutional adjudication in the region (Navia and Rios Figueroa, 2005). The new framework was supposed to facilitate its emergence as an assertive judicial institution in a politically volatile environment (See Sanchez Urribarri, 2011, 2017). This was especially the case of the Venezuelan Constitutional Chamber, a constitutional adjudication institution that was crafted as a constitutional court within the context of a Supreme Tribunal, i.e., with wide constitutional review powers vis-à-vis the other branches of the Tribunal, the rest of the judiciary, and other branches of government.[1] This institutional design also encompassed very generous access rules, against the backdrop of a domestic and regional context characterized by an emerging culture of rights protection.[2] At least on the surface, one could mistake it for a strong judicial institution in a region where there's significant institutional variation.

Yet the TSJ, including the Constitutional Chamber, functioned in the context of a protracted process of democratic backsliding led by a populist administration, where many conditions impaired its ability to challenge the regime—including low *de facto* judicial independence, low legitimacy, and high levels of corruption (Sanchez Urribarri, 2022). Moreover, the regime's transition to authoritarian rule, involved ongoing demand for judicial support on behalf of the government, which the Chamber provided via a wide variety of rulings since its creation. During the troubling environment of the regime's transition and subsequent consolidation, the TSJ—and especially the Constitutional Chamber—positioned itself as a bulwark of regime stability and, eventually, authoritarian rule. This role continues to the present day, despite the definitive collapse of democracy and the openly autocratic nature of the Chavista regime under President Nicolás Maduro (Corrales, 2015, 2023; López Maya, 2021). This process included the Chamber's expansive interpretation

1 This less-common constitutional adjudication framework has the potential to elicit very interesting dynamics, including dialogue, tensions, or collaboration between the chambers to achieve common goals. In Latin America, countries with a Constitutional Chamber under the umbrella of a Supreme Tribunal include Costa Rica (the well-known *Sala Cuarta* analyzed by Wilson in his chapter in this volume), El Salvador, Guatemala, Nicaragua, and Paraguay (discussed by Castagnola et al in their chapter).

2 See article 336 of the 1999 Constitution of the Bolivarian Republic of Venezuela. Also, in this chapter, any time I mention 'the Constitution' refers to the 1999 Constitution. For a brief description of the creation of the Venezuelan Constitution and its key features, *see* García Soto et al. (2021).

of its own powers vis-à-vis the rest of the judiciary and other actors, and the creative use of these prerogatives to protect and advance regime interests. It was a nonlinear process (Sanchez Urribarri, 2011), but it followed the overall trajectory of the Venezuelan regime all the way from its origins—when the Chamber served as guardian and steward of the 1999 constitutional project and the transition to the new regime—to its overtly 'activist' phase to obstruct the opposition-controlled National Assembly during 2015–2020 (Casal, 2021).

Thus, I show how in an authoritarian context, where we traditionally expect the judiciary to fulfill a lesser role or become a marginal actor (or, occasionally, stand against the regime); there could also be instances of *authoritarian judicial activism* where the court becomes a key tool for autocratic consolidation, and regime optimization and survival. In an age when judicial institutions fulfill key roles in different autocratic contexts, making sense of this phenomenon becomes particularly important (Moustafa and Ginsburg, 2008; Moustafa, 2007, 2014; Solomon, 2007; Shen-Bayh, 2018). As we see in the Venezuelan case, a court of last resort can still be 'activist' in more than one way, surviving and thriving as an authoritarian institution. More worryingly, even a tribunal widely seen as lacking independence (and discredited at home by the opposition, and abroad), can remain legitimate vis-à-vis key audiences, thus fulfilling an important role to contribute to regime stability and longevity (Gerschewski, 2013).[3]

In what follows, I briefly rehearse the notion of judicial activism in comparative perspective, in line with other chapters in the present volume. Of particular importance here is the link between judicial activism and debates about the judiciary as a counter-majoritarian institution, and the broader role of courts in connection to regime politics. These two debates are useful to think about judicial activism during periods of democratic deterioration and/or authoritarian consolidation. As part of this discussion, I posit the notion of *authoritarian judicial activism*, to identify and critique episodes where high courts—especially those endowed with constitutional adjudication prerogatives—display features typically associated with judicial activism, but do so during rising authoritarianism. It's a notion that encompasses different forms of conducts typified as activism during the key stages of the regime's

3 The Venezuelan case stands in contrast to other judicial adjudication institutions in Latin America that have been singled out as 'activist institutions' that have acted on behalf of liberal democracy in a context of turmoil (sometimes with mixed results, see Rodríguez-Garavito, 2011). Key examples have been explored in this book's chapters on Colombia (*see* also Cepeda-Espinosa, 2004), Brazil (see also Benvindo, 2010), and Costa Rica.

trajectory, including abuses of jurisdictional prerogatives; the Chamber's role as a decider of salient political cases at different points; the development of binding jurisprudence vis-à-vis the rest of the judiciary, and even the open confrontation with the Legislature when it fell in opposition hands.

I examine those features in the Venezuelan context, briefly exploring the rise of judicial power during the late years of Venezuela's democracy (1990s), and then looking at the TSJ's performance of 'authoritarian judicial activism' at different times throughout the regime progression towards authoritarianism. I finish the chapter with a short reflection on the difficulties of the analytical use of judicial activism as a concept, but also on its (potential) advantages to illustrate and communicate troubling behavior by judicial institutions in weakly institutionalized democracies and emerging autocracies.

Judicial Activism, Democratic Deterioration and Authoritarian Consolidation

As mentioned above, judicial activism is a concept widely employed in scholarship and public discourse, with a wide variety of meanings in mind (Kmiec, 2004). This volume's Introduction and various chapters across this collection, have highlighted its different meanings. The implications present an analytical problem, especially for comparative analysis; different meanings of 'judicial activism' make it difficult to compare phenomena ascribed to the concept across different countries/political units, and over time.[4] Thus, when discussing judicial activism in a particular context, it is imperative to clearly establish what we mean by judicial activism and specify (if possible) how it is assessed. More importantly, if the case in question is analyzed comparatively, then it is important to be cautious about the extent to which the lessons of the setting under analysis are applicable to other contexts (Miller, 2018; see also Garoupa, 2016).

Usually, the notion of 'activist judges' transcending or significantly departing from the acceptable boundaries of their role—in a political, public-policy or jurisprudential sense—presupposes certain features typical of: (a) A liberal

4 Moreover, meanings ascribed to the concept in high-profile, well-researched judicial adjudication institutions, particularly those endowed with judicial review prerogatives (e.g., judicial activism in reference to the U.S. Supreme Court), tend to have a disproportionately large influence on the use of the term in other countries—an issue that has also been pointed out in this volume (in particular, see the excellent conceptual discussion in this volume, in Benítez et al.'s chapter on Colombia).

democratic order that is more or less functional and, thus, implies expectations about the compliance and enforcement of its institutional framework across its relevant actors and vis-à-vis the public; (b) A particular understanding of judicial authority, which informs the existence of key conditions that allow for such authority to be exercised and widely respected. This includes a shared respect for the rule of law among political actors and the legal complex; a minimum of judicial independence to engage in judicial activism without fearing significant repercussions, the existence of rules of access that allow key actors with standing to activate judicial protection mechanisms, among other conditions.

Thus, when judicial activism is said to be deleterious to the functioning of other branches of government—especially the legislature, but even the executive branch or other state institutions—we are assuming that such institutions fulfill key roles established in a liberal democratic environment and constitutional order, and that the authority of their leaders flow from electoral politics or is otherwise legitimate. Moreover, the behavior of the judges is meant to conform to the roles and normative imperatives of such settings, with judges expected to decide cases according to their jurisdiction, based on clear and pre-established constitutional and legal premises, respecting precedent, caring about respecting existing understanding of rights, and so forth.

Thus, in analysis of judicial activism (or restraint) in democratic contexts, normative discussions and empirically-grounded analyses are usually anchored in shared core premises, including the following: A central role for the constitution and legal principles, and their ability to structure political behavior and social life; a respect for the principle of separation of powers; the role of courts as neutral adjudicators of conflict vis-à-vis a variety of actors; an acceptance of judiciaries as relevant actors to adjudicate certain political or policymaking conflicts; among other aspects of interest. Usually, it is against this backdrop that we talk about the 'proper' use of judicial authority and, conversely, about transgressions; and it is with this background in mind (and the need to preserve its integrity) that judicial activism is used as a 'pejorative term', i.e., to express disagreement (or even disdain) for an unelected/undemocratic court and its rulings. Hence, for instance, when a court repeatedly strikes down legislation by reinterpreting constitutional norms or turning down precedent, and/or when such reinterpretation bends or openly transgresses the interpretive boundaries of a given norm, or when it develops a jurisprudence by repeatedly siding (explicitly or implicitly) with an ideological agenda, we say it is 'activist' because it is acting in a way that is 'inappropriate' on one or more of those counts.

However, the discussion might take a different turn if we relax some of the underlying assumptions about the regime conditions vis-à-vis these discussions are usually articulated. Is it still possible to talk about judicial activism in non-democratic contexts? If so, how do we make sense of 'activism' in such environments, and how would the term help us make sense of the varied roles courts fulfill in non-democracies? (Moustafa and Ginsburg, 2008).

On this note, comparative judicial scholars have strived to make sense of the role of courts in processes of democratic deterioration or openly autocratic polities (Solomon, 2007; Moustafa, 2014). They have noted different types of dynamics, depending on a variety of factors related to varied regime features and the different conditions that shape patterns of judicial assertiveness, including jurisdiction, rules of access and decision-making powers (*see* Kapiszewski, 2012; Brinks and Blass, 2018). Additionally, in weakly institutionalized democracies and authoritarian polities, where particularistic interests often influence power relations in the socio-political and legal realms, it is also important to consider different aspects of the informal dimension of courts (on the relevance of links see also Basabe Serrano, 2015; Dressel et al., 2017; Kosar, 2016; Popova, 2012). This includes paying attention to the judges' loyalty commitments vis-à-vis key political actors (such as political leaders, powerful politicians in a political party or movement, or other influential informal figures). Other things equal, these links can also help explain why judges engage in instances of 'activist' decision-making and are willing to go beyond what is expected from them to favor their allies (or, instead, engage in resistance with a little help from other allies, see Trochev and Ellett, 2014).

We should bear in mind, though, that a pliant or enthusiastic court in favor of a regime undergoing democratic erosion is not a given. There are multiple studies focused on judicial institutions in embattled democracies that show how courts can resist, with varied success, regime efforts to control the courts in some circumstances (e.g., Moustafa, 2007; Quansah and Fombad, 2009; Kureshi, 2021; Schaaf, 2022). Even in dire circumstances, judges sometimes use their agency, responding to shifting incentives and conditions in unstable political contexts, as is often the case of regimes enduring authoritarian pressures (*see* Helmke, 2005). In a situation of a transition from democratic rule towards autocracy, in which the court system has not been captured, it is possible that we witness benevolent forms of judicial activism, this is, courageous judges who use their prerogatives in a way that transcends one or more of the 'dimensions of activism' (Kmiec, 2004) to protect democratic rule (e.g., Kureshi, 2021, see Reid's chapter on Mexico in this volume).

Yet, the rise of courts against authoritarian rule is not free from risks (Daly, 2017, see also Bustamante and Meyer's chapter on Brazil in this volume), including the possibility that judges get used to the 'activist' role they fulfill. Hence, the path of exercising a virtuous form of activism against authoritarian rule may be desirable, but it's often perilous. This is particularly the case in times of crisis, when courts could be constrained by a strong executive and/or public opinion to rule independently (Belov, 2021). And, in any case, precisely because authoritarian rulers may anticipate judges' reaction to their attempts to subvert the law, they can engage in efforts to control it *ex ante* (See Sanchez Urribarri, 2022), or *ex post*, i.e., punishing courts for challenging their rule, or simply engaging in systematic efforts to capture a high court, or even the judicial system as a whole (Sadurski, 2019), in tandem with a systemic dismantlement or subversion of constitutional democracy (Scheppele, 2018). Once captured, courts can at best be helpless devices to hold back overzealous authoritarian rulers—or, even worse, become enthusiastic actors and collaborators in a process of democratic deterioration and autocratic consolidation.

Which takes us back to a case of courts under authoritarian rule that has become symbolic of the role of courts in democratic erosion: Venezuela under Chávez (Brewer-Carías, 2010; Corrales, 2015; Sanchez Urribarri, 2011; Casal, 2021). In the case of Venezuela, we witness a situation in which the Supreme Tribunal (TSJ)—and, in particular, the Constitutional Chamber—engages in judicial activism in a variety of ways in tandem with a process of dismantlement of democratic institutions, consolidation of a new ruling elite, and eventual transition to autocratic rule in a polarized, conflict-ridden political context. It's an instance of *authoritarian judicial activism*, in which the Chamber engaged in different excesses usually characterized as 'activism' to help Chavismo protect its rule, control the regime's different contestation arenas (Levitsky and Way dixit, 2010), and eventually help craft an authoritarian regime with distinct features, which persists until today under Nicolás Maduro's rule.

In what follows, I identify these different manifestations of authoritarian judicial activism. I first discuss developments prior to the arrival of Chávez in power—and the reform of the Constitution and creation of the Constitutional Chamber—to assess how, and to what degree, Venezuela was already allowing for an expansion of judicial power during the late years of the country's previous democratic rule. This is an important exercise to understand the subsequent court's institutional role and its attitude towards rights adjudication

(Couso and Hilbink, 2011). Then, I turn my attention to the court's participation in Chávez's authoritarian project. To these ends, I discuss three eras: The creation-consolidation of the regime transition towards a hybrid authoritarian regime (2000–2004); the judicial collaboration role in the implementation of 21st Century Socialism (2005–2012); and the deliberate anti-opposition role as a bulwark of authoritarian rule during the Nicolás Maduro years, following Hugo Chávez's death (2013–*current*). These three eras coincide with broader trends of regime trajectory in the country (López Maya, 2021), and are largely consistent with research I have previously carried out on the Venezuelan TSJ (see Sanchez Urribarri, 2022). Moreover, as I explain below, in all three eras we see different 'dimensions' of authoritarian judicial activism taking place as a vital component of *Chavismo*'s evolving regime framework.

The Supreme Court during the Decline of Democracy and the Onset of Chavismo

How did the judiciary emerge as an important political actor in Venezuela in recent decades? What was the role of Venezuela's high court in the country's political life, and as a guarantor of fundamental rights? And in what way was it an 'activist' institution, and to what effect?

As explained in previous scholarship (see Perez Perdomo, 2005), the Venezuelan judiciary was traditionally a conservative institution, endowed with a variety of institutional mechanisms to intervene in political affairs and secure constitutional rights, but not too keen to get involved in political affairs (Sanchez Urribarri, 2011). Although judicial independence had been defined as a constitutional principle since the 19th century; and the Supreme Court had long enjoyed judicial review prerogatives, Venezuela was an authoritarian state until the mid-20th century, when it finally transitioned to a pacted democracy (Berríos Ortigoza and Sanchez Urribarri, 2023). Even if the expansion of the judiciary began before democracy, the court system would not emerge as a notable actor until much later, assuming a more prominent role in legal matters and public affairs as the democratic regime consolidated (1960s–1970s), and its administrative law prerogatives were further defined by law (1976).

From the 1980s on, though, the Supreme Court began taking a more visible role across different areas, in connection with the country's rising social and economic crisis. There was increasing demand for conflict adjudication in public law matters, including due process rights, labor rights, tenant rights, administrative litigation and others. A major expansion of constitutional litigation began taking place, especially after the coming into force of the Organic Law on Constitutional *Amparo*, which created procedures for processing urgent relief claims against constitutional rights violations (Sanchez Urribarri, 2011). The number of cases rose significantly, both in first instance and on appeal. However, paradoxically, this also happened during a time of rising corruption and decreasing regime legitimacy. It was also an era of mounting conflict—riots in 1989 and two failed coup attempts in 1992 made evident the decline of the regime. Against this backdrop, during the 1990s, the judiciary began increasing its presence in civic and political life, with the ongoing judicialization of different issues (including a notable participation in the impeachment of President Pérez in 1993). Judicial reform and the expansion of judicial power became important matters as part of a broader institutional agenda (Perez Perdomo, 2005). However, Venezuela did not experience a 'rights revolution' (Epp's dixit, 1998) similar to what Costa Rica or Colombia experienced in the 1990s.[5] Despite the growing fragmentation of the political system; a rapidly deteriorating socio-political environment; a haphazard, interrupted course of policy reform promoted from discredited, unpopular governments; and, perhaps more importantly, the overall discontent of the population with the leading political class, the judiciary did not become a major leading institution at a time of change.

This does not mean, however, that it did not try, or that its role during these years did not shift and became more prominent, leading to a rise of cases and heralding times of greater judicial intervention. There were at least three key factors worth mentioning during this period that help explain the eventual rise of the country's high court, especially the Constitutional Chamber, as an 'activist' institution. First, the use of *amparo* proceedings and other constitutional review procedures became increasingly common. Although this did not necessarily translate into an assertive institution against the government in a consistent fashion (Sanchez Urribarri, 2011), it did increase the social and political relevance of the Court. Second, during this time there were important judicial reform efforts promoted by the World Bank and the Inter American Development Bank, among other institutions, together with a growing civil society sector that pushed an agenda inspired in human rights, rule of law protection, and greater transparency (Hammergren, 2007). Finally, on this last note, the 1990s also witnessed an increase in human rights education by academics, civil society and the judiciary itself, leading to an increasing awareness

5 See Wilson's chapter on Costa Rica in this volume.

of the role of courts in policy change. Therefore, against this backdrop, the emergence of the Supreme Court as a key venue to adjudicate political conflict during the onset of *Chavismo* and, subsequently, the rise of prominence of the Supreme Tribunal is not entirely surprising.

Hugo Chávez capitalized on the country's strong desire for social and political change in the 1990s, winning the Presidency by a landslide against the main democratic parties AD and COPEI (McCoy, 1999). The general story of the collapse of Venezuela's 'partyarchy' democracy (See McCoy and Myers, 2006), Chávez's arrival in power, and the rise of the Bolivarian Revolution are well known (Corrales and Penfold, 2011). He came to the fore in Venezuela's political history as the leader of a coup against President Pérez in 1992. He was eventually pardoned and ran for the presidency in 1998 as a charismatic outsider with a strong transformative populist discourse. His most important promise was to replace the 1999 Constitution via a Constituent Assembly—an option that was not available in the 1961 democratic Constitution—allegedly to make Venezuela's faltering democracy more participatory and inclusive (See García Soto et al. 2021). After winning by a substantial margin and taking office, he proceeded to push for a new constitution, openly challenging the other branches of power.

From the beginning, there was an inherent contradiction or 'original sin' in the *Chavista* (i.e., pro-Chávez) Bolivarian Revolution: Whilst it was said to be a democratic change driven by the people, which was supposed to respect democratic institutions and the rule of law, it relied largely on top-down authoritarian populist logics centered on Chávez as the leader (Corrales and Penfold, 2011). This originated significant tensions within *Chavismo* as well, as diverse actors in the ruling coalition had different takes on how to push the Revolution forward (Hawkins, 2010).

With this context in mind, an embattled Supreme Court was asked to rule on key questions related to the constitutionality of the different stages of the proposed constitutional reform (Colón Ríos, 2020; Braver, 2016). The cases represented an unprecedented juncture for the Supreme Court in a political context that was increasingly polarized and uncertain, and where the institution's authority (and survival) was at stake. At the same time, the proposed changes did not count on explicit constitutional basis, as the Constitution only contemplated partial amendments or reform procedures (García Soto et al. 2021). In subsequent cases in January and April 1999, the Venezuelan Supreme Court declared the constitutionality of both organizing a referendum to ask the Venezuelan people if they wished to convoke a Constituent Assembly to replace the Constitution (January 1999), and then declared the constitutionality of President Chávez's decree convoking the referendum (April 1999). These decisions were 'activist' in different ways (they were 'mega-political' cases, that involved major constitutional interpretation developments). However, until then, it is hard to state that they were expressly supportive of authoritarianism. Instead, they seem a strategic reaction to a harsh political environment.

Yet, once elected and functioning (July 1999), the Constituent Assembly not only began working towards writing a new Constitution, but also moved against the other branches of power, ordering the intervention of both the legislature (*Congreso*) and the judiciary as a whole—including the Supreme Court. Facing the loss of its independence vis-à-vis the Chavista regime, and its authority over the court system—plus, openly currying favor with Chávez and his allies—the Supreme Court issued an *Acuerdo* (public notice) agreeing to collaborate with the Assembly's new measure (August 1999). Subsequently, in September 1999, it issued a ruling that effectively endorsed the power-grab attempted by the Chavista-dominated Constituent Assembly. This was not an activist ruling in the sense of challenging the government of the day—quite the opposite, it refused to control Chávez and the nascent Bolivarian Regime at a time when it was most needed. However, by refusing to oppose the regime and, conversely, providing footing for the regime's questionable intervention of the branches of power it did not control, it also showed its willingness to interpret the constitution in a way that best fit the regime's best political interests. This, right at a time when navigating political uncertainty and adjudicating conflicts in a legitimate fashion was most needed.

Therefore, the Court acquired a novel role, potentially very powerful, that of ally of the regime in its quest for stability and governance—without clear limits as to how far it was willing to go to protect regime interests by: a. Expanding its jurisdiction; b. Distancing itself from previous jurisprudential and doctrinal debates; and c. Engaging in politically sensitive matters across a variety of issue areas, among other 'activist' goals. It is unclear to what degree the Court's support for the Chavista regime at this critical time helped persuade Chavista leaders and constitution-makers to bolster the court's institutional prerogatives and effective power in the novel constitutional order, but it was definitely a factor that helped pave the way to the high court's role in the new regime era.[6]

6 See discussion of the prominence of constitutional review on politics at Berríos Ortigoza (2013a, 2015).

The 1999 Constitution, *Chavismo* and an Activist Constitutional Chamber (2000–2004)

The new 1999 Constitution envisioned a new Supreme Tribunal (*Tribunal Supremo de Justicia* or TSJ), that was supposed to be different from the *Suprema Corte*. The Constitution contemplated the creation of a Constitutional Chamber (*Sala Constitucional*) in a separate section, ostensibly to preserve and 'secure' the Constitution's integrity and helping dismantle the 1961 constitutional order and develop the 1999 constitutional project. The Constitution gave the *Sala* all the prerogatives of a constitutional tribunal, establishing more modalities of constitutional adjudication and intervention in legal, social, and political matters that it had ever been contemplated for Venezuela's apex court (Sanchez Urribarri, 2011).

Additionally, there were other features that would also influence the character of the novel Constitutional Chamber and the TSJ as a whole. On one hand, the judicial appointments that took place in December 1999 and inaugurated the Tribunal were not definitive, but *interim*, subject to review at a later time (i.e., a whole year). This created a strong incentive on the judges not to defect and remain loyal to the regime (or otherwise lose their seat). Additionally, the new judges included several justices with strong ties with the different political forces that coexisted in *Chavismo*.[7] This reduced judicial independence *de facto* and allowed for greater input from political actors into the judges' preferences and decision-making (Sanchez Urribarri, 2010). This also happened across the rest of the judiciary—the blanket replacement of most judges ordered by the Constituent Assembly, in the context of a 'judicial revolution' (Molina Galicia, 2002), was supposed to replace judges connected with the *ancien regime* and craft a less corrupt, more professional judiciary. Instead, it increased the dependence of the court system on the political establishment (Castaldi, 2006), facilitating the politicization of the judicial system (Casal, 2017). After all, building a different rule of law would require persistence and a change of ethos across the judiciary and other actors in the legal system (Kosar, 2016). Unfortunately, that would be easier said than done, since corruption, inefficiency and commitment to the honest interpretation and application of the law were problems that were present across the whole legal system (including the High Court). It was not a problem of a few 'rotten apples', but rather

7 An ex-ante modality of politicization, as I have mentioned in previous work (See Sanchez Urribarri, 2022).

a systemic phenomenon that shaped the expectations and performance of all actors involved.

With all of this in mind—did the Supreme Tribunal, and particularly the Constitutional Chamber, become an activist institution in the aftermath of regime change? The short answer is yes, it did, but not as an institution committed to controlling the government in the name of the constitution but, gradually, the opposite—to interpret and shape the constitutional project to protect regime interests. This trend became increasingly evident over time in a variety of ways—not only in terms of the raw number of cases, types of cases and outcomes, but also in relation to the way the decisions were justified and structured (Berrios Ortigoza and Sanchez Urribarri, 2024). As we can see in Figure 9.1 below, the first few years of the last twenty years or so of constitutional litigation before the Constitutional Chamber witnessed a rise of constitutional review cases, signifying both a mounting interest in using its powers to protect rights and adjudicate a wide range of constitutional conflicts, and assert its authority as a new powerful pro-regime institution.

There were pressing needs during this time: a. Securing the new regime's governance in a volatile political context vis-à-vis external political actors; b. developing a rights agenda based in the 1999 Constitution; and c. Control the rest of the Supreme Tribunal and the judiciary—among other tasks. To these ends, the Constitutional Chamber engaged in 'creative jurisprudence' that

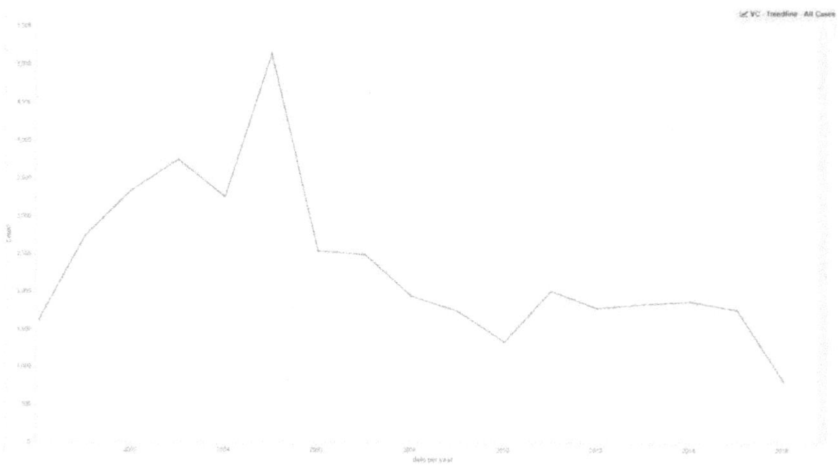

Figure 9.1: Venezuelan Supreme Tribunal—constitutional review Chamber (raw cases per year)

deliberately broke apart from prior case-law developed by the Supreme Court (Berríos Ortigoza and Sanchez Urribarri, 2023). For example, this included cases that established the Chamber's prerogatives to adjudicate constitutional cases, interpreting article 336 of the Constitution (which listed the Chamber's powers), among other provisions related. Right at the start, the Chamber even redefined the process by which constitutional *amparo* cases would be decided (e.g., see the Chamber's rulings 01/2000 and 02/2000 of January 20, 2000; and 0007/2000 of February 1, 2000). Another important example of the Chamber configuring its own powers during this era involved the jurisdiction to hear constitutional interpretation abstract petitions, a type of procedure that allowed the Chamber to interpret the Constitution in 'definitive' fashion, and which would become a very important form of constitutional litigation for years to come (ruling 2000-1077; see also Brewer-Carías, 2005). This aspect of the Chamber's activism—defining and interpreting its own powers in the name of its role as constitutional guarantor—would become an important role, often with equivocal commitment to its own case law.

During this era, the Chamber also decided salient cases of major political import, such as the decision to suspend the 2000 'mega-election' to elect a new President, Legislature, and other elected officials across the country (ruling 483/2000 of May 29, 2000, see Sanchez Urribarri, 2011). This phase also included very innovative jurisprudence, sometimes beyond the boundaries of what the Chamber could do, stretching its resources and making it look like an over-eager court that could take any case in the name of material justice. For instance, in the ASODEVIPRILARA case, decided through a series of judgments (e.g., August 22, 2001); the Chamber upheld a collective or 'diffuse' rights petition against two Executive agencies, one in charge of overseeing the banking system (SUDEBAN) , and the other in charge of the protection of the rights of users and customers (INDECU); with regards to their failure to provide protection against credit schemes that abused the rights of borrowers (*See* Badell Madrid, 2009). This involved an indefinite number of users, who were supposed to then become part of the collective action procedure. This type of judicial intervention in policymaking would have been hard to envision years prior.

Later on, as the political situation worsened and the government and the opposition entered a more conflictive phase (including a coup attempt against Chávez in April 2002, and a major general strike in December 2002), there was increasing demand for the Court to intervene as a legitimate actor to help solve the political stand-off. Although this is only a short account of a longer saga that requires much careful elaboration, it is important to highlight that the Constitutional Chamber was a key protagonist to decide cases concerning the creation of an electoral pathway to solve the conflict, leading to the referendum against President Chávez in August 2004. This included the appointment of the National Electoral Authority (CNE), and the governance of the electoral process that led to a recall referendum. To these ends, the Constitutional Chamber created major jurisprudential innovations, and fulfilled a major political role unprecedented in the country's political history. Moreover, the judicialization of politics also included the selective involvement of other branches of the Supreme Tribunal in the open warfare that took place between the government and the opposition in an extreme polarised environment (*see* Brewer-Carías, 2004). However, the price of this intervention was twofold: the definite politicization and division of the Chamber (and the Court as a whole) into pro-regime and opposition factions, and the eventual response of the pro-regime majority of the Legislature, which decided to reform the Supreme Tribunal legislation and pack the Court. In turn, re-packing the Court served two valuable purposes: It allowed for the continuing control of the Court in the event of a loss at the referendum (i.e., 'judicial insurance', Ginsburg *dixit*, 2003); whilst updating the composition of the Court in a way that mirrored the relative power of the political forces that coexisted in the Chavista ruling coalition. As we see in the next section, what emerged was a tamed Chamber that maintained its *activist* vocation and pro-regime stance, whilst abandoning any expectations of emerging as an independent actor.

Activism to Consolidate Chávez's Populist Authoritarian Rule

After Chávez won the 2004 election, we begin witnessing a slightly different role for the Constitutional Chamber, further consolidating its position at the peak of the judicial ranks (especially vis-à-vis the other Chambers), whilst continuing to make major decisions that affected politics and policymaking. The newly renovated, expanded Chamber had a greater presence of justices with strong political affiliations or prior political experience.[8] Unfortunately, the

8 In fact, the Constitutional Chamber's new three justices were: A politician and National Assembly member (Velásquez Alvaray); the previous President of the Electoral Authority (who had actually been appointed by the Constitutional Chamber, Carrasquero), and a judge with alleged connections with Chávez himself, Luisa Estela Morales, who was then

government's dominance of the Supreme Tribunal ended up using the Chamber to provide additional support to a government that already enjoyed too much power (from 2005, the government also controlled the parliament after the opposition refused to participate in the election in protest). Whilst we witness during the first period under analysis that the Constitutional Chamber was preoccupied with defining its competences and key constitutional interpretation principles—sometimes in such a way that it would be called 'activist' by critics—during this new phase the most salient rulings now focused on protecting government's interests in a wide range of cases (Berríos Ortigoza and Sánchez Urribarrí, 2023). This included a variety of controversial cases that were related to the government's increasing restrictions on the different contestation arenas—including the distribution of powers to authorize/control political demonstrations; freedom of expression; constitutional reform and different political rights (see Sánchez Urribarrí, 2022).

For the government, controlling the judiciary was good in on itself. A judiciary populated with judges who had ties with Chavismo afforded key advantages to the regime, including the allocation of judgeships and other jobs in the judicial system to individuals who had various connections with the regime (i.e., judicial clientelism, see Basabe-Serrano, 2015). But, more importantly, it allowed for the use of the judicial system (across the whole structure of the Venezuelan judiciary, but especially at the apex court level), to prevent the opposition from using the judiciary as an effective contestation arena to counter Chavismo's political clout and executive decision-making, and even to enable pro-government actors to use the court system to the regime's advantage. In some of these cases, the Chamber would go out of its way in terms of the interpretation of its own powers, or the substance of the ruling itself, to support a project with clear authoritarian traits. Moreover, the Chamber would become a participant in the development of a new legal framework that purported to establish a socialist project ("21st Century Socialism", see López Maya, 2016), sidelining the 1999 Constitution. During this phase, the opposition (and citizens in general) no longer saw the Chamber—or the Supreme Court, for that matter—as a venue to challenge the regime. In fact, there have been studies that suggest that for most of its existence, and particularly in this period, there were no decisions that actually challenged regime interests in the Court (Canova et al., 2014).

appointed President of the Chamber and the Court as a whole (Berríos Ortigoza and Sánchez Urribarrí, 2023). There was only one justice left in the Chamber who had a pro-opposition stance.

Whilst a longer analysis is out of the scope of the present chapter, there are several examples that illustrate the importance of the Chamber in this emerging regime architecture, and that could well be considered 'activist'. First, in 2007, shortly after Chávez's re-election in 2006, the government made a major move to control the media space by refusing to renew RCTV's broadcasting license (one of the major TV operators in the country, and well-known for its opposition to the regime). This was a case of major importance to the President himself, who publicly vouched to fight against opposition TV stations and other media platforms. It is well known that the Chamber not only refused to intervene to prevent the questionable closure of the TV station from taking place, but actually went as far as ordering that a new government TV station could take control of all the equipment necessary to continue broadcasting using the same frequency (Decision 07-957, May 25, 2007, see *Reporteros Sin Fronteras*, 2007). This case was a good example of the Chamber not only supporting the government in a *reactive* fashion, but even going further and using its prerogatives to craft a ruling that best reflected the government's specific policy needs and political interests. In a pro-regime form of activism, it helped narrow down a vital arena for contestation against Chavismo (i.e., the closure of an important TV station), sending a signal that similar government measures would not only be tolerated, but actively supported if needed, and showcasing that the judiciary would use its powers in discretionary fashion as required to favor specific outcomes.

Another excellent example of 'abusive constitutionalism' (Landau, 2013), from the bench was the Constitutional Chamber's decisions regarding the failed constitutional reform attempted by Chávez in 2007 to facilitate the transition to a socialist state and adopt key institutions to these ends. These goals were later achieved by way of different normative instruments and by judicial decisions issued by the Constitutional Chamber over the course of the following years (see Brewer-Carías, 2014; Casal, 2021). On one hand, there is the Constitutional Chamber's decision not to block the constitutional referendum from taking place, a decision that it on itself might not be surprising at this stage. However, the Chamber's activist stance became more critical on, first, allowing the government to move forward with another attempt to modify the constitution, this time by way of a constitutional amendment to allow the President, and other elected officials across the state, to seek office again without facing term limit constraints (Decision 0053-2009, February 2, 2009).

Moreover, after the attempted constitutional reform was blocked on December 2, 2007, the government went on carrying out institutional reforms to articulate several of the modifications proposed in the constitutional reform (Maigon and Welsch, 2009; Brewer-Carias, 2014), seeking to further move in the direction of a 'hybrid' socialist regime (despite the 2007 constitutional reform's rejection at referendum). The Constitutional Chamber lent legitimacy to several of these reforms, by recognizing their superior hierarchical relevance in the legal system (e.g. ruling 10/1330, on December 12, 2010, on the Organic Law of the Communes that intended to establish a communal state, see Brewer-Carias, 2014, pp. 52–53; or ruling 10/1329, on December 16, 2010, re the Organic Law of the Communal Economic System). These rulings *per se* might not be overtly activist, as the Chamber here is not using its powers beyond what would reasonably be expected or lending its support to the regime in a particularly contested matter. They are, however, pro-regime decisions that are part of an overall trend of support for the government's questionable reform agenda.

Subsequently, the Constitutional Chamber continued playing an important role as Chávez's term went on. Perhaps the most noticeable instance of its vocation to secure the stability of the regime was after Hugo Chávez's fell sick, in late 2012. Chávez was re-elected in October 2012, and underwent treatment for cancer in Cuba later in the year, eventually dying in January 2013. During this time, the Constitutional Chamber fulfilled an important role interpreting the constitution regarding Chávez's absence and succession by Nicolas Maduro (*See* Brewer-Carías, 2013). Once again, despite being discredited, dependent and widely criticized at home and abroad, the Chamber afforded the regime a modicum of legitimacy, intervening with timely judicial rulings to help establish a constitutional footing to the regime at a time of crisis. The Court went out of its way to consistently issue pro-regime decisions in controversial fashion, first by guaranteeing the continuous exercise of power by the sitting government, despite Chávez's physical inability to be sworn in after his recent re-election in October 2012 (see ruling 0002/2013, January 3, 2013). Next, after Chávez's death, the Chamber, in the occasion of interpreting article 233 of the 1999 Constitution, which establishes who should step in as interim President in the event of the President's absence, (i.e., the Vice-President or the President of the Legislature), used the chance to interpret another article of the Constitution, which dealt with the Vice-President's inability to act as President in certain circumstances (article 299 of the Constitution, see ruling 0141/2013, March 8, 2013). In both decisions, the Chamber decided the cases *en banc* (a rarity for the Chamber) and refused to open the proceedings to allow for debates on argument or evidence (that is, treated the cases as 'mero derecho', i.e., as dealing only with matters of constitutional interpretation). Berríos Ortigoza has cited this decision as a "clear example of the activist intervention by the Constitutional Chamber in the political process" (Berríos Ortigoza, 2013b, p. 155). I could not agree more.

As we see in the next section, the Chamber's support would also serve Chávez's successor, Nicolás Maduro, very well. Once in power (elected in April 2013 by a small margin), he would preside over the most challenging period in the country's contemporary history. The most activist phase on behalf of the regime was still yet to happen. Here, I offer a few reflections to highlight the importance of an 'activist authoritarian' Chamber at a time of the country's transition to a more overt autocratic regime under Maduro.

Judicial Activism in Overt Authoritarian Conditions: The Maduro Era (2013–*Current*)

Once Maduro arrived in power, the country began experiencing an increasingly volatile environment. Maduro had been elected by a slim margin, the country's economy was already faltering, and the opposition seemed to enjoy increasing support among the population. A variety of protest demonstrations against the government were met with openly repressive strategies, including the persecution and incarceration of political opponents. In 2015, for the first time since Chavismo arrived in power (over 15 years), the opposition won the National Assembly elections (December 2015), taking control of an elected branch. In theory, this afforded the opposition new avenues to challenge and control the regime, enact legislation, and have a say in the designation of key authorities, among other constitutional functions. Yet, from the point of view of the government, this represented serious risks to the way they had exercised power since Chávez was first elected. Moreover, a pending presidential election in 2018/9, coupled with the possibility of removing Maduro by activating a recall referendum against Chávez—according to the Constitution—meant that the stakes of losing the Assembly were quite high for the regime, especially for the radical wing of the *Chavista* movement.

Thus, only weeks after the opposition's victory at the polls became apparent, the departing pro-government National Assembly proceeded to, once again, replace several of the members of the TSJ (including the Constitutional Chamber, see Perdomo and Santacruz, 2016). The new justices of the Constitutional Chamber had various links to the Maduro regime, lacked substantial prior experience, and overall did not comply with the requirements in the

Constitution (Casal, 2021). In their hands, the expectation became that the Chamber would fulfill a deliberate anti-opposition role, as a bulwark of authoritarian rule (Moustafa and Ginsburg dixit, 2008). And, to this end, it already counted, not only an institutional framework that would allow for a strong position vis-à-vis the legislature, but also a prior *activist* record, so it was safe to assume that it would fulfill an assertive political role on behalf of the regime's survival interests.

What followed went even beyond expectations: The Constitutional Chamber was systematically employed to question, delegitimize, and effectively block the National Assembly's functions throughout its term. Shortly before the Assembly was installed, the Constitutional Chamber issued an order to prevent the opposition majority from being sworn in and taking office, because of alleged fraud in the election of three members of parliament. Once the Assembly was installed, it declared the Assembly in 'contempt of court' for having incorporated the members to the Assembly (See Ayala Corao and Chavero Gazdik, 2017). This clarion call was followed by a true evisceration of the National Assembly's functions. During the five years that followed (the normal term of the National Assembly), the Chamber decided at least 145 decisions against the Legislature (Acceso a la Justicia, 2021), a noteworthy record given that for the vast majority of its existence it had simply refused to act against the Executive, or against the executive-dominated parliament.

The Chamber's stance against the National Assembly was not completely linear. It varied in its proclivity to take on a case, how quickly to decide it against opposition interests, and how far to go to support the government in particular cases. However, its unambiguous willingness to serve as an instrument to prevent an opposition majority in the Legislature to carry out their mandate is the pinnacle of the Chamber's process of expansion of authority over time (Casal, 2021), and could only happen in a context where an excessively assertive, openly discretionary role for the Chamber, i.e., *activist*, is not only expected, but considered an integral part of the system. In a nutshell, at this stage the Chamber's decision to flaunt its institutional legitimacy in the name of safeguarding the regime's interest did not surprise anyone. It was also a key precondition of the eventual constitutional crisis the country would face in 2019, following Maduro's illegitimate election in 2018 (Sanchez Urribarri and Garcia Soto, 2019). After all, the Assembly was effectively sidelined—it could not even elaborate the national budget, which was adopted by President Maduro by decree with the approval of the Chamber (ruling 0814/2016, October 11, 2016). The Chamber went as far as attempting to strip the National

Assembly of its legislative powers, in two infamous rulings (decisions 0156/2017 and 156/2017) that would start a saga of protests, repression, and eventual democratic breakdown with the creation of the fraudulent 2017 Constituent Assembly (Sanchez Urribarri and Garcia Soto, 2019).

There are several notable features in this phase. First, the Chamber's focus on playing the role of blocking the legislature happened in a context where the TSJ as a whole (including the Chamber) had seen a significant decline in number of cases (See Figure 9.1 above). This reflected the Chamber's lack of legitimacy and several institutional changes that had made it more difficult to bring cases to the attention of the Court. Additionally, the types of cases that the Chamber was interested in solving also changed in nature (Berrios Ortigoza and Sanchez Urribarri, 2023). Another interesting development that also characterized this 'activist' phase included the rise of cases filed by President Maduro himself, including many that sought to suspend the validity of the Legislature's actions or annulling them on constitutional grounds. In any case, the Chamber had shifted its attention away from protecting rights a long while ago (a function that declined in the previous phase) yet, as we can see, it had retained a significant role as an authoritarian governance tool. This role would diminish towards the late phase of the Maduro years, after the regime was able to impose a Constituent Assembly and, via a distorted interpretation of the theory of constituent power, impose their rule by way of the supposed constituent organ (Sanchez Urribarri and Garcia Soto, 2019).

Concluding Remarks

In this chapter, I have sought to articulate and discuss the notion of authoritarian judicial activism, with a special focus on the TSJ—Venezuela's highest court – and with an emphasis on the Constitutional Chamber as the ultimate constitutional adjudicator in the land according to the 1999 Constitution.

The idea of judicial activism in an authoritarian context is, as we discussed above, problematic. Traditionally, we think of the judiciary under authoritarian conditions as a submissive, marginal actor that passively serves the interests of the regime without going beyond its allocated role. Whilst abundant research has debunked this assumption, the emergence of an activist court in an authoritarian context is, at face value, an enigma. Why would a regime need an activist tribunal, or otherwise allow the emergence of a judicial institution that is willing to go beyond its allocated functions—and take on a central role in the regime's performance over time?

The specific juncture that the new Supreme Tribunal faced involved the possibility for the new Court to act beyond its traditional role and being 'activist' in different ways—as a political actor (one way or the other); as a rights guarantor, and/or in terms of legal and constitutional interpretation. However, the fact that the expansion of Venezuela's constitutional review system was taking place at the same time (and as an integral part of) a political reform that had clear authoritarian traits from its start involved a difficult contradiction. The Supreme Tribunal was supposed to be—at least according to the Constitutional text—a strong institution to support the development of a new, modern *democratic* state that sought to enhance social progress whilst respecting the Constitution and the rule of law. Yet, at the same time, the overall zeitgeist was different. Based on Chávez's rhetoric as leader of the *proceso revolucionario* (revolutionary process), it involved the expectation that all state institutions were at the service of political change as first and main premise, i.e., that the advancement of the government's interests came first (Pérez Perdomo, 2005; Brewer Carías, 2010). This would have important implications for the new Constitutional Chamber—and the Supreme Court as a whole—in terms of how it addressed any eventual tensions between the government, citizens' rights, and the law.

In the end, the incipient pro-rights activism that took place during the early phase was quickly sidelined by the extraordinary political role the Chamber was asked (and obliged) to fulfill. The Chamber, as the peak institution of the Venezuelan High Court, emerged as a judicial adjudicator whose main political role was to solve salient conflicts involving the government and/or opposition interests in favor of the regime's interests. As part of this process, it found itself progressively less tied to past doctrinal and jurisprudential constraints. The Constitutional Chamber was able to create new constitutional review procedures from scratch; reinterpret the conditions under which these procedures applied depending on its own perceived need to use its powers; sideline its own jurisprudence when needed, and revise decisions by all other judicial instances—including itself. Thus, from different standpoints, the Venezuelan Supreme Tribunal, especially its Constitutional Chamber, can be offered as an example of judicial activism in an authoritarian context—a rare, yet worrying example of what a Tribunal endowed with strong powers can do when it is captured, lacks *de facto* judicial independence, and becomes a key ally in the process of democratic backsliding and autocratic consolidation.

The Venezuelan case is useful to help us theorize about why authoritarian courts may emerge in autocratic conditions, particularly in regimes that experience democratic backsliding. In this regard, the Venezuelan experience shows one worrying possibility: A judicial system with ambivalent or no principled commitment to the normative underpinnings of constitutional adjudication and/or judicial review—i.e., controlling the government and protecting citizen rights—can end up becoming a very powerful tool in the wrong hands. Thus, a court that had been created to protect the constitution and the rule of law, ended up as an activist institution acting on behalf of a new authoritarian regime.

References

Acceso a la Justicia. (2021) *El TSJ vs. la AN*. Last checked on December 9, 2022, at: https://accesoalajusticia.org/el-tsj-vs-la-an/

Ambrosio, T. (2014). Beyond the transition paradigm: A research agenda for authoritarian consolidation. *Demokratizatsiya, 22*(3), 471.

Ayala Corao, C. M., & Chavero Gazdik, R. J. (2017). *El Libro Negro del TSJ de Venezuela: Del secuestro de la democracia y la usurpación de la soberanía popular a la ruptura del orden constitucional (2015–2017)*. Caracas: Editorial Jurídica Venezolana.

Badell Madrid, R. (2009). La tutela de los intereses colectivos y difusos en Venezuela como medio de protección constitucional. *Revista de la Maestría en Derecho Procesal, 3*(1). https://revistas.pucp.edu.pe/index.php/derechoprocesal/article/download/2115/2048

Basabe-Serrano, S. (2015). Informal institutions and judicial independence in Paraguay, 1954–2011. *Law & Policy, 37*(4), 350–378.

Belov, M. (Ed.). (2021). *Courts and judicial activism under crisis conditions: Policy making in a time of illiberalism and emergency constitutionalism*. Routledge.

Benvindo, J. Z. (2010). *On the limits of constitutional adjudication: Deconstructing balancing and judicial activism*. Springer Science & Business Media.

Berríos Ortigoza, J. A. (2013a). El concepto constitucional de democracia y la judicialización de la política en Venezuela. *Cuestiones Políticas, 29*(50), 13–46.

Berríos Ortigoza, J. A. (2013b). La judicialización de la transición política en Venezuela. Estudio sobre la decisión 141/2013, de 8 de marzo de la Sala Constitucional del Tribunal Supremo de Justicia. *Frónesis: Revista de Filosofía Jurídica, Social y Política, 20*(1), 149–156.

Berríos Ortigoza, J. A. (2015). *El control jurisdiccional de la constitucionalidad y la política en Venezuela: estudio sobre la sala constitucional (2000–2010)*. Universidad Nacional de Educación a Distancia (España). Facultad de Derecho, Departamento de Derecho Político.

Berríos Ortigoza, J. A., & Sanchez Urribarri, R. (*forthcoming*, 2024). Constitutional interpretation in an ever-authoritarian context: The Constitutional Chamber of the Venezuelan Supreme Court. In J. Frohlich (Ed.), *Constitutional interpretation in Latin America*. Hart Publishing.

Braver, J. (2016). Hannah Arendt in Venezuela: The Supreme Court battles Hugo Chávez over the creation of the 1999 constitution. *International Journal of Constitutional Law, 14*(3), 555–583.

Brewer-Carías, A. R. (2004). El secuestro de la Sala Electoral por la Sala Constitucional del Tribunal Supremo de Justicia. In *La guerra entre las Salas del TSJ frente al referéndum revocatorio* (pp. 13–58).

Brewer-Carías, A. R. (2005). Quis Custodiet ipsos Custodes: De la interpretación constitucional a la inconstitucionalidad de la interpretación. In *VIII Congreso Nacional de derecho constitucional* (pp. 463–489). Perú.

Brewer-Carías, A. R. (2010). *Dismantling democracy in Venezuela: The Chávez authoritarian experiment*. Cambridge University Press.

Brewer-Carías, A. R. (2013). Crónica constitucional del proceso venezolano de transición gubernamental, ocasionado por la enfermedad y muerte del presidente Hugo Chávez, y de la instauración por el juez constitucional de un gobierno sin legitimidad democrática (Diciembre 2012/Abril 2013). *Pensamiento Constitucional, 18*, 265–314.

Brewer-Carías, A. R. (2014). ¿Reforma constitucional, o mutación constitucional?: La experiencia venezolana. *Revista de Derecho Público, 137*, 19–65.

Brinks, D., & Blass, A. (2018). *The DNA of constitutional justice in Latin America*. Cambridge University Press.

Canova González, L. A., Herrera Orellana, E., Rodríguez Ortega, E., & Graterol Stefanelli, G.. (2014). *El TSJ al servicio de la revolución*. Caracas: Editorial Galipán.

Casal, J. M. (2017). *Justicia y política: El caso de la jurisdicción constitucional en Venezuela*. Konrad Adenauer Stiftung. Last Accessed online on November 24, 2022 at: https://www.kas.de/es/web/rspla/einzeltitel/-/content/justicia-y-politica-el-caso-de-la-jurisdiccion-constitucional-en-venezuela

Casal, J. M. (2021). The Constitutional Chamber and the erosion of democracy in Venezuela. *Zeitschrift für ausländisches öffentliches Recht und Völkerrecht/Heidelberg Journal of International Law*, 80, 913.

Castaldi, L. (2006). Judicial independence threatened in Venezuela: The removal of Venezuelan judges and the complications of rule of law reform. *Georgetown Journal of International Law, 37*(3), 477–506.

Cepeda-Espinosa, M. J. (2004). Judicial activism in a violent context: The origin, role, and impact of the Colombian Constitutional Court. *Washington University Global Studies Law Review, 3*, 529.

Colón-Ríos, J. (2020). *Constituent power and the law*. Oxford University Press.

Corrales J. (2015). The authoritarian resurgence: autocratic legalism in Venezuela. *Journal of Democracy, 26*(2), 37.

Corrales, J. (2023). *Autocracy rising: How Venezuela transitioned to authoritarianism*. Brookings Institution Press.

Corrales, J., & Penfold-Becerra, M. (2011). *Dragon in the tropics: Hugo Chávez and the political economy of revolution in Venezuela*. Brookings Institution Press.

Couso J., & Hilbink L. (2011). From quietism to incipient activism: The institutional and ideological roots of rights adjudication in Chile. In G. Helmke & J. Ríos-Figueroa (Eds.), *Courts in Latin America* (pp. 99–127). Cambridge University Press.

Daly, T. (2017). *The alchemists: Questioning our faith in courts as democracy-builders*. Cambridge University Press.

Dressel, B., Sanchez Urribarri, R., & Stroh, A. (2017). The informal dimension of judicial politics: A relational perspective. *Annual Review of Law and Social Science, 13*, 413–430.

Epp, C. R. (1998). *The rights revolution: Lawyers, activists, and supreme courts in comparative perspective*. University of Chicago Press.

García-Soto, C., Martínez Meucci, M. A., & Sanchez Urribarri, R. (2021). Winds of change: Comparing the early phases of constitutional redrafting in Chile and Venezuela. *Hague Journal on the Rule of Law, 13*(2), 315–334.

Garoupa, N. (2016). Comparing judicial activism: Can we say that the U.S. Supreme Court is more activist than the German Constitutional Court?. *Revista Portuguesa de Filosofia, 72*(4), 1089–1105.

Gerschewski, J. (2013). The three pillars of stability: Legitimation, repression, and co-optation in autocratic regimes. *Democratization, 20*(1), 13–38.

Ginsburg, T. (2003). *Judicial review in new democracies: Constitutional courts in Asian cases*. Cambridge University Press.

Hammergren, L. (2007). *Envisioning reform: Conceptual and practical obstacles to improving judicial performance in Latin America*. Penn State University Press.

Hawkins, K. A. (2010). *Venezuela's Chavismo and populism in comparative perspective*. Cambridge University Press.

Helmke, G. (2005). *Courts under constraints: Judges, generals, and presidents in Argentina*. Cambridge University Press.

Kapiszewski, D. (2012). *High courts and economic governance in Argentina and Brazil*. Cambridge University Press.

Kmiec K. (2004). The origin and current meanings of "judicial activism". *California Law Review*, 92(5), 1441–1477.

Kosar, D. (2016). *Perils of judicial self-government in transitional societies*. Cambridge University Press.

Kureshi, Y. (2021). When judges defy dictators: An audience-based framework to explain the emergence of judicial assertiveness against authoritarian regimes. *Comparative Politics, 53*(2), 233–257.

Landau, D. (2013). Abusive constitutionalism. *UCDL Review, 47*, 189.

Levitsky, S., & Way, L. A. (2010). *Competitive authoritarianism: Hybrid regimes after the Cold War*. Cambridge University Press.

López Maya, M. (2016). *El ocaso del chavismo: Venezuela 2005–2015*. Editorial Alfa.

López Maya, M. (2021). *Democracia para Venezuela: ¿representativa, participativa o populista?* Editorial Alfa.

Maigon, T., & Welsch, F. (2009). Venezuela 2008: Road map towards authoritarian socialism. *Revista de Ciencia Política, 29*(2), 633–656.

McCoy, J. L. (1999). Latin America's imperiled progress: Chavez and the end of "partyarchy" in Venezuela. *Journal of Democracy, 10*(3), 64–77.

McCoy, J. L., & Myers, D. J. (Eds.). (2006). *The unraveling of representative democracy in Venezuela.* Johns Hopkins University Press.

Miller, L. L. (2018). The use of case studies in law and social science research. *Annual Review of Law and Social Science, 14*, 381–396.

Molina Galicia, R. (2002). *Reflexiones sobre una visión constitucional del proceso y su tendencia jurisprudencial ¿Hacia un gobierno judicial?* Caracas: Ediciones Paredes.

Moustafa, T. (2007). *The struggle for constitutional power: Law, politics, and economic development in Egypt.* Cambridge University Press.

Moustafa, T. (2014). Law and courts in authoritarian regimes. *Annual Review of Law and Social Science, 10*, 281–299.

Moustafa, T., & Ginsburg, T. (2008). Introduction: The functions of courts in authoritarian politics. In T. Ginsburg & T. Moustafa (Eds.), *Rule by law: The politics of courts in authoritarian regimes* (pp. 1–27).

Navia, P., & Ríos-Figueroa, J. (2005). The constitutional adjudication mosaic of Latin America. *Comparative Political Studies, 38*(2), 189–217.

Perdomo, R. P. (2005). Judicialization and regime transformation: The Venezuelan Supreme Court. In R. Sieder, L. Schjolden, & A. Angell (Eds), *The judicialization of politics in Latin America* (pp. 131–159). Palgrave Macmillan.

Perdomo, R.P., & Santacruz, A. Y. (2016). La legitimidad de jueces y legisladores en el Estado constitucional de derecho: la Asamblea Nacional y el Tribunal Supremo venezolano. *Doxa. Cuadernos De Filosofía Del Derecho*, (39), 405–423.

Popova, M. (2012). *Politicized justice in emerging democracies: A study of courts in Russia and Ukraine.* Cambridge University Press.

Quansah, E. K., & Fombad, C. M. (2009). *Judicial activism in Africa: Possible defence against authoritarian resurgence?* Paper presented at the Annual Conference of the African Network of Constitutional Lawyers' on "Judicialism and Good Governance," in Cape Town, 25-28 August 2009.

Reporteros Sin Fronteras. (2007). Venezuela: *Cierre de Radio Caracas Televisión: La consolidación de una hegemonía mediática.* Reporteros sin Fronteras por la Libertad de Prensa, last accessed on December 6, 2022, at: https://rsf.org/sites/default/files/Informe_Venezuela.pdf

Rodríguez-Garavito C. (2011). Beyond the courtroom: The impact of judicial activism on socioeconomic rights in Latin America. *Texas Law Review, 89*, 1669.

Roux, T. R. (2021). Judicial activism. In *Elgar encyclopedia on comparative law.* Downloaded at: https://papers.ssrn.com/sol3/papers.cfm?abstract_id=3923921 on August 8, 2022.

Sadurski, W. (2019). *Poland's constitutional breakdown.* Oxford University Press.

Sanchez Urribarri, R. A. (2010). *Judges and their loyalties: A comparative study focused on the Venezuelan Supreme Court.* Doctoral dissertation, University of South Carolina.

Sanchez Urribarri, R. A. (2011). Courts between democracy and hybrid authoritarianism: Evidence from the Venezuelan Supreme Court. *Law & Social Inquiry, 36*(4), 854–884.

Sanchez Urribarri, R. A. (2017). Between power and submissiveness: Constitutional adjudication in Latin America. In *Comparative constitutional law in Latin America* (pp. 276–299). Edward Elgar.

Sanchez Urribarri, R. A. (2022). Populism, constitutional democracy and high courts—lessons from the Venezuelan case. In M. Krygier, A. Czarnota, & W. Sadurski (Eds.), *Anti-constitutional populism* (pp. 185–217). Cambridge University Press.

Sanchez Urribarri, R., & García-Soto, C. (2019). A primer to Venezuela's constitutional crisis. *IACL-AIDC Blog* (29 April, 2019) See: https://blog-iacl-aidc.org/crisis-in-venezuela/2019/4/29/a-primer-to-venezuelas-constitutional-crisis

Schaaf, S. (2022). When do courts constrain the authoritarian state? Judicial decision-making in Jordan and Palestine. *Comparative Politics*, *54*(2), 375–399.

Scheppele, K. L. (2018). Autocratic legalism. *The University of Chicago Law Review*, 85(2), 545–584.

Shen-Bayh, F. (2018). Strategies of repression: Judicial and extrajudicial methods of autocratic survival. *World Politics*, *70*(3), 321–357.

Solomon, P. H. (2007). Courts and judges in authoritarian regimes. *World Politics*, 60(1), 122–145.

Trochev, A., & Ellett, R. (2014). Judges and their allies: Rethinking judicial autonomy through the prism of off-bench resistance. *Journal of Law and Courts*, *2*(1), 67–91.

· 10 ·

JUDICIAL ACTIVISM IN PARAGUAY: A REACTIVE FORM OF COMPENSATORY JUSTICE

Andrea Castagnola, Gabriela Bonzi, Shirley Franco and Aníbal Pérez-Liñán

What is the role of constitutional justice in countries with low levels of judicial independence? Under those circumstances, most scholars expect to observe weak and deferential courts (Ríos-Figueroa, 2007; Domingo, 2004, 2009). Two reasons make judicial activism unlikely in this context. First, in countries with captured courts (i.e., courts or tribunals that are controlled by the actors that they are supposed to hold accountable), justices usually have close connections with the ruling elites. Thus, they have few incentives to invalidate norms. Second, justices who lack connections with the ruling party have few incentives to take an activist stand, since they can be punished for defying the government.

Against this common wisdom, we find that in Paraguay—a country with long tradition of political manipulation, lack of judicial independence, and strong party hegemony (Pérez-Liñán and Castagnola, 2009 Basabe-Serrano, 2015)—the Supreme Court has ruled systematically against the government. Original data reveals that, between 1995 and 2015, the Court decided in favor of plaintiffs in seven (7) of every 10 actions of unconstitutionality challenging executive decrees or congressional laws. How can we interpret these results? Is the judiciary settling political disputes between partisan elites? Or are all these rulings a form of anti-government judicial activism, addressing a diverse agenda of citizens' rights?

This chapter aims to address these questions by providing a quantitative and qualitative analysis of Supreme Court rulings in actions of unconstitutionality. We identify on which type of controversies justices have invalidated norms, seeking to understand the justices' role in dealing with horizontal and vertical accountability disputes. Horizontal accountability disputes refer to cases in which the judiciary resolves controversies between partisan elites (like Congress and the Executive), while vertical disputes involve controversies between citizens and the State.

We argue that institutional design has shaped the role of the judiciary in ways that transcend partisan politics. In Paraguay, judicial review is concentrated in the Constitutional Chamber of the Supreme Court. The Chamber does not control its docket, the effect of its sentences are *inter partes*, and there is no binding principle of *stare decisis* for its rulings. This hybrid institutional design, which combines features of concentrated and diffuse judicial review, promotes the arrival at the courts of constitutional or legal controversies already addressed in previous decisions. Consequently, the Chamber ends up reasserting its position in multiple cases. Because of this practice, a high frequency of decisions against the government does not necessarily reflect a proactive Chamber creating innovative jurisprudence, but rather a reactive role that demands the replication of rulings in similar cases. While a proactive court can control case stimulus (control the docket and consequently the litigation agenda), a reactive court simply responds to the stimulus (the cases that reach the tribunal). In the following pages we show that, due to the institutional design of constitutional justice, Paraguay's judicial "activism" is a reactive form of behavior.

Even though scholars recognize the importance of repetitive cases at the high court level in many jurisdictions, studies of this problem are rare, both in the Paraguayan context and elsewhere. We offer an empirical assessment of the problem, identifying distinct constitutional controversies that reemerge in repetitive cases. The 4,947 rulings analyzed in this chapter involve only 430 unique controversies, indicating that over 90% of the docket involves matters of law on which the Chamber has ruled previously. Moreover, only four (4) controversies out of 430 cases concentrated 72% of the docket. The Chamber's agenda concentrated on social security issues, civil servants' rights, the adoption of a new criminal procedure, and municipal powers. The Chamber has dealt primarily with vertical disputes, with only a few instances of low-profile horizontal disputes involving the prerogatives of municipalities. Altogether, we find that constitutional activism is a reactive form of compensatory justice (key for regulating the social security system) and not necessarily a form of mediating conflicts between political elites.

The chapter is structured as follows. Before analyzing the Chamber's docket, we first lay out the political context in which the rulings took place. In the second section, we describe judicial review in Paraguay and provide a conceptual framework for analyzing the Chamber's behavior. In the third section, we present the findings of a novel dataset that identifies constitutional controversies and repetitive cases. In the following section, we present a qualitative analysis of the four controversies that have recurrently appeared in the Chamber.

Courts and Politics in Paraguay

Paraguay's judicial politics takes place in the context of a system dominated by the Colorado Party (Republican National Association-ANR) which has been a dominant party for over seven decades. The transition to democracy started in 1989, when General Alfredo Stroessner was ousted from office. During the transition, political competition flourished between parties and among party factions within the Colorado Party. Still, it was not until 2008 when Fernando Lugo from the Christian Democratic Party put an end to the continuous rule of the Colorado Party, although not for long. President Lugo was impeached and removed from office within a few years of arriving in office, and the Colorado Party eventually returned to power. The emergence of electoral party competition had a positive effect on the legal system since it reduced undue partisan influence on the judiciary (Basabe-Serrano, 2015).

In 1992, the Paraguayan Constitution underwent significant reform, with three substantial changes aimed at promoting judicial autonomy and independence. First, the new Constitution introduced life terms until the retirement age of 75 (Article 261), and reduced the role of the president in the appointment of judges. Previously, judges were appointed for a fixed number of years, concurrent with the president's term. Moreover, an informal requisite required candidates to be affiliated to the Colorado Party. Second, Article 249 granted financial autonomy to the judiciary by establishing a fixed budget of "no less than three percent of the budget of the Central Administration". Third, Article 132 established the principle of judicial review, embodied in a Constitutional Chamber within the Supreme Court. The Chamber reviews claims that challenge norms on concrete cases and *a posteriori*. Its decisions have effects *inter partes* (article 260). Because justices lack the power to remove norms from the legal framework on unconstitutionality grounds (acting as a veto power or "negative legislator"), ruling in favor of the plaintiff in a particular case usually opens the floodgate for repetitive cases that increase the justices' workload.

Regardless of these profound transformations, political manipulation of the judiciary has persisted. In Paraguay, as in other countries of the region, politicians have systematically manipulated the Supreme Court by pressuring justices to resign and opening vacancies for allied judges (Pérez-Liñán and Castagnola, 2009). Based on qualitative and quantitative research, we identify at least three mechanisms by which Paraguayan politicians have consistently controlled the court: *cuoteo*, attempts to alter the constitutional interpretation of life tenure, and purges.

Cuoteo: This practice consists of distributing the vacancies in the Court among the parties or factions necessary to form a majority to approve nominations. For *cuoteo* to take place, the Senate and the president typically bargain over multiple vacancies in the court at the same time, to allocate them among coalition members. For example, three years after the enactment of the 1992 Constitution, politicians filled the new seats in the Court by *cuoteo*. The nine seats were distributed in the following way: five to the Colorado Party, three to the Authentic Radical Liberal Party (PLRA), and one to the Christian Democratic Party (Molina et al., 2018).

Constitutional (re)interpretation of the justices' tenure: A conflict surrounding the tenure of justices has been taking place between Congress and the Court, based on the articles of the 1992 constitution each institution cites to determine the tenure of justices. Congress refers to Article 252, while the Court refers to Article 261. Article 252 refers to the tenure of all judges, establishing that they are appointed for periods of five years, and that those judges who had been confirmed for two periods acquire life tenure until retirement age. On the other hand, Article 261 refers exclusively to the tenure of Supreme Court justices, stating that the only way to remove a justice is by impeachment.

The first controversy on this issue arose in 1999 when the Senate, invoking Article 252, opened the floor to decide which of the nine justices of the Court should be confirmed after their first five years on the bench. On that occasion five justices were confirmed, and the rest were dismissed. The members of the Court ruled instead that justices have life tenure based on Article 261 (Agreements and rulings N ° 222/2000 and 223/2000). The Court won the battle, but the constitutional controversy over the interpretation of life tenure remains open. The Senate continued to challenge life-term appointments, while the

Constitutional Chamber has reaffirmed the previous interpretation of the Supreme Court (rulings 557/2007, 1149/2008, 947/2009, 949/2009, 1010/2015).

Purges: Purges or reshuffles have also been part of the repertoire of political manipulation. One of the most notable moments during the presidential campaign of Nicanor Duarte Frutos was when he promised to "pulverize the Court" if elected. After Duarte Frutos took office in 2003, he threatened to impeach six justices; four of them resigned and the remaining two were impeached and removed from the bench. The ruling coalition filled the six vacancies by *cuoteo* from a list of close candidates.

The mechanisms just described help explain the recurrent pattern of instability of the justices on the bench. As Figure 10.1 shows, the Court was reshuffled on 20 occasions between 1900 and 2021.

According to Basabe-Serrano (2015, 2022) there is a strong presence of informal practices like cooptation, clientelism and corruption for capturing the judiciary. A comparative study recently revealed that in Paraguay, judicial operators have consistently recognized the existence of subtle modes of interference in justices' decisions, mainly through bribes and clientelist relations. In contrast, direct methods, like threats and verbal or physical attacks, have been unusual during the democratic period (Llanos et al., 2016).

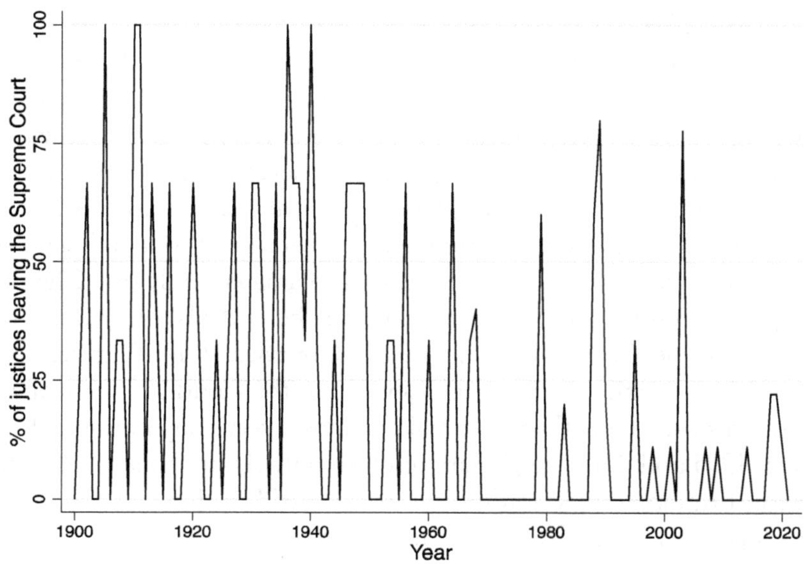

Figure 10.1: Reshuffles in the Supreme Court of Paraguay since 1900–2021

Countries like Paraguay, with a legacy of political manipulation of the Supreme Court, appear to be unlikely places to find activist courts. However, between 1994 and 2014, the Constitutional Chamber ruled against the Executive or Legislature on 70% of the cases. In the next section, we analyze the implications of this type of judicial behavior and its impact on the legal system.

Judicial Activism and Judicial Review in Paraguay

There are different interpretations about what constitutes judicial activism and, therefore, how to identify it. Judicial activism is often related to the idea that courts, through their rulings, protect and expand individual rights by departing from the "official" interpretation of norms (Cross and Lindquist, 2007). Judicial restraint, on the other hand, presupposes the opposite: courts have a narrow or limited interpretation of norms (Skelly, 1968). Both types of behaviors are part of the justices' repertoire, and it is expected that courts will balance activism and self-restraint. Yet, the presence of more activist justices would imply that government acts are found unconstitutional more often. In Latin America and other developing countries, there is a prominent literature on judicial activism on socioeconomic rights as well (for example, see Gauri and Brinks, 2008; Wilson, 2005; Motta Ferraz, 2009, among others).

Kmiec (2004) and Cohn and Kremnitzer (2005) systematize the main approaches to assess judicial activism and related debates in the literature, as discussed in Staton's chapter earlier in this volume. Some of these approaches can be applied to our case. In this research, we associate activism with constitutional rulings that challenge the existing legal framework, thus modifying the status quo. The model of judicial activism characteristic of Paraguay's Constitutional Chamber results from its *sui generis* institutional design, which sets the pace and scope of judicial action. In Paraguay, only one Chamber of the Supreme Court—the Constitutional Chamber—deals with judicial review (Lezcano Claude, 2000; Mendonça, 2012; González, 2014; Ramírez Candia, 2019). Although some cases may be elevated to the Court's nine-member plenary, the three-member Chamber makes almost every constitutional decision; between 1995 and 2015 the plenary resolved only six of about 5,000 petitions of unconstitutionality. According to article 8 of Law No. 609/95, the three judges appointed to the Chamber remain on those seats for one year. However, the informal rule is that once a justice has been appointed to a Chamber she will remain throughout her tenure. Contrary to other concentrated judicial review systems, Paraguayan justices do not control their docket, and their decisions have an *inter partes* effect. Even though the Court created a doctrine that suggests that rulings issued by the plenary of the court (and not the chamber) could have *erga omnes* effects (Agreement and Sentence No. 222/2000), this doctrine has been highly controversial and inconsistently applied (Moreno Rodriguez Alcalá, 2018). The possibility that the rulings of the Supreme Court may have *erga omnes* effect comes from article 259 (5) of the Constitution, which establishes that the Court as well as the Chamber can exercise judicial review. So far, the Supreme Court issued decisions claiming *erga omnes* effects in only four cases.[1] Nevertheless, it is precisely the *inter partes* effect and the mandatory docket what create a reactive form of judicial activism in Paraguay.

Inter partes effects: The *inter partes* effect promotes repetitive cases, creating not only a significant workload but also the illusion of a highly proactive court. The Chamber's decisions do not necessarily affect policymaking since they only affect litigants in the case. Moreover, our research shows that the norms that are most frequently challenged have not been reformed or repealed by the elected branches, despite thousands of declarations of unconstitutionality by the Chamber. This situation has been exposed by the media, but the legislature did not address those complaints (Ramírez Bogado, 2018). Some scholars argue that this type of judicial review system transfers control over bureaucratic outcomes from the executive or legislature to the judiciary (Chutkow, 2008). In the long run, the constant filing of cases on the same topic could produce a snowball effect, influencing policymaking. However, this has not been the case in Paraguay.

Mandatory docket: The lack of control over the docket also influences the nature of judicial review exercised by the Constitutional Chamber. The literature has shown that docket control can affect the efficiency and quality of the decisions (e.g., if justices only have a short time to devote to each case), shaping the Court's role within the legal system (Clark and Strauss, 2010). According to Clark and Staton (2015), courts can be *law-applicant* (when having large dockets) or engage in *rule construction* (when having small dockets). In law-applicant courts with mandatory dockets, justices do not necessarily develop new rules but instead apply the same rule on multiple cases. This feature, combined with the *inter partes* effects mentioned above, boosts the proliferation of new claims on the same topic. In contrast, in rule-constructing courts with discretionary dockets, justices select the cases, and have more time and resources

1 Those cases were the rulings Nos. 183/1994; N° 415/1998; 222/2000, and 223/2000, respectively.

to spend on each of them. It is precisely in this type of court that justices can best make policy or influence the legal system.

In Paraguay, the Constitutional Chamber is a law applicant institution. Judicial activism becomes a reactive behavior conditioned by the type and volume of demands from litigants. It is *reactive* because justices must process the demands (claims) and the number of cases filed. The type of demands defines the agenda (i.e., determines which rights are more frequently under dispute in the Chamber). The number of cases reflects the importance of that right for society and a potential area for activism. Because of these reasons, the most appropriate way for studying judicial activism in Paraguay implies identifying, first, which claims have been the most recurrent ones before the courts—especially the Constitutional Chamber—and, second, how the Court has ruled in those cases.

Judicial activism is often associated with independent courts or enclaves of judicial autonomy. However, in this chapter, we reexamine this assumption. Conventional theories predict judicial activism in countries with high levels of judicial independence, since politicians will not punish justices for their rulings. Yet, subnational studies in the US reveal that judicial activism is more likely to occur in states where justices reach office through elections than on states in which justices remain insulated from partisan politics (Wenzel et al., 1997). Politics and electoral accountability also explain judicial activism in subnational courts in the US and in some other countries in the region, such as Chile (Royce and Tiede, 2011). In Paraguay, justices are selected through competitions held by the Council of the Judicature, the Senate nominates a candidate from the shortlist provided by the Council and the President appoints the candidate in the Court. Partisan politics often plays an essential role in that process. Still, due to the *sui generis* institutional design, it is not clear *a priori* whether judicial activism represents a form of judicial independence. In the following sections, we present both quantitative and qualitative analyses of the Constitutional Chamber's rulings to shed light on these issues.

Empirical Data about Constitutional Justice in Paraguay

We use a novel dataset to analyze the role of the Constitutional Chamber in Paraguay, to help elucidate whether the Court has engaged in judicial activism. The dataset contains all actions against the President (executive decree) and/or Congress (law) between 1995 and 2015. During this period, the Chamber decided on 14,744 actions, of which 4,947 (34%) challenged a decree and/or a law.[2] The Chamber ruled about 70% of them unconstitutional. Again, due to the *inter partes* effect of the rulings, many of those decisions were repetitions of previous controversies.

To distinguish unique cases from repetitive ones, we adopted a three-step methodology. First, we determined the norm or combination of norms challenged in each case. Second, we grouped the cases by the norm or norms challenged. As a result of these two steps, we identified a total of 444 "unique cases", i.e., clusters of cases that challenged the same norm/s. Third, once we identified these unique cases, we analyzed the clusters of claims to check for consistency during the coding process. During this phase we found that there were 14 unique cases that could be re-clustered or re-grouped with other unique cases because they all relate to the same issue. The social security cluster is a good example of this phenomenon. When analyzing the clusters of claims, we identified that there were 12 unique cases related to social security issues, and that all of these unique cases could be re-grouped together in one unique case because they were all against norms regulating the public (Decree No.1579/04, Laws No. 2345/03 and 3542/08) and non-contributory systems (Laws No. 525/94, 1534/00, 1661/01, and 1857/02). Another example is the municipal autonomy cluster of cases. When analyzing these "unique cases", we found two clusters of cases targeting the same type of claim: protecting the autonomy of municipalities. One unique case challenged Law No. 3850 (2009) that established that municipalities should transfer to the central government the prerogative of technical inspection of vehicles, while another unique case challenged Law No. 3966 (2010) that dictated that municipalities should transfer to central authorities the control of national routes. Both cases were grouped together rather than separately. As a result of this re-examination of cases, we identified a total of 430 unique cases for the whole period.[3] This means that 4,517 cases (91% of the docket) repeated some of those 430 controversies already decided by the Chamber. Moreover, four (4) of those 430 controversies concentrated 72% of the total docket (3,561 cases). This dramatic docket concentration

2 The remaining of the cases of the docket were actions against a ministerial resolution and/or local authorities.

3 This means that a total of 14 "unique cases" identified in step-two were re-grouped in step-three: 11 "unique cases" were re-grouped within the social security cluster, 2 "unique cases" were re-grouped within the civil servants' rights cluster and 1 "unique case" was re-grouped within the municipal autonomy cluster.

Table 10.1: Most frequent types of cases resolved by the Constitutional Chamber (1995–2015)

Cluster of Cases	No. of Cases	% Unconstitutional Ruling
Social security system	2661	84%
Civil servants' rights	557	31%
Transition to a new Criminal Procedure System	192	100%
Municipal autonomy	151	72%

raises questions about the Court's efficiency and the value of legal mobilization for legal actors and citizens.

A preliminary analysis of the four most frequent cluster of cases, presented in Table 10.1, reveals that judicial activism has been the most likely behavior adopted by Chamber in these highly repetitive cases. In three of the four clusters of cases the Chamber has declared the norm inapplicable in more than 70% of the individual cases (see Column 3, Table 10.1). Most of these decisions centered on disputes between the state and citizens and not necessarily on conflicts among political elites (except in municipal autonomy cases).

A vast majority of the decisions of the Chamber between 1995 and 2015 therefore referred to controversies already resolved. Figure 10.2a compares the total number of unique controversies decided per year vis-à-vis the total number of cases (the figure employs different scales for readability). For instance, in 2002, only eight (8) of the 793 rulings corresponded to novel controversies, i.e., 99% of the decisions referred to already resolved disputes. A similar situation occurred in 2012 and 2013, when 93% and 91% of the rulings (respectively) referred to previous controversies. Moreover, the Chamber resolved less than ten novel controversies per year in seven of the 21 years under analysis,[4] while it solved 50 novel controversies or more in three years (2006, 2012, and 2013). On average, the Chamber resolved about 21 unique controversies per year.

When accounting for repetitive cases, the percentage of norms declared unconstitutional declines from 70% to 46% of the docket (Figure 10.2b).[5] However, the analysis that does not weight cases according to their repetitive status, represented by the darker line, overestimates the Chamber's activist role.

4 In 1995, 1998, 2002, 2003, 2004, 2011, and 2015.

5 The brown line denotes the decisions declared unconstitutional over total cases, whereas the gold line shows the actual new cases declared unconstitutional per year over the actual new cases per year, expressed as a percentage.

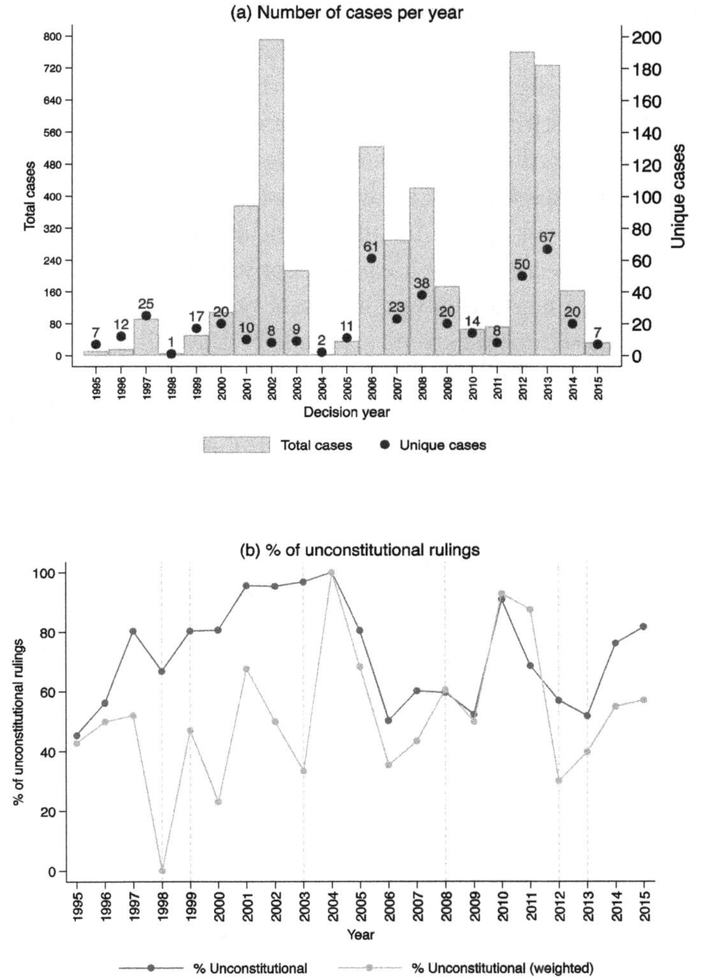

Figure 10.2: Unique vs total cases per year
Note: the bar graph captures the total number of rulings (primary axis) and the dotgraph the total number of unique ruling (secondary axis).

The weighted examination—treating all cases referring to the same constitutional controversy as a unit, represented by the grey line—produces similar results to other courts in the region. For example, in Costa Rica, between 1990 and 2015, the Constitutional Chamber declared a norm unconstitutional in 47% of the cases (Poder Judicial, 2017). In Colombia, between 1992 and 2006, the Constitutional Court ruled norms unconstitutional 38% of the times

(Rodríguez-Raga, 2011). Between 1935 and 1998, the Argentinian Supreme Court ruled 37% of the cases as unconstitutional (Bercholc, 2004). In Mexico, the Supreme Court declared it on 18% of the Constitutional Controversies and 24% of the Constitutional Actions (Castagnola and López-Noriega, 2017).

A closer analysis of the Chamber's rulings on the four most frequent controversies, though, suggests that early decisions are decisive because those rulings, on average, are upheld in subsequent instances (see Figure 10.3). For example, on social security cases, early unconstitutional rulings remained for subsequent years, while the opposite was the case for civil servants' rights cases. Criminal Code cases are an extreme example because all the cases appeared in 2003 and were declared unconstitutional.

In sum, one of the most salient features of the Constitutional Chamber is the high number of repetitive cases. This information becomes crucial for studying judicial behavior. Lack of acknowledgment of repetitive cases can cause an inference problem because the high number of decisions of unconstitutionality may result from the institutional design, not from an equivalent number of unique norms violating the constitution. In addition, because

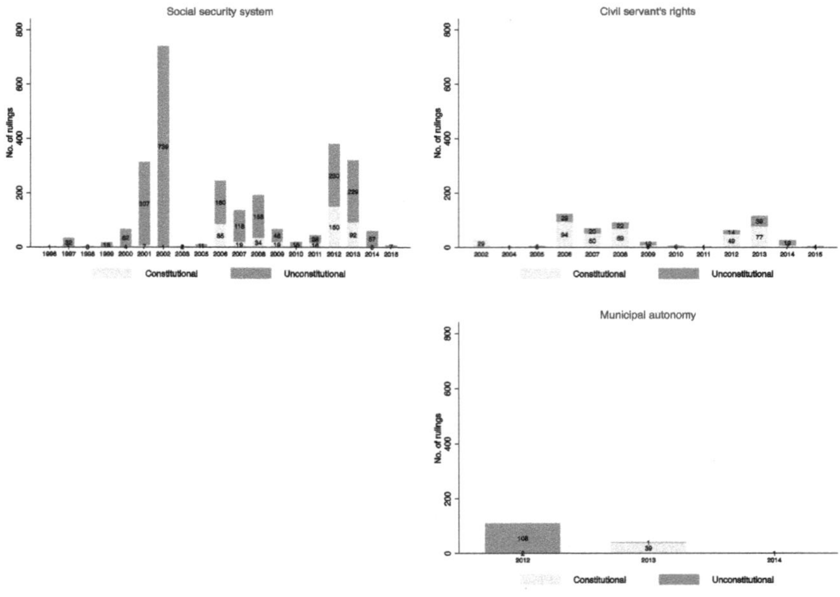

Figure 10.3: Rulings of the Constitutional Chamber on the three most repeated cases
Note: Criminal Code controversies do not appear because all of them were filled in 2003 and were declared unconstitutional.

Table 10.2: Main role of the Constitutional Chamber on judicial review

Unique Cases	Rights under dispute	Role of the Court	Behavior of the court	Conflict
Social Security System	Social Security and equality	Protector of core values	Activism	State vs. society
Civil servants' rights	Work and equality	Mediator in state bureaucracy	Self-restraint	State vs. civil servant
Transition to a new Criminal Procedure System	Equality	Auxiliary within the judicial system	Activism	Potential conflict in the administration of justice
Municipal Autonomy	Municipal autonomy	Arbitrator in the separation of powers	Activism	Central vs. local government

justices rule similarly in the same type of cases, their votes are not independent, and econometric models should model this behavior to compute unbiased coefficients. In the next section, we present a detailed analysis of the four most repeated controversies.

The Roles of the Constitutional Chamber

This section analyzes the Chamber's role in the four most frequent cluster of controversies to understand the particularities of societal, legal mobilization, and justice behavior. Table 10.2 systematizes the critical findings, and highlights similarities and differences. Overall, the Chamber has acted as an activist body on claims involving the social security system, the transition to a new criminal procedure, and the regulation of the autonomy of municipalities. Meanwhile, on cases regulating state-work relations, the Chamber has restrained itself.

Social Security System

The Paraguayan social security system is a classic case of judicial activism. The Constitutional Chamber intervened to remedy the social conflicts caused by faulty social security legislation. Despite changes in the composition of the Court, judges tended to rule in the same way over time. The judiciary seemed to intervene when violations of fundamental rights occurred. Affected persons filed lawsuits against norms regulating the public (Decree No.1579/04, Laws No. 2345/03 and 3542/08) and non-contributory systems (Laws No. 525/94, 1534/00, 1661/01, and 1857/02).[6] The plaintiffs alleged that these laws were unconstitutional since they infringed their rights or did not guarantee their access to their retirement funds. The Constitutional Chamber declared these norms unconstitutional. The Chamber's unconstitutional rulings were recurrent for non-contributory cases. It ruled against the annual budget approved by Congress every year since it limited or excluded Chaco War veterans' and families' rightful access to their retirement funds. Regarding the public sector, the Chamber decided not to analyze the unconstitutionality of its legislation because the legislature had already replaced it (Law No. 1802/01). However, the new law has the same defects as the previous one (except for an additional requirement of seniority). Therefore, courts should declare it void or inapplicable to protect petitioners' access to their retirement funds.

Rights of Civil Servants

The Chamber reviewed lawsuits filed by civil servants and government agencies that challenged two laws that regulate work relationships. One group of civil servants challenged Law 700/1996 that banned them from receiving more than one government salary, while another group disputed Law No. 1626/2000 that disqualified retired civil servants from being re-hired to a public function and receiving retirement funds and current salary. The plaintiffs alleged that these laws were unconstitutional since they infringed their rights to work and equal treatment.

The Chamber's verdicts varied according to the nature of the plaintiff. It declared the disputed laws unconstitutional, displaying a certain predisposition to reverse or annul the Legislature's provisions. Although formally only

6 Different overlapping institutions governs the Paraguayan social security system. A public, a private, and a non-contributory sector coexist in the system. The first sector administers funds for public officials and the banking industry's pension funds. The private structure comprises mutual funds, and the non-contributory system encompasses pensions granted to Chaco War veterans and their families. The entire social security structure runs under the norms enacted by the Paraguayan Congress and the Executive. However, the absence of a single regulatory entity puts intense pressure on the national budget. For example, the pensions of the non-contributory system are established in the annual budget and they entail major financial outlays.

affecting the parties, since the litigant was a public entity, the Chamber's decision impacted all the entity's public servants. In this case, the ruling departed de facto from an *inter partes effect*, and embraced instead an *erga omnes* effect. Although it argued that its actions were to protect fundamental rights and constitutional principles, they represented, in fact, an act of mediation between the parties in conflict. This type of disputes should be handled by an Administrative Court rather than a Constitutional Chamber, but due to the lack of a consistent legal system that regulates on the issue, it is the Chamber that ends up resolving the controversies.

Unlike the Social Security controversy, in this case the Chamber adopted a position of self-restraint when mediating conflicts between the State and its employees. When individual civil servants filed lawsuits, the Chamber mostly rejected the claims. It is a classic example of judicial restraint: the Chamber showed deference towards the legislator and ruled in favor of the State.

Transition to the New Criminal Procedure

The transition to a new Criminal Procedure System involved two significant reforms. First, in 1989 the reform of the 1890 Criminal Procedure system, and second, in 1997, the reform of the 1914 Criminal Code. Along with these reforms, transition acts were also established to regulate the passages from the old to the new systems, with Transition Act No. 1444/99 as one of them. Law No. 1444/999 established that all criminal trials had to end before the new code took effect. The Public Ministry of Paraguay filed lawsuits against Transition Act No. 1444 (specifically art. 5) because it established that all claims under the old Criminal Procedure system of 1890 that were not concluded before February 28, 2003 would expire. The Attorney General argued that the law was unconstitutional because it violated the principle of equality, extinguishing unfinished criminal proceedings without an acquittal or conviction.

This is one of the few controversies decided by the Plenary of the Supreme Court and not by the Constitutional Chamber. The Court ascertained in decision No. 979 that art. 5 of Law No. 1444/99 was unconstitutional since it violated the guarantee to effective judicial protection. This interpretation led to other similar judicial decisions, which declared the law inapplicable not just with respect to art. 5, but also with regards to all other articles that could endanger the completion of the criminal proceedings. The practical effect was that criminal cases initiated under the previous criminal procedure did not expire when the new system entered into force.

The Court played an auxiliary role in allowing criminal processes to conclude in time, preventing criminal proceedings from ending without a final verdict. Otherwise, the Criminal Procedure would have failed its primary duty of protecting defendants, bearing a considerable political cost for the judiciary as a whole.

In this case, the Court's Plenary claimed *erga omnes* effects for the sentence. However, as noted above, the conventional interpretation is that the Constitution only allows for *inter partes* effects. The Court claimed *erga omnes* effects to prevent the multiplication of disputes about pending criminal cases. Nevertheless, prosecutors promoted claims in all the cases, since it was the first time that the Court's Plenary enlarged the scope of the effect of its decisions. The Constitutional Chamber handled the repetitive cases, and it systematically supported the Plenary's initial position from sentence No. 979. The Chamber did not address the substance of the cases, but just ratified the precedent.

Municipal Autonomy

Municipalities filed lawsuits against two laws that affected their autonomy by limiting their competence and shifting some of their powers to the central government: Law No. 3850 (2009), which transferred to the central government the technical inspection of vehicles, and Law No. 3966 (2010), which conceded to central government authorities the control of national routes. The Constitutional Chamber mediated conflicts concerning the decentralization of executive functions.

Generally, the Chamber reversed the acts of the Legislature by ruling in favor of municipal entities, to which it granted exclusive prerogatives on the issues submitted for consideration. In doing so, the Chamber delineated each body's prerogatives, thus enforcing the separation of powers principle. The case challenges the traditional idea of the judge as a mere enforcer of the law, subject to the Legislature's will. In this example, the Chamber overturned the Legislature's work, displaying an activist profile in favor of subnational municipal authorities. After the Court's verdicts against the Legislature, Congress removed the legislation from the legal system, engaging in an institutional dialogue between powers.

Conclusion

At the beginning of this article, we wondered about the role of constitutional justice in countries with low levels of judicial independence. Our analysis of Paraguay shows that, even in a new democracy where the judiciary has traditionally been subject to political influence, judicial review deserves careful attention. The goal of this chapter was to understand the roles played by the Constitutional Chamber of the Supreme Court, using a quantitative and qualitative methodology to identify patterns of judicial activism.

The results show that the Constitutional Chamber has not been deferential to the legislature. Even after accounting for an institutional design that produces repetitive cases and artificially inflates the number of decisions against the government, we find that the Chamber's frequency of decisions overturning government acts is fairly high, similar to the one observed in Costa Rica. Paraguay's constitutional case docket, however, focused during the years under analysis on four types of controversies: social security, civil servants' rights, the criminal procedure reform, and municipal autonomy. In three of these controversies, the Chamber ruled against the national government in over 70% of the individual cases. It generally played an activist role in the protection of rights, but it refused to intervene in relations between the State and civil servants.

Constitutional justice in Paraguay is a reactive form of compensatory justice, and not necessarily a form of mediating conflicts between political elites. Paraguay's *hybrid* institutional design of judicial review creates the illusion of a highly activist institution, but this chapter has shown that the figures above should be interpreted carefully. The lack of *certiorari* (i.e., the presence of a mandatory docket) and the *inter partes* effect of the rulings promotes the arrival at the courts of repetitive cases. The absence of any systematic response on the part of the legislature to correct the constitutional deficits of the legislation questioned by the Chamber further exacerbates this situation. For example, the legislative deficit of the pension system forced justices to take an activist role to address individual claims. These types of constitutional rulings do not necessarily represent an attack to the ruling elites, since they do not affect the partisan balance in the institutions, and instead offer compensations for individuals.

These findings do not undermine the importance of the Chamber, nor of its role within the political system, but help to shed light on the scope of constitutional justice in Paraguay and the types of cases that tend to be adjudicated—including several in which Paraguay's judges have taken an interest and acted. Judicial activism is therefore a form of compensatory justice for a very specific number of individual rights (and just occasionally to exercise horizontal accountability). It is not necessarily a mechanism for regulating partisan politics or resolving political disputes.

References

Basabe-Serrano, S. (2015). Judicial Independence in Paraguay. *Law & Policy, 37*, 350–378.

Basabe-Serrano, S. (2022). Judicial corruption: The constitutional court of Ecuador in comparative perspective. In B. Sandra, D. M. Brinks, & E. A. Gonzalez-Ocantos (Eds.), *The limits of judicialization: From progress to backlash in Latin America*. Cambridge University Press.

Bercholc, J. (2004). *La Independencia de la Corte Suprema a través del control de Constitucionalidad respecto a los otros poderes políticos del Estado (1935–1998)*. Edited by Ediar. Buenos Aires, Argentina.

Castagnola, A., & López-Noriega, S. (2017). Are Mexican justices true abiters among political elites? An empirical analysis of the court's rulings from 2000–2011. In A. Castagnola & S. López-Noriega (Eds.), *Judicial politics in Mexico. The Supreme Court and the transition to democracy*. New York: Routledge.

Chutkow, D. M. (2008). Jurisdiction stripping: Litigation, ideology, and congressional control of the court. *Journal of Politics, 70*(4), 1053–1064.

Clark, T. S., & Staton, J. K. (2015). An informational model of constitutional jurisdiction. *The Journal of Politics, 77*(3), 589–607.

Clark, T. S., & Strauss, A. B. (2010). The implications of high court docket control for resources allocation and legal efficiency. *Journal of Theoretical Politics, 22*(2), 247–268.

Cohn, M., & Kremnitzer, M. (2005). Judicial activism: A multidimensional model. *Canadian Journal of Law & Jurisprudence, 18*, 333–356.

Corte Suprema de Justicia (Ed.). (2008). *Digesto de Derecho Administrativo. Tomo II*. Asunción: División de Investigación, Legislación y Publicaciones. Centro Internacional de Estudios Judiciales.

Cross, F. B., & Lindquist, S. A. (2007). The scientific study of judicial activism. *Minnesota Law Review, 652*, 1752–1784.

Domingo, P. (2004). ¿Judicialitasion of politics or politication of judiciary? Recent trends in Latin America. *Democratisation, 1*(11), 104–126.

Domingo, P. (2009). Ciudadanía, derechos y justicia en América Latina. *CIDOB d'Afers Internacionals*, 85–86, 33–52.

Ferraz, O. L. M. (2009). The right to health in the courts of Brazil: Worsening health inequities?. *Health & Hum. Rts. J., 11*(2). Colombia.

Gauri, V., & Brinks, D. M. (2008). *Courting social justice, judicial enforcement of social and economic rights in the developing world*. Cambridge University Press.

González, R. M. (2014). Capítulo VII. El Control de constitucionalidad en el Paraguay. En J. A. Amaya (Ed.), *La Jurisdicción Constitucional. Control de constitucionalidad y de convencionalidad* (pp. 177–205). Asunción: La Ley S.A..

Kmiec, K. (2004). The origin and current meanings of judicial activism. *California Law Review*, 92. DOI: 10.2307/3481421.

Lezcano, C. L. (2000). *El Control de Constitucionalidad en el Paraguay*. Asunción: La Ley Paraguaya S.A. Editora.

Llanos, M., Tibi Weber, C., Heyl, C., and Stroh, A. (2016). Informal interference in the judiciary in new democracies: A comparison of six African and Latin American cases. *Democratization*, *23*(7), 1236–1253.

Mendonça, J. C. (2012). Inconstitucionalidad. In Mendonça, D. (Coord.) *Derecho Procesal Constitucional. Régimen procesal de las garantías constitucionales* (pp. 21–75). Asunción: Centro de Estudios Constitucionales y la Ley Paraguaya S.A. Editora.

Molina, A., Costa R., J.M., and Berioshka, T. (2018). *Fragmentación Política e Independencia Judicial: Un Estudio de las Acciones de Inconstitucionalidad, 1995–2015*. Asuncion: Edicion Instituto Desarrollo.

Moreno Rodríguez Alcalá, D. (2018). Veinticinco años de evolución de la justicia constitucional. In C. Montanía Cibils & E. Santander Donna (Eds.), *Comentario a la Constitución—Tomo V—Homenaje al Vigésimo Quinto Aniversario* (pp. 279–312). Asunción: Corte Suprema de Justicia – Instituto de Investigaciones Jurídicas.

Pérez Liñán, A., & Castagnola, A. (2009). Presidential control of high courts in Latin America: A long term view (1904–2006). *Journal of Politics in Latin America*, *1*(2), 87–114.

Poder Judicial. (2017). El Control Constitucional: patrones de votación de la Sala Constitucional. In *Estado de la Justicia*. San Jose: Poder Judicial de Costa Rica.

Ramírez Bogado, R. (2018). Cientos de leyes siguen rigiendo, pese a ser inconstitucionales. *Ultima Hora*. February 11th 2018. https://www.ultimahora.com/cientos-leyes-siguen-rigiendo-pese-ser-inconstitucionales-n1133105.html

Ramírez Candia, Manuel de Jesús. (2019). *Control de Constitucionalidad*. Asunción: Editorial Arandurã.

Ríos-Figueroa, J. (2007). Fragmentation of power and the emergence of an effective judiciary in Mexico, 1994–2002. *Latin American Politics and Society*, 49(1), 31–57.

Rodríguez-Raga, J. C. (2011). Strategic deference in the Colombian constitutional court, 1992–2006. In G. Helmke & J. Ríos-Figueroa (Eds.), *Courts in Latin America* (pp. 81–98). New York: Cambridge University Press.

Royce, C., & Tiede, L. (2011). Judicial behavior on the Chilean constitutional tribunal. *Journal of Empirical Legal Studies*, 8(4), 856–877.

Skelly, W. J. (1968). Role of the Supreme Court in a democratic society–judicial activism or restraint. *Cornell Law Review*, 54(1).

Wenzel, J. P., Bowler, S., & Lanoue, D. J. (1997). Legislating from the state bench: A comparative analysis of judicial activism. *American Politics Quarterly*, 25(3) (July), 363–79.

Wilson, B. M. (2005). Changing dynamics: The political impact of Costa Rica's constitutional court. In R. Sieder et al. (Eds.), *The judicialization of politics in Latin America* (pp. 47–65). Studies of the Americas. Palgrave Macmillan, New York.

· 11 ·

JUDICIAL ACTIVISM IN HUMAN RIGHTS: IACTHR, CONVENTIONALITY CONTROL, AND THE MEXICAN SUPREME COURT

Rebecca A. Reid

First coined in 1947, judicial activism describes the use of judicial power to prescribe social goods, rather than allowing other branches of government to legislate the results that society wants (Schlesinger, 1947). Since then, the term has evolved, becoming both more commonplace and more varied in its definition (Green, 2009; Kmiec, 2004). Nonetheless, judicial activism usually refers to judicial behavior where a court takes on policymaking powers that are typically reserved for other branches of government. This conceptualization of judicial activism—and its usual pejorative rhetoric—is dependent upon a separation of powers framework, where activist courts are perceived as usurping policymaking powers at the expense of the appropriate (i.e., democratically elected) government authorities.

However, this same judicial behavior takes on an entirely different normative character when evaluated within human rights contexts. Within a rights framework, judicial activism becomes a positive mandate, where courts are critiqued if they fail to act when they have a duty to (Dawson, De Witte, and Muir, 2013). In this sense, judicial activism reflects a mandated function of the court, where the court should *not* be deferential to government authority and should go *beyond* the letter of the law to consider the broader societal implications of its decisions. Indeed, an adequate protection of human rights often requires that courts take on a significant policymaking role so as to effectively define rights and their violation, evaluate government actions, and hold violators accountable. Effective human rights regimes thus require activist courts.

In this chapter, I conceptualize judicial activism within a human rights context as a mandate that courts identify lacunae in existing law, and step in to create law or adjudicate cases that would otherwise be left vacant or unaddressed (Thirlway, 2002). In other words, judicial activism consists of judicial self-expansion, filling legal and policymaking spaces through (a) increased adjudication of rights cases, particularly those typically outside court jurisdiction, and (b) increased legal innovation. Legal innovation includes the generation of new law, a new interpretation of the law, or the novel application of existing law to new situations or cases. This definition of legal innovation as activism encompasses judicial reliance on international law and jurisprudence as "novel forms of engagement with the law and legal instruments" that align and synthesize international and domestic rights standards (Domingo, 2010, p. 269).

I evaluate both avenues of judicial activism looking at the interactive dialogue between two courts: the Inter-American Court of Human Rights (IACtHR) and the Mexican Supreme Court (*Suprema Corte de Justicia de la Nación* or SCJN). Specifically, I examine SCJN response to the IACtHR's development of the doctrine of conventionality control, which compels domestic courts to interpret domestic laws in accordance with rights treaty obligations and IACtHR jurisprudence (Castán, 2013). Conventionality control represents judicial activism by the IACtHR in that it is a legal innovation designed to establish a direct procedural link between the IACtHR and domestic legal regimes in order to make international law immediately enforceable domestically (García Ramírez, 2015; Malarino, 2012). Yet, the success of this doctrine—and the ability for the IACtHR to continue to engage in judicial activism—depends upon domestic courts' reception to IACtHR's legal innovation. National court compliance to conventionality control legitimizes and reinforces this legal innovation and the judicial activism of the IACtHR, while the rejection of conventionality control undermines the doctrine and constrains IACtHR behavior. Using human rights case data from 1996 to 2019 from Mexico's SCJN, I examine the extent to which the SCJN has accepted conventionality control's invitation for judicial activism to harmonize domestic and international law. I find that IACtHR activism via conventionality control is supported by the SCJN. Further, the SCJN has responded by expanding its adjudicative role in human rights cases, redefining domestic judicial power, and increasingly relying upon international law and jurisprudence in its decision-making. Thus, the SCJN has accepted the IACtHR's invitation for judicial activism.

The chapter proceeds as follows. Section I discusses the IACtHR and doctrine of conventionality control, and Section II introduces the SCJN and identifies its initial responses to the doctrine. Section III presents a descriptive empirical analysis of how the SCJN decision-making has changed in response to the development of conventionality control, focusing on expansion of SCJN purview and citations to international law and jurisprudence. Section IV offers some concluding thoughts.

IACtHR Judicial Activism and Conventionality Control

The Inter-American Court of Human Rights (IACtHR) was established by the American Convention on Human Rights in 1979, derived from the overlapping regional agreements of the American Declaration of the Rights and Duties of Man (1948) and the American Convention on Human Rights (1969). It is a part-time institution composed of seven independent judges, headquartered in San José, Costa Rica. Judges are nominated by Organization of American States (OAS) member states and elected by the OAS General Assembly, serving six-year terms with one possible reelection for another six-year term. All judges have legal backgrounds although only a limited number ever served as a judge in the home country. Most judges have been academics or have experience in diplomacy and politics (Harris, 2004).

The main function of the IACtHR is to oversee compliance with the American Convention on Human Rights through adjudicating contentious cases and issuing advisory opinions. States must be parties to the Convention and voluntarily submit to the IACtHR's jurisdiction for the Court to be competent to hear cases involving that state. Most of the region has granted blanket compulsory jurisdiction to the Court, including Mexico which acknowledged the court's jurisdiction in 1998. The IACtHR has no formal enforcement mechanism, though it provides annual compliance reports to the OAS General Assembly, who can issue sanctions. However, the OAS has never sanctioned a state for noncompliance to the IACHR (Pasqualucci, 2013). Hence, the IACtHR induces compliance through its public compliance reports[1] and conventionality control.

The IACtHR established the doctrine of conventionality control in *Almonacid Arellano et al. v. Chile* (2006)[2] to ensure that domestic laws and constitutional provisions do not impede the protection of rights established in the American Convention. Conventionality control asserts a direct obligation on all domestic courts and judges, by asserting a direct procedural link for the domestic application and enforcement of IACtHR jurisprudence (García Ramírez, 2015). In essence, conventionality control mandates that domestic judges ensure that domestic laws are in conformity with IACtHR jurisprudence and international human rights standards. In case of conflict between domestic law and norms and international legal standards, judges are to give preference to international legal standards. In fact, judges are to disregard domestic laws that contravene international human rights laws (Contesse, 2017). In addition, conventionality control should be exercised on all domestic laws and legal norms—including constitutional provisions—regardless of whether the litigating parties request it or not. This legal innovation also

1 In 1996, the IACtHR took it upon itself to issue yearly compliance reports that monitor state compliance. These compliance reports are based upon reports from victims, from the Inter-American Commission of Human Rights, and from the State.

2 The IACtHR continued to develop the doctrine until 2009 through its case law. Specifically, the IACtHR expanded upon the doctrine in *Dismissed Congressional Employees v. Peru* (2007), where the IACtHR explicitly (a) links the obligation of conventionality control to the duty of judges, (b) determines that conventionality control should be exercised *ex officio* (regardless of whether the parties request it or not), (c) decides that conventionality control shall be exercised by domestic judges in accordance with procedural regulations applicable to a particular case except when the enforcement of the rule violates rights protected by the American Convention, and (d) clarifies that conventionality control does not confer powers on domestic judges to act outside their respective sphere(s) of competence under domestic law. In *Boyce et al. v. Barbados* (2007), the IACtHR determined that judges must exercise conventionality control even on constitutional norms and laws. In *Heliodoro Portugal v. Panama* (2008), the IACtHR determined that domestic judges are required to exercise conventionality control to fill legal lacunae in domestic laws in order to guarantee rights, even if that violation of rights is not defined as a crime under domestic law. Finally, in *Radilla Pacheco v. Mexico* (2009), the IACtHR made explicit the judicial duty to interpret all domestic legal laws and norms in accordance to IACtHR's jurisprudence and international law. In other words, this case requires that judicial interpretation and implementation of domestic laws conform to international law and jurisprudence, even if the law itself is not necessarily incompatible. Through these cases, the IACtHR clarified domestic judicial obligations under the doctrine of conventionality control (González-Domínguez, 2018; Carmelina Londoño-Lázaro and Carrillo-Santarelli, 2019).

instructs domestic courts to engage in judicial activism, as the doctrine directs domestic courts to fill legal lacunae in domestic laws in order to guarantee rights, even if a violation of particular rights is not defined as a crime under domestic law. Conventionality control thus invites domestic courts into direct dialogue (Bazán, 2011) and to engage in judicial activism by asking them to apply IACtHR legal doctrines within their own decisions and to take a more expansive approach in human rights cases.

Conventionality control reinforces notions that domestic legal systems can serve as enforcement mechanisms for international human rights law (Simmons, 2009; Alter, 2011; Powell and Staton, 2009; Koh, 1996, 1997, 1998) and can foster "compliance partnerships" where domestic courts and the IACtHR can interact as allies to secure rights protections (Huneeus, 2011; Alter, 2011). By fostering cooperative and complementary relationships with national courts, the IACtHR invites national courts to engage in judicial activism and rely upon the IACtHR to realize their own empowerment. In other words, national courts are empowered through their partnership with the IACtHR, where their judicial activism is legitimized by IACtHR mandate, thereby reducing the likelihood of negative responses domestically. Furthermore, a national court's acceptance of this invitation of judicial activism and reliance on IACtHR empowers the supranational court, as its jurisdiction and impact are both consent-based, making it a more powerful institution and enabling future judicial activism. Thus, conventionality control can empower both courts by creating a partnership that enables judicial activism in both international and domestic spheres. However, relatively little scholarship has systematically examined the extent to which domestic courts have responded to this call for judicial activism (though see Aguiar-Aguilar, 2016; Maués et al., 2021).

Further, this unique legal innovation remains controversial. The doctrine of conventionality control originates as an agreement of IACtHR judges, rather than from the states. As such, the generation of this doctrine is an example of judicial activism where critics view it as a shameless power grab by the IACtHR, serving to impose its supremacy by creating self-proclaimed precedent with *erga omnes* effects, forcing monism upon states with little regard for sovereignty and domestic constitutional processes, taking direct control of domestic courts, and ignoring or violating the traditional principles of international law (Candia, 2012). This doctrine is thus viewed as anti-democratic and lacking legal grounding in the text or intent of the American Convention of Human Rights (González-Domínguez, 2018; Contesse, 2018; Binder, 2011).[3]

3 According to the IACtHR, conventionality control is based upon Articles 1 and 2 of the American Convention and Articles 26 and 27 of the Vienna Convention.

For instance, Contesse (2018) argues that this doctrine is (a) problematically intrusive, usurping domestic constitutional decisions about the incorporation of international law; (b) unnecessary, since most Latin American states were monist prior to conventionality control and thus incorporated international rights laws anyway; (c) inefficient, where a legal tool to solve the political problem of noncompliance offers little solution; (d) unclear, creating legal inconsistencies and incompatibilities; and (e) potentially delegitimizing for the Court's international legal authority. Dulitzky (2015) describes the doctrine as overreaching and absolutist, placing the IACtHR as a regional constitutional court and granting domestic courts powers of judicial review even when not constitutionally granted. Similarly, Contesse (2017) suggests that, rather than the IACtHR inviting domestic judiciaries into conversation or dialogue on the protection of rights, conventionality control relies upon IACtHR's asserting their presumed legal and moral superiority to issue top-down mandates. Gargarella (2015) expresses concern about the IACtHR's lack of deference to domestic democratic processes. Tsereteli (2016) highlights concerns pertaining to the IACtHR's lack of willingness to defer, or even carefully consider, interpretation by national courts. The establishment of conventionality control has thus divided legal scholars and practitioners, making domestic court response far from certain.

The next section investigates how the Mexican high court has responded to the IACtHR's judicial activism in establishing this doctrine, and whether the high court has accepted or rejected the invitation for their own judicial activism through the implementation of conventionality control.

SCJN and Reception of Conventionality Control

The SCJN sits atop the judicial hierarchy much like the U.S. Supreme Court.[4] Historically, the SCJN has played only a limited role as a protector of human rights (Pozas-Loyo and Ríos-Figueroa, 2017; Castagnola and Noriega, 2017; Castillejos-Aragón, 2013; Helmke and Ríos-Figueroa, 2011; Ansolabehere, 2010; Magaloni, 2007). Indeed, traditionally SCJN justices have exhibited a

4 As the highest federal court, it consists of eleven members: the elected President of the Supreme Court (similar to the United States' Chief Justice) and ten justices. Justices are proposed by the President of Mexico and confirmed by the Senate, and each justice is appointed to serve 15 years.

judicial ideology that prioritizes judicial restraint (Magaloni et al., 2011). Rights cases have been no exception, where the SCJN tends to develop both pro-rights and rights restrictive criteria in their decisions (Ansolabehere, 2010). Advances in rights jurisprudence have been incrementally made, partly due to SCJN restraint but also because of procedural requirements that vary across jurisprudential mechanisms. These requirements have limited accessibility to the SCJN in that only certain parties have standing to bring certain suits, and rights decisions are limited in their applicability beyond the parties of the case. Similarly, the ability of the SCJN to alter precedent is limited to certain types of cases and often requires the Court to issue multiple, identical rulings in a consecutive fashion. For instance, many rights cases appear before courts as *amparo* cases, which have not established precedent until the Court issues five consistent, consecutive decisions.[5]

However, some significant shifts in rights jurisprudence have recently appeared. The SCJN originally adjudicated based upon the principle of constitutional supremacy, where treaties and federal law were equal yet both below the Constitution hierarchically.[6] This standard was revised in 1999 to place treaties as hierarchically superior to federal and local laws but beneath the Constitution.[7] In 2007, the SCJN revised the hierarchy again, placing treaties and constitutional law as equal and superior to federal and local legislation.[8] In June 2011, Mexico amended its constitution to create a "new juridical system of human rights protections" (Collí-Ek, 2012, p. 1) that places international human rights treaties and the Constitution on the same footing. This amendment, largely based upon proposals sponsored by the SCJN (Medécigo, 2013), assigns responsibility on all Mexican authorities to take into account treaties to which Mexico is a party (i.e., conventionality control or *interpretación conforme*) and requiring them to always favor rules that most benefits the person (*pro personae* principle).

With the amended constitution, the SCJN began to issue decisions delimiting how domestic courts would comply and implement conventionality control (Contesse, 2017). Specifically, in the ruling *Expediente Varios* 912/2010, the SCJN developed standards about the character of international judgments and conventionality control obligations in their decision implementing IACtHR's *Radilla Pacheco v. Mexico* (2009). The SCJN determined that

5 This requirement was amended in 2021.

6 Amparo en revision 2069/91 [1992].

7 Amparo en revision 1475/98 [1999].

8 Amparo 815/2006 [2007].

IACtHR decisions were binding as *res judicata* and thus could not be revised by the SCJN. The SCJN also declared that all Mexican courts are to follow the doctrine of conventionality control applied *ex officio*. The SCJN expanded this legal doctrine in *Expediente Varios* 1396/2011, where the SCJN incorporated the IACtHR judgments on *Fernández Ortega et al. v. Mexico* (2010) and *Rosendo Cantú et al. v. Mexico* (2010), and clarified the set of obligations for all federal judicial authorities that expanded the *ex officio* conventionality control mandate and implemented administrative measures. Similarly, in *Contradiccion de Tesis 293/2011*, the SCJN recognized the normative principle of *pro personae* as established by constitutionally-granted rights and rights by international sources, so that courts were to use the most expansive or protective norms available from either source—so long as the constitution does not contain express restriction of that right. The SCJN also determined that international human rights and IACtHR jurisprudence are binding to national courts even if Mexico is not party to the case.

This deliberation by the SCJN illustrates its dialogue with the IACtHR, providing concrete and specific guidance on the implementation of conventionality control, lending domestic judicial legitimacy, and accepting state responsibility for implementing international human rights laws (Contesse, 2017). Without this SCJN jurisprudence, the 2011 constitutional amendment could have been relegated to being "aspirational" rather than binding and enforceable (Zamora et al., 2004). The SCJN thereby implies its approval of this legal innovation and offers its domestic judicial support and legitimacy to the doctrine and IACtHR.[9] Further, the SCJN's intentional domestic incorporation of the doctrine reflects judicial activism in their own part. The Court overruled its own precedent so as to allow a broad use of conventionality control (Aguiar-Aguilar, 2016). Furthermore, the 2011 amendment—and even IACtHR decisions—do not mandate this broad interpretation of conventionality control. Instead, they provide for more limited versions of conventionality control that recognize existing competencies and procedural regulations

9 Fortunately for the IACtHR as well, Mexico's constitutionalization of conventionality control and subsequent SCJN landmark decisions coincided with the "strengthening process" that took place from 2011 to 2013, where states re-evaluated the IACtHR in light of the "region's new context" and criticism (Kletzel, 2017). This period was a tenuous and difficult time for the supranational court, where proposals sought to reduce IACtHR authority. Mexican constitutionalization and incorporation of conventionality control embedded the IACtHR into the domestic legal system, which contributed to the supranational court's resilience to this backlash (Gonzalez-Ocantos and Sandholtz, 2022).

(Medecígo, 2013). The SCJN's interpretation, however, functionally granted constitutional review powers to state courts, which had been forbidden to interpret the constitution or apply international law (Collí Ek, 2012).

The SCJN's decisions to implement conventionality control—and their decisions on *how* it should be implemented—fundamentally altered the traditional structure of Mexican judicial powers. Thus, the SCJN's interpretation of conventionality control represents a radical shift. In short, the constitutional amendment (based upon the SCJN's own proposals), SCJN's incorporation of constitutionality control, and its incorporation of a broad, wide-reaching version of conventionality control that unilaterally reshaped judicial power all reveal the SCJN's activism. However, new domestic constitutional architecture is itself not sufficient to produce the desired changes in legal culture and human rights practices (Torelly, 2019). In fact, SCJN justices were "ferociously divided" in their decision in *Expediente Varios 912/2010* (Pou Giménez, 2017, p. 123). The SCJN tried to resolve this division by developing a unified majority opinion in *Contradiccion de Tesis 293/2011*, but the result was a majority opinion with "complex criteria and internal contradictions" along with two dissenting opinions and five concurring opinions (Pou Giménez, 2017, p. 123). Thus, despite the official stance supporting conventionality control, it remains unclear whether these constitutional changes have led to systemic changes in the SCJN decision-making.

Analysis of SCJN Judicial Activism

In what follows, I examine the extent to which conventionality control has affected SCJN decision-making and litigation beyond these landmark decisions. In particular, I compare SCJN behavior across three time periods: prior to the advent of conventionality control (1996–2005), the establishment and the development of conventionality control (2006–2010), and after the constitutionalization of conventionality control in Mexico (2011–2019). I investigate evidence of two forms of SCJN judicial activism across these periods. First, I examine the possibility of increased adjudication of rights cases so as to expand judicial purview. In particular, I am interested if the SCJN is active in expanding its influence through taking on more cases to set policy and/or taking on cases that may not originally fall under its jurisdiction. Second, I examine citation patterns regarding international law and jurisprudence as a form of legal innovation. Increased reliance on international law and jurisprudence in SCJN decisions represents changes in SCJN decision-making, reflecting legal innovation through increased reliance on international norms to bolster or inform domestic legal outcomes and/or using international law to fill domestic legal lacunae.

For my analysis, I use the universe of human rights cases before the SCJN for *facultad de atracción* cases, made available in the SCJN website, from 1996 to 2019. *Atracción* cases are cases that usually fall outside of SCJN jurisdiction, where litigants are appealing to the SCJN, asking it to 'attract' the case because elements of the case present fundamental implications for the law. Hence, these cases reflect the Court's (only) discretionary jurisdiction where the Court can decide whether or not to hear a case. This case type is thus the most amenable to activist Courts, which are more likely to take on additional cases that would otherwise fall outside of their jurisdiction—thereby expanding their policy-making power to areas that normally would exclude Court influence. Furthermore, conventionality control mandates alignment of domestic laws and international human rights law, yet domestic courts are dependent upon their jurisdictional authority and litigation before them. Hence, *atracción* cases are the space within which the SCJN can maneuver most freely to either reject conventionality control mandates or accept invitations for judicial activism.

Similarly, because all other case types are part of its mandatory docket, changes in citations and outcomes in other case types may be less reflective of SCJN preferences and more determined by underlying changes in litigation. In other words, changes in Court decisions may be reflecting changes in the cases the SCJN receives rather than its own decision-making. I reduce this possibility by using *atracción* cases, where the Court can decide to hear the case or not, thereby better indicating Court preferences. I also trace litigation patterns to better compare changes in litigation versus changes in SCJN decisions. Tracing litigant citation patterns is further informative in that it offers insights to how conventionality control has shifted national rights discourse through its reception by the SCJN. While conventionality control itself offers a strategic framework for domestic litigation, SCJN decisions determine the extent to which this framework is effective. *Atracción* cases signal Court preferences for the types of litigation amenable to the Court and the types of frameworks that are effective in garnering favorable judicial outcomes. *Atracción* cases allow the Court to guide the direction of *atracción* litigation over time based upon their decisions to hear the case (Baird, 2007). In other words, SCJN treatment of international law and jurisprudence determines future litigation frameworks so they better align with Court preferences and priorities over time.

The universe of human rights *atracción* cases from 1996 to 2019, consist of a total of 5,827 human rights cases, of which 1,659 cases include citations to international law or jurisprudence. These citations can appear in the litigant petition (*solicitud*), SCJN decision (*sentencia*), and/or separate judicial opinions. The data consist primarily of litigant and SCJN citations, where a separate vote (i.e., concurring or dissenting opinion) by a justice occurs in one case between 1996 and 2005, eight cases between 2006 and 2010, and six cases between 2011 and 2019. A separate vote citation where neither the petition nor majority opinion cite international law or jurisprudence occurs only in four cases total.[10] I focus primarily on litigant and SCJN citations rather than these separate votes. Citations to international jurisprudence typically arise in conjunction with citations to international law, and I rely on the SCJN definition of international jurisprudence, consisting of international and foreign case law as well as reports from international organizations and foreign states. Of particular interest is IACtHR jurisprudence, as conventionality control obligates domestic judges to use the IACtHR's interpretation of international human rights laws in aligning domestic law with international law.

Expansion of SCJN Rights Adjudication and Citation Patterns

The expansion of SCJN purview over human rights *atracción* cases is evident over time—particularly since 2011. Figure 11.1 depicts the total number of human rights *atracción* cases submitted to the SCJN and the total number of cases 'attracted' by the SCJN, as well as the proportion of these cases that cite international law and jurisprudence. Figure 11.1 also includes two reference lines for the years 2006 and 2011, to represent the establishment of conventionality control and its constitutionalization, respectively.

Figure 11.1 shows that litigation has significantly increased since 2008, skyrocketing by 2010, and hovering around the 600-case mark since 2014.[11] Yet,

10 These four cases appear: (1) in 2006, in a joint opinion by Justice José de Jesús Gudiño Pelayo and Justice José Ramón Cossío Díaz; (2) in 2009, in two opinions, one by Justice Olga María del Carmen Sánchez Cordero de García Villegas and one joint opinion by Justice José Ramón Cossío Díaz and Justice Olga María del Carmen Sánchez Cordero de García Villegas; and (3) in 2012, in one opinion by Justice José Ramón Cossío Díaz.

11 Fluctuations in litigation and 'attraction' are likely due to ongoing judicial reforms. For instance, in 2014, Mexico approved a new National Penal Procedures Code (*Código Nacional de Procedimientos Penales*) that establishes uniformity in the application of criminal

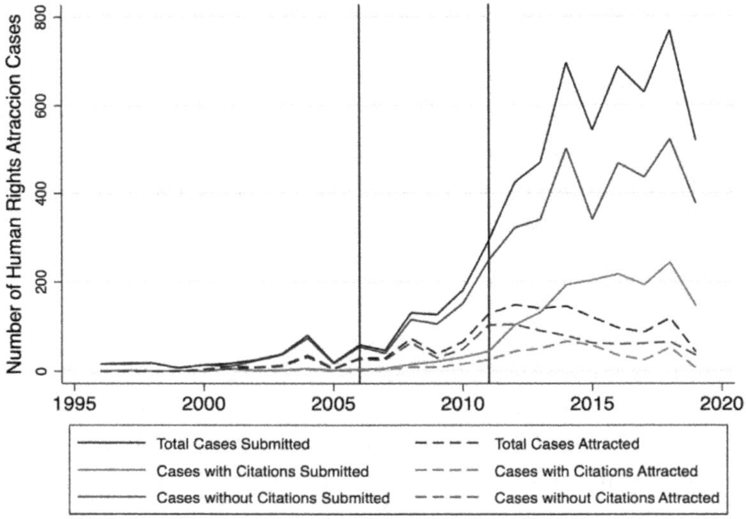

Figure 11.1: Number of human rights atracción cases submitted and 'Attracted' by SCJN

while litigants are increasingly seeking SCJN attention for their rights cases, the SCJN 'attracts' only a relatively small proportion of these cases. Nonetheless, submitted cases with international law and jurisprudence citations significantly increased from zero cases prior to 2006, to around 200 cases in recent years. This increase reflects a significant shift in litigation strategies and SCJN decision-making, where international law and jurisprudence has become an increasingly important framework for decision-making. In terms of 'attracted' cases with citations to international law and jurisprudence, the modest increase depicted here is still a meaningful change. Between 1996 and 2005, the SCJN 'attracted' an average of only two cases with international citations. After conventionality control (between 2006 and 2010), the SCJN 'attracted' an average of eight cases with international citations. After the

law, standardizes the classification of crimes, and sets clear guidelines to preserve individual rights. Part of the rehaul of the criminal justice system initiated in 2008, these reforms are often implemented in stages and their functioning and effectiveness vary across states. Thus, these reforms may create additional uncertainty and inconsistency as the nation adjusts to the new system, diagnoses unanticipated consequences, addresses state capacity differences, and faces divided public responses. While these issues are beyond the scope of this chapter, they reflect the ongoing national discourse and activities to realize human rights and justice.

constitutionalization of conventionality control in 2011, the SCJN 'attracted' an average of 40 cases with international citations. Hence, not only is the SCJN 'attracting' more cases, it is 'attracting' more cases that rely upon international law and jurisprudence. Considering the already overwhelming docket and backlog the SCJN faces (Pou Giménez, 2017), these 'attracted' cases reflect the prioritization of the SCJN to adjudicate in these cases, thereby taking on more policymaking space in the human rights arena.

Figure 11.2 illustrates the different citation patterns of international law and jurisprudence between litigants and the SCJN itself. Both litigants and the SCJN tend to rely more heavily upon international law than on international jurisprudence, though citations to both significantly increase after 2011. Specifically, the number of cases where the petition cites international jurisprudence reaches a maximum of 72 cases in 2018. The maximum number of cases where the SCJN itself cites international jurisprudence is 23 cases in 2014. A similar trend appears for international law, where the SCJN uses international law less frequently in its decision-making than does litigation. Nonetheless, conventionality control has shifted SCJN decision-making to take into consideration international law and jurisprudence, though more modestly than litigation.

Figure 11.3 depicts the breakdown of 'attracted' cases citing international law versus international jurisprudence in the petitions versus SCJN decisions

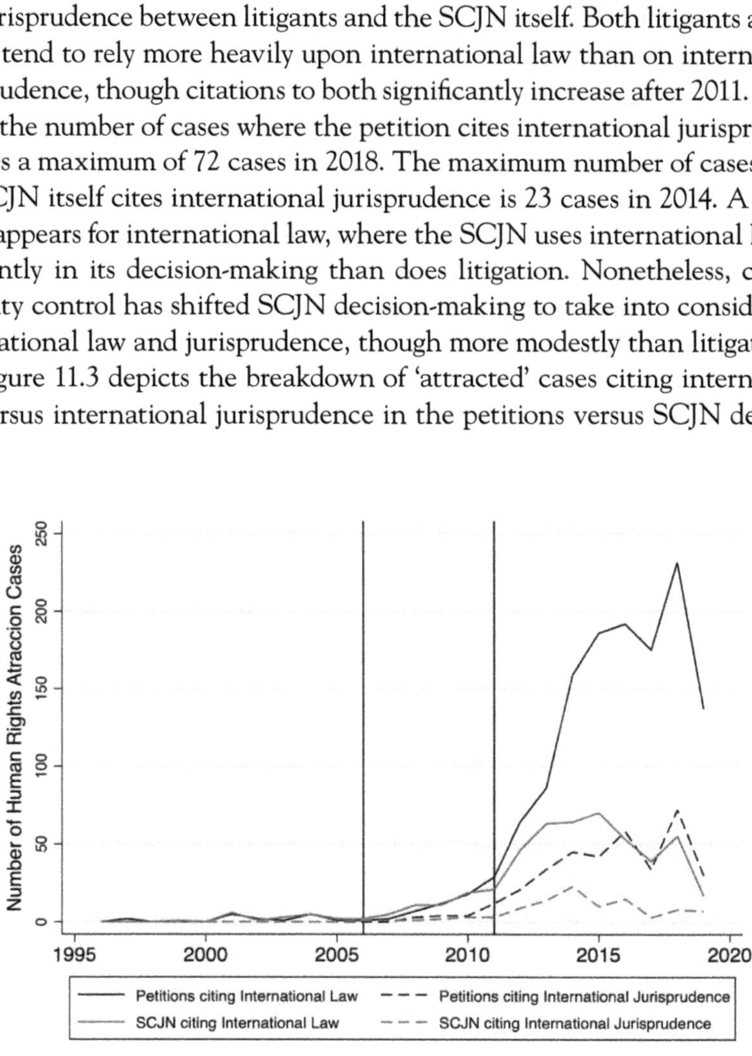

Figure 11.2: Patterns of citations across litigant petitions and SCJN decisions

themselves. In other words, Figure 11.3 shows the proportion of cases with citations to international law versus citations to international jurisprudence in the litigant petitions that were 'attracted' by the SCJN. It also shows the proportion of cases where the SCJN cites international law versus jurisprudence in their 'attracted' decisions. Importantly, the number of 'attracted' litigant petitions citing international jurisprudence occurs *after* the SCJN begins to cite international jurisprudence in their 'attracted' decisions. The number of 'attracted' SCJN decisions citing international jurisprudence increases slightly after the advent of conventionality control but more substantively increases after the constitutionalization of the doctrine.

More specifically, the average number of 'attracted' litigant petitions citing international law between 1996 and 2005 was one case, which increased to an average of three cases between 2006 and 2010. Between 2011 and 2019, the average number of 'attracted' petitions citing international law was 24 cases. Similarly, there is an increase in 'attracted' cases where petitions rely upon international jurisprudence. Between 1996 and 2005, the annual number of 'attracted' petitions citing international jurisprudence was consistently zero, while between 2006 and 2010 the average increased to one case. Between

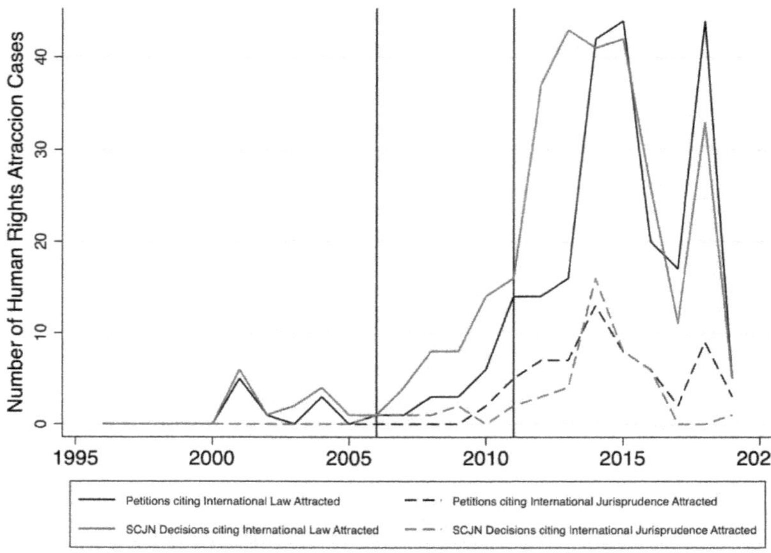

Figure 11.3: Number of human rights atracción cases 'Attracted' by type and location of citations

2011 and 2019, the average number of 'attracted' petitions citing international jurisprudence was seven cases. While these changes 'attracted' petitions are relatively modest, they nonetheless reflect a shift from total absence of international jurisprudence and limited international law in domestic litigation and SCJN decision-making, towards a more prominent feature of domestic judicial activity.

Turning to SCJN decisions, the average number of 'attracted' cases where the SCJN cites international law is one case between 1996 and 2005, increasing to an average of seven cases between 2006 and 2010. After 2011, the average number of 'attracted' cases with SCJN citations to international law increases to 28 cases. This pattern is similar for international jurisprudence, though the increase is more modest. Between 1996 and 2005, the number of 'attracted' cases where the SCJN cites international jurisprudence is consistently zero every year. Between 2006 and 2010, the average number of 'attracted' cases where the SCJN cites international jurisprudence is one case. After 2011, the average number of 'attracted' cases with SCJN citations to international law is six cases. Thus, while this increase is slight, international jurisprudence had no explicit impact on domestic litigation and judicial decision-making in Mexico prior to 2006. With the development and constitutionalization of conventionality control, international jurisprudence has begun to directly impact both litigation and SCJN decision-making.

While these data reflect the general trends of how international law and jurisprudence has impacted Mexican litigation and SCJN decision-making since the development of conventionality control, what about the role of IACtHR specifically? Figure 11.4 shows the annual number of petitions and SCJN decisions that cite the IACtHR, as well as the proportion of these cases that are 'attracted' by the SCJN.

Figure 11.4 reveals that litigants only began to consistently cite the IACtHR in their petitions to the SCJN in 2011. Indeed, none of the petitions prior to 2005 ever cited the IACtHR, and the average number of petitions citing the IACtHR between 2006 and 2010 was one petition. However, after 2011, the average number of petitions citing the IACtHR increased to 30 petitions. Of these petitions submitted to the SCJN, a small proportion are 'attracted' each year. Between 1996 and 2005, the SCJN did not 'attract' any petition citing the IACtHR, and between 2006 and 2010 the SCJN 'attracted' no more than 1 case per year. After 2011, the SCJN 'attracted' an average of 5 petitions citing the IACtHR. Similarly, the IACtHR was never cited by the SCJN prior to 2006. Between 2006 and 2010, the SCJN cited the IACtHR an average

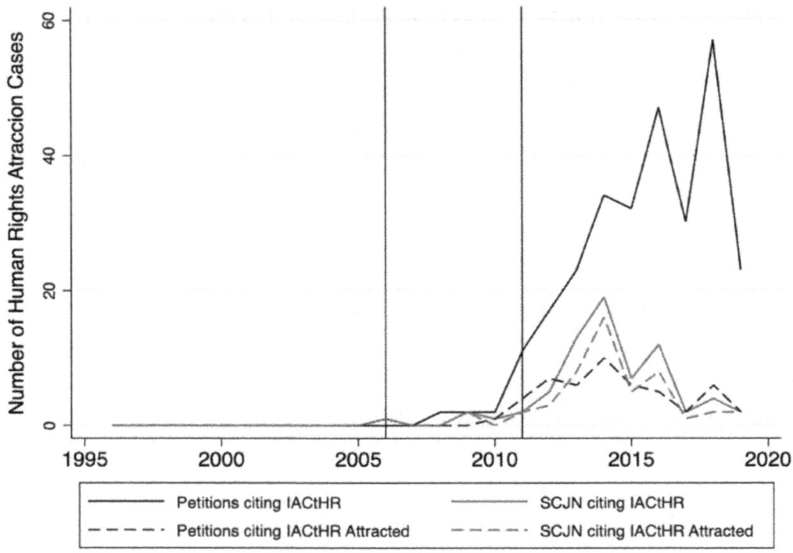

Figure 11.4: Number of human rights atracción cases citing IACtHR

of one case, and 'attracted' an average of one case citing the IACtHR. After 2011, the SCJN cites the IACtHR an average of seven cases, and the SCJN 'attracts' an average of five cases itself citing IACtHR. Thus, the IACtHR went from obscurity prior to 2006, to an influential player in domestic litigation and SCJN decision-making.

In sum, these data reveal several important trends. First, Mexican litigation has increasingly relied upon international law and jurisprudence—and the IACtHR specifically—in their petitions to the SCJN. Prior to conventionality control, the IACtHR and international jurisprudence generally was lacking in domestic litigation frameworks. While petitions occasionally cited international laws prior to conventionality control, the doctrine expanded litigant reliance on international human rights laws significantly, with an average of 140 cases citing international law, 39 cases citing international jurisprudence, and 31 cases citing the IACtHR since 2011. Thus, international law and jurisprudence appears to be a prominent framework in modern human rights litigation in Mexico.

Second, SCJN decisions have increasingly relied upon international law and jurisprudence as well, including the IACtHR specifically. The IACtHR and international jurisprudence were completely absent from SCJN decisions prior to the establishment of conventionality control. The SCJN consistently cites more international laws than jurisprudence, and the SCJN consistently 'attracts' more cases citing international laws than jurisprudence. While the SCJN 'attracts' only a modest proportion of cases, the Court increasingly relies on international law and jurisprudence in their decisions for both 'attracted' and 'non-attracted' cases. Still, the SCJN is increasingly deciding to 'attract' human rights cases, suggesting that the Court is deciding to take on a more prominent role in human rights protections in Mexico. Despite their already overburdened workload, the SCJN has sought to increasingly insert itself to fill the spaces sought by rights litigants, even when the Court does not have authority or jurisdiction in these cases originally.

To gain a better picture of the substantive nature of the international law and jurisprudence citations and potential dialogue between litigants and SCJN (and IACtHR), I investigate the specific patterns of citations at the SCJN. This allows me to isolate citations to human rights law and to identify if SCJN citations occur only in response to litigant citations. SCJN citations only in response to litigant citations do not directly demonstrate SCJN preferences or application, since the SCJN may merely be addressing litigant queries and arguments. Hence, I consider citations as SCJN activism only if the SCJN cites international law even when it is not required to. For the sake of space, I summarize this qualitative analysis, focusing on the major trends and turning points across each of the three timeframes: prior to the establishment of conventionality control (1996–2005), the establishment and development of conventionality control (2006–2010), and the constitutionalization of conventionality control (2011–2019).

Prior to Conventionality Control (1996–2005). Between 1996 and 2005, no international jurisprudence or IACtHR decisions were ever cited. Furthermore, while international laws were occasionally cited during this time frame, most pertain to economic, criminal, education, and assembly rights. For example, in 1996, none of the cases before the SCJN included any citation to international law or jurisprudence, whether by the petitioners or Court. In 1997, two cases cite NAFTA in the petition, but neither case was 'attracted'. In 1998, no cases included international citations; in 1999, one case includes a SCJN citation to United Nations Convention Against Illicit Traffic in Narcotic Drugs and Psychotropic Substances (1988). In 2000, no cases include international citations. In 2001–2003, several petitions include citations to (1) *Acuerdo entre el Instituto Latinoamericano de la Comunicación Educativa y los Estados Unidos Mexicanos*, (2) *Convenio de Cooperación de los Países de América Latina y el Caribe para la Reestructuración del Instituto Latinoamericano de la Comunicación Educativa* (1983), and (3) ILO Convention 87 (Freedom of Association and Protection of the Right to Organize). In these cases, the SCJN generally cites the same international laws in their decision, reflecting a response to litigation and case issues rather than judicial activism.

Substantive international human rights laws emerge in the data only in 2004. Specifically, litigants begin to cite the International Covenant on Civil and Political Rights (1966) and ILO Convention 169 (Indigenous and Tribal Peoples Convention), which are 'attracted' by the SCJN. SCJN cites its first substantive international human rights law in 2004 as well, citing the Universal Declaration of Human Rights. However, SCJN citations remain as responses to litigants, and the IACtHR and Inter-American human rights system is overlooked by domestic litigation and SCJN decision-making during this time frame.

Establishment and Development of Conventionality Control (2006–2010). After the establishment of conventionality control, a shift begins to appear before the SCJN. For the first time, in 2006, litigants cite the American Convention on Human Rights (1969) and, in a separate case, the SCJN cites IACtHR decision *Olmedo Bustos et al. v. Chile* (2001), along with the Constitution of Spain; International Covenant on Civil and Political Rights (1966); and American Convention on Human Rights (1969). Thus, this is the first time the American Convention on Human Rights, Inter-American human rights system, and the IACtHR enter domestic litigation in Mexico for *atracción* cases. Furthermore, for the first time, SCJN citations are not in response to litigant petitions.

The SCJN and litigation then begin to increasingly rely on international human rights laws, IACtHR jurisprudence, and foreign law. This period thus marks the beginning of a more globalized court, entering into a dialogue with international and foreign law. While SCJN reliance on IACtHR jurisprudence remains nascent, the SCJN begins to consistently cite regional human rights laws that undergird the Inter-American system and IACtHR, specifically the American Convention on Human Rights (1969), its additional protocols, and the American Declaration on the Rights and Duties of Man (1948). Importantly, this application of IACtHR jurisprudence is reflective of SCJN preferences as conventionality control has been established but not yet constitutionalized in Mexico.

Similarly, litigation in *atracción* cases increases significantly—particularly starting in 2008—and begin to increase their reliance on international human rights law frameworks. In fact, 2008 marks the first time that litigants begin to rely on IACtHR jurisprudence in their *atracción* petitions. This implies that litigants are receptive to the shift in SCJN decision-making in 2006. In other words, litigants modified their litigation strategy to include IACtHR jurisprudence *after* the SCJN began to cite the IACtHR. The SCJN further advances this shift to increasingly rely upon international law and jurisprudence even when litigants do not. Thus, SCJN decision-making reflects a consistent prioritization of international law and IACtHR jurisprudence, reinforcing these litigation strategies and demonstrating judicial activism in signaling to litigants their desired rights frameworks and issue areas.

In sum, a substantial shift in the use and type of citations to international law and IACtHR jurisprudence occurs in 2006. Prior to 2006, the IACtHR simply was not a part of judicial discourse in the SCJN. After 2006, the IACtHR becomes as a significant focal point in legal dialogue, where both the SCJN and litigation begin to rely upon its jurisprudence. The SCJN also significantly widens their sources of citations during this period, citing numerous IACtHR advisory opinions and contentious cases, as well as regional laws, UN Committee reports, European conventions, and other international treaties. Thus, this period reflects the changing rights discourse, the evolving legal culture, and shifting role of the SCJN.

Constitutionalization of Conventionality Control in Mexico (2011–2019). The domestic constitutionalization of conventionality control further expands upon these trends, pushing litigation to increase even higher as litigants seek the SCJN to take an expanded role in human rights adjudication and policymaking. While the SCJN only modestly responds to this call in terms of the number of cases they add to their docket, the SCJN remains consistent in its frequent use of international laws and jurisprudence. Indeed, the Inter-American legal system and IACtHR have become permanent, prominent features of SCJN decision-making. For example, litigants now frequently cite multiple IACtHR decisions in their petitions, ranging from one to three IACtHR decisions to regularly citing 14–20 IACtHR decisions in each petition.

The SCJN also regularly cites IACtHR jurisprudence, as well as case law from other international and foreign courts, thereby embracing conventionality control as well as a more globalized stance to human rights adjudication. In terms of foreign courts, the SCJN cites the U.S. Supreme Court, the European Court of Human Rights, and the International Court of Justice. The SCJN also cites several sources of international and foreign law within their decisions. For instance, SCJN decisions can each include one to 20 citations of IACtHR judgments, with a mode of around nine judgments cited in each. In addition to these citations, the SCJN most frequently cites, in descending order: the American Convention on Human Rights (1969); International Covenant on Civil and Political Rights (1966); Universal Declaration of Human Rights (1948); Convention on the Rights of the Child (1989); International Covenant on Economic, Social and Cultural Rights (1966); American Declaration on the Rights and Duties of Man (1948); Additional Protocol to the American Convention in the Area of Economic, Social and Cultural Rights (1988); Vienna Convention on the Law of Treaties (1969); and NAFTA (1994). Thus, the SCJN appears to have embraced an expansive approach to their application of international law and jurisprudence.

Summary

In sum, this short history reveals three significant trends. First, the Inter-American human rights system and IACtHR was nonexistent in Mexican litigation and SCJN decision-making in *atracción* cases prior to the establishment of conventionality control. Since its establishment, however, IACtHR and regional human rights laws—as well as international law and jurisprudence generally—have become important frameworks for SCJN adjudication. The domestic constitutionalization of conventionality control seems to have cemented and expanded these trends to increasingly rely upon international law and jurisprudence. The American Convention on Human Rights (1969) is now one of the most frequently cited laws in both litigation and SCJN decisions, and a variety of IACtHR decisions in contentious cases and advisory opinions appear regularly in litigation and SCJN decisions.

Second, the number of citations to international law and jurisprudence has generally increased within each case, where each case is informed by a wide range of international laws and supranational court jurisprudence. These citations go beyond jurisprudence directly affecting Mexico and the Inter-American system to include not only IACtHR cases to which Mexico is not a party, but also reference foreign law and other international court decisions in other regions. Hence, the SCJN has taken an expansive approach to conventionality control, as invited by the IACtHR, to align domestic law with international human rights regimes broadly.

Third, the SCJN reveals judicial activism in three ways. First, SCJN engages in judicial activism by their increasing adjudication of rights cases that would normally fall outside its jurisdiction. This represents additional avenues for SCJN to set law and policy in each case but also represents an expansion of jurisdiction. Second, the SCJN demonstrates judicial activism through increasing citations of international law and jurisprudence, particularly the IACtHR, in their decision-making even before conventionality control was constitutionalized or approved in principle by Mexico. Third, the SCJN took the lead in introducing international law and IACtHR jurisprudence into the Mexican legal regime, signaling to litigants, lawyers, and rights support structures their desired areas of influence and effective litigation strategies (Baird, 2007; Epp, 1998). The changes in litigation are largely caused by changes in SCJN citation and decision-making, thereby making the SCJN activist in altering domestic litigation and rights discourse.

Conclusions

These results suggest that the SCJN has accepted IACtHR's judicial activism in creating conventionality control by constitutionalizing and enforcing international rights standards in domestic courts. The SCJN's positive response to the IACtHR reinforces the possibility that domestic legal systems can serve as enforcement mechanisms for international human rights law (Simmons, 2009). The SCJN's acceptance and implementation of the IACtHR's doctrine promotes the IACtHR and Inter-American system to prominence by making them influential institutions within domestic law, thereby legitimizing and empowering the IACtHR as well as enabling the IACtHR to engage in future judicial activism. Similarly, the IACtHR has supported the SCJN explicitly in their decisions and compliance reports, applauding Mexico for its constitutionalization of conventionality control and the SCJN enforcement of this doctrine. Thus, conventionality control appears to have successfully fostered a "compliance partnership" where domestic courts and the IACtHR can interact as allies to secure rights protections that mutually empower and support each other (Huneeus, 2010, 2011; Alter, 2011). Through conventionality control, the IACtHR and SCJN have led to the reframing of issues and reshaping social values using the language of law (Alter, 2011).

In response to the IACtHR's invitation, the SCJN demonstrates multiple examples of judicial activism: (1) SCJN activism in policymaking through the proposal of constitutional amendments and judicial reform, such as the 2011 constitutional amendment; (2) SCJN activism in deliberately incorporating a broad, expansive version of conventionality control that unilaterally expands judicial power; (3) SCJN activism through increased activity deciding rights-related cases and taking on cases that would otherwise fall outside its jurisdiction, and (4) legal innovation through (increasingly) utilizing new legal sources like the IACtHR to (re)interpret, justify, and align domestic law with international rights standards. Successfully developing constitutional amendments enabled the SCJN to direct rights development in Mexico and determine how conventionality control would be implemented. The incorporation of conventionality control allowed the SCJN to expand judicial power to grant constitutional review to state courts and promote greater judicial influence over rights protections. Despite the SCJN being limited by an overwhelming workload of thousands of cases each year, the SCJN has expanded their role in rights adjudication, showing signs of taking on agenda-setting powers and guiding rights litigation. In addition, the SCJN actively determined to take advantage of conventionality control, even before its domestic constitutionalization, to increasingly rely upon international law and the IACtHR in its decision-making. While international human rights regimes and the IACtHR were ignored by Mexican litigation and SCJN decision-making in *atracción* cases prior to conventionality control, the SCJN initiated their implementation in domestic law and promoted them to become fundamental frameworks for litigation and judicial decision-making. The Inter-American system has now achieved prominence as a dominant source for rights interpretation and enforcement.

Future judicial capacity to expand their role in human rights will likely require judicial reforms to consolidate cases, establish precedent, and refine their mandatory docket to reduce backlog and make the workload manageable. Indeed, such judicial reforms have already been approved. A judicial reform bill, drafted by President of the Supreme Court Arturo Zaldívar and endorsed by President Andrés Manuel López Obrador in February 2020, proposed the establishment of precedent through single SCJN decisions and includes a reform to make additional rights-related cases (*amparo directo*) part of the SCJN's discretionary docket (*Mexico* 2020). While this reform has some potential weaknesses regarding judicial independence (Ríos-Figueroa, 2020), the SCJN seems to be reevaluating its history of its limited role as a protector of rights. Mexico approved these reforms and amended Amparo Law in June 2021, making all SCJN decisions with eight majority votes (issued after June 7, 2021) obligatory precedent immediately (rather than setting precedent only after five consecutive, consistent decisions). This establishment of precedent can improve the consistency and predictability in the law, as well as reduce SCJN caseloads by eliminating redundant cases. In addition, the reform moves *amparo directo* cases from the SCJN's mandatory docket to its discretionary docket. Combined with the SCJN's September 2021 decision that all federal judges can review the constitutionality of laws in *amparo* cases rather than keep that power reserved for the SCJN, *amparo* cases are likely to be determined by the lower courts and reaching the SCJN only in exceptional circumstances. These reforms can reduce the SCJN's mandatory caseload and offer the opportunity to realize conventionality control's promise of decentralized constitutional scrutiny for human rights, reducing the "excessive dependence" of rights enforcement on federal courts by empowering lower courts to play a more significant role in constitutional review and rights protections (Medécigo, 2013, p. 42). While Mexico's judicial trajectory remains far from certain, conventionality control has successfully created a space for expanded activism for promoting human rights for both the IACtHR and the Mexican high court.

References

Additional Protocol to the American Convention on Human Rights in the Area of Economic, Social and Cultural Rights, "Protocol of San Salvador". (Adopted in San Salvador, November 17, 1988).

Aguiar-Aguilar, A. (2016). Harmonizing national law with Inter-American human rights law: Evidence from Mexico. *Journal of Human Rights, 15*(4), 477–495.

Almonacid Arellano et al. v. Chile (2006). Inter-American Court of Human Rights (series C) No. 154 (September 26, 2006).

Alter, K. (2011). Tipping the balance: International courts and the construction of international and domestic politics. *Cambridge Yearbook of European Legal Studies, 13*, 1–22.

American Convention on Human Rights (1969). (Adopted at the Inter-American Specialized Conference on Human Rights, San José, Costa Rica, November 22, 1969).

American Declaration on the Rights and Duties of Man (1948). (Adopted by the Ninth International Conference of American States, Bogotá, Colombia, 1948).

Ansolabehere, K. (2010). More power, more rights? The Supreme Court and Society in Mexico. In Javier Cuoso, Alexandra Hunneus, & Rachel Sieder (Eds.), *Cultures of legality: Judicialization and political activism in Latin America*. New York: Cambridge University Press.

Baird, V. (2007). *Answering the call of the court: How justices and litigants set the Supreme Court agenda*. Charlottesville, VA: University of Virginia Press.

Bazán, V. (2011). Control de convencionalidad, aperturas dialógicas e influencias jurisdiccionales recíprocas. *Revista Europea de Derechos Fundamentales, 18*(2), 63–67.

Binder, C. (2011). The prohibition of amnesties by the Inter-American Court of Human Rights. *German Law Journal, 12*(5), 1203.

Boyce et al. v. Barbados (2007). Inter-American Court of Human Rights (series C) No. 169 (November 20, 2007).

Candia, G. (2012). The conventionality control: Moving the Inter-American system of human rights to judicial supremacy. *Social Science Research Network*. Available at SSRN:< http://ssrn.com/abstract=2406725>.

Carmelina Londoño-Lázaro, M., & Carrillo-Santarelli, N. (2019). The control of conventionality: Developments in the case law of the Inter-American Court of Human Rights and its potential expanding effects in international human rights law. *Max Planck Yearbook of United Nations Law Online*, *22*(1), 319–346.

Castagnola, A., & Noriega, S. (2017). The Supreme Court and the (no) rights revolution. In A. Castagnola & S. López Noriega (Eds.), *Judicial politics in Mexico: The Supreme Court and the transition to democracy* (pp. 95–116). Routledge.

Castán, D. (2013). *The transformation of the Inter-American system for the protection of human rights: The structural impact of the Inter-American court's case law on amnesties*. European Inter-University Centre for Human Rights and Democratization.

Castillejos-Aragón, M. (2013). The transformation of the Mexican Supreme Court into an arena for political contestation. *Consequential Courts*, 138–160.

Colli-Ek, V. M. (2012). Improving human rights in Mexico: Constitutional reforms, international standards and new requirements for judges. *Human Rights Brief*, *20*(1), 7–14.

Contesse, J. (2017). The final word? Constitutional dialogue and the Inter-American Court of Human Rights. *International Journal of Constitutional Law*, *15*, 414.

Contesse, J. (2018). The international authority of the Inter-American Court of Human Rights: A critique of the conventionality control doctrine. *The International Journal of Human Rights*, *22*(9), 1168–1191.

Convention on the Rights of the Child (1989). (UN General Assembly resolution 44/25, November 20, 1989).

Dawson, M., De Witte, B., & Muir, E. (2013). *Judicial activism at the European court of justice*. Edward Elgar.

Dismissed Congressional Employees v. Peru (2007). Inter-American Court of Human Rights (series C) No. 174 (November 30, 2007).

Domingo, P. (2010). Novel appropriations of the law in the pursuit of political and social change in Latin America. In J. Cuoso, A. Hunneus, & R. Sieder (Eds.), *Cultures of legality: Judicialization and political activism in Latin America*. New York: Cambridge University Press.

Dulitzky, A. E. (2015). An Inter-American constitutional court? The invention of the conventionality control by the Inter-American Court of Human Rights. *Texas International Law Journal*, *50*(1), 45–93.

Epp, C. (1998). *The rights revolution*. University of Chicago Press.

García Ramírez, S. (2015). The relationship between Inter-American jurisdiction and states (national systems): Some pertinent questions. *Notre Dame Journal of International & Comparative Law* 5(1), 115–152.

Gargarella, R. (2015). Symposium: The constitutionalization of international law in Latin American democracy and rights in *Gelman v. Uruguay*. *AJIL Abound*, 109, 115–119.

González-Domínguez, P. (2018). *The doctrine of conventionality control: between uniformity and legal pluralism in the Inter-American human rights system*. Intersentia.

Gonzalez-Ocantos, E., & Sandholtz, W. (2022). The sources of resilience of international human rights courts: The case of the Inter-American system. *Law & Social Inquiry, 47*(1), 91–131.

Green, C. (2009). An intellectual history of judicial activism. *Emory Law Journal, 58*(5), 1195–1264.

Harris, D. J. (2004). *Cases and materials on international law.* London: Sweet & Maxwell.

Heliodoro Portugal v. Panama (2008). Inter-American Court of Human Rights (series C) No. 186 (August 12, 2008).

Helmke, G., & Ríos-Figueroa, J. (2011). Introduction: Courts in Latin America. In G. Helmke & J. Ríos-Figueroa (Eds.), *Courts in Latin America.* Cambridge: Cambridge University Press.

Huneeus, A. (2010). Rejecting the Inter-American Court: Judicialization, national courts, and regional human rights. In J. Couso, A. Huneeus, & R. Sieder (Eds.), *Cultures of legality: Judicialization and political activism in Latin America.* Cambridge: Cambridge University Press.

Huneeus, A. (2011). Courts resisting courts: Lessons from the Inter-American Court's struggle to enforce human rights. *Cornell International Law Journal, 44*(3), 493–533.

International Covenant on Civil and Political Rights (1966). (UN General Assembly resolution 2200A (XXI), December 16, 1966).

International Covenant on Economic, Social and Cultural Rights (1966). (UN General Assembly resolution 2200A (XXI), December 16, 1966).

Kletzel, G. (2017). The Inter-American Commission on Human Rights' new strategic plan: An opportunity for true strengthening. *The International Journal of Human Rights, 22*(9), 1249–1266.

Kmiec, K. D. (2004). The origin and current meanings of 'Judicial Activism.' *California Law Review,* 92(5), 1441–1477.

Koh, H. (1996). Transnational legal process. *Nebraska Law Review, 75*(181), 183.

Koh, H. (1997). Why do nations obey international law?. *Yale Law Journal, 106,* 2599.

Koh, H. (1998). How is international human rights law enforced?. *Indiana Law Journal, 74,* 1397.

Magaloni, A. L. (2007). ¿Por qué la Suprema Corte no ha sido un instrumento para la defensa de derechos fundamentales? *Documento de Trabajo CIDE.* <http://www.cide.edu/publicaciones/status/dts/DTEJ%2025.pdf.>

Magaloni, B., Sánchez, A., & Magar, E. (2011). Legalists vs interpretativists: The Supreme Court and the democratic transition in Mexico. In G. Helmke & J. Ríos-Figueroa (Eds.), *Courts in Latin America* (pp. 187–218). New York: Cambridge University Press.

Malarino, E. (2012). Judicial activism, punitivism and supranationalisation: Illiberal and antidemocratic tendencies of the Inter-American Court of Human Rights. *International Criminal Law Review, 12*(4), 665–695.

Maués, A. M., Magalhães, B. B., Nassar, P. A., & Sena, R. (2021). Judicial dialogue between national courts and the Inter-American Court of Human Rights: A comparative study of Argentina, Brazil, Colombia and Mexico. *Human Rights Law Review, 21*(1), 108–131.

Medécigo, A. N. (2013). Enforcement of fundamental rights by lower courts: Towards a coherent system of constitutional review in Mexico. *Mexican Law Review,* 6(1), 3–44.

Mexico: President López Obrador Endorses Proposed Judicial Branch Reform. (2020). Web Page. Retrieved from the Library of Congress, <www.loc.gov/item/global-legal-monitor/2020-02-27/mexico-president-lpez-obrador-endorses-proposed-judicial-branch-reform/>.

Olmedos Bustos et al. v. Chile (2001). Inter-American Court of Human Rights (series C) No. 73 (February 5, 2001).

Pasqualucci, J. M. (2013). *The practice and procedure of the Inter-American Court of Human Rights*. Cambridge University Press.

Pou Giménez, F. (2017). Constitutional change and the Supreme Court constitutional architecture. In A. Castagnola & S. L. Noriega (Eds.), *Judicial politics in Mexico: The Supreme Court and the transition to democracy* (pp. 117–146.) Routledge.

Powell, E., & Staton, J. (2009). Domestic judicial institutions and human rights treaty violation. *International Studies Quarterly*, *53*, 149–174.

Pozas-Loyo, A., & Ríos-Figueroa, J. (2017). The transformations of the role of the Mexican Supreme Court. In A. Castagnola & S. L. Noriega (Eds.), *Judicial politics in Mexico: The Supreme Court and the transition to democracy* (pp. 8–40.) Routledge.

Radilla Pacheco v. Mexico (2008). Inter-American Court of Human Rights (series C) No. 209 (November 23, 2009).

Ríos-Figueroa, J. (2020). Mexico's constitutional reforms: Threats to judicial independence from within?. *ConstitutionNet: International IDEA*. < https://constitutionnet.org/news/mexicos-constitutional-reforms-threats-judicial-independence-within>.

Schlesinger, Jr., A. (1947). The Supreme Court: 1947. *XXXV Fortune Magazine*, *73*.

Simmons, B. (2009). *Mobilizing for human rights: International law in domestic politics*. New York: Cambridge University Press.

Thirlway, H. (2002). Judicial activism and the international court of justice. In N. Anda, E. McWhinney, & R. Wolfrum (Eds.), *Lib Amicorum Judge Shirgeru Oda* (Vol. 1, pp. 75–105). Kluwer Academic Publishers.

Torelly, M. (2019). From compliance to engagement: Assessing the impact of the Inter-American Court of Human Rights on constitutional law in Latin America. In Par Engstrom (Ed.), *The Inter-American Human Rights System: Impact beyond compliance* (pp. 115–141). London, UK: Palgrave MacMillan.

Tsereteli, N. (2016). Emerging doctrine of deference of the Inter-American Court of Human Rights?. *The International Journal of Human Rights*, *20*(8), 1097–1112.

Universal Declaration of Human Rights (1948). (UN GeneralAssembly resolution 217A, December 10, 1948).

Vienna Convention on the Law of Treaties (1969). (UN Treaty Series vol. 1155, May 23, 1969).

Zamora, S., Cossío, J. R., Pereznieto, L., Roldán-Xopa, J., & Lopez, D. (2004). *Mexican law*. Oxford University Press.

· 12 ·

MEASURING JUDICIAL LEGITIMACY AS AN EXPLANATORY FACTOR OF JUDICIAL ACTIVISM

Lee Demetrius Walker

In 2003, Costa Rica's Constitutional Chamber ('Sala Cuarta', or 'Sala IV') voted 5-2 to allow presidential reelection despite the fact that the same Chamber had ruled only three years earlier that the Costa Rican Constitution prohibited the reelection of the president (Martinez-Barahona, 2010). In approving reelection, the Chamber concluded that the constitutional provision prohibiting the reelection of former presidents violated individual citizens' human right to vote for the candidate of their choice. The Chamber's ruling included the proviso that former presidents could seek reelection after sitting out two electoral cycles, even though the constitution made no mention of an eight-year hiatus. Meanwhile, the Honduran Supreme Court also dramatically reversed itself concerning presidential reelection. In May of 2009, the Honduran court voted 15-0 that then President José Manuel Zelaya's attempt to seek a public vote on reelection constituted an abuse of presidential power. The ruling, in part, validated the Honduran military's forceful removal of President Zelaya in June of 2009. In 2015, in a stunning reversal, the Constitutional Chamber of the court voted 6-0 to allow presidential reelection (Toledo, 2015).

In a previous chapter, Staton explains that a key element of activism is the departure from precedent. In theory, Civil law countries like Costa Rica and Honduras are not bound formally or informally by judicial precedent, allowing courts to vacillate on a point of law. Historically, however, civil law courts tend to accede to past decisions when there is a sufficient level of consistency in case law (Fon and Parisi, 2006, p. 519) and to play a passive role in the resolution of highly political questions (Wilson and Handberg, 1999). Given this backdrop, one useful definition of judicial activism is "the degree to which a judicial decision supersedes serious consideration of the same problems by other political actors" (Cross and Lindquist, 2007, p. 1763, see also Cannon, 1982–1983). This definition of judicial activism does not account for the normative nature of the concept of judicial activism (as stated in Staton's earlier discussion), in that a court stepping into a conflict that previously has been resolved by other political actors will likely be greeted with approval by some and derision by others.

Given the normative nature of judicial activism, opponents of presidential reelection may view the court ruling in favor of presidential reelection as activist because this highly political question has been resolved generally by other mechanisms (constitutional reform or referendum processes) (Carey, 2003) and because the court is departing from the previously accepted interpretation of the constitution. As a result, political leaders will seek to influence the public discourse concerning public perception about the court. Consequently, rulings that the public perceives activist are expected to affect the court's legitimacy (Gibson et al., 2003b; Smithey and Ishiyama, 2002; Dawson et al., 2013).

In Western established democracies, conventional wisdom assumes that a court will draw on its legitimacy when it makes a decision that a significant proportion of the public believes to be activist. For example, Gibson et al. (2003b) show that the legitimacy of a highly legitimate court may increase as a result of a court making a controversial ruling in a highly political case. Meanwhile, based on various measures of legitimacy, courts in newer democracies often have yet to establish or maintain high levels of institutional legitimacy. Nonetheless, courts in developing democracies make authoritative decisions on highly political questions that the public may consider activist (Martinez-Barahona, 2010; Taylor-Robinson and Ura, 2013; Corrales and Penfold, 2014). Accordingly, scholars connect judicial activism to judicial legitimacy by insinuating that activism by a court affects either positively (Gibson et al. 2003b) or negatively (Dawson et al., 2013) the court's legitimacy.

The assumption that a pre-existing level of legitimacy undergirds the link between activism and legitimacy motivates this chapter. I examine, in cross-national context, three manifestations of judicial legitimacy that impact courts' tendencies to make activist rulings on highly political questions. This evaluation demonstrates that the public's institutional commitment to courts is a resource from which highly legitimate courts draw support to rule against powerful political actors. Meanwhile, I also find that courts that lack institutional legitimacy rely on direct political support to make activist decisions in highly charged political cases. Given that reelection of the president is one of a set of important political questions about the balance of power between the formal institutions of government that high courts are increasingly asked to decide (Perea, 2008; Wise, 2010), I use this area of constitutional conflict in Latin America to examine the relationship between judicial legitimacy, decision making, and judicial activism.

Representations of Legitimacy

Judicial scholars have yet to incorporate and operationalize effectively judicial legitimacy as an explanatory factor in empirical models that seek to understand judicial activism. This omission is largely related to three factors. First, scholars often present legitimacy as a fixed and implied aspect of the country-level context. This approach is evident in law and courts studies that involve a single country or a small set of countries. Second, judicial scholars have assumed that a court's legitimacy is relatively static overtime. This assumption is grounded in the fact that scholars initially performed judicial legitimacy research in Western established democracies with highly legitimate judiciaries. Third, unlike judicial independence, there is still little consensus on what constitutes a useful cross-national measure of judicial legitimacy. Partly due to this lack of consensus on measurement, there has been little work that attempts to examine the effect of judicial legitimacy on judicial activism in cross-national perspective.

Two studies are useful to demonstrate the current state of judicial legitimacy research in political science. Helmke (2010) uses judicial legitimacy as an explanatory variable to explain institutional crises in Latin America. She uses confidence in the judiciary as a proxy for judicial legitimacy. Meanwhile, in an experimental study, Gibson (2008b) measures judicial legitimacy through a series of vignettes that seek to capture subjects' appraisals of the legitimacy of the Supreme Court of Kentucky. Fundamentally, judicial legitimacy is concerned with the public's diffuse support for judges and courts.

While these studies examine judicial legitimacy, neither uses legitimacy as a variable that explains judicial decision making or judicial activism. Moreover, Gibson's (2008b) study illustrates the limitations of both single state (nation-state) and experimental studies in providing a mechanism to study legitimacy across time and space. The study examines legitimacy as the dependent variable and at a single point in time. Meanwhile, the confidence in the judiciary proxy that Helmke uses in the above mentioned study is a form of public support for judiciary and is more akin to specific political support than diffuse support (Caldeira and Gibson, 1992; Dougherty et al., 2006; Walker, 2016). These two studies propose an institutional commitment and confidence in the judiciary as representations of judicial legitimacy and demonstrate that scholars use measures to approximate judicial legitimacy because of the lack of an overtime, cross-national measure of an institutional commitment for the judiciary. In the balance of this section, I discuss three such representations of judicial legitimacy (Institutional Commitment, Confidence in the Judiciary, and Procedural Justice) in more detail.

Institutional Commitment as Legitimacy

Like Gibson, Caldeira and their co-authors, I propose that institutional commitment is the most useful way to conceptualize legitimacy. For example, Gibson et al. (1998) posit diffuse support for courts as a representation of judicial legitimacy. They use a set of survey questions that concerns the public's commitment to the institutional functions of the high court in the respondent's respective country. Their study is cross-sectional and includes 17 European countries. The survey questions that Gibson et al. (1998) use have not been standardized on cross-national survey instruments. This is unfortunate as these questions are likely the best representation of diffuse support for the judiciary. Subsequently, others use variants of institutional-commitment questions to assess judicial legitimacy (Baird, 2001; Gibson and Caldeira, 2003; Gibson et al., 2003a; Gibson, 2008a; Bartels and Johnston, 2013; Gibson and Nelson, 2015). Baird (2001, p. 339) argues that diffuse support is best defined by a negative response to the question "if the Court started making decisions that nobody liked, it might be better to do away with the Court altogether" (Caldeira and Gibson, 1992).

Confidence in the Judiciary as an Antecedent to Legitimacy

Confidence in the judiciary has become an important and dynamic proxy that scholars use to approximate judicial legitimacy, or at least public support for courts (Mondak & Smithy, 1997; Benesh, 2006; Dougherty et al., 2006;

Kelleher and Wolak, 2007; Clark, 2009; Bühlmann and Kunz, 2011; Helmke, 2010). For example, Mondak and Smithey (1997) argue that confidence in the judiciary captures the dynamic nature of support for courts. While conceding the weakness of the confidence in the judiciary measure, Bühlmann and Kunz (2011, p. 321) argue that the "confidence measure [using the World Value Survey] serves as at least a proxy for diffuse support in a mid-range position between the most diffuse or abstract and the most specific form of support." In essence, Bühlmann & Kunz respond to the criticisms of Gibson et al. (2003a), who argue convincingly that confidence in the judiciary represents mostly specific support for the judiciary. Meanwhile, in a study of U.S. state supreme courts, Dougherty et al. (2006, p. 187) find that confidence in the judiciary "is more closely associated with institutional competence than with fiduciary responsibility." Furthermore, Levi et al. (2009) posit trustworthiness of government as one of two antecedents to institutional legitimacy. In this context, if a significant proportion of the public perceives a court's ruling as activist, these public perceptions are likely to affect the public's overall trust in the court, at least in the short term.

Procedural Justice as an Antecedent to Legitimacy

Concurrently, Tyler and his various co-authors make a case that scholars relate legitimacy to procedural justice. Levi et al. (2009) argue that procedural justice is one of two antecedent conditions of institutional legitimacy (see also Tyler, 1990; Tyler and Rasinski, 1991). Tyler (2006) argues further that the relationship between assessment of procedural justice and legitimacy is robust across legal and political environments. If Tyler is correct, then like judicial confidence, we can think of perceptions of fairness in the justice system as a proxy for judicial legitimacy.

Nonetheless, many scholars contest the notion that perceptions of procedural fairness can predict perspectives on judicial legitimacy (Gibson, 1989; Mondak, 1993; Baird, 2001). Here, Gibson (1989) and Mondak (1993) are unified in their criticism of the procedural justice/legitimacy linkage. They both argue that people lack knowledge of specific procedures of courts. Because of this lack of knowledge, individuals are more likely to generate perceptions of fairness based on their support for the institution. Furthermore, Baird (2001) contends that it is not that procedures are fair (or exposure to process) that elicit support for institutions. Rather, it is more that the "legalistic" nature of

Relating these two approaches to judicial activism, I expect that a judiciary that has greater legitimacy to be more strategic in making activist rulings. In other words, I expect greater legitimacy to induce courts to be strategic about drawing on its legitimacy, developing my research hypotheses from Clark's (2009) Separation-of-Powers Court-curbing theoretical model. Clark (2009, p. 977) offers hypotheses in terms of interaction between court curbing and public support, i.e., highly legitimate courts must consider the effect of making an activist ruling on both the potential response of other institutional actors and the public at large. Clark's model has two pre-conditions: (1) the position of actors must be public (the court, the legislature, and the executive), and (2) the court must be aware that the visibility of the position of actors reflects on its public support. Given these pre-conditions, I offer the following hypotheses:

H1→Antecedent Hypothesis: A court is more likely to vote to make an activist decision as specific public support increases.

H2→Institutional Commitment Hypothesis: A court is more likely to make a strategic ruling as the public's institutional commitment to the court increases.

Data and Methods

I use a dataset of 22 incidents of reelection in Latin America that was compiled by Walker, Schorpp, and Songer (WSS) (2014) to test the implications of competing theoretical and empirical approaches to operationalizing judicial legitimacy on courts' decision-making processes in highly public and political cases that can be described as either judicial activism, or judicial restraint. Political observers may view presidential-reelection cases that a court decides in favor of the executive as activist (1) because other political actors have decided traditionally these political-charged questions and (2) because the court's decision in favor of reelection expands beyond language that is found in the country's written constitution. This idea of expanding beyond explicit language in the written constitution relates to Staton's argument in Chapter 2, concerning fidelity to precedent and avoiding the negation of public policy.

Several descriptive case-study papers seek to explain the role of courts in presidential reelection in Latin America (Perea, 2008; Martínez-Barahona, 2010; Wise, 2010; Martínez-Barahona and Brenes-Barahona, 2012; González

Marrero, 2012).[1] Currently, no work offers a theoretical and analytical model that explains the process by which courts cross-nationally come to their respective decisions on the highly political question of presidential reelection and the outputs of these cases as they relate to judicial activism.

I use all cases of change or attempted change in the terms of presidential reelection in Latin America from 1990 to 2015. These cases are shown in Table 12.1. These 22 cases include constitutional reform on reelection that involves legislative-based constitutional change (Argentina 1994, Colombia 2005, Venezuela 1999, Peru 1993, and Ecuador 2008), referendum-based reform (Venezuela 2009, Peru 2000, Colombia 2009, Bolivia 2009 and Nicaragua 2014), and court action (Colombia 2005 and 2009; Peru 1997, Costa Rica 2000 and 2003; Guatemala 1990, 1995, 2003; Honduras 2009 and 2015; Nicaragua 2009; Bolivia 2013; Ecuador 2014). Table 12.1 also shows the distribution of votes in the 13 supreme-court cases of reelection in which high courts rendered decisions.

Dependent Variable: Vote on Reelection Decision

When the court has an opportunity to vote on reelection, the decision process of voting on presidential reelection is a dichotomous choice, and many in the public may interpret the decision of the court as activism or restraint. In many circumstances, the court does not control completely its ability to select into the reelection process. This lack of control is related to the fact that the executive and legislative branches can implement constitutional change without the inclusion of the court.[2]

In the WSS data, there are seven “Yes” votes, six “No” votes, and nine situations in which the court does not participate. In other words, the outcome of interest is a nested process in which the court selects into, or is selected into the process, and then decides to vote “Yes” or “No” on the question. I consider a “Yes” vote on presidential reelection as an instance of judicial activism because (1) the vote is a departure from past rulings on reelection, and (2) there

1 Additionally, other papers focus more generally on the manipulation of presidential term limits in Latin America but do not focus explicitly on the role of courts (Taylor-Robinson and Ura, 2013; Corrales and Penfold, 2014).

2 Moreover, the court could evoke the “political question” doctrine, which allows the court to remove itself from some political disputes (Sunstein, 1989, p. 337).

Table 12.1: Conditions in reelection vote

Country and Year	Court Prefer	Judicial Ideology	Judicial Vote	Legislative Strength	RRReelect Y/N	Vote
	Legislature in Accord					
Argentina 1994	0.425	0.667	0	0.556	N	None
Bolivia 2009	0.490	1.000	0	0.532	N	None
Ecuador 2008	0.434	1.000	0	0.893	N	None
Ecuador 2014	0.407	1.000	1	0.000	Y	9-0
Colombia 2005	0.421	0.111	1	0.872	Y	5-4
Columbia 2010	0.470	1.000	1	0.812	N	7-2
Honduras 2015	0.398	0.500	1	0.757	Y	6-0
Nicaragua 2014	0.619	0.500	0	0.714	N	None
Peru 1993	0.211	1.000	0	0.991	N	None
Peru 1997	0.276	1.000	1	0.991	N	3-2*
Venezuela 1999	0.433	0.000	0	0.986	N	None
Venezuela 2009	0.312	1.000	0	0.000	N	None
	Legislature Divided or Opposed (Discord)					
Bolivia 2013	0.526	0.000	1	0.321	Y	7-0
Costa Rica 2000	0.922	0.570	1	0.751	N	4-3
Costa Rica 2003	0.919	0.000	1	0.855	Y	7-2
Guatemala 1990	0.308	1.000	1	0.431	N	9-0
Guatemala 1995	0.348	0.000	1	0.794	N	13-0
Guatemala 2003	0.435	0.285	1	0.521	Y	4-3
Honduras 2009	0.387	0.533	1	0.809	N	15-0
Nicaragua 2009	0.575	1.000	1	0.714	Y	6-0
Paraguay 2011	0.588	0.222	0	0.561	N	None
Peru 2000	0.355	1.000	0	0.991	N	None

Data Sources: For Independence: Linzer and Staton's (2015) latent measure of judicial independence. Ideology = % of judges on constitutional court or constitutional chamber selected during the term of the president's party. *Latinobar´ometro*, various years. *Two of the seven judges abstained from voting.

Table 12.2: Reelection and measures of legitimacy

Country and Year	Institutional Commitment = Perceived Independence	Judicial Confidence	Procedural Justice = Fair Justice
Argentina 1994	-0.023	0.005	-0.062
Bolivia 2009	-0.372	0.027	-0.258
Ecuador 2008	-0.401	-0.175	-0.350
Ecuador 2014	-0.057	0.086	-0.340
Colombia 2005	0.001	0.084	-0.104
Columbia 2010	0.029	0.258	0.159
Honduras 2015	-0.172	-0.130	-0.171
Nicaragua 2014	-0.315	0.016	-0.170
Peru 1993	-0.215	0.001	-0.180
Peru 1997	-0.215	-0.061	-0.221
Venezuela 1999	-0.272	0.160	-0.092
Venezuela 2009	-0.573	0.188	-0.101
Bolivia 2013	-0.086	-0.001	-0.226
Costa Rica 2000	0.401	0.398	0.280
Costa Rica 2003	0.115	0.366	0.328
Guatemala 1990	-0.344	0.138	-0.116
Guatemala 1995	-0.344	0.138	-0.116
Guatemala 2003	-0.344	-0.026	-0.190
Honduras 2009	-0.115	0.062	-0.179
Nicaragua 2009	-0.344	0.003	-0.170
Paraguay 2011	-0.458	-0.070	-0.247
Peru 2000	-0.430	-0.156	-0.350

Data Sources: For the Perceived Independence, Judicial Confidence and Fair Justice: Bühlmann et al. (2011) Democracy Barometer dataset.

of justice in the society."[6] Table 12.3 shows that the three measures of judicial legitimacy are highly reliable with values closer to 1 indicating greater reliability and stability (Heise, 1969, p. 93).[7]

6 At the aggregate level, the values are rescaled and range from -37 to 101 for all countries in the DB dataset. I divide the values by 100. Table 2 shows that the values that I extract for the country-years of our study from the DB range from -.350 to .328.

7 I compare the Pearson correlation between the measures for 2000, 2003, 2009 and compute the "true reliability" and "stability coefficient" of the correlation between the respective measures. Values closer to 1 indicate greater reliability and stability.

Table 12.3: True-reliability and stability of legitimacy proxy indicators

	Between 2000 and 2003	Between 2003 and 2009	Between 2000 and 2009	Reliability	Stability 2000-2009
Perceived Ind	0.777	0.916	0.724	0.984	0.726
Judicial Confidence	0.912	0.944	0.851	1.012	0.841
Fair Justice	0.920	0.798	0.867	0.846	1.020

Reliability estimates by create multiplying the Pearson correlation for between 2000 and 2003 by the Pearson correlation for between 2003 and 2009 and then dividing by the Pearson correlation for between 2000 and 2009. The sample size for all correlations is the 17 countries of Central and South America.

Judicial Vote Model and Predictive Validity of Judicial Legitimacy Proxies

In all cases that I consider, I expect the Judicial Legitimacy proxy to interact with the Judiciary's Preference on reelection. This interaction occurs because the court is compelled to modify its sincere preference given its relative level of public support. This idea of the court seeking to advance its own preference links to judicial activism in the sense that citizens who believe that a court is activist (or deciding in activist fashion) are also likely to believe that the judges of that court are imposing their personal preferences on to the society. The public would view these preferences as biased based on partisan, political, social, or economic considerations. In this section, I assess the predictive validity of the three judicial legitimacy proxies given the two theoretical hypotheses.[8] My model is:

"Yes" Vote on Reelection~Judicial Legitimacy+ Judicial Preference+(Judicial Legitimacy-Judicial Preference) +Judicial Ideology +Legislative Strength*

8 Predictive validity relates to construct validity and is a "more rigorous test than face or content validity" (Dilliplane et al., 2013, 241). For the statistical models, I standardize the three Judicial Legitimacy measures to place them on similar scales. The measures range from -1.65 to 2.75.

Relating this model to the theoretical hypotheses and judicial activism, I use a "Yes" vote on reelection as a representation of a decision that some of the public may view as activist. For the Institutional-Commitment hypothesis (H2), I expect a court that is highly legitimate to be more likely to vote "Yes" on reelection when it prefers reelection, all things equal. Meanwhile, legitimacy and judicial preference interact negatively to affect the vote on reelection. This negative interaction reflects the strategic nature of the decision process. As the court becomes more legitimate, it also becomes more likely to vote strategically to make an activist ruling when it would prefer to vote No at low levels of independence. A high legitimacy and low independence court is willing to tap *its reservoir of goodwill* to make an activist ruling on reelection.

Alternatively, we can think of Hypotheses 1 as directly *related to specific political support for the court*. In this instance, the court leverages its political support against its preference for reelection. These theoretical expectations apply to both the Judicial Confidence and Fair Justice models, the two antecedent models. The interaction reflects the positive relationship between the interaction term and a "Yes" vote on reelection. As both the court's specific political support and preference for reelection increases, the court becomes increasingly likely to make an activist vote and rule in favor of presidential reelection.

In the overall model above, Judicial Independence represents the court's preference on reelection. I expect a more independent court to seek to protect its higher level of judicial independence, all things being equal. For this reason, a highly independent court should have a higher preference for reelection than a dependent court. A more independent court desires to retain the level of control that it has over policy outcomes that it prefers (Clark, 2009). Moreover, Smithey and Ishiyama (2002) show that judicial independence is empirically related to judicial activism. I use the Linzer and Staton (2015) latent measure of judicial independence, which is a composite/overtime measure of judicial independence from all existing *de jure* and *de facto* measures of judicial independence from 1960 to 2012.[9] This measure is currently the most comprehensive measure of judicial independence and ranges from 0 to 1. Table 12.1 shows that Costa Rica in 2000 has the highest level of judicial independence (.922) and Peru in 1993 has the lowest level of judicial independence (.211).

9 Using a Bayesian IRT estimation procedure, the measure systematically aggregates multiple comparative indicators without substantial loss of information.

In the model, I account for other factors that may influence the court's decision on the presidential reelection decision. These factors include the Legislature's Strength *vis-a-vis* the executive, the Legislature's preference on reelection, and the ideological orientation of the Court in relations to the president. Taken from the Democracy Barometer, Legislative Strength measures the balance of power between the government and the opposition in the national legislature and ranges from 0 to 1.[10] Table 12.1 is divided into two sections: (1) Legislature in Accord (twelve observations), and (2) Legislature in Discord (ten observations). Legislative in Accord or Discord is the representation of the legislature's preference on the reelection question. Finally, Judicial Ideology is the percentage of judges on constitutional court or constitutional chamber selected during the term of the current president's party (see Table 12.1).

Results of Predictive Validity Test

In this section, my statistical analysis considers the court's decision on reelection as a dichotomous choice in a nested decision-making process on a highly political issue that some citizens may consider activist. Figure 12.1 shows the findings graphically from three statistical models that use a Bayesian Hierarchical Logistic Regression (BHLR) approach (see Appendix 1 for actual estimates). For the three models, I plot the probability of a "Yes" vote for reelection by Judicial Independence for different levels of Judicial Legitimacy to demonstrate the effect of legitimacy, judicial preference (Judicial Independence), and the interaction of legitimacy*preference on voting "Yes" on presidential reelection. The figure shows that the Fair Justice and Judicial Confidence models produce similar results, while Institutional Commitment model that uses Perceived Independence produces a unique result in which highest legitimacy courts are predicted to vote "Yes" on reelection at lower levels of judicial independence. Moreover, using the Deviance as a measure of model fit, the Institutional Commitment model produces the best fit with a Deviance value of 20.17 in comparison to 24.55 and 24.195 for the Judicial Confidence and Fair Justice models, respectively.[11]

10 It is computed by 1-(absolute value (Government seat share—Opposition seat share)/100).

11 The Deviance is a measure of discrepancy between observed and fixed values, and smaller values indicate better fit. It is twice the sum of observed times the log of observed values over expected values, where the sum is over both these successes and the failures.

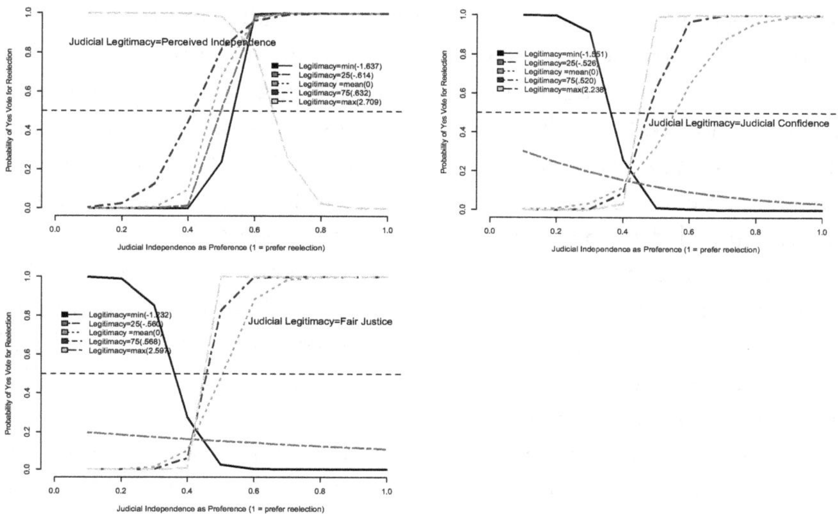

Figure 12.1: Posterior estimates of Yes vote on reelection

Furthermore, the Institutional Commitment panel of Figure 12.1 shows that courts with lower levels of legitimacy (solid-black, dashed-red) are more likely to vote their preference on reelection. These courts are more likely to vote "No" when they prefer to vote "No" (low judicial independence) and "Yes" when they prefer to vote "Yes" (high judicial independence). The sincere vote by low legitimacy and low independent courts conforms to Helmke's (2002) argument that judges in a nothing-to-lose position are free to vote sincerely.[12] In this instance, courts lacking in legitimacy and institutional autonomy, can rule against an executive seeking to extend his term in office because the court anticipates no benefits in further empowering the executive. Alternatively, courts at lower levels of legitimacy can make an activist ruling when they have higher levels of institutional autonomy (independence).

Meanwhile, courts with very high legitimacy (light-blue-dashed line) appear to vote strategically. These courts tend to vote Yes when they prefer to vote No (an activist ruling) and No when they prefer to vote Yes. At low levels of independence, a high-legitimacy court is willing to tap the reservoir of goodwill that it has established with the public to make the activist ruling. In other words, highly legitimate courts can use their legitimacy to make activist

12 See also Helmke and Rosenbluth (2009).

rulings to perhaps curry some favor with a potentially empowered executive, even though the public may view this specific ruling negatively.

Testing the Antecedent Hypothesis (H1) using Judicial Confidence and Fair Justice models, I find that a low legitimacy court (lacking public support) will make a strategic vote of "Yes" on reelection when it prefers to vote "No". In this outcome, the executive has captured this low legitimacy court, and the court is compelled to make an activist vote to support the executive's desire for reelection. Meanwhile, Panels 2 and 3 of Figure 12.1 show that higher legitimacy courts (the blue dotted-dashed line, the light blue dashed line, and the green-dotted line) that have higher levels of independence vote "Yes" on reelection because they prefer presidential reelection. This finding indicates that a court with higher legitimacy (public support) will make an activist ruling because the public generally agrees with the court's true preference. Alternatively, the two Antecedent models predict that a court with low, but not the lowest, legitimacy has a low probability of making an activist vote regardless of the court's own preference. In other words, this court lacks sufficient specific public support to make an activist vote.

Case Studies of Legitimacy and Judicial Activism

At this point, I return to discuss further the two country cases that motivated this chapter concerning legitimacy and activism (Costa Rica 2000, 2003; and Honduras 2009, 2015). These two country cases offer variation on the level of legitimacy and allow for different interpretations of the court's reelection vote given different approaches to judicial legitimacy (as an institutional commitment or an antecedent to legitimacy).

Costa Rica: A High Legitimacy Court

As a reminder, the Costa Rican Constitutional Chamber switches from a 4-3 "No" vote against reelection in 2000 to a 5-2 "Yes" vote for reelection in 2003. In approving reelection, the Chamber determined that former presidents could seek reelection after a hiatus of eight years. How does the Chamber get to a "Yes", activist ruling on the reelection question? The impetus for the change in the terms of reelection came from the supporters of former president and Nobel Prize Winner Oscar Arias who sought to return to the presidency

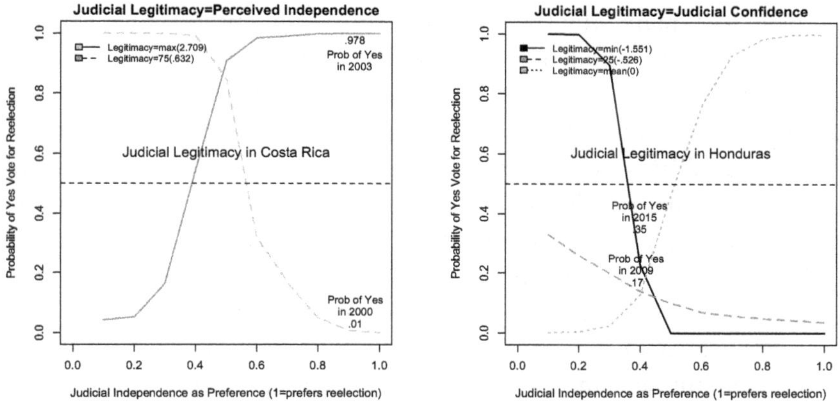

Figure 12.2: Predicted probability of Yes on reelection in Costa Rica and Honduras

after having served as president from 1986 to 1990.[13] After the Chamber's "Yes" vote, Arias ran for office and won the 2006 Presidential election.

Under the Institutional Commitment as Legitimacy model, in 2000, the legitimacy of the Costa Rican Supreme Court is the highest of all courts in this study at 0.401, and its level of institutional autonomy (judicial independence) is also the highest at 0.922. The model predicts that the Chamber should vote "No" (see Figure 12.2). Providing a No ruling is exactly what the Chamber does, as it is willing to draw on its public support to rule against Arias's supporters desire for reelection. Meanwhile, in 2003, the legitimacy of the Costa Rican Court declines somewhat to 0.115. This value is still the second highest among the legitimacy figures in the study, but the decline from 0.401 (2.709 standardized) to 0.115 (1.415 standardized) is the second greatest decline in legitimacy experienced by a court in this study (produces a probability of "Yes" vote of .978).[14] While the independence (autonomy) of the Costa Rican court remains high at 0.919, the Chamber makes an activist ruling, votes "Yes" on reelection, and expands on the written Costa Rican constitution concerning the terms of presidential reelection.

Conversely, the Antecedent Models predict that the Costa Rican Constitutional Chamber should vote "Yes" on reelection in both 2000 and 2003, and

13 During the 2000 and 2003 periods, Miguel Angel Rodriguez (1998–2002) and Abel Pecheco (2002–2006) served as president. After the Chamber's "Yes" vote, Arias won the 2006 Presidential election.

14 Venezuela has the greatest decline in legitimacy and declines from -.272 (-.295 standardized) to -0.573 (-1.638 standardized).

are unable to explain why the Chamber votes differently in the two decision years. For Judicial Confidence, prior studies show that Judicial Confidence is highly correlated with the institutional confidence of other formal institutions (Caldeira and Gibson, 1992; Kelleher and Wolak, 2007; Gibson and Nelson, 2015; Walker, 2016). Consequently, I interpret the model's prediction in two ways: (1) the court is able to vote its preference on reelection because it has high specific support to do so, or (2) the court determines that the executive (or his supporters) has sufficient public support to eventually force through presidential reelection and decides to side with the executive. Either way, the court's activism is a function of specific political support. The fact that Institutional Commitment model predicts better the high-legitimacy Costa Rican case suggest that judicial legitimacy places a major role in highly legitimate courts making activist decisions.

Meanwhile, the Institutional Commitment and Antecedent models offer predictions of the Honduran case that differ only slightly. This slight difference occurs because of the dynamic nature of the Judicial Confidence measure. The Institutional-Commitment model predicts that the Honduran Supreme Court should vote "No" on both the unanimous 2009 ruling that facilitated the 2009 coup against Jos´e Manuel Zelaya (Liberal Party) and the unanimous 2015 ruling that allowed presidential reelection.[15] The Institutional-Commitment measure of legitimacy of the Honduran court changes little between 2009 and 2015, and the lack of change produces similar probability of the Court ruling against reelection. The Antecedent models also predict that the Honduran Supreme Court should vote "No" on both the 2009 ruling that prevented a public vote on reelection and the 2015 ruling that allowed presidential reelection. Nonetheless, the Judicial Confidence model (see Figure 12.2) shows that there is a slightly higher probability that the court would vote "Yes" in 2015 (0.35) than in 2009 (0.17). In other words, the Judicial Confidence Antecedent model predicts that the court has a slightly higher probability to make an activist ruling. Even still, all three models predict that the court should refrain from making an activist ruling. As an alternative, the preference of the Honduran legislature is a possible explanation for these divergent predictions between 2009 and 2015. In 2009, the legislature opposes Zelaya's attempt to seek a public vote to extend his term. In contrast, the legislature does not

15 Toledo, E. (2015, April 23). Fallo de la Corte Suprema Allana Camino a la Reelección en Honduras. *PanAm Post.* https://panampost.com/elena-toledo/2015/04/23/fallo-de-la-corte-suprema-allana-camino-a-la-reeleccion-en-honduras/

actively contest the reelection efforts of then President Juan Orlando Hernández of the National Party in 2015. Hernandez was reelected in 2017 after the Honduran Constitutional Chamber validated presidential reelection.

Conclusion: Judicial Legitimacy and Judicial Activism

If we define judicial activism as a court deciding in a manner that deviates from past restraint on societal disputes that are resolved traditionally by more political actors, this study offers some explanation as to how the court makes its decisions by specifying judicial legitimacy as key variable in the court's decision-making process. The lack of a useful cross-national measure of judicial legitimacy has been a major impediment to the study of the relationship between legitimacy and activism. As Gibson and Nelson (2014, p. 215) point out "the most pressing need for those seeking to understand judicial legitimacy is data capable of supporting dynamic analysis." In this chapter, I establish that various approaches to measuring judicial legitimacy have different interpretations when related to judicial activism.

Using an Institutional Commitment approach, I infer that high legitimacy courts use institutional legitimacy to make strategic votes against more powerful political actors. The court can make these decisions because it has a reservoir of institutional support from which to draw public support (Gibson et al., 1998; Walker, 2016). More specifically, when the court lacks judicial independence (institutional autonomy), it can decide cases in an activist manner, assured that the public will concede to its decision because of the goodwill that it has accumulated as an institution. Furthermore, low legitimacy courts use their lack of institutional legitimacy to inform their decision to vote their true preference in an activist manner on important political issues. A lack of institutional support from the public prompts the court to seek to protect its institution autonomy (judicial independence) by siding with the executive. To be clear, I am not referring to individual judges because judges do have individual-level personal and political cost to pay for defying powerful political actors.

Meanwhile, Antecedent models that are based on measures of specific support as legitimacy indicate that courts with high specific support will vote their true preference in an activist manner on important political issues. Accordingly, a court that believes it has public support in the issue area of contestation (e.g., human rights protection) can make an activist ruling because the public likely favors the constitutional outcome derived from the court's ruling. The court uses its high political support from the public to reinforce its decision to vote its preference. In this way, a "Yes" vote by the court on the reelection question could be considered activism given that the constitution has not explicitly defined the terms of presidential reelection. Alternatively, a court with low specific support will vote strategically against its sincere preference because it lacks both specific public support and institutional autonomy. Because of these deficiencies, a court with low specific support will make an activist "Yes" vote to gain favor with a potentially empowered executive. Furthermore, a court with low specific support but high institution autonomy will make the alternative "No" vote because it wishes to maintain its institutional autonomy.

Finally, both the Institutional-Commitment and the Antecedent models presented here do a relatively poor job in predicting activism by mid-level legitimacy courts. In these mid-level legitimacy cases, courts likely give greater weight to aligning with other political actors in making the decision on how and when to make an activist ruling.

Method Appendix: Statistical Model

I use a Bayesian Hierarchical Logistic Regression (BHLR) model with the Chib and Carlin's (1999) blocked Gibbs sampler (see Martin, Quinn and Park, 2011). The BHLR model is similar to a selection model and allows me to model the effect of the court selecting into or being selected into the presidential reelection process. I run three models, one with each of the three different proxies for judicial legitimacy. The BHLR model takes the form of $y_i \sim Bernoulli(\theta_i)$, and latent variables $\phi(\theta_i)$, with ϕ being the logit link function:

$$\phi(\theta_i) = X_i\beta + W_i b_i + \varepsilon_i$$

Each group i has k_i observations. The random effects take the form $b_i \sim N_q(0, V_b)$, and the over-dispersion terms are given by $\varepsilon_i \sim N(0, \sigma^2 I_k)$. We use a standard conjugate prior ($\beta \sim N_p(\mu_\beta, V_\beta)$). In this configuration, $\sigma^2 \sim IGamma(\nu, 1/\delta)$, and $V_b \sim IWishart(r, rR)$ (Chib and Carlin, 1999; Gill and Walker, 2005; Martin et al., 2011).

I use relatively non-informative priors, set the prior mean on the fixed effects at 0, set the prior variance on the fixed effects at 0.01, run three chains with 2,000,000 iterations for each chain, use a burnin = 20,000, and use a thinning interval = 1000. The beta-start values for the three chains are -1, 0, and 1 for each of the three models. This results in a sample size of 6,000 for each of the models. I estimate the models in R using MCMCpack (Martin et al., 2011) and obtain the posterior means, standard deviations, and 90% Bayesian credible intervals. I use the Geweke diagnostic to assess model convergence.

This material is based upon work produced by the author while serving at the National Science Foundation. Any opinion, findings, and conclusions or recommendations expressed in this material are those of the author and do not necessarily reflect the views of the National Science Foundation.

Appendix 1

Table 12.A1: Bayesian hierarchical logistic regression model of Yes reelection vote

	Judicial Legitimacy = Perceived Independence (Institutional Commitment)		Judicial Legitimacy = = Judicial Confidence (Specific Support)	
Parameter	post mean(sd) 90% BCI		post mean(sd) 90% BCI	
	Fixed Effects		Fixed Effects	
Intercept	-18.260(8.193)	[-29.29: -8.55]	-7.522(4.804)	[-13.67: -1.61]
Judicial Legitimacy	11.400(4.755)	[5.73: 17.80]	-12.800(8.131)	[-23.95: -3.38]
Judicial Preference	30.150(12.687)	[15.05:47.27]	13.160(8.800)	[2.87: 24.78]
Judicial Ideology	-2.607(2.377)	[-5.61: 0.33]	-2.988(2.035)	[-5.61: -0.45]
Legislative Strength	8.207(4.236)	[3.13: 13.89]	3.038(2.824)	[-0.48: 6.73]
Preference* Legitimacy	-20.440(8.321)	[-31.71:-10.64]	30.430(19.036)	[8.21: 56.06]
Deviance	20.170(4.478)	[14.94: 26.09]	24.550(5.186)	[18.43: 31.13]

Judicial Legitimacy
Fair Justice (Procedural Justice)

Parameter	post mean(sd)	90% BCI
Fixed Effects		
Intercept	-11.617(6.884)	[-20.65: -3.42]
Judicial Legitimacy	-16.634(9.952)	[-29.80: -5.09]
Judicial Preference	21.083(13.056)	[5.66: 38.40]
Judicial Ideology	-2.622(2.035)	[-5.21: -0.18]
Legislative Strength	3.825(3.180)	[0.05: 7.99]
Preference*Legitimacy	39.065(23.017)	[12.05: 69.33]
Deviance	24.195(5.088)	[18.17: 30.94]

Model estimated using MCMCPack. post mean= Posterior Mean; sd= Standard Deviation; BCI= Bayesian Credible Interval.

References

Baird, V. A. (2001). Building institutional legitimacy: The role of procedural justice. *Political Research Quarterly*, *54*(2), 333–354.

Bartels, B. L., & Johnston, C. D. (2013). On the ideological foundations of supreme court legitimacy in the American public. *American Journal of Political Science*, *57*(1), 184–199.

Benesh, S. C. (2006). Understanding public confidence in American courts. *The Journal of Politics*, *68*(3), 697–707.

Bühlmann, M., & Kunz, R. (2011). Confidence in the judiciary: Comparing the independence and legitimacy of judicial systems. *West European Politics*, *34*(2), 317–345.

Caldeira, G. A., & Gibson, J. L. (1992). The etiology of public support for the Supreme Court. *American Journal of Political Science*, *36*(3), 635–664.

Canon, B. (1982–83). Defining the dimensions of judicial activism. *Judicature*, *66*(2), 236–239.

Carey, J. M. (2003). The reelection debate in Latin America. *Latin American Politics and Society*, *45*(1), 119–133.

Chib, S., & Carlin, B. P. (1999). On MCMC sampling in hierarchical longitudinal models. *Statistics and Computing*, 9(1), 17–26.

Clark, T. S. (2009). The separation of powers, court curbing, and judicial legitimacy. *American Journal of Political Science*, *53*(4), 971–989.

Corrales, J., & Penfold, M. (2014). Manipulating term limits in Latin America. *Journal of Democracy*, *25*(4), 157–168.

Cross, F. B., & Lindquist, S. A. (2007). The scientific study of judicial activism. *Minnesota Law Review*, 91, 1752–1784.

Dawson, M., De Witte, B., & Muir, E. (2013). *Judicial activism at the European Court of Justice*. Cheltenham, UK: Edward Elgar.

Dilliplane, S., Goldman, S. K., & Mutz, D. C. (2013). Televised exposure to politics: New measures for a fragmented media environment. *American Journal of Political Science*, *57*(1), 236–248.

Dougherty, G. W., Lindquist, S. A., & Bradbury, M. D.. (2006). Evaluating performance in state judicial institutions: Trust and confidence in the Georgia judiciary. *State and Local Government Review*, *38*(3), 176–190.

Fon, V., & Parisi, F. (2006). Judicial precedents in civil law systems: A dynamic analysis. *International Review of Law and Economics*, *26*(4), 519–535.

Gibson, J. L. (1989). Understandings of justice: Institutional legitimacy, procedural justice, and political tolerance. *Law & Society Review*, *23*(3), 469–496.

Gibson, J. L. (2008a). Campaigning for the bench: The corrosive effects of campaign speech? *Law & Society Review*, *42*(4), 899–928.

Gibson, J. L. (2008b). Challenges to the impartiality of state supreme courts: Legitimacy theory and 'New-Style' judicial campaigns. *American Political Science Review*, *102*(1), 59–75.

Gibson, J. L., & Caldeira, G. A. (2003). Defenders of democracy? Legitimacy, popular acceptance, and the South African Constitutional Court. *The Journal of Politics*, *65*(1), 1–30.

Gibson, J. L., & Nelson, M. J. (2014). The legitimacy of the US Supreme Court: Conventional wisdoms and recent challenges thereto. *Annual Review of Law and Social Science*, *10*, 201–219.

Gibson, J. L., & Nelson, M. J. (2015). Is the U.S. Supreme Court's legitimacy grounded in performance satisfaction and ideology. *American Journal of Political Science*, *59*(1), 162–174.

Gibson, J. L., Caldeira, G. A., & Baird, V. A. (1998). On the legitimacy of national high courts. *The American Political Science Review*, *92*(3), 343–358.

Gibson, J. L., Caldeira, G. A., & Spence, L. K. (2003a). Measuring attitudes toward the United States Supreme Court. *American Journal of Political Science*, *47*(2), 351–367.

Gibson, J. L., Caldeira, G. A., & Spence, L. K. (2003b). The Supreme Court and the US presidential election of 2000: Wounds, self-inflicted or otherwise? *British Journal of Political Science*, *33*(4), 534–556.

Gill, J., & Walker, L. D. (2005). Elicited priors for Bayesian model specifications in political science research. *Journal of Politics*, *67*(3), 841–872.

Gonz ález Marrero, S. (2012). Las elecciones Nicaragüenses de 2011. *Anuario de Estudios Centroamericanos*, 38(April), 137–176.

Heise, D. R. (1969). Separating reliability and stability in test-retest correlation. *American Sociological Review*, *34*(1), 93–101.

Helmke, G. (2002). The logic of strategic defection: Courts and executive relations in Argentine under dictatorship and democracy. *American Political Science Review*, 96(2), 301–326.

Helmke, G. (2010). The origins of institutional crises in Latin America. *American Journal of Political Science*, *54*(3), 737–750.

Helmke, G., & Rosenbluth, F. (2009). Regimes and the rule of law: Judicial independence in comparative perspective. *Annual Review of Politics*, *12*, 345–366.

Kelleher, C., &Wolak, J. (2007). Explaining public confidence in the branches of state government. *Political Research Quarterly*, 60(4), 707–721.

Levi, M., Sacks, A., & Tyler, T. (2009). Conceptualizing legitimacy, measuring legitimating beliefs. *American Behavioral Scientist*, *53*(3), 354–375.

Linzer, D. A., & Staton, J. (2015). A measurement model for synthesizing multiple comparative indicators: The case of judicial independence. *Journal of Law and Courts*, *3*(2), 223–256.

Martin, A. D., Quinn, K. M., & Park, J. H. (2011). MCMCpack: Markov Chain Monte Carlo in R. *Journal of Statistical Software*, *42*(9), 22–33.

Martínez-Barahona, E. (2010). Las cortes supremas como mecanismo de distribución de poder: El caso de la reelección presidencial en Costa Rica y Nicaragua. *Revista de Ciencia Poltica*, 30(January), 723–750.

Martínez-Barahona, E., & Brenes-Barahona, A. (2012). 'Y Volver, Volver, Volver . . .'. Un analisis de los casos de intervenci´on de las cortes supremas en la reelecci´on presidencial en Centroamerica. *Anuario de Estudios Centroamericanos*, *38*(1–2), 109–136.

Mondak, J. J. (1993). Institutional legitimacy and procedural justice: Reexamining the question of causality. *Law and Society Review*, *27*(3), 599–608.

Mondak, J. J., & Smithey, S. I. (1997). The dynamics of public support for the Supreme Court. *Journal of Politics*, *49*(4), 1114–1142.

Perea, J. F. (2008). Of presidents and precedents: The role of judicial review in recent presidential elections in Peru, Costa Rica, and the United States. *Florida Journal of International Law*, *20*, 201–353.

Smithey, S. I., & Ishiyama, J. (2002). Judicial activism in post-communist politics. *Law and Society Review*, *36*(4), 719–742.

Staton, J. K. (2010). *Judicial power and strategic communication in Mexico*. New York: Cambridge University Press.

Staton, J. K. (2023). Judicial activism in comparative law and politics. In L. Hausegger, R. L. Pacelle Jr., & R. A. Sanchez Urribarri (Eds.), *Judicial activism in comparative perspective* (pp. 1–16). Peter Lang.

Sunstein, C. R. (1989). Is there an unconstitutional conditions doctrine? *San Diego Law Review*, *26*, 337–345.

Taylor-Robinson, M. M., & Ura, J. D. (2013). Public opinion and conflict in the separation of powers: Understanding the Honduran coup of 2009. *Journal of Theoretical Politics*, *25*(1), 105–127.

Toledo, E. (2015, April 23). Fallo de la Corte Suprema Allana Camino a la Reelección en Honduras. *PanAm Post*. https://panampost.com/elena-toledo/2015/04/23/fallo-de-la-corte-suprema-allana-camino-a-la-reeleccion-en-honduras/

Tyler, T. R. (1990). *Why people follow the law: Procedural justice, legitimacy, and compliance*. New Haven, CN: Yale University Press.

Tyler, T. R. (2006). Psychological perspectives on legitimacy and legitimation. *Annual Review of Psychology*, *57*(1), 375–400.

Tyler, T. R., & Rasinski, K. (1991). Legitimacy and the acceptance of unpopular Supreme Court decisions: A question of causality. *Law and Society Review*, *2*(3), 621–630.

Walker, L. D. (2016). A multi-level explanation of mass support for the judiciary. *Justice System Journal*, *37*(3), 194–210.

Walker, L. D. (2017). Courts and decisionmaking in developing democracies. In R. M. Howard & K. A. Randazzo (Eds.), *Routledge handbook of judicial behavior* (pp. 406–426). Routledge.

Walker, L. D., Schorpp, S., & Songer, D. A. (2014). The judicial politics of presidential reelection. *Paper presented at the 2014 Midwest Political Science Association Annual Meeting*, April 2014.

Wilson, B. M., & Handberg, R. (1999). From judicial passivity to judicial activism: Explaining the change in Costa Rica's Supreme Court. *Law and Business Review of the Americas*, *5*, 522–543.

Wise, M. B. (2010). Judicial review and its politicization in Central America: Guatemala, Costa Rica, and constitutional limits on presidential candidates. *Santa Clara Journal of International Law*, *7*(2), 145–180.

· 13 ·

AN INSTITUTIONAL APPROACH TO JUDICIAL ACTIVISM

Susan Achury

The challenges of defining judicial activism have long been discussed in the literature (Canon, 1982). At the core of this discussion lies a normative aim to distinguish between the 'legitimate' exercise of judicial review powers to maintain the supremacy of the constitution (Harwood, 1992; Cohn and Kremnitzer, 2005; Bolick, 2019; Grover, 2020) and the antidemocratic usurpation of political discretion from the elected branches by the courts (Sunstein, 2009). As various chapters have pointed out in this volume, some scholars argue the need to abandon the term 'judicial activism' because of its lack of clarity and political connotations (Easterbrook, 2002; Lawrence, 2015; Schacter, 2018), while others still use it in various circumstances, including to describe judicial behavior perceived as abusive of its institutional role in democracies (Green, 2008; Coutinho et al., 2015).

In this chapter, I propose a definition of judicial activism that focuses on the institutional expectations created by formal rules granting judicial review prerogatives. Rather than assuming the existence of universal standards to identify activist courts, it recognizes that judicial review powers vary across jurisdictions; therefore, their legitimate exercise also varies. This approach accounts for the differences in the scope of judicial intervention across countries, depending on three institutional features: who has legal standing (*access*), what can be reviewed (*jurisdiction*), and when and how courts intervene (*procedures*). Courts situated in constitutional justice systems accessible to citizens, addressing society's critical problems, and with procedures that facilitate political deliberation are granted a wider space for legitimate intervention than courts working in more limited institutional settings. I use the expected level of judicial intervention created by these formal powers to assess anti-majoritarian behavior as 'activist.' This approach challenges definitions of judicial activism that assume that courts have the same legitimacy to intervene in policymaking. Instead, it brings variation in courts' formal authority (i.e., accessibility, jurisdictional reach, and the decisiveness of their decisions) into discussions of legitimacy and decision-making across constitutional justice systems. Courts' interventions are identified as activist when the extent of such participation does not align with the expectations created by the institutional setting.

To contribute to the conceptualization and measurement of judicial activism, this chapter is divided into four sections. First, it identifies *anti-majoritarianism* and *legal stability* as the main subdimensions of the concept of judicial activism. In section two, I present formal judicial authority as a benchmark to differentiate when anti-majoritarianism and legal instability are indicators of judicial activism. Section three provides empirical evidence of how this benchmark can be implemented by ranking judicial activism in ten Latin American high courts. Finally, the chapter highlights the advantages of an institutional approach to conceptualizing judicial activism and the implications for the scientific study of the phenomenon.

Conceptualizing Judicial Activism: The Controversy

Most accepted definitions of judicial activism identify the phenomenon as instances in which courts encroach on the role of elected branches or abuse their discretion (Canon, 1982; Cohn and Kremnitzer, 2005; Cross and Lindquist, 2006; Lindquist and Cross, 2009). Like other multidimensional concepts in the field, activism refers to courts' behaviors that can be identified through their different manifestations or dimensions, although they are not directly observable. Multiple indicators have been employed to try to provide a "holistic representation of a complex phenomenon that allows researchers to match broad predictors with broad outcomes and increase the explained variance" (Edwards, 2001, 145).

Current definitions aim to capture the multidimensional nature of the concept by listing court outcomes that broadly differentiate two types of judicial behavior. The first type refers to instances in which courts invalidate legislation, although they have reasonable interpretations that justify their constitutionality (Coutinho et al., 2015). The second type includes judicial decisions holding policies constitutional when the literal meaning of the provisions is clearly unconstitutional (Bolick, 2019; Lawrence, 2015; Lindquist and Cross, 2009).

Table 13.1 classifies the indicators previously used in the literature as expressions of *anti-majoritarianism* and *legal instability*. Indicators used to measure degrees of anti-majoritarianism aim to capture the frequency and impact of court intervention in policymaking (i.e., striking down legislation or executive orders). Legal instability, on the other hand, refers to behavior that violates the accepted norms for the use of judicial discretion, for example, engaging in judicial aggrandizement or contradicting well-established doctrine. The columns list the different indicators used in judicial activism. Each row lists the definitions and measures proposed in the literature to highlight the inconsistent use of these two elements. Notice that although most accepted definitions of judicial activism have incorporated indicators of *anti-majoritarianism* and *legal instability* to identify instances of courts encroaching on the role of the elected branches, (Canon, 1982; Cohn and Kremnitzer, 2005; Cross and Lindquist, 2006; Lindquist and Cross, 2009), focusing on abuses of judicial discretion can still be useful for comparative analysis.

Anti-majoritarianism

Anti-majoritarianism, as an expression of judicial activism considers that, other things equal, high numbers of decisions declaring laws and executive orders unconstitutional are a symptom of courts abusing their discretion (Column 1). This can be directly observed and measured as the frequency with which decisions strike down legislation or executive orders. This measurement, however, is not sensitive to instances of anti-majoritarianism that are not necessarily illegitimate. Consider, for example, the judicial reaction to populist leaders. Attacks on liberal democracies can trigger anti-majoritarian decisions without engaging in the abusive use of judicial power. Moreover, this approach may overlook instances of judicial activism in which strategic courts friendly to the political regime engage in selective anti-majoritarianism by declaring only secondary or minor policies unconstitutional while being deferent to the government on the more impactful legislation (see Sanchez Urribarri's discussion of the Venezuelan case in this volume).

Current conceptualizations of activism address these concerns by including indicators of the court's deviation from the preferences of public opinion (Column 2), the extent to which decisions create public policies or reflect result-oriented judging (Column 3), or the role of courts vis-à-vis the other political branches (Column 4). Although these characteristics of judicial decision-making qualify purely anti-majoritarian approaches, there are at least two reasons to disregard them as indicators of activism. First, while the responsiveness of judges to public opinion impacts courts' institutional legitimacy, it does not necessarily signal judges are overstepping their discretion. These indicators conflate potential causes of anti-majoritarian behavior rather than defining aspects of activism, contributing to the inconsistent use of the term. For example, ideological judging may be associated with anti-majoritarianism as an expression of activism when courts' ideological preferences oppose those in power. Ideological judging also manifests when courts support policies enacted by governments closer to their ideological preferences despite the policies being unconstitutional. In such cases, anti-majoritarianism fails to identify activism.

Similarly, a lack of public support might be normatively related to the negative connotation of anti-majoritarianism, but it is not necessarily an indicator of judicial activism. For example, high levels of confidence in courts relative to the support of other elected branches may lead courts to be more assertive (see Walker's chapter in this volume). In both cases, qualifications of anti-majoritarianism must be subject to causal examination rather than incorporated as components of the definition. Also, looking at the judges' self-perception of their role and ideological voting, notice that, regardless of how judges consider their function within a checks and balances system, the idea of activism as an illegitimate use of judicial behavior implies the characterization of judges' behavior by external actors. In this sense, decisions are not more legitimate because judges believe their role is to have more intervention. Adopting such criteria implies that judicial discretion depends on the judges' beliefs and perceptions of what are legitimate institutional constraints that grant them the power to intervene in policymaking.

In sum, ideological judging and a lack of public support might be normatively related to judicial assertiveness (Weiden, 2011). However, these assertions must be subject to causal examination rather than incorporated as definitional components of judicial activism.

Table 13.1: Dimensions of judicial activism

	Dimensions of judicial activism						
	Anti-majoritarianism				*Legal instability*		
Concepts	1. Invalidation of laws and executive actions	2. Influence of the decisions	3. Specificity of judicial policymaking	4. Availability of an alternative policymaker	5. Institutional aggrandizement	6 Interpretive stability	7. Interpretive fidelity
Cannon (1983)*	Policies adopted through democratic processes are negated by justices	Decisions make substantive policy choices	Decision establishes policy itself	Decision supersedes consideration by other governmental actors		Earlier court decisions are altered	Constitutional provisions are contrary to the clear intentions of their drafters
Harwood (1992)	-	-			Relaxing requirements for justiciability	Breaking precedent	Interpretation venturing beyond any plain meaning of a statute
Kmiect (2004)	Invalidation of the arguably constitutional actions of other branches	-	Result-oriented judging	Judicial "legislation"	-	Failure to adhere to precedent	Departures from an accepted interpretive methodology
Cohn and Kremnitzer (2005)**	Overstep judicial role of dispute resolution	Deviation from the social consensus or social equilibrium	Deviation from the protection of core values of the constitution				
Lindquist & Cross (2010)	Majoritarianism and deference to other branches		Result-oriented judging		Institutional aggrandizement***	Legal stability****	
Coutinho, La Torre, and Smith (2015)					Nature and scope of legal reasoning led to different degrees of tolerance regarding what should be admissible to courts.		

Notes: Based on Canon (1982) and Lindquist and Cross (2009). *See also Marshall (2002) and Young (2002). For a further description of the similarities, see Cohn and Kremnitzer (2005, 339). **Similarly, Anand (2006) provides a definition based exclusively on the majoritarian dimension: the tendency for judges to make, as opposed to simply interpret, the law; the willingness of courts to issue rulings reversing or altering the legislative enactments of Parliament and the provincial legislatures; and the inability of legislatures to effectively respond to such rulings, thereby giving judges the last word over matters involving rights and freedoms. ***See also Posner (1999) describing activist decisions as those that expand judicial power over other branches of the national government or state governments—also endorsed by Hellman (2001). ****See also, de Almeida Ribeiro (2015).

Legal Instability

Legal instability refers to the instances in which judicial decision-making fails to provide an outcome that follows the accepted norms of judging in the legal profession. The illegitimate use of judicial discretion involves influencing the policymaking process by violating the boundaries created by applicable methods of constitutional interpretation, including constitutional doctrines or precedents. Decisions are labeled as an expression of activism when adopted beyond the predictable outcome based on such norms. Thus, legal instability as an indicator of activism is mainly instrumental in examining courts' aggrandizement (i.e., decisions increasing courts' power vis-à-vis elected branches). While this dimension of activism addresses some of the main concerns of using pure anti-majoritarian approaches, looking at legal reasoning in judging also raises important questions about using legal instability as an indicator of judicial activism. Consider, for example, decisions introducing instability, such as those overturning precedents that reduce or prevent judicial intervention in policymaking. While such decisions can go against legal professional norms, they can also constrain (rather than expand) judicial discretion.

Table 13.1 portrays the inconsistent use of the two critical dimensions of the concept. Based on the assumption that each indicator can capture activism as a latent variable, current studies often involve only one dimension. Quantitative studies of judicial activism usually focus on anti-majoritarianism, and qualitative works are more commonly focused on legal instability (Lindquist and Cross, 2009), each facing different challenges and criticisms. Qualitative approaches to activism based on legal instability have repeatedly been criticized for their subjectivity. Judicial decisions are based on legal interpretations, and determining when they imply abuse of judicial discretion often becomes impossible. These issues are related to the ability to systematically identify changes of precedent across legal cultures and whether it is possible to identify such changes using universal criteria. Also, the intensive data-collecting process of qualitative research often limits the study of activism to within-country analysis, as Hausegger and Sanchez Urribarri pointed out in the introduction to this volume.

The controversy in conceptualizing activism is much on whether the phenomenon is related to how much courts intervene in the policymaking process, labeled as anti-majoritarianism, or whether it relates to courts respecting the institutional boundaries of its jurisdiction and legal reasoning, labeled as legal instability (Kapiszewski and Taylor, 2008; Hirschl, 2008; Hamlin and Sala, 2018). Here, I reconsider the apparent consensus in the literature about anti-majoritarianism as a definitional aspect of activism by looking at legal instability as a necessary component of the concept. Despite the rich debate on the conceptualization of activism, the structure of the concept remains understudied. Little work has examined how those subdimensions contribute to recovering activism as a latent variable. Notice that my critique of purely anti-majoritarian and purely legal instability approaches coincides with the idea that the concept's dimensions are greater than the sum of its parts, which is a characteristic of coexisting non-compensatory subdimensions (Wuttke et al., 2020, p. 359). Think, for example, when higher values on anti-majoritarianism cannot offset lower values on legal instability. To that extent, activism refers exclusively to instances in which both subdimensions, anti-majoritarianism and legal instability, coexist. Similar to recent empirical work on populist attitudes (Wuttke et al., 2020), this piece points out the need to examine the structure of the concept. It claims that it is critical to recognize the non-compensatory nature of subdimensions. This approach to the conceptualization of judicial activism clarifies the differences with neighboring concepts like judicial assertiveness or the judicialization of politics, especially for comparative studies on judicial activism, where contextual factors may trigger anti-majoritarian patterns that do not necessarily involve legal instability.

The Conceptual Structure of Judicial Activism

In current conceptualizations, the anti-majoritarianism and legal instability subdimensions are considered intearchangeable contributors to activism. Frequent judicial invalidation of policies reduces law's predictability and stability (Lindquist, 2017). Moreover, activists' courts must be encouraged to engage with changes in the interpretation of the law to achieve specific policy outcomes. Conceptually, this approach builds upon the idea of reflective causality, in which the observed measures of the dimensions reflect activism as an unobservable concept. However, there is no agreement in the scholarship about each dimension's ability to tease out instances of activism when they do not coexist. Notably, thinking about instances of anti-majoritarianism that may not compromise legal stability or vice versa highlights the conceptual and pragmatic problems of treating activism as a latent construct.

Indeed, there are no theoretical reasons to expect that anti-majoritarianism and legal instability can be treated as interchangeable expressions of activism. For example, we may observe either high anti-majoritarianism in the absence of legal instability (or high levels of legal instability in the absence of anti-majoritarianism) for which there is no illegitimate use of judicial discretion. For example, constitutional courts in Colombia, India, and South Africa have played a decisive role in shaping public policy and have developed significant legal stability (Rodríguez-Garavito, 2010; Kapiszewski et al. 2013). Should we consider decisions failing to adhere to the precedent but not departing from the accepted interpretive methodology as activism? Is judicial activism when decisions are adopted at odds with the norms of judging, regardless of whether the court upheld the preferences of the elected branches? To answer these questions, we need to examine the structure of the concept to design measuring strategies that target the coexistence of anti-majoritarianism and legal instability.

Across the different proposals exploring the multidimensionality of the term, previous efforts have not intended to measure both dimensions simultaneously, thus failing to operationalize them consistently. In what follows, I argue that judicial activism implies the presence of both dimensions (Polites et al., 2012, 32), and I introduce the need for identifying a more apt dynamic benchmark to differentiate when anti-majoritarianism is an indicator of judicial activism.

Formal Judicial Authority: The Creation of a Moving Institutional Benchmark

Comparative studies of judicial activism are hindered, partly because researchers look at anti-majoritarianism and legal instability separately. Studies across countries rarely include a comprehensive analysis of the dimensions of the term, and the few exceptions aggregate them through cumulative scales (Lindquist and Cross, 2009, p. 135). Cross-country studies are rare and mostly use qualitative approaches to conceptualize and measure activism (Porat, 2018). Neither of these approaches offers a fair comparison across cases capturing the legitimacy of the courts' intervention. Thus, I propose using an institutional benchmark that conceptualizes activism as a function of institutional expectations, and its connection with the legitimate exercise of the power of judicial review. In order to do this, judicial activism is defined as a breach of those institutional expectations, as a source of illegitimate use of political power based on a moving institutional benchmark. Hence, I account for instances in which institutional arrangements allow courts a greater intervention in policymaking, considering it legitimate in comparison to instances of pure anti-majoritarianism displayed by courts with lower levels of formal authority. This approach offers a systematic assessment of the degree to which high levels of judicial intervention in public policymaking are more likely to be related to legal instability, representing instances of illegitimate use of judicial power.

Formal authority refers to the "nature and scope of courts' potential sphere of action: its formal capacity to intervene efficiently and decisively in a broad range of politically significant disputes on behalf of a broad range of actors" (Brinks and Blass, 2018, p. 28). It comprises three institutional features of constitutional justice: the courts' jurisdictional reach, its accessibility, and the decisiveness of their decisions (Brinks and Blass, 2017). Institutional features of judicial review do not account for what courts actually do. As we know, there tends to be a gap between *de jure* and *de facto* aspects of judicial decision-making, especially judicial independence.

The *de jure* aspects of judicial authority shape courts' authority to influence different policy outcomes, defining the 'demand side' of constitutional justice. These rules legitimate courts' broader intervention in public policy by allowing small interests in society and those underrepresented in government to voice their preferences through constitutional debates. To the extent that diverse and politically marginalized voices in society access courts, judges are called to develop a richer jurisprudence about a higher number of policies, providing courts with greater opportunities to influence policy (Wilson 2009; Gauri and Brinks 2008; see Wilson's chapter on Costa Rica). These courts are more successful at gathering information from the different parties in conflict, and thereby more likely to develop creative and forward-looking jurisprudence (Ríos-Figueroa, 2017, p. 10). Collectively, these rules determine the breadth of cases that get to the courts and the courts' ability to provide a resolution.

A fundamental implication of this approach to judicial activism is that it captures instances in which greater judicial intervention in public policymaking can be attributed directly to courts' powers. The more formal rules help explain the courts' activist behavior, the less likely it would be attributed to instances in which courts compromise the legal stability, or to the court's reliance on institutional aggrandizement to affect the preferred policies enacted by the elected branches.

Also, if judicial activism is the illegitimate use of judicial power and courts' formal authority determines when, how, and what is subject to judicial intervention, the latter constitutes an institutional benchmark to assess courts' legitimacy. According to Kelsenian doctrine, courts participate in politics to ensure the constitutions' supremacy. This participation lies at the core of an intertwined relationship between politics and law in which "law is the formalization of politics; [and] politics is formalized through discrete acts taken by those actors who are authorized to produce and enforce legal norms, including judges" (Stone Sweet, 2007, 72). While there is no perfect correlation between formal rules and the exercise of political power authorized by such rules (Ríos-Figueroa and Staton, 2014; Epp, 1998; Rosenberg, 2008; Rodríguez-Garavito, 2010), these rules create a benchmark to assess when the influence of constitutional justice on policy is legitimate. Therefore, courts' deviation from the expected behavior, given a particular authority configuration, might help to identify the court's proclivity to engage in judicial activism. The central assumption made under this approach refers to the ability of formal authority as a concept to capture differences across constitutional justice systems.

Once we move away from anecdotal or historical approaches in which anti-majoritarianism and the lack of legal stability are studied as independent manifestations of activism, comparing the infrastructure of constitutional justice can help understand an important variable of the phenomenon in comparative perspective. To better describe the legitimate use of judicial power across countries (and over time), we need to include this aspect in the conceptualization and measurement of activism. While most studies of activism include institutional variables as explanatory variables of the phenomenon, most of them exclusively focus on rules related to independence or mixed *de jure* and *de facto* components. However, notice that here we are presenting a different argument. Formal authority, by definition, provides a dynamic point to encompass different *de jure* aspects of constitutional justice. Formal authority might help researchers differentiate assertiveness (the frequency to which courts overrule the preferences of the elected branches) from judicial activism (the instances in which this happens in the absence of formal authority for courts to do so). This results in a definition and measurement suitable for comparing rates of unconstitutionality across countries, helping us identify when it is more likely to indicate activism.

Revising Judicial Activism in Latin America

Arguably, there are different methods to gather information about legal instability. However, collecting and coding such fine-grained data has proven difficult in Latin America, as it often requires expertise that is hard to find. Courts do not state changes in precedent explicitly or consistently. Therefore, it demands an extensive understanding of the evolution of constitutional concepts for each jurisdiction that cannot be systematized using current text analysis techniques. Recognizing such shortcomings and challenges in the operationalization of activism, I implement a new methodology to facilitate its analysis. The goal is to provide a substitute for cases in which researchers rely exclusively on the anti-majoritarian subdimension. Thus, this approach aims to make comparisons across jurisdictions more accessible for empirical analysis and time-series for within-countries studies.

I use cross-sectional data that includes all decisions of constitutionality adopted by courts of last resort in ten Latin American countries in 2003. The analysis consists of two levels of variation. Case-level data from the

CompLaw database Carrubba et al. (2015) provide information about the court rulings and case characteristics such as the type of complainant, the type of review, the type of policy, and the year of enactment. I also included country-level information, such as Brinks and Blass's (2018) Index of courts' authority and autonomy, and contextual factors of political fragmentation.

I estimate a bivariate multilevel logit model with random intercepts by country and robust standard errors. The dependent variable is a binary variable that indicates whether the decision is to declare the law unconstitutional, and the independent variable is the measurement of formal authority. Surprisingly, courts' authority is not a statistically significant predictor of the probability of a decision judging a particular policy to be unconstitutional. Figure 13.1 identifies cases of judicial activism as outliers displaying values greater than two.[1] Also, notice that there are no outliers among the decisions in which the court defers to the preferences of political actors.

The results of the bivariate regression provide an inversed rank of judicial activism. Figure 13.2 presents the predicted posterior means by country. Countries such as Argentina and El Salvador represent courts for which the formal authority better predicts the level of assertiveness. On the other hand, countries such as Chile and Colombia represent instances in which authority poorly correlates with courts' patterns of unconstitutionality. Overlapping confidence intervals in Figure 13.2 denote a lack of significant statistical difference among the countries. However, the ranking provides two relevant insights about activism in the region. First, countries with formal authority higher than the regional mean, such as Venezuela and Colombia, display assertiveness like Chile's (which has the lowest such levels in the region). Under this conceptualization, the Chilean Constitutional Tribunal is an example of activism with rates of unconstitutionality greater than expected given its formal authority, and the Colombian Constitutional Court is activist because it ruled less unconstitutionality than expected.

I have argued here that there are good reasons to believe that we can only talk about the lack of legitimacy in courts' decision-making after accounting for differences across their formal powers. Table 13.2 presents three models comparing the ability of the same independent and control variables to predict judicial assertiveness *versus* judicial activism. All models include the three types of regressors. First, the models account for *institutional variance* between

1 I use Anscombe residuals because they are designed to be approximately normally distributed; thus, we can check for outliers by plotting Anscombe residuals against observation numbers and seeing which residuals are greater than two in absolute value.

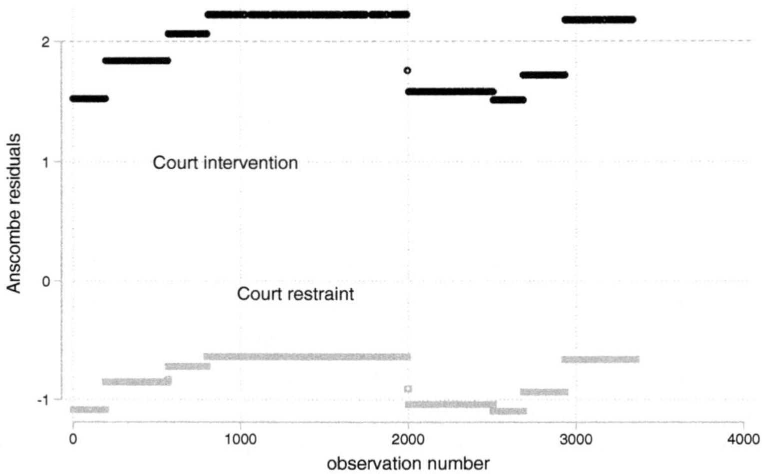

Figure 13.1: Anscombe residuals
Notes: Figure 13.1 displays the Anscombe residuals from multilevel logit bivariate regression between the dichotomous variable indicating decisions striking out policies and the formal authority.

countries regarding the characteristics of the judiciary, including authority and autonomy, and the prerogatives of the president over legislation. I measure courts' formal autonomy using the average scores of Brinks and Blass's ex-ante and ex-post indices (2017).[2] To measure the president's powers over legislation, I use Negretto's index (2013), which measures the executive's constitutional capacity to issue legislative content decrees without a previous delegation by the legislature.

Secondly, the models include *contextual factors* previously identified in the literature affecting the willingness of courts to be deferent to the preferences

2 The ex-ante index provides information about the rules that affect the level of influence that political actors have in the nomination and selection process of judges. It aggregates information about the number of institutional veto players with two multipliers: one that accounts for the collective nature of the veto players (the legislature as opposed to the executive) and another for whether there is a supermajority requirement at any stage that affects the formation of the court's majority. The ex-post index includes information about the level of influence that political actors have to modify the court's current composition, including the length of judicial terms, the difficulty of removal, and constitutional protections of the number of judges and judges' salary. The first type of constitutional guarantee makes court packing more difficult, and the second isolate the courts from financial threats.

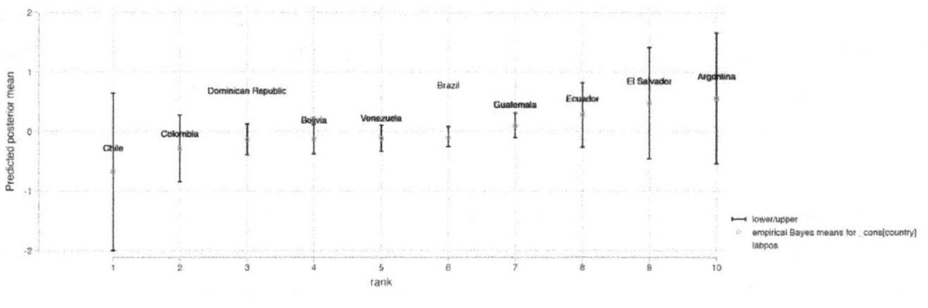

Figure 13.2: Ranking of activism in Latin America
Notes: Figure 13.2 displays the ranking of activism among 10 Latin American courts of last resort in 2003 based on the posterior means.

of the elected branches. Courts are expected to be more activist when facing fragmented governments. I include different aspects of political fragmentation: the effective number of legislative parties and the executive's control over the court and the legislature. Finally, the models include control variables for *case characteristics* such as whether the sitting government enacted the policy under review, whether the case was initiated by a citizen, whether it reviews a national versus regional or local policy, and whether it was presented as a concrete review.[3]

Table 13.2 shows three models. In Model 1, I use judicial assertiveness as a measurement of activism. Given the hierarchical nature of the data, I estimate a multilevel logit model with random intercepts by country and robust standard errors that use assertiveness to measure activism. In Model 2, I use the Anscombe residuals as fit as a matching construct of judicial activism. Because the dependent variable is continuous, I ran a multilevel regression with random intercepts by country and robust standard errors. The proposed operationalization of the dependent variable aims to capture the instances in which assertiveness is not expected, given the powers granted to the courts. Finally, Model 3 presents a two-step model representing the conceptual relationship between assertiveness and activism as a linear regression with a binary endogenous covariate. In the first step, assertiveness is the dependent variable, explained as a factor of formal authority. I use the Anscombe residuals as the dependent variable in the second step. This model captures the fact that

3 Concrete cases are those in which, for the courts to get jurisdiction, the plaintiff must demonstrate they have been directly affected by the policy and the decision has only inter-partes effect.

assertiveness is conceptually part of activism, but they are distinguished by how much formal authority explained the anti-majoritarian courts' behavior. Theoretically, not all instances of assertiveness are indicators of activism, as some courts, by design, are expected to have a more legitimate influence on policy than others.

The models show that contextual factors are significant in explaining activism and not assertiveness. Both measurements of political fragmentation, the effective number of parties and executive control over the legislature, are statistically significant in Model 3 and not significant in Model 1. Moreover, notice that formal authority is a relevant predictor of both assertiveness and activism. Adopting operationalization that conflates the conceptual nuances of each of them will obscure the causal mechanism at work.

Concluding Remarks

This article has aimed to make a threefold contribution to the current debate on judicial activism. The first contribution is to the identification of the multidimensional nature of the term. Moreover, I highlight the implications of discussing its conceptualization and operationalization. I have noted that activism, defined as the illegitimate use of judicial discretion to intervene or not in public policymaking, involves both anti-majoritarianism and legal instability. By comparing these expressions of the phenomenon, I examine the taxonomy and characteristics of activism as a multidimensional construct.

Secondly, I address the concept's structure and recognize it as being more than the sum (or average) of its subdimensions. A construct based on a dynamic benchmark of formal authority provides an objective expectation of how much of its assertiveness is legitimate. Deviations from the expectations created by the institutional powers granted to courts are considered activism. Studies of assertiveness cannot resolve questions of judicial activism. It is necessary to develop theoretical expectations about when it is legitimate for a court to intervene in the policymaking process. I argue that the formal aspects of constitutional review create a parameter to compare courts' behavior across constitutional systems. Thirdly, the empirical analysis identifies the practical consequences of adopting a flawed conceptualization of judicial activism based exclusively on measuring one of its dimensions, drawing from the results obtained from studying ten Latin American countries in 2003.

This raises questions about the proper interpretation of empirical findings connecting institutional and political features to judicial activism, especially if

Table 13.2: Ranking of activism in Latin America

	Model 1: Judicial Assertiveness (Dichotomous: 1 strike down policy)	Model 2: Judicial Activism (Continuous: Anscombe residuals	Model 3: Judicial Activism (Continuous: Anscombe residuals)
Institutional context			
Formal authority	-1.470*	-0.702**	-0.0968**
	(0.755)	(0.277)	(0.0444)
Formal autonomy	1.488	-0.0771	-1.254***
	(1.257)	(0.560)	(0.0630)
Executive powers over legislation	0.0200***	0.00572***	-0.00453***
	(0.00389)	(0.00183)	(0.000158)
Political context			
Effective number of political parties	-0.140	0.261	0.357***
	(0.371)	(0.163)	(0.0196)
Executive control over the legislature	0.195	1.274**	1.362***
	(1.331)	(0.517)	(0.0772)
Executive control over the cc	0.352	0.191*	-0.0106
	(0.241)	(0.111)	(0.00860)
Case characteristics			
Policy enacted by sitting gov	0.327	0.157	0.00294
	(0.253)	(0.116)	(0.00205)
Citizens' complaint	-0.137	-0.0766	-0.0103**
	(0.529)	(0.264)	(0.00423)
National Policy	0.288	0.173	0.0110
	(0.234)	(0.127)	(0.00878)
Executive Policy	1.037***	0.468**	0.00663***
	(0.395)	(0.209)	(0.00251)
Concrete	0.320	0.177	0.00999**
	(0.516)	(0.285)	(0.00495)
var(_cons[country])	0	-24.11	
	(0)	(89.86)	
var(_resd[country])		0.118***	
		(0.0447)	
Constant	-2.794	-1.926*	-1.620***
	(2.178)	(1.004)	(0.0434)
Observations	3,152	3,152	3,152
Number of groups	10	10	
First Stage: strike_1			
Formal authority			-0.366***
			(0.0320)
cons			0.512***
			(0.0254)
var(e.L1_resid)			0.00282***
			(0.000314)
var(e.strike_1)			0.182***
			(0.00374)
corr(e.strike_1,e.L1_resid)			-0

*Notes: Estimates are based on regressions including all decisions of constitutionality adopted by courts of last resort in 10 Latin American countries in 2003. Standard errors in parentheses *** is significant at the 1% level; **is significant at the 5% level; and * is significant at the 10% level.*

measuring only the anti-majoritarian dimension of the concept. There are at least two reasons to believe the degree to which aspects of the political context may be more likely to affect activism than assertiveness. Judicial assertiveness may be primarily defined by the institutional distribution of power rather than by the political context. In contrast, courts' reactions to fragmented as opposed to unified governments may lead to judicial activism. Further studies should explore the differences in the significance of contextual factors in explaining activism compared to assertiveness. This can shed light on the role of courts in protecting human rights and establishing fair rules for political participation (Faundez, 2005; Levitsky and Murillo, 2013; for an exception see Leishman, 2006).

In sum, courts' differences in formal authority are an important aspect to identify judicial activism because it allows researchers to analyze behavioral responses otherwise treated as equivalent. For example, decisions on the legalization of abortion and same-sex marriage are often described as instances of judicial activism across countries. However, considering the legalization of abortion in Colombia and Argentina as judicial activism can be deceiving as they constitute contrasting models of constitutional justice. The Argentinean Supreme Court is characterized by being constrained and organized more for politicians than citizens, and the Colombian Constitutional Court is considered a dynamic actor in policymaking, open to the direct claims of citizens (Palacio, 2006; Rodríguez-Garavito 2010; Helmke, 2012). Similarly, can we say that courts in Brazil, Colombia, Costa Rica, Ecuador, and Mexico that legalized same-sex marriage are more activist than their Chilean counterpart that declared the legal definition of marriage as a contract between a man and a woman not unconstitutional? *A priori* comparisons of assertive decisions, even if substantially equivalent, cannot be used as examples of activism without qualifying whether the courts were legitimated to intervene (Ruibal and Fernandez Anderson 2020; Ruibal 2021). Judicial activism is a latent concept for which anti-majoritarianism and legal instability are definitional dimensions that should be incorporated in any conceptualization and measurement endeavor that tries to capture the concept's unique properties. The data analysis demonstrates that using an institutional benchmark is an alternative to capture the different expectations created by each court in its own context, allowing studies to incorporate elements differentiating legitimate behavior, and facilitating behavioral studies across constitutional justice systems. To that extent, this chapter aims to provoke further discussions on the structure of the concept that opens the way for comparative analyses of judicial activism.

References

Anand, S. (2006). The truth about Canadian judicial activism. *Const. F.*, *15*, 87.

Bolick, C. (2019). The proper role of judicial activism. *Harv. JL & Pub. Pol'y*, *42*, 1.

Brinks, D. M., & Blass, A. (2017). Rethinking judicial empowerment: The new foundations of constitutional justice. *International Journal of Constitutional Law*, *15*(2), 296–331.

Brinks, D. M., & Blass, A. (2018). *The DNA of constitutional justice in Latin America politics: Governance, and judicial design*. Cambridge University Press.

Canon, B. (1982). Defining the dimensions of judicial activism. *Judicature*, *66*, 236.

Carrubba, C. J., Gabel, M., Helmke, G., et al. (2015). When parchment barriers matter: De jure judicial independence and the concentration of power, manuscript (on file with authors).

Cohn, M., & Kremnitzer, M. (2005). Judicial activism: A multidimensional model. *Can. JL & Jurisprudence*, *18*, 333.

Coutinho, L. P., La Torre, M., & Smith, S. D. (2015). *Judicial activism: An interdisciplinary approach to the American and European experiences* (Vol. 44). Springer.

Cross, F. B., & Lindquist, S. A. (2006). The scientific study of judicial activism. *Minn. L. Rev.*, *91*, 1752.

de Almeida Ribeiro, G. (2015). Judicial activism and fidelity to law. In *Judicial activism* (pp. 31–46). Springer.

Easterbrook, F. H. (2002). Do liberals and conservatives differ in judicial activism. *U. Colo. L. Rev.*, *73*, 1401.

Edwards, J. R. (2001). Multidimensional constructs in organizational behavior research: An integrative analytical framework. *Organizational research methods*, *4*(2), 144–192.

Epp, C. R. (1998). *The rights revolution: Lawyers, activists, and supreme courts in comparative perspective*. University of Chicago Press.

Faundez, J. (2005). Democratization through law: Perspectives from Latin America. *Democratisation*, *12*(5), 749–765.

Gauri, V., & Brinks, D. M. (Eds.). (2008). Courting Social Justice: Judicial Enforcement of Social and Economic Rights in the Developing World. Cambridge University Press.

Green, C. (2008). An intellectual history of judicial activism. *Emory LJ*, *58*, 1195.

Grover, S. C. (2020). *Judicial activism and the democratic rule of law: Selected case studies*. Springer Nature.

Hamlin, R., & Sala, G. (2018). The judicialization of politics disentangled. In *Oxford research encyclopedia of politics*.

Harwood, S. (1992). *Judicial activism: A restrained defense*. PhD thesis, Cornell University.

Hellman, A. D. (2001). Judicial activism: The good, the bad, and the ugly. *Miss. CL Rev.*, *21*, 253.

Helmke, G. (2012). *Courts under constraints: judges, generals, and presidents in Argentina*. Cambridge University Press.

Hirschl, R. (2008). The judicialization of mega-politics and the rise of political courts. *Annu. Rev. Polit. Sci.*, *11*, 93–118.

Kapiszewski, D., & Taylor, M. M. (2008). Doing courts justice? Studying judicial politics in Latin America. *Perspectives on Politics*, 741–767.

Kapiszewski, D., Silverstein, G., & Kagan, R. A. (2013). *Consequential courts: Judicial roles in global perspective*. Cambridge University Press.

Lawrence, A. (2015). Judicial activism: Clearing the air and the head. pp. 15–20.

Leishman, R. (2006). *Against judicial activism: The decline of freedom and democracy in Canada*. McGill-Queen's Press-MQUP.

Levitsky, S., & Murillo, M. V. (2013). Lessons from Latin America: Building institutions on weak foundations. *Journal of Democracy, 24*(2), 93–107.

Lindquist, S. A. (2017). Judicial activism in state supreme courts: Institutional design and judicial behavior. *Stan. L. & Pol'y Rev., 28*, 61.

Lindquist, S. A., & Cross, F. B. (2009). *Measuring judicial activism*. Oxford: Oxford University Press.

Marshall, W. P. (2002). Conservatives and the seven sins of judicial activism. *U. Colo. L. Rev., 73*, 1217.

Palacio, M. (2006). Between legitimacy and violence. A history of Colombia, 1875–2002. Duke University Press.

Polites, G. L., Roberts, N., & Thatcher, J. (2012). Conceptualizing models using multidimensional constructs: A review and guidelines for their use. *European Journal of Information Systems, 21*(1), 22–48.

Porat, I. (2018). *Proportionality and judicial activism: Fundamental rights adjudication in Canada, Germany and South Africa. International Journal of Constitutional Law*, 16, 1035–1041.

Posner, R. A. (1999). *The federal courts: Challenge and reform*. Harvard University Press.

Ríos-Figueroa, J. (2017). Radical deprivation on trial: The impact of judicial activism on socioeconomic rights in the global south. *International Journal of Constitutional Law, 15*(2), 545–548.

Ríos-Figueroa, J., & Staton, J. K. (2014). An evaluation of cross-national measures of judicial independence. *Journal of Law, Economics, and Organization, 30*(1), 104–137.

Rodríguez-Garavito. C. (2010). Beyond the courtroom: The impact of judicial activism on socioeconomic rights in Latin America. *Tex. L. Rev.*, 89, 1669.

Rosenberg, G. N. (2008). *The hollow hope*. University of Chicago Press.

Ruibal, A. (2021). Using constitutional courts to advance abortion rights in Latin America. *International Feminist Journal of Politics, 23*(4), 579–599.

Ruibal, A., & Fernandez Anderson, C. (2020). Legal obstacles and social change: strategies of the abortion rights movement in Argentina. *Politics, Groups, and Identities*, 8(4), 698–713.

Schacter, J. S. (2018). Putting the politics of 'judicial activism' in historical perspective. *The Supreme Court Review, 2017*(1), 209–272.

Stone Sweet, A. (2007). The politics of constitutional review in France and Europe. *International Journal of Constitutional Law*, 5(1), 69–92.

Sunstein, C. R. (2009). *Radicals in robes*. Basic Books.

Weiden, D. L. (2011). Judicial politicization, ideology, and activism at the high courts of the United States, Canada, and Australia. *Political Research Quarterly*, 64(2), 335–347.

'ilson, B. M. (2009). Institutional reform and rights revolutions in Latin America: The cases of Costa Rica and Colombia. Journal of Politics in Latin America, 1(2), 59–85.

Wuttke, A., Schimpf, C., & Schoen, H. (2020). When the whole is greater than the sum of its parts: On the conceptualization and measurement of populist attitudes and other multidimensional constructs. *American Political Science Review, 114*(2), 356–374.
Young, E. A. (2002). Judicial activism and conservative politics. *U. colo. L. rev., 73*, 1139.

· 14 ·

CONCLUDING REMARKS: TOWARDS A COMPARATIVE THEORY OF JUDICIAL ACTIVISM

Lori Hausegger and Raul Sanchez Urribarri

This book has sought to study judicial activism in comparative perspective, bringing together scholars with expertise in the study of law and courts from different disciplines, and with specialized knowledge of a variety of jurisdictions across the common law world and Latin America. It was designed as a genuine cross-national project, as part of a long-term agenda that we hope will lead to developing theory on judicial activism and subsequent analyses.

From the start, our purpose was not to push for a particular theoretical approach to the study of judicial activism or endorse one of the different understandings of the term over others. Instead, we shared with our colleagues a concern about the capricious use of judicial activism in different realms, and about the lack of conceptual and methodological clarity surrounding judicial activism, particularly when engaging in debates beyond a single jurisdiction. We also agreed, from the start, that the discussion of judicial activism was dominated by visions generated in the U.S. context and, especially, with the U.S. Supreme Court in mind. As a result, our work from the beginning sought to question existing distortions about the concept and, as much as possible, acknowledge and recognize its emergence in historical perspective and grapple with the specific social, legal, and political contexts that condition the concept's use and its interpretation. We hope the present volume has accomplished these goals, helping to open pathways for a more principled—yet nuanced—analysis of judicial activism across different systems.

Beyond the disagreements and complications that gave origin to this book, there are some areas of consensus that have emerged as well. First, in order to deal with an 'essentially contested concept', the authors in this book have strived to be clear about what specific conceptual meaning they are following, and what specific empirical implications follow from their adoption. This approach allows us to see beyond the moniker of activism, and instead compare specific behaviors and their patterns—whether it is a propensity to challenging the legislature, to engage in policy-making beyond usual expectations, to expand jurisprudential boundaries in controversial fashion, to use (or even create) competences or prerogatives where there are not any, or, simply to become a militant actor on behalf of a political party. Looking at these specific behaviors and patterns allows us to move beyond U.S. centric definitions of activism to consider different situations; for instance, where behaviors like overturning precedent or striking down legislative acts might not qualify as activism at all, but rather might be an expected or approved part of the court's role.

Following the suggestions of Jeffrey Staton in Chapter 2 of this volume, we argue that one way of circumventing the challenges of multiple meanings and cross-national contexts is to be very explicit, from the start, about what specific behavioral phenomenon is referred to with the term. Or—if it will be used with more than one conception in mind—to signpost this from the start of the research project. As Staton pointed out, this is not very different from what happens when using other contested concepts such as the concept of democracy. What matters, then, is to be clear about what is studied, and why. We must consider in a careful way the methodological and normative implications of the definition employed, as well as how it is linked to existing discussions on judicial activism in a theoretical sense and to the specific context under analysis.

Our common law chapters start off the volume attempting to do just that, and in doing so, illustrate something reiterated in every chapter: the impact of institutional differences and judicial constraints on the behaviors that make up a conception of activism. Richard Pacelle (Chapter 3), focusing on the much-studied U.S. case, argues that context matters even for the U.S. courts, and behaviors classified as activist and restrained are part of a judicial balancing act. Monica Lineberger (Chapter 4) notes the difficulties of applying a U.S. centric concept of activism in a country ruled by Parliamentary supremacy, and carefully details the institutional developments that allow activist behavior to grow. And Troy Riddell et al (Chapter 5) detail the unique Canadian institutional and constitutional makeup that affect definitions of activism in that country, and the judicial context which makes behavior such as overturning precedent not fit neatly in the traditional activist category.

Out of these chapters also comes the first suggestion of a related theme that will recur throughout the volume: that examining specific behaviors can give a more nuanced reflection of activism and restraint—terms which may depend on the eye of the beholder and the context in which they are found. Thus, behavior typically thought of as restrained, such as following precedent, may in fact be considered activist in some situations. This theme is reiterated clearly later in the volume by Bruce Wilson (Chapter 7), for example, when he notes that the Costa Rican courts exercising restraint were often actively supporting the status quo and the elites that benefited from it.

Andrea Castagnola et al (Chapter 10) add a different dimension to this theme when they note how a traditionally weak court in Paraguay, one traditionally lacking in independence, has ruled against the government in a systematic fashion. The chapter examines this surprisingly 'activist' behavior more closely, arguing that institutional design plays a large role, and that much of that behavior is actually reactive rather than activist. While the Paraguay high court does indeed undertake behaviors that can be characterized as 'activist', this chapter's nuanced analysis of the concept demonstrates it is only in particular areas—ones not attacking ruling elites. Thinking about the ability of these different courts—with varying levels of assertiveness and independence—to be activist, Lee Walker (Chapter 12) discusses the connection between legitimacy and activism. Undertaking a cross national study, Walker argues that courts that lack institutional legitimacy may rely on direct political support to make activist decisions, whereas highly legitimate courts can draw support from the public's institutional commitment to rule against political elites.

Of course, being clear on the conceptual meaning should not prevent scholars from engaging in critique about judicial activism and improving upon existing conceptual tools. In this sense, several chapters of this book not only emphasized clear definitions from the start, but also came up with novel ways to theoretically approach judicial activism, such as Lineberger's chapter in the British context (Chapter 4), and Vicente Benítez et al's chapter on the Colombian case (Chapter 6). In both chapters, the authors offer a good template for scholars interested in exploring the theoretical boundaries of the concept, first by surveying key literature on the topic and then by clearly delineating the concept and its empirical implications. The authors of each of these chapters propose a conceptual framework that should travel well across borders, while questioning the use of definitions that fail to capture the concept's complexity (Lineberger) or its essence (Benítez et al.). This is a concern that should also guide efforts that go beyond single-country analyses. For instance, it guides Susan Achury's cross-national contribution (Chapter 13), in which she carefully considers alternative dimensions of the concept of judicial activism and proposes a definition of activism that focuses on the "institutional expectations created by formal rules granting judicial review prerogatives." Looking at a selection of ten Latin American countries, Achury reflects on the need to analyze the complex phenomenon of judicial activism, bearing in mind that the phenomenon is tied to the broader question of when it is legitimate for a court to intervene—not *all* judicial action against other branches of power is activist.

A similar kind of principled approach can guide normative debates on judicial activism as well. As Thomas Bustamante and Emilio Peluso Neder Meyer show in their discussion of the Brazilian case (Chapter 8), claims endorsing (or disapproving of) judicial activism often rest against certain epistemological or normative backgrounds. Thus, one should be cautious when equating judicial activism to good or bad behavior or outcomes. Again, as illustrated by several of the book's chapters, it depends on the context, on the particular behavior we are emphasizing—and, sometimes, it will still be a contested matter whether the activist conduct in question is welcome or not. What might be 'good' judicial activism to one side could well be 'bad' judicial activism for another. But, at least in scholarship, either claim needs to be properly buttressed. If judicial activism is pernicious, problematic, constructive, beneficial or any other adjective, scholars should try to clarify, as much as possible, what they mean by their word choice, in what context, and to what ends.

For instance, our volume offers very good examples of judicial activism that can be productive for democratic consolidation, whether by enhancing horizontal accountability (O'Donnell, 1998), or protecting the rights of citizens in a weakly institutionalized democratic context (Epp, 1998). There are multiple ways in which the 'activist' exercise of judicial power can protect democracy. For example, in the Mexican case (Chapter 11), Rebecca Reid identifies how the Mexican Supreme Court exhibited multiple forms of activism in integrating international law and the Inter-American Court of Human Rights' jurisprudence into the Mexican legal system. As a result, the Mexican Supreme Court increased its activity in rights related jurisprudence and "enforced international rights standards in domestic courts." On a related note, Bruce Wilson (Chapter 7) tracks a similar transformation of Costa Rica's high court, after the creation of the Sala IV, which opened access to the court, and resulted in a court willing to protect rights and hold other branches of government accountable. The Court's decisions are not without controversy, but Wilson argues behavior categorized as 'activist' is often necessary for the protection of rights.

By contrast, Bustamante and Meyer (Chapter 8), use the Brazil case, with its extremely powerful high court, to warn of the dangers judicial activism can create when engaging in fraught and polarized political battles in the name of moral principles or virtue. Detailing the rise of judicial activism in the Federal Supreme Tribunal during Brazil's tumultuous political recent past (and present), their work helps us reconsider normative debates about the desirability of specific types of judicial intervention in weakly institutionalized democracies, particularly those where judicial authority and legitimacy can be at serious risk. Moreover, assuming that judges should act as safeguards of democracy without considering the specific institutional trajectory of a specific judicial system, its usual nomination politics, its relationship with other political actors, and the socio-political context where it functions, can have very dangerous consequences. Consider for example the Venezuelan case explored by Sanchez Urribarri (Chapter 9), where a captured judiciary ended up becoming a key institutional ally to a regime that engaged in dismantling democracy and eventually embraced an authoritarian project. In the wrong environment, judicial activism can also emerge and destroy the very regime it is supposed to protect.

All in all, the chapters in this book, with their explicit focus on specific situations and conducts as they relate to activism in varied socio-political and institutional contexts, provide important lessons to continue on the path towards a well-grounded comparative theory of judicial activism. They do not coalesce around one conception of judicial activism and they do not resolve its status as a contested concept. Instead, they accept, and indeed embrace, its complexity and normative ambiguity, and carefully dissect each in the context of the courts they analyze. In doing so, they open the door to future conversations on judicial activism across different contexts, by questioning more traditional conceptions of judicial activism, discussing how this contested concept should be studied, and debating whether it is a desirable phenomenon in some circumstances. As a result, this book contributes to push the boundaries of the ongoing debate on judicial activism, a key theme in comparative law and courts scholarship.

References

Epp, C. R. (1998). *The rights revolution: Lawyers, activists, and supreme courts in comparative perspective*. University of Chicago Press.

O'Donnell, G. A. (1998). Horizontal accountability in new democracies. *Journal of Democracy*, 9(3), 112–126.

NOTES ON CONTRIBUTORS

Raul Sanchez Urribarri
Associate Dean (Academic and International Partnerships) and Senior Lecturer in Crime, Justice and Legal Studies, La Trobe University

Lori Hausegger
Professor of Political Science and Director of Canadian Studies, Boise State University

Jeffrey K. Staton
Senior Associate Dean, Laney Graduate School and Professor of Political Science, Emory University

Richard Pacelle Jr.
Professor of Political Science, University of Tennessee

Monica Lineberger
Assistant Professor of Politics, Government and Law, University of Wisconsin-Whitewater

Troy Riddell
Associate Professor and Chair of Political Science, University of Guelph

Nicole Scott
JD Student, Osgoode Hall Law School

Vicente F. Benítez-R.
Associate Professor of Law, School of Law and Political Sciences, Universidad de La Sabana

Fabio Pulido-Ortiz
Associate Professor of Law, School of Law and Political Sciences, Universidad de La Sabana

Pablo Rivas-Robledo
Institute for Logic, Language and Information, University of Amsterdam

Bruce M. Wilson
Professor and Interim Director, School of Politics, Security and International Affairs, University of Central Florida

Thomas Bustamante
Federal University of Minas Gerais, National Council for Scientific and Technological Development

Emilio Peluso Neder Meyer
Federal University of Minas Gerais, National Council for Scientific and Technological Development

Andrea Castagnola
Adjunct Professor, Universidad Torcuato Di Tella, and Fellow, LawTransform CMI

Gabriela Bonzi
Independent Scholar

Shirley Franco
Professor of Constitutional Law, Universidad Nacional del Este

Aníbal Pérez-Liñán
Professor of Political Science and Global Affairs, University of Notre Dame

Rebecca A. Reid
Associate Professor of Political Science and Director of Graduate Studies, University of Texas at El Paso

Lee Demetrius Walker
National Science Foundation

Susan Achury
Assistant Professor of Political Science, Lycoming College

INDEX

Global Perspectives on Judicial Politics

Richard Pacelle, Raul Sanchez Urribarri, and Lori Hausegger
Series Editors

The late 20th and early 21st century have been marked by the growth and expansion of government, and the increasing role of courts in politics and policymaking at a global scale. However, the study of the courts and legal systems has been dominated by attention to high courts (especially the U.S. Supreme Court), at the cost of understanding the judiciary as a whole and across different countries.

This interdisciplinary book series seeks to help fill this gap. Bringing together scholars from different theoretical fields and methodological traditions, it focuses on studies examining the role of courts across different legal and political systems, to understand better how different judicial actors -including high courts- respond to the contemporary challenges of administrating justice and good governance

For additional information about this series or the submission of manuscripts, please contact:

Richard Pacelle, Professor of Political Science, University of Tennessee
Raul Sanchez Urribarri, Senior Lecturer in Crime,
Justice and Legal Studies, La Trobe University

Lori Hausegger, Associate Professor of Political Science and Co-Director of the
Canadian Studies Program, Boise State University

To order other books in this series, please contact our Customer Service Department:

peterlang@presswarehouse.com (within the U.S.)
orders@peterlang.com (outside the U.S.)

Or browse online by series:

www.peterlang.com

Milton Keynes UK
Ingram Content Group UK Ltd.
UKHW020735300924
1916UKWH00005B/36

9 781433 198120